D1566555

Theory and Practice in the Teaching of Writing: Rethinking the Discipline

Edited by Lee Odell

Southern Illinois University Press

Carbondale and Edwardsville

Library of Congress Cataloging-in-Publication Data

Theory and practice in the teaching of writing: rethinking the discipline /
edited by Lee Odell.
        p.   cm.
    Includes bibliographical references and index.
    1. English language—Composition and exercises—Study and
teaching. 2. English language—Rhetoric—Study and teaching.
I. Odell, Lee, 1940– .
PE1404.T475   1993
808'.042'07—dc20   92-40547
ISBN 0-8093-1755-9 (cloth)   CIP
ISBN 0-8093-1947-0 (pbk.)

"The Christmas Tree" is reprinted by permission of The
Putnam Publishing Group for *On the Road with Charles
Kuralt* by Charles Kuralt. Copyright © 1985 by CBS, Inc.

The paper used in this publication meets the minimum requirements of
American National Standard for Information Sciences—Permanence
of Paper for Printed Library Materials, ANSI Z39.48-1984. ⊖

Contents

Introduction: Theory and Practice

Lee Odell

In one of his more recent books, Peter Elbow argues that teachers need to adopt a "theoretical stance" (49–66). Since Elbow is himself a teacher of writing, he's hardly suggesting that theory is more important than practice. But he is recommending that all of us need to be more conscious of the fundamental assumptions that underlie our work, identifying and questioning them in light of other assumptions and in light of our experiences as teachers and writers. In other words, Elbow seems to be suggesting that we need to take an active role in shaping and reshaping the theories that underlie our daily practice as writers and as teachers of writing.

All of the chapters in this book are intended to help us do just that. Each is intended to help us reflect on what we do and why we do it. The problem is that some recent discussions of theory raise questions as to whether we should bother with this sort of effort. Donald Schon, for example, denies that theory can help with the day-to-day practice of any profession, and Stanley Fish has specifically denied that theory can serve as a foundation for the teaching of writing. In addition, Fish has attacked the premise that theoretical knowledge has some special status, that it is somehow more true or more reliable than other sorts of knowledge.

What's more, these critics of theory have a point. Teachers have always known that individual students don't fit neatly into the categories and generalizations of theory. Further, in most of our dealings with students there just is not time to stop and carefully work out a syllogism that says, in effect, X principle applies to Y situation in the following ways; therefore it logically follows that the only valid thing

1

to do next is Z. And finally, scholarship in a wide variety of disciplines makes a strong argument that all human knowledge—theory in- cluded—appears to be limited, tentative, subject to ongoing revision. If we're expecting theory to provide us with unchanging, universally applicable principles, we're deluding ourselves, indulging in what Fish refers to as "theory hope" (342).

So far, so good. The arguments of Fish, Schon, and others help us see the limits of theory. But they don't give a very complete account. They don't consider some of the strong reasons we have for believing that theory is implicit in everything we do, in our routine work as writers and teachers as well as in major developments in our disci- pline. Moreover, the critics of theory don't help us understand that theory and practice are interactive, each capable of informing and remaking the other.

Acknowledging Theory

As Schon has pointed out (see his critique of what he calls the "myth of technical rationality"), we tend to act intuitively, spontane- ously, without explicitly referring to abstract principles. That's true, but it's not the whole story. For one thing, theory often figures promi- nently in efforts to bring about fundamental changes in practice. For example, in assigning and evaluating writing, we have become very aware of context, especially of ways audience and purpose influence the efforts of a writer and the judgments of an evaluator. In helping bring us to this awareness, people such as Richard Lloyd-Jones have explicitly drawn on scholarship in rhetoric and discourse theory and have consciously used that scholarship to guide practice. Similarly, those who advocate the use of informal, expressive writing base their argument in part on Vygotsky's theory of thought and language. (See, for example, Britton's discussion of "shaping at the point of utterance.")

In addition to serving as a force for change, theory also underlies our daily practice as teachers and as writers. Implicit in this practice are powerful sets of assumptions—about knowledge, for example, about our own and our students' role in the educational process, about what we are trying to do and why we are trying to do it.[1] These assumptions are not necessarily articulated in the abstract terminology we may associate with theory. Indeed, there is a good chance that our most basic assumptions will not be articulated at all. They may have become so deeply internalized that they have become second nature; we act upon them without even recognizing that that's what we are doing.[2] But these assumptions function in the way theory is presumed to function—they constitute generalizations, predictions, interpretations of what is or should be, and we often act as though they were widely applicable principles. They seem to account for a lot of what we do.

Here's one example: When Douglas Barnes and Denis Shemilt surveyed a number of teachers about the ways they used writing in their classes, Barnes and Shemilt found that responses could be grouped into two major categories, which they labeled *transmission* and *interpretation*. Responses in the transmission category suggested that some teachers saw writing principally as a means of recording information provided by a teacher or a textbook. By contrast, responses in the interpretation category suggested that other teachers saw writing as a means of learning to think independently, to come to understand one's experiences or feelings, to construct one's own meanings.

These general patterns imply fundamentally different attitudes toward knowledge. Barnes and Shemilt found that teachers who held the transmission view were likely to feel that knowledge exists "out there," in a book, for example, and the student's job is to ferret out and remember that knowledge. By contrast, those who held the interpretation view were likely to see knowledge as something that students have to construct for themselves, using, for example, assertions found in a book as one basis (along with prior experience, assertions in other books, etc.) for constructing meaning.

Moreover, results of Barnes and Shemilt's survey suggest that these different assumptions about knowledge are likely to be associated with different ways of teaching and evaluating student work. Survey responses indicate that teachers who took a transmission view were likely to see their job as one of conveying information and were likely to evaluate student writing on the basis of how well it met predetermined standards of accuracy and correctness. Once a piece of writing had been "marked" or "corrected" these teachers were unlikely to make any further use of it, except, perhaps to show it to the class as a "model of good or bad practice" (219). By contrast, teachers who held an interpretation view were likely to see their job as one of creating classroom conditions that would allow students to explore ideas and deepen personal understandings of their world.

These teachers were more likely to respond to students' writing by setting up a dialogue with students and encouraging them to use a given piece of writing as a "springboard" (218) for new individual or class projects.

Composing Theory

So we have profound assumptions and, deliberately or intuitively, we appear to act upon them in surprisingly coherent ways. How do we acquire these assumptions? What is our role in creating, forming, revising them? Do we even have such a role? To this last question, Fish would answer no. We acquire our assumptions (and a repertoire of "unreflective actions" associated with them) as a result of being "embedded" in a particular "context of practice" (ix) or "interpretive community" (141).

Again, Fish has a point. We do seem to internalize a lot of our assumptions and habits without conscious reflection. Moreover, we are fortunate that we don't have to make a conscious effort to learn everything we somehow come to know. There is, after all, only so much we can consciously attend to at any one time. But there are a couple of reasons why we can't rely solely on tacit assumptions and unreflective actions.

For one thing, we may have spent a lot of time embedded in contexts of practice that we may not want to perpetuate. For example, it's very likely that many of us grew up in an educational system where most of our teachers, consciously or not, adopted a "transmission" view of education. Their job was to provide us with information, and our job was to get it straight and remember it.[3] Moreover, to the extent that we received any writing instruction at all, there's a good chance it grew out of the practical stylist tradition that emphasized correctness, ignored the process of constructing meaning, and assumed that we should know what we want to say *before* we started to write.[4]

A second reason for not relying solely on intuition and habit is that we routinely encounter a variety of conflicts (dissonances, uncertainties, questions) that cannot be resolved by conducting business as usual. For example, we may find ourselves working in what Schon calls a "zone of indeterminate practice," that is, in a situation where accepted theory or customary practice just doesn't seem to apply (6–7). A sense of dissonance may also occur because we're aware of the disparity between our ambitions (or values, knowledge, hopes) and our abilities, or between our own level of expertise and that of someone else—a mentor, perhaps, or our students. Or we may feel conflict or uncertainty because we're aware, to a greater or lesser degree, of a variety of contexts of practice, each of which entails a somewhat different set of assumptions and habitual ways of doing business. That is, we are conscious not only of the classrooms in which we currently teach, but also those we inhabited as students; not only of our own present or past classrooms but also those of colleagues with whom we work; and not only of the world of classrooms but also the worlds outside school where writing is done and valued.[5]

Part of resolving these dissonances entails a process that Schon refers to as "reflection in action" (26–31). As Schon describes it, this process engages us in a transaction between what we know (hope, value, expect, fear) and what we encounter in a specific situation. We begin a project relying on "spontaneous, routinized responses" (28). But almost inevitably we encounter some sort of surprise—an unexpected problem arises, for example, or our actions have implications we hadn't anticipated. Consequently, we reflect on what we're doing: How am I approaching this problem? What am I really trying to do? What would happen if . . . ? Grappling with such questions "serves to reshape what we are doing while we are doing it" (26).

This attention to the here and now, this "conversation with [our] situation" (78) is central to our teaching. But it is not enough. As Schon points out, his notion of reflection-in-action depends upon a "constructionist" view of knowledge (36), a view that closely resembles the "interpretation" view described by Barnes and Shemilt (see above, "Acknowledging Theory"). That is, our knowledge is not something that exists independently of us but rather is something we must articulate for ourselves. If we accept this view of knowledge, we cannot be concerned solely with getting on with the business at hand. We have to use this reflection as part of our effort to construct—and reconstruct—the theories, the assumptions that underlie our actions. In short, being teachers means we must also be students of what we are trying to teach and of our reasons for trying to teach it.

The goal of this constructive process is not simply to produce more theory or to discover the one true way of writing or of teaching writing. Instead, the goal is to try to contribute to an ongoing dialogue, a transaction in which (1) increased awareness of our basic assumptions leads us to rethink our practice as teachers or writers and, at the same time, (2) our practice serves as a way to test and modify those assumptions. From the perspective of this book, theory needs practice and practice needs theory; each continually challenges and refines the other. Consequently, our understanding of our discipline is not simply knowledge of theory or knowledge of practice. Our knowledge of composing consists of the claims we can make as the result of the ongoing interaction between theory and practice.

Essays in this book are an effort to take part in, perhaps even stimulate, this interaction. Consequently, it might be useful to think of each essay in terms of the questions or issues it raises. The first pair of essays focus on how we might engage in the process of knowing. Jane Peterson asks, What are the institutional/cultural forces that hinder our efforts to use teaching as an occasion for our own learning? And how can we overcome those forces? Anne Herrington identifies the assumptions implicit in a social constructivist view of knowledge and asks what responsibilities those assumptions impose on researchers.

The next set of essays leads us to consider our work in a larger interdisciplinary, historical, or social context. David Kaufer and Richard Young raise the related issues of how writing is related to "content" and of the nature of the expertise writing teachers can offer colleagues in other disciplines. Shirley Heath asks, How did we arrive at our current conception of the school essay and what are the limitations of that conception? Beverly Moss and Keith Walters identify the social and cultural values that are implicit in teachers' classroom behavior and question not only our usual assumptions about what constitutes "Standard English" but also our tendency to define *diversity* too narrowly. Sally Hampton looks at the assumptions underlying the education of "at-risk" students and considers ways we might develop new assumptions and, consequently, more appropriate educational practice.

The final section focuses specifically on teaching. Lee Odell explores the relation between conscious inquiry ("strategy") and intuition ("surprise") in the composing process and asks how we might teach strategy while encouraging surprise. George Hillocks asks, How do we need to structure our classes to promote active learning? And why does the sort of structure he proposes seem to have such a powerful effect on students' writing? Jim Corder raises questions about the current interest in collaboration, acknowledging that collaboration is inevitable, but cautioning that we must not lose sight of the individual in this process. And Lee Odell focuses on the process of assessment, asking how this process can serve as, in Dennie Wolf's phrase, "an episode of learning."

In these essays, the authors identify a number of assumptions that underlie some aspect of our daily work as teachers. In all cases, authors stake out their own positions as clearly and forcefully as they can. But in all cases, the authors realize that their statements are simply one more turn in the ongoing conversation that is at the center of our effort to help our students continue to grow as writers.

Notes

1. We have various ways of labeling these assumptions—Kenneth Burke calls them *terministic screens*, George Kelly calls them *personal constructs*, and reading theorists call them *schema*. These terms, of course, are not exact synonyms. But they share one fundamental premise: we approach experience with a complex set of background experiences, expectations, values, assumptions, and feelings. All of this material shapes the way we make sense of new information and guides the way we act.

2. See Fish's "Preface" to *Doing What Comes Naturally*.

3. See John Mayher's criticism of this "commonsense" view of education.

4. Unfortunately, there is always the chance that we will, wittingly or not, do unto others as we have been done unto. That is, because we have internalized sets of assumptions and unreflective actions, we are likely to treat our students the same way our teachers treated us, even if we have both personal and professional reasons not to want to do this. For instance, if we have spent most of our student lives in classrooms where the teacher was an absolute authority, there's an excellent chance we will find ways to exert our own authority. Intending to invite students' judgments, we may ask questions ("Yes, but don't you think the author really meant . . . ?") whose rhetorical nature is apparent to students if not to us. Or hoping to get students to see the need to substantiate their more debatable assertions, we may become especially critical of statements with which we happen to disagree, passing by other statements that are no less debatable but that we find more consistent with our own views.

5. See Heath's discussion of literacy practices in families and communities and also discussions in Odell and Goswami's *Writing in Non-Academic Settings* of writing in business and government settings.

Works Cited

Barnes, Douglas, and Denis Shemilt. "Transmission and Interpretation." *Educational Review* 26 (1974): 213–28.

Britton, James. "Shaping at the Point of Utterance." *Reinventing the Rhetorical Tradition*. Ed. Aviva Freedman and Ian Pringle. Conway, AR: L & S Books for the Canadian Council of Teachers of English, 1980. 61–65.

Burke, Kenneth. "Terministic Screens." *Language as Symbolic Action: Essays on Life, Literature, and Method*. Berkeley: U of California P, 1965. 44–62.

Elbow, Peter. *What Is English?* New York: Modern Language Association, 1990. 49–66.

Fish, Stanley. *Doing What Comes Naturally: Change, Rhetoric, and the Practice of Theory in Literary and Legal Studies*. Durham, NC: Duke UP, 1989.

Heath, Shirley. *Ways with Words*. Cambridge: Cambridge UP, 1983.

Kelly, George. "The Autobiography of a Theory." *Clinical Psychology and Personality: The Selected Papers of George Kelly*. Ed. Brendan Maher. New York: Wiley, 1969.

Lloyd-Jones, Richard. "Primary Trait Scoring." *Evaluating Writing: Describing, Measuring, Judging*. Ed. Charles R. Cooper and Lee Odell. Urbana: NCTE, 1977. 33–66.

Mayher, John. *Uncommon Sense*. Portsmouth, NH: Boynton/Cook, 1990.

Odell, Lee, and Dixie Goswami. *Writing in Non-Academic Settings*. New York: Guilford, 1985.

Schon, Donald. *Educating the Reflective Practitioner*. San Francisco: Jossey-Bass, 1990.

1

Learning Through Teaching

Jane Peterson

In the fall of 1968, I taught my first two classes of freshman composition. I don't remember much about those classes except that students sat in neat rows, wrote a theme in class each Friday, and took grammar and usage tests that I slowly typed on ditto pages with a razor blade handy to scrape away the unwanted purple. I don't know what happened in class between themes and tests, but I can guess because I remember vividly the required graduate course I had taken that summer to be eligible to teach. Every day we did nothing but discuss the exercises we had completed from the two workbooks that would be our students' texts: *Writing Good Sentences* and *Writing Good Prose* (both written by the chair of the department, Claude Faulkner, who also taught that graduate course). We never read a single article, never looked at a student paper, never discussed how to teach. We just analyzed sentences and paragraphs. Although I considered it a dismal experience at the time (partly because my Chinese boxes only matched Faulkner's often enough to earn a B), I am sure that I dutifully tried to duplicate it for my students that fall.

My own experience in freshman composition had been quite different. With the entire freshman class of a small liberal arts college, I attended two lectures a week, usually given by tenured English faculty but sometimes by a sociologist, psychologist, or anthropologist. The readings and lectures introduced us to linguistics—surveying not only theories of language origin, development, acquisition, and use but also several approaches to describing our language. One day a week we attended discussion sections that were taught by those who graded our papers and who may or may not have had anything to do with the lecture component of the course. For discussion sessions, we read short stories and wrote papers analyzing them. The two components remained as distinct as my feelings about them: I found the information from the lecture component fascinating and the work for the discussion component confusing. In fact, I failed my first freshman theme.

Those first experiences with freshman composition did not provide an auspicious beginning for a career. From them, I could not have imagined ever *wanting* to teach writing. But much has changed in the intervening years—and changed for the better. Both what we teach and how we teach differ dramatically from what was common not very long ago. Although we are aware of the differences and often talk about the changes in our theories of reading, writing, and learning, and in our practices, I think we haven't fully realized how radical those changes have been and how significantly they have transformed the nature of our work. In particular, we have not recognized the range of opportunities for our own learning that now exist in our daily encounters with students and their writing.

The idea that we, as teachers, can learn through teaching is not new, but what it means is. In the past, we only thought of teaching as a way to learn "something," to help us retain information. The adage "The best way to learn something is to teach it" assumed a transmission model of teaching that focused on content—on information to be retained—and succeeded primarily through repetition. Most important, it implied clear limits to the learning potential of teaching. We had to either teach new courses or bring new material into existing ones to continue "learning" through the act of teaching. Today, however, we are in a different situation, one rich with opportunities. We now have theories of reading, writing, and learning that not only allow us to engage in a different form of learning through teaching but actually promote our own substantive learning.

I will argue, in fact, that when we act on current theories, we surround ourselves with important opportunities for constructing knowledge—for internalizing what we are learning as a profession about reading, writing, and learning and for raising new questions about those theories and proposed models. With language as both our subject matter and our means of teaching, we have an advantage over those in other disciplines, as Moran and Penfield suggest: "English is a discipline that is fundamentally connected to teaching in a way that the physical, natural, and social sciences are not" (3). This connection enables a powerful interplay of theory and practice because, as Lee Odell points out in the introduction to this collection, opportunities for applying and challenging theory exist in our daily encounters with students and their writing. And in the introduction to *Textual Power*, Robert Scholes emphasizes the interplay of theory and practice, claiming that "theory can help us solve curricular and pedagogical problems" and "teaching can help theory pose and articulate those problems" (ix). Despite such comments, many of us do not see teaching as a potentially powerful mode of learning. We talk about theory affecting practice but seldom about practice informing and shaping our theoretical constructs. And even those who understand intellectually the potential interplay of theory and practice seldom experience it. Why? What makes it difficult for us to engage in an interplay of theory and practice and experience teaching as a mode of learning?

There is, I believe, no simple answer to that question, but it is a question worth exploring, for it impinges on our sense of what it means to be an English teacher today. And the question needs to be explored, I believe, within the context of larger social change, for, whether we like it or not, our lives and roles as teachers are inextricably linked to the larger social order through the schools in which we work, which constitute one of our society's major social institutions. Acknowledging and examining that link is particularly important now because we live in an era of major social change—in the midst of the transition from the more than two-hundred-year-old social order known as the Industrial Age to a new age, one not yet adequately labeled because its character is still emerging. Many of the traits of this new age, however, are not only visible but reflected in the changes we have seen in our discipline over the last twenty-five or thirty years, and they are significant changes that are transforming the nature of our work.

In this essay, then, I want to explore the impact of both social and disciplinary changes on us as teachers from several angles. I hope first to clarify the *fundamental* nature of the recent changes in our theories of reading, writing, and learning by pointing out how they parallel changes in the larger society. Second, I will demonstrate, through an extended example, how current theories promote our own learning through teaching, enabling us to become knowledge makers. Third, with that potential for learning established, I will sketch out some of the ways in which our socially constructed knowledge of our field and of our role may interfere with our enacting current theories in our classrooms and so keep us from tapping the potential for learning that those theories promote. Finally, I'll suggest a reconception of our role and offer strategies to internalize a new set of assumptions about our work—what constitutes reading, writing, and learning—about students, and about ourselves.

Fundamental Changes in Society and Our Discipline

In *The Third Wave*, Alvin Toffler argues that we live in a time of fundamental social change, moving from the Industrial Age to a new age variously dubbed Post Modern or Post Industrial, the Space Age or Electronic Era, the Age of Information or Communication.[1] Whatever the label, the reality is pervasive change that profoundly affects our personal and professional lives. It is also rapid change: while the transition from the Agricultural Age to the Industrial Age took about three hundred years, Toffler predicts that this change, which he finds "beginning about 1955" (14), will take only decades so that by about 2025 a new set of assumptions will dominate our institutions. That puts us in the midst of major change now, making us, as Toffler notes, "the final generation of an old civilization and the first generation of a new one" (12).

When most of us grew up, one belief system prevailed, the one that had gradually come to dominate industrial societies and institutions. That belief system, which Toffler calls indust-reality, consisted of a specific set of interwoven assumptions about nature, time, space, matter, and causality. Those assumptions included the idea that humans were superior to nature; that time and space were independent, absolute, and divisible into smaller and smaller standardized units; and that causality was linear, mechanical, and predictable (96–115). This mechanistic view of the universe was extended to society, suggesting "that not only the cosmos and nature but society and people behaved according to certain fixed and predictable laws" (113). It assumed, for instance, that people would respond to stimuli in predictable ways, that students would move from one isolated activity or piece of information to another and "learn" (i.e., passively receive) what the teacher "taught." This industrial worldview also assumed closed systems and one-to-one correspondences. With it came unwavering belief in logic and order, a sense of certainty that everything could be known because rules or laws could be discovered through analysis, empirically validated, and used to predict. As Toffler puts it, "All that was needed was to find the critical variable to explain any phenomenon" (114).

Today, however, that mechanistic belief system is disintegrating and a very different set of assumptions is emerging. Drawing on the work of scientists and philosophers, Toffler describes this new belief system as one that "emphasizes contexts, relationships, and wholes" (301), that acknowledges interdependence and mutuality, and that appreciates the dynamism and complexity of relationships. It defines our relationship to nature as symbiotic, not domineering, and includes dynamic, relativistic concepts of time and space that differ dramatically from those of the Industrial Age. Toffler clarifies the difference by noting, for example, that the static, absolute Industrial Age concepts of time and space assumed "that 'before' or 'after' had a fixed meaning independent of any observer" (297), but that current dynamic, relativistic concepts even recognize "that there is no single 'right' map, but merely different images of space that serve different purposes" (300). Complementing these new views of nature, time, and space is a new concept of causality that focuses on "mutually interacting forces" (308). It is not linear, predictable, or closed, for it acknowledges the possibility that an interplay of forces can create something wholly new.

This shift from Industrial Age assumptions to a new set is reflected in changes in our discipline. Not many years ago, we considered reading largely a matter of decoding. We thought of texts as determinate and talked about finding *the* meaning or *the* message in what was read. We saw writing primarily as encoding: the writer knew what he or she wanted to say, so the issue was transcribing correctly. Learning theories were based on transmission models—getting information from the teacher into students' heads—and knowledge was assumed to be explicit. We defined it as information (measurable, discrete data—and the more the better) or as highly skilled performance (meaning standardized performance that could be objectively measured). Accepting the general belief in the whole equaling the sum of its parts, we privileged analysis in our classrooms and spent hours explicating poems and diagraming sentences. We also relied on analysis for curriculum design. We divided complex tasks into discrete components and created assembly lines for learning. Largely ignoring context, we embraced logical, sequenced part-to-whole methods in both writing and reading—first words, then sentences, paragraphs, three-paragraph essays, five-paragraph essays. Our "logical" stair-step methods and closed-system models were unidirectional and linear—fully consonant with the mechanistic belief system of our larger industrial society.

That belief system informed every aspect of our work. It not only affected how we taught but what we taught, for it shaped our theories, our ideas about what constitutes reading, writing, and learning. To appreciate how deeply the basic assumptions of the Industrial Age affected the thinking of our discipline and how fundamental the changes in our theories and models have been during the past twenty-five years, we can juxtapose current views of reading, writing, and learning with those from our recent past. Let's begin with reading.

Today, in place of a single formalist theory of reading, we have several interpretative frameworks: deconstructionism, poststructuralism, cultural criticism, and reader response theories. And although these theories differ from one another in ways important to those within our field,[2] they all view texts as indeterminate and share a constructivist base in the broad sense that they all assume that readers create meaning and that reading is an interactive, recursive process, not a mechanical, linear one. Still immersed in Industrial Age concepts, we as a profession were not ready for this view of reading when Louise Rosenblatt's *Literature as Exploration* first appeared in 1938.[3] In fact, it was years before we were ready to seriously consider the possibility that readers interact with texts to create meaning, years during which we ignored our own experiences as readers. We all had, for instance, experienced reading a book and finding it incredibly moving or meaningful and then rereading it two or five or ten years later and wondering what we had been so excited about. So we "knew" that readers create meaning—that a single meaning does not reside in the text. As a profession, however, we ignored that tacit knowledge. After all, it contradicted our explicit knowledge of our field, our basic assumptions about readers and texts and our rather mechanical, closed, unidirectional model of reading as a decoding process. The fact that it took most of us so long to consider alternative views of reading, despite our own experiences and Rosenblatt's work, begins to suggest, I hope, both how much the belief system of the Industrial

Age permeated the thinking of our discipline and how radical the recent changes in our theories have been.

For more examples, we have only to consider some of the changes in our views of writing. In the past twenty-five years, we have moved from the idea of a solitary writer sitting down and encoding a particular known message to the idea of writing as an active, interactive, and recursive process with writers often discovering meaning as they think (perhaps in the shower, perhaps as they drive or read), write, interact with their own emerging texts, listen to responses from others, and revise. Although many of us didn't fit the old solitary, linear, encoding model, we ignored that, apparently preferring to assume there was something wrong with us rather than something wrong with the model. And when accounts from novelists, poets, playwrights, and essayists differed from the model, we attributed their processes to creative genius instead of questioning the model. It seems our internalization of indust-reality made it easier to invoke variants of "the exception proves the rule" than to acknowledge the possibility of a messy, rather unpredictable reality.

Today, we not only acknowledge that possibility but embrace it, as any review of recent literature in our field will attest. And as we have developed new theories of reading and writing, we have also espoused new theories of learning and knowledge. Instead of defining knowledge as merely information to be transmitted (learned in the sense of memorized) or as skills to be mastered in the sense of predictable rote movements that meet some standard, we now think of knowledge in broader terms—as concepts and understanding that must be constructed by an active learner. Drawing on the work of philosophers such as Polanyi, psychologists such as Bruner, Luria, Vygotsky, and sociologists such as Berger and Luckmann, we have come to see learning as dynamic, interactive, and recursive, not linear or predictable.

These theories of learning complement current theories of reading and writing. They are all constructivist in the broad sense of assuming that knowledge and meaning are created by readers, writers, and learners.[4] Together, these theories give us a new foundation for our work, a base that is fundamentally different from that of our recent past. And this base supports the emerging belief system of a new age, one which views the world as highly interactive, interdependent, unpredictable and which increasingly values principles such as cooperation and collaboration, diversity, and flexibility over the Industrial Age need for competition, uniformity, and standardization. The congruity between constructivist theories and the emerging belief system suggests that neither our current theories nor the practices associated with enacting them can be dismissed as surface changes or fads that will soon be displaced by variants of past models and methods.

Although our theories and models will continue to evolve, the direction is not likely to change any time soon, for as a profession, we have already aligned ourselves with the future. Consider, for example, the recommendations for the study of English developed at the 1987 English Coalition Conference by sixty participants chosen to represent eight national English associations (Lloyd-Jones and Lunsford). That mixed group of literary theorists, researchers, rhetoricians, English education specialists, and classroom teachers from all levels endorsed resolutions emphasizing the need for students at every level to be actively engaged in meaningful tasks and to reflect on their own reading, writing, and learning processes. Informed by constructivist theories, participants rejected the traditional transmission model of teaching and its goal of having students accumulate a standard bank of information that can be learned through memorization and measured by standardized tests. To the extent that the recommendations of the Coalition Conference, and the assumptions on which they are based, reflect our position as a profession, we are aligned with the emerging values of the new age and against attempts, including Hirsch's call for cultural literacy, to return to what was—to get back to the basics. In *The Third Wave*, Alvin Toffler characterizes the back-to-the-basics movement as a doomed reactionary effort: "Legitimately outraged by the disaster in mass education, it does not recognize that a de-massified society calls for new educational strategies, but seeks instead to restore and enforce Second Wave [Industrial Age] uniformity in the schools. Nevertheless, all these attempts to achieve uniformity are essentially the rearguard actions of a spent civilization" (256).

Most of us, it seems, have chosen to move forward, to invest our energies in the emerging future rather than the fading past, and it's time to think about the implications for us as teachers.

The Potential of Teaching as a Mode of Learning

As long as our theories of reading, writing, and learning were grounded in the assumptions of the Industrial Age, there was not much point in thinking about teaching as a mode of learning. Given those assumptions, the teacher's job was to parcel out isolated bits of fixed information in an appropriate sequence. But if we accept and enact current theories—replacing that closed-system transmission model and its static, linear, unidirectional assumptions with an open, interactive model based on dynamic, relativistic, nonlinear assumptions—then we can discover rich opportunities for learning through teaching.

In 1977, Janet Emig argued that writing itself is a mode of learning. After identifying clusters of characteristics that foster learning, Emig pointed out how the act of writing fulfills those characteristics ("Writing" 124–25). As I have suggested elsewhere, we can use the same approach to demonstrate the potential of teaching as a mode of learning (30–31). This potential for constructing knowledge through teaching, however, is not merely a theoretical possibility, but a probability for those who think in terms of the *inter*play of theory and practice and replace the usual unidirectional "from theory to practice" model with an interactive, dynamic one. But how might this interplay of theory and practice work? What makes it possible for teaching to become a mode of learning?

The potential for learning through teaching begins with our daily attempts to enact constructivist theories, for these theories promote our own learning in two basic but interrelated ways. First, when we internalize and act on our theories, we see students as subjects, as actors and agents who create meaning and construct concepts, not as objects or passive recipients of "knowledge." And if we see students as meaning makers, we not only develop a better sense of what we are asking them to do but also a new respect for them, one which enables us to envision the student-teacher relationship as a partnership in learning. Second, when we act on current theories, we become immersed in "data," surrounded by opportunities to observe and interact with students engaged in reading and writing and in reflecting on their own processes. In other words, any serious attempt to make daily practices congruent with constructivist theories creates a rich context for our own learning. However, for that possibility to become reality, for teaching to become a way of learning and knowing, we must add the catalyst of regular reflection on what we see and hear, reflection that increases our sense of ourselves as learners and that respects the knowledge and abilities students possess when they enter our classrooms.

One of our most prominent exemplars of reflective practice was Mina Shaughnessy. Although many models of teacher as learner now exist in our professional literature, Shaughnessy was among the first, and her work has not only inspired individual teachers but influenced research and scholarship in our field. In the preface to *Errors and Expectations*, Shaughnessy recalls the afternoon her work on that significant book began:

> I remember sitting alone in the worn urban classroom where my students had just written their first essays and where I now began to read them, hoping to be able to assess quickly the sort of task that lay ahead of us that semester. But the writing was so stunningly unskilled that I could not begin to define the task nor even sort out the difficulties. I could only sit there, reading and re-reading the alien papers, wondering what had gone wrong and trying to understand what I at this eleventh hour of my students' academic lives could do about it. (vii)

Her work, begun in a classroom with student papers, developed through ten years of interaction with underprepared students who enrolled under CUNY's then new open-admissions policy that only required a high school diploma. And for her and her colleagues, that work involved "many shifts in attitude and methodology" (4).

Shaughnessy's own attitude of deep respect for students permeates her descriptions of their writing and speaking. Seeing them as meaning makers and knowledge builders, she talks about "the logic that is usually implicit in what they are saying" (34); "the obvious sophistication of so many of these students as speakers" (87); and their prior knowledge of grammar as native speakers, emphasizing that "most of what they need to know has already been learned—without teachers" (129). Rejecting deficit models that center on what students do not know or cannot do, Shaughnessy focuses on what they already know and can do. She portrays students as important resources for teachers and for other students, even when dealing with matters of punctuation:

> The teacher must try to decipher the individual student's code, examining samples of his writing as a scientist might, searching for patterns or explanations, listening to what the student says about punctuation, and creating situations in the classroom that encourage students to talk openly about what they don't understand. One of the great values of the decentralized classroom where students participate as teachers as

> well as learners is that it opens up the students' "secret" files of misinfor-
> mation, confusion, humor, and linguistic insight to an extent that is not
> often possible in the traditional setting. However committed teachers
> are to starting from "scratch," they have difficulty deciding where
> "scratch" is without this kind of help from their students. (40)

This passage suggests not only her view of students as resources but a high level of interaction with students individually and in groups. And through interacting with students and respecting them enough to value their knowledge and see them as resources, Shaughnessy surrounded herself with "data," creating a rich context for her own learning.

This potential for her own learning became reality through her commitment to reflect on what she saw and heard—to search for patterns, articulate assumptions, and pose questions about the nature of error (90–91), attitudes toward error outside our profession (119–22), academic culture and the stance associated with academic discourse (85–86, 240, 292), and the development of writing abilities in adults (119, 158–59). Her discussions of student problems in *Errors and Expectations* modeled new ways of reading student work that continue to shape scholarship in the field. Consider, for instance, the continuing work of David Bartholomae, Sondra Perl, and Mike Rose, who are among those acknowledging in their early work Shaughnessy's influence on their readings of students' writing processes and products. And the questions Shaughnessy raised about error, academic discourse, and the development of writing abilities stimulated diverse research and discussions that remain lively today.

Had Shaughnessy lived to see any of the work generated in the fifteen years since the publication of *Errors and Expectations*, she probably would not have been surprised. Based on her own experience and that of her colleagues, she predicted the powerful interplay of practice and theory that we can trace retrospectively in the work of many basic writing teacher-scholars:

> From these [BW] students we have also begun to learn much about
> learning and teaching. Capable because of their maturity of observing
> the processes they are going through as learners, they can alert us easily
> and swiftly to the effects of instruction. They work, in this sense, collabo-
> ratively with teachers in ways that are impossible with child learners.
> In a hurry, also, to learn what we have to teach them, they press us to
> discover the most efficient ways of presenting what we would have them

understand. The result will be, in time, not so much a simplified view
of written English as a more profound grasp of what lies below the
prescriptive bits and pieces of instruction we once called English composition. (291–92)

Shaughnessy believed that daily work with basic writers—practice—leads to the recognition that we do "not know enough about
how people learn to write or about what writing is" (293). And she
believed in the power of that recognition to motivate the teacher "to
venture into fields where he is not a scholar—into psycholinguistics,
perhaps, or learning theory, or discourse analysis—in search of fresh
insights and new data" (293). In other words, Shaughnessy suggests
that the interplay of theory and practice that she experienced is an
almost "natural" result of teaching—of daily encounters with students. Yet many who teach and regularly read professional books and
journals experience little, if any, *inter*play of theory and practice.
What we read may affect our practices, but our classroom experiences
seldom lead us to explore new areas or to question existing models
and assumptions. We live on a one-way street.

What made Shaughnessy's experience different? What made
teaching a way of learning for her? The answer seems to be a combination of attitude and practices. As we have seen throughout *Errors
and Expectations*, Shaughnessy exhibits characteristics that seem to be
essential to realizing the potential of teaching as a mode of learning:
a strong sense of respect for students, a high level of interaction
with students, and a commitment to reflect on what she observed,
searching for patterns, questioning assumptions, generating and playing with new possibilities. But what theories informed her work? Is
there any basis for using her experience to connect current theories
of reading, writing, and learning with the idea of daily teaching as a
way of learning and knowing for teachers?

Although Shaughnessy did not outline the theoretical foundations of her teaching as such, her comments reflect the constructivist
theories that have become increasingly dominant. For example, when
she discusses the role of reading in a writing class, she describes "a
writing approach to reading" through which "the student begins to
sense that the meaning of what he reads or writes resides not in the
page nor in the reader but in the encounter between the two" (223).
She defines writing as "a social act, a kind of synthesis that is reached

through the dialectic of discussion" (83) and emphasizes the recursive and interactive nature of writing when she describes the process:

> Paradoxically, we tend to discover what we as individuals have to say by talking with others. Here, in the give-and-take of discussion, we see our experiences in larger contexts: what seemed idiosyncratic or unimportant before now illuminates a general truth; what seemed obvious must now be defended; what seemed inexplicable now begins to make sense. Ideas come out of the dialogue we sustain with others and with ourselves. Without these dialogues, thoughts run dry and judgment falters. Even accomplished writers, deep into the sense of their subjects, doubt at moments the worth of what they are saying and wait uneasily to be judged by their readers. (82)

Shaughnessy's comments reveal not only her view of reading and writing as meaning-making processes but her ability to identify with basic writers and her strong commitment to engage them in meaningful tasks, a commitment that informed every aspect of her work with basic writers. She believed in "letting the student in on what is happening" (127) and encouraged students to theorize and construct concepts. For example, her chapter on "Common Errors" emphasizes the importance of students' exploring language variation and developing concepts: "Without a clearer understanding of the reasons behind language variations and of the difference between being effective in any dialect and being right according to the conventions of a particular dialect, the student is not psychologically ready to work on common errors in formal English" (126). And when students are ready, *they* search for and describe patterns of error in their work that enable them to construct new views of themselves and become more confident writers.

As these examples suggest, constructivist theories of reading, writing, and learning informed Shaughnessy's teaching, and her reflection transformed her teaching into a way of learning and knowing. Through teaching she became a knowledge maker. And so can we. Surrounded by opportunities to observe and interact with students engaged in meaning-making processes, those of us who act on current theories are potential knowledge makers. We don't have to design special research projects to be learners in our classrooms, although that possible subtext appears in much of the work growing out of the teacher-researcher movement. And though that movement has improved the image of teachers and produced some valuable insights, especially through ethnographic studies, it has also implied that teachers can only become learners and knowledge makers through special projects.

Certainly the transformation from teacher to learner does not occur automatically, and for many, research projects may be useful in promoting the kind of thinking about students and teaching that transforms teachers into learners. But, as Shaughnessy has shown us, when teachers enact constructivist theories, that transformation can also occur "naturally," as part of our daily work with students. What's required is not a special project but a high level of commitment and openness: a willingness to reflect on what we observe, to question our assumptions, and to play with possibilities in ways that generate new questions, uncover previously hidden connections among processes, or suggest alternate models. With most teachers so committed to teaching that they see it more as a vocation than a job, why is it so difficult for those of us who spend hours each week in classrooms to enact our theories and see, let alone seize, the opportunities for learning that surround us? What shadows fall between the idea and the reality?

Obstacles to Realizing the Potential for Learning

Many shadows obscure our vision of teaching as a mode of learning and interfere with our efforts to enact current theories. Some of these shadows emanate from the institutions in which we teach and others from our selves, from the knowledge we constructed as children when Industrial Age assumptions remained dominant. Whatever the source, most of us feel their presence, especially in our institutions, so those are the shadows to consider first.

Like most institutions in this transitional era, schools and colleges continue to operate on principles that Toffler identifies as characteristic of the Industrial Age, principles that, not surprisingly, were necessary for factories to run well:

1. standardization (of products and procedures)
2. specialization (of labor)
3. centralization (of power and authority)
4. concentration (of money, energy, resources, and people)

5. maximization (of production)
6. synchronization (of activities)

Although we may first associate those principles only with factories, Toffler argues that they "affected every aspect of life from sex and sports to work and war" (46) because they shaped the development of every social institution, from banking and government to families and schools. One way that we as teachers might assess the continuing presence and power of those principles in our professional lives is to weigh the effort required to free ourselves of them.

One of the more pernicious principles has been standardization. From the beginning of mass education, a belief in the desirability of standardization led to increasingly standardized curricula with standardized texts and standardized tests, and now many of our professional interests and activities directly challenge that principle. For example, we fight for alternatives to standardized objective tests, seeking to replace them with writing samples or portfolios of work. We question the existence of *an* academic discourse and challenge the canon of literary works that Hirsch, Bennett, and others strive to protect. We work to replace basal readers in elementary schools with "real books" chosen by individual teachers or students, not by district or state committees. As a profession, we struggle to move away from standardization toward customization, one of the new principles Toffler sees emerging.

We also now work against the unquestioning belief in the value of specialization. That belief brought a proliferation of disciplines and majors in colleges and universities and institutionalized separation and fragmentation. Through our departments, we institutionalized the separation of reading from writing and of both from speaking and listening. Within our programs and courses, we divided what we taught into ever smaller units and increasingly isolated those units from one another so that we ended up with not only separate literature and composition courses but separate reading, vocabulary, writing, and grammar courses made up of isolated units on specific errors, parts of speech, or methods of development.

Today, as a profession, we are challenging the value of specialization in multiple ways, from the whole language movement of elementary teachers to the emphasis on the interdisciplinary nature of composition studies. At every level we search for connections among processes, consider rhetorical contexts, and question formalistic ap-

proaches to reading and writing that isolate features, prescribe procedures, and ignore the interplay of reader, writer, and text. More
holistic, naturalistic research methods gain credibility while attacks
on positivistic models grow. And these efforts parallel the larger movement away from specialization and toward synthesis, a movement
Toffler predicted in 1980:

> Today I believe we stand at the edge of a new age of synthesis. In
> all intellectual fields, . . . we are likely to see a return to large-scale
> thinking, to general theory, to the putting of the pieces back together
> again. For it is beginning to dawn on us that our obsessive emphasis
> on quantified detail without context, on progressively finer and finer
> measurement of smaller and smaller problems, leaves us knowing more
> and more about less and less. (130)

Although specialization and standardization were particularly po-
tent influences, the other four Industrial Age principles, working
together and reinforcing one another, also shaped our institutions
and professional lives in ways that can be seen by the attacks now
under way from inside and outside our educational systems. As part
of the attack on centralization of power and authority, consider the
movement to site-based management for schools, a drive to endow
teachers with authority over curriculum, or the parallel emergence of
home-schooling outside of the system. Or think about the effort to
shift from teacher-centered to student-centered or learning-centered
classrooms and the rise of workshop models with students responding
to their peers' drafts. For sample attacks on concentration—the assumption that those with similar characteristics should be brought
together—consider current efforts to mainstream physically disabled
and learning-disabled students and to end ability grouping in elementary classrooms and tracking in high schools.

The belief in maximization, that more or bigger is better, is being
displaced by notions of the importance of context, appropriate scale,
and the value of depth of understanding over breadth of information.
We no longer assume that a theme a week is innately better than one
every three, four, or five weeks or that having read every one of
Shakespeare's plays is necessarily better than having read and reread
a few. Even synchronization is under attack as public school systems
look at alternate calendars and colleges offer mini-semesters during
the regular year and flex-entry courses. In our classrooms, portfolios
mean not every student is working on the same assignment at the

same time, and collaborative learning may mean groups are grappling with different texts at the same time.

Despite these attacks, the guiding principles of the Industrial Age, which reinforce one another, still dominate our schools. As teachers we are caught trying to act on theories based on new principles—the valuing of customization over standardization, diversity and flexibility over uniformity, cooperation over competition, integration and synthesis over compartmentalization and fragmentation—while operating in institutions developed to meet the needs of an industrial society. Historically, schools met those needs through what Toffler calls the "covert curriculum" and describes as "three courses: one in punctuality, one in obedience, and one in rote, repetitive work. Factory labor demanded workers who showed up on time, especially assembly-line hands. It demanded workers who would take orders from a management hierarchy without questioning. And it demanded men and women prepared to slave away at machines or in offices, performing brutally repetitious operations" (29). Today, however, companies do not need workers able to perform rote tasks without questioning but workers able to ask questions, assess situations, and solve problems. In fact, *Work in the 21st Century*, published by the American Society for Personnel Administration, emphasizes that the need for workers "with discretion"—those able to exercise judgment, adapt, cooperate, and collaborate—is growing at *all* job levels because, as machines take over more of the rote tasks of comparatively low-level jobs such as bank tellers, the workers must assume responsibility for nonroutine tasks (Zaleznik 4–5; Yankelovich and Immerwahr 13–16). The problem, of course, is that the covert curriculum continues to inform institutional priorities and policies even though the mind-set and values it engenders do not match today's realities.

So part of the difficulty of enacting our theories is that we work in institutions designed to serve purposes no longer valid and built on principles that conflict with the emerging values of a new age and with current theories in our field. An even greater obstacle, however, may be found within each of us—the "knowledge" of our world and our discipline that we have individually internalized.

Most of us who teach composition (or design the programs in which graduate students teach) were reared when Industrial Age principles and assumptions remained largely unchallenged. So, the "reality" we internalized as children was, for the most part, the socially constructed objective reality of industrial society. We first acquired

that reality through primary socialization, a process Berger and Luckmann describe as powerful because of its emotional context. During
primary socialization, which occurs in early childhood through interaction with primary caretakers, we internalize as "the truth" what
our parents or other caretakers tell us (through words and actions)
about ourselves, others, and the "world." Their objective reality becomes our subjective reality or truth—what we "know" in the sense of
everyday knowledge about people, relationships, expected behaviors,
what it means "to be" a man or woman or parent or child in a given
society. And despite the dialectical relationship between objective
reality and subjective reality (between, for instance, an idea, belief,
or assumption and "the truth" or "what I am certain of"), Berger and
Luckmann emphasize the difficulty of unlearning or transforming the
subjective reality or worldview constructed as a child: "It takes severe
biographical shocks to disintegrate the massive reality internalized in
early childhood" (142). And that massive reality is only part of what
we have to contend with.

In addition to the concepts we internalized as children through
primary socialization, we also have more specific knowledge and concepts constructed later through secondary socialization processes. Secondary socialization, which Berger and Luckmann describe as similar
to primary socialization, involves constructing knowledge of sub-
worlds—what it means to be an employee of a particular company
or what it means to be a judge or a teacher. Although some information
about a subworld might be transmitted formally, most of it comes
through observing and interacting with others to discover and then
adopt the assumptions, values, and behaviors associated with that
subworld. Secondary socialization, then, results in our everyday
knowledge of our field, what Robert Scholes labels "the arche-depart-
ment of English that presently authorizes our professional behavior"
(4) and "the arche-institution of English [that] lives in each one of us
as a professional unconscious, revealing itself in actions and aversions
that we experience in our roles as institutional beings" (4). For example, as part of our socialization into the field of English, our subworld,
most of us accepted two basic value-laden distinctions, which Scholes
calls the "organizing gestures" of our field: valuing literature over
non-literature and privileging the consumption of texts over the production of texts (4–5). And we accepted those gestures or assumptions
because they were so institutionalized in our departmental structures

and hierarchies that they remained invisible as assumptions; instead, they seemed to be "true."

The invisibility and power of those assumptions are not surprising in terms of social constructionist theory. According to Berger and Luckmann, several factors affect the power of concepts formed through secondary socialization: the degree of institutionalized support for the concepts associated with that subworld; the time invested in the process of socialization; and the level of emotional intensity associated with the process (138–49). For us as college English teachers, these factors spell trouble. Many of our ideas about what it means "to be a teacher" were first constructed years ago when we were elementary school students, and they came with strong emotional ties and heavy institutional support. Then we spent years as undergraduate English majors and graduate students being inducted into the world of the English professor. No wonder change is difficult.

As evidence of the presence and power of some of those old internalized concepts, consider the many teachers who, acting on what research suggests, try not marking every error but continue to feel guilty about it. Despite the growing research on responding, they feel that they are somehow "not doing their job." Or consider Jane Tompkins's description of the distressing effects on her of trying to enact current theory in a new graduate course. Though she calls the outcome exciting, she reports experiencing so much guilt and self-doubt during the course that she "started getting migraines after every class" (639). Like Tompkins, most of us have internalized a set of assumptions about our role—what being an English teacher means—that makes acting on our current theories difficult. And without enacting these theories, we have little chance of constructing new concepts of what it means to be a teacher today. Instead, we are left with the notion that teaching has only the very limited potential as a mode of learning that it had when mechanistic assumptions and transmission models dominated our field.

Given the pervasiveness of social and disciplinary change and its radical nature, it's not surprising that, despite our good intentions, we find it difficult to enact current theories in our classrooms and tap the potential for learning through teaching. To enact new theories and construct new concepts of our role and our work, we must first make the invisible, visible: recognize our assumptions as assumptions and scrutinize them. As long as we consider them reality or truth, we can neither question old concepts nor begin to internalize new ones. And intellectual acceptance is not sufficient. The changes in our theories run deep, representing new values, new ways of thinking and being. They mean that teaching composition today challenges us in *fundamental* ways that reverberate with the challenges inherent in our era as well as in our individual lives. And just as disciplinary lines blur in the larger academic world and lines between genres fade, so the lines between teacher and learner, between the person and the role, become less visible, more admittedly arbitrary.

Reconceiving Our Role as Teachers

What we are trying to do in classrooms today is substantively different from what occurred even twenty-five years ago. We are trying to enact a new set of theories, theories congruent with one another and with the emerging values of the new age, but at odds with many of the attitudes and assumptions we have internalized as individuals and as teachers. When we prepare for a class, we don't just focus on content—on what *we* will talk about—we think about how to structure the class so that students can learn. And we don't just think about *our* interactions with students, but *their* interactions with one another. We want students to be engaged readers, writers, and learners and our classes to somehow become communities where multiple voices can be heard and respected. But how do we accomplish this?

Simply putting students in small groups or having them read their work aloud to one another—or any other change in practice—will not, by itself, transform 20, 25, or 30 students into a community of engaged learners. They have learned too well the "covert curriculum" that continues to inform public education, fostering passivity, obedience, and competition over the active engagement, critical thinking, and cooperation we wish to promote. To become the engaged learners we want, students need to develop a different attitude toward their work, one another, and themselves—an attitude or stance they see in us. But what does that mean? What stance or set of attitudes can foster communities of engaged learners?

One answer can be found in *Pedagogy of the Oppressed* where Paulo Freire sketches out such a stance—that of the humanist or dialogic educator—and discusses the attitudes associated with that stance as conditions necessary for dialogue. Critical thinking is one: "Only dialogue, which requires critical thinking, is also capable of generating critical thinking. Without dialogue there is no communication, and without communication, there can be no true education" (81). Before reaching critical thinking, however, Freire discusses five other conditions necessary for dialogue—love, humility, faith, mutual trust, and hope (77–80). When I first read Freire, I found those terms very uncomfortable, despite his definitions, because the terms themselves reverberated too much with memories from a childhood and youth dominated by a fundamentalist Swedish Baptist upbringing. Yet the sense that trying to act on our theories demands more of me as a person and that the "more" it demands falls within the humanizing/transforming arena of dialogue has enabled me to stick with Freire's terms and definitions:

> love = commitment to others; a basic attitude or orientation toward people, the world, and life that requires courage
>
> humility = acknowledgement of one's own limits; a willingness to learn from and with others; openness
>
> faith = belief in the power of humans "to make and remake, to create and recreate" (79)
>
> trust = the feeling that emerges through dialogue and experiences of congruity between belief and action, what is said and done
>
> hope = the expectation that something will come of the encounter

If Freire is right in asserting these conditions for dialogue apply to *all* participants in the encounter, then we as teachers need to develop a different stance, that of committed learner and risk taker. For, as Freire asks, "How can I dialogue if I always project ignorance onto others and never perceive my own?" (78) or "How can I dialogue if I am closed to—and even offended by—the contribution of others?" (79) The answer is, of course, I can't. If there is to be a community engaged in dialogue, Freire says there can be "neither utter ignoramuses nor perfect sages" but only people "who are attempting, together, to learn more than they now know" (79). For this stance as community member and learner to be more than a role we play, we need to internalize the assumptions and values inherent in our current theories, to develop a different attitude toward our work, students, and ourselves. But what might that mean? How do we begin?

Internalizing New Concepts

We begin, I think, by understanding that enacting our theories requires more than surface changes in our practices. To structure situations for learning and enter our classes honestly expecting that something will come of the encounter, we need to see students as people to learn from and with. For most of us, this means not only becoming more knowledgeable about learning but also developing a deeper respect for students and increasing our sense of ourselves as learners. And those changes do not occur quickly or automatically. They require effort—time and energy devoted to the activities we associate with learning: focused writing, reading, discussion, and thinking. Because we each begin in a different place, what each of us needs to do and *can* do will differ. I can only sketch out what I mean by the process of change—internalizing different assumptions—and then suggest a few strategies for getting started that have, at different points, served as catalysts for change, helping me develop a deeper understanding of current theories and a different set of attitudes toward students and myself.

An Overview of the Process

For me, this process began early in my career. I remember, for example, not only reading Emig's *Composing Processes of Twelfth Graders* but rereading the transcript and interviews with Lynn several times. Lynn's attitudes toward "school writing" stunned me, and the questions and concerns she expressed in self-assigned writing tasks fascinated me. Both the content and Emig's exploratory tone led me to think and write about my own attitudes toward writing in different situations, to "test" the validity of what Lynn reported against my own experience. Soon I was writing in my journal about my students' being like Lynn, like me. Not long after, I began to think that maybe— just maybe—the mediocre writing I was seeing said more about my assignments than about the students' abilities. The process of questioning my assumptions about students and their work had begun. Although the catalysts change, the critical ingredient in the process remains the same—conscious and regular reflection on what I observe and how I interpret those observations.

For me, reflection means monitoring my actions and questioning what I'm doing and why I'm doing it. What, for instance, am I trying to accomplish through reading and responding to this draft or journal entry? How might I best accomplish my goal in responding? I also question the effects of what I do. What happens when students receive my responses? How do students interpret my questions or comments? And most important, I question the basis of my own answers. How do I know what I think I know? What assumptions about students' knowledge and attitudes underlie my "answers"? How do those assumptions fit my broader knowledge of students or of an individual student? What if I'm wrong? How can I find out?

Sometimes simply asking students is enough, but not always. For example, when I asked students to comment on the value of written responses to their drafts from me and peers, they were enthusiastic. Yet questions designed to help them rethink seldom led to substantive revisions. Instead of assuming widespread obstinacy or laziness, I decided to listen to students' interpreting my comments. As I returned drafts, I asked them to read my responses aloud and tell me what they thought those comments meant. The sarcastic and shaming tones used by some students shocked me as did the frustration my questions often engendered. That first experience of hearing students read my comments generated many questions for me about reading and writing, about my own experiences as an undergraduate, about when and how I seek feedback from colleagues, about when I do and don't use that feedback. It led me to a new round of professional reading on both reading and responding and a series of changes in practice as well as a renewed sense of how significantly expectations shape readings—both students' and our own.

Developing a Deeper Respect for Students

Because students easily detect incongruities between words and actions, my reflection includes monitoring my attitude toward students. They know when a question represents a genuine prompt for information or ideas and when their responses will be valued. And they know when a question means "Tell me what I want to hear or what I already know." Most are sophisticated readers of teachers and classrooms with many years of experience in playing transmission games. Confronted with different expectations, a few seem relieved, but most don't. Instead they shift into what feels like a "red alert" phase, looking for incongruities that will enable them to dismiss me and my expectations as a variant of the old game. Faking interest doesn't work. If I expect honest responses, I need to be engaged in the process and really see students as worthy partners in learning.

And so I monitor my attitude toward students. When I catch myself focusing on what students "don't know" or can't do, I take time to list what I don't know and can't do or what some of my current students do know that I don't. Calculus, physics, business law, robotics, microeconomics, electronics—the lists quickly get long. I think about the skills and abilities students have developed and use in other courses, in other areas of their lives. And, like Shaughnessy and others, I think about what they already know about language, reading, and writing that they are not aware they know. How can they make that tacit knowledge explicit and accessible? What expectations or assumptions do they have that block that process? What expectations or assumptions do I have that interfere? Then I question my "answers." Increasingly I look to students for help, taking them my questions as I did my concern about how students read comments. And through them, I continue to learn and change.

Self-assigned journal entries also help deepen my respect for students and increase my awareness of the role they play in my professional life. Instead of writing about teachers who have had an impact on me, every week or two I take time to write about students who have had an impact on me. Sometimes I think of Lydia, the first severely learning-disabled student I met. In the fall of 1971, she was a junior enrolled in freshman composition for the fifth time. And the disparity between her writing and her astute comments in class shocked me into asking her to come in for a conference, where she told me about having been tested the previous summer and found "dyslexic." But Lydia had no ideas about what might help her, and I had never before heard of dyslexia. Her intelligence, extreme frustration, and willingness to work led me to find a couple of articles on dyslexia and devise a way for us to work together: we talked, she wrote, I read aloud what she had written, then she read and taped it, we talked, she listened to the tape and rewrote. With multiple conferences each week, she passed the course, and I discovered the challenge and satisfaction of working with one kind of "underprepared" writer. Lydia destroyed my assumption that writing accurately reflects intelligence and catapulted me into the world of basic writing, where I chose to work for the next fifteen years.

Although I occasionally dip far into my past when I think about the impact students have had on me, I usually write about recent or current students and how they influence me. Some reinforce my beliefs about professional concerns. When the issue of placement into writing courses through objective tests arises, I see and hear the frustration and anger of students I have worked with who were placed needlessly into developmental courses or into freshman composition with little chance of success. When discussions about ability grouping and tracking in public schools begin, I think of Allison who was told as a senior by her high school counselor that she could not attend college because she had not taken the college preparatory course and that, in fact, it had been clear since eighth grade that she was not "college material." Allison's outrage motivated her to discover her options, enter a community college, and enroll in developmental courses, but I also see many students each semester who accepted what they were told at 17, found jobs, and then realized at 22 or 28 or 40 that they were as intelligent as their degreed supervisors. Now, however, when they attend college, they juggle multiple responsibilities—full-time jobs, families, and school. And they face not four years of college as full-time students, but six or eight years as part-time students. Donna, Linda, John, Jimmy, Phyllis, Kim, Ken, Steve, Annette, Jay—all current students enrolled in my day sections of technical writing, a sophomore course.[5] All were tracked out of college, and all now seek degrees. Most work full-time and have families. Will they make it? Donna, a single parent and full-time worker, had to withdraw from school early in the semester when her father who lived with her and helped with child care died suddenly of a heart attack. Her mother had died six months earlier after a long illness. Without parents to provide child care, will she be able to return to school any time soon to complete her engineering degree?

Thinking about the lives of these students not only reinforces my belief that tracking serves institutions and not students, but it also motivates me to continue reflecting on what I am seeing and doing. I think, for instance, of Robert, a twenty-seven-year-old paraplegic enrolled in my freshman research and argumentation course two summers ago. Near the end of the course, Robert was talking about a possible audience for an argumentative piece, and I discovered that he had only been injured about nine months before. Having assumed his injury had occurred several years earlier, I felt shocked and soon wondered what had led me to think he had been paralyzed for years. I reread Robert's work—his journal, his documented report on spinal cord injuries, his research log with accounts of trips to other libraries. Reading with new information and questions for myself, I found no references to his life before the accident and felt overwhelmed by his courage in trying to understand his injury and face his loss of mobility. Thinking about Robert's courage in the weeks following that course enabled me to face the impending loss of a very close friend, understand his need to discuss his dying, and make myself available to him. So Robert had a very direct and personal effect, but he also deepened my understanding of the nature of reading: rereading Robert's work vividly reminded me of what I believe—that readers construct meaning and that multiple factors, both conscious and unconscious, affect any reading; it also raised new questions for me as both reader and writer, questions about the power of what is not said.

As I write for myself about students who have had an impact on me—shaping my beliefs about professional issues, helping me understand the processes of reading and writing, and even affecting personal decisions—my respect for students deepens and my sense of myself as a learner grows.

Seeing Ourselves as Learners

Although conscious reflection on my attitude toward students helps increase my sense of myself as learner, I also find it useful to think directly about past and current learning experiences, both professional and personal. Buying my first microcomputer in 1980 and feeling compelled to learn how to program in Basic. Teaching my first course for managers in a large electronics firm. Participating in the 1987 English Coalition Conference. Becoming an investor in joint land ventures. Designing a data base. Having a family member undergo bypass surgery. As I review experiences like these when I have been a vulnerable learner in some important way, I focus on different aspects of the situations. For instance, what have I been able to hear and not hear in new situations? How have analogies used by an authority figure affected me? When do someone else's analogies help? When do they interfere? What happens when I can generate my own analogies to test my understanding? When does talk alleviate anxiety and when doesn't it? What factors affect its value to me? What kinds of writing have I done as part of learning and why? What kinds of reading? What affects my view of the value of "assigned" reading? What prompts me to seek additional information?

Applying questions like these to my own school experiences also helps. Sometimes I focus on negative experiences and sometimes on positive ones—what I remember learning in grade school, junior high, high school, and college. A group project in third grade to write a script and make puppets for a show for first graders. A fourth grade group project on the industries of our state. A mock election in fifth grade. A debate on presidential candidates in eighth grade. In high school, a paper on the Scopes trial for history and one on Hedonism for English. And two science fair projects. In college, taking weekly oral quizzes in Spanish, reading aloud in Middle English each time our Chaucer class met, defending my senior "thesis." I ask questions about individual experiences and look for common traits in these and other positive school experiences. Two keep surfacing. The experiences that led to learning I still remember either engaged me in multi-sensory activities over an extended time, often in collaboration with others, or represented topics I chose based on concerns originating outside of school.

Whether reflections like these are triggered by a student's comment or question, a mediocre class session, or the need to prepare a syllabus, they help me remember what it means to be a student and a learner. They authenticate my belief in the value of engaging students as fully as possible in their own learning and motivate me to continue questioning what I do and reflecting on what I observe. And through this process, I become more conscious of myself as a reader, writer, and learner. Through teaching, I learn.

Realizing the Potential for Learning Through Teaching

Through teaching, we can learn—but it's not easy. We live and teach in an era of major transition, and the changes within our profession parallel those Toffler identifies for the larger society. Our current constructivist theories of reading, writing, and learning and our evolving organic, interactive models are far more congruent with the emerging principles of the new era than with those of the Industrial Age. So, as a profession, we seem to be married to the future, but as individuals, we live and work in the present, in institutions still dominated by Industrial Age principles. And although we may intellectually embrace constructivist theories, as children most of us internalized indust-reality, a belief system that conflicts with current theories and makes enacting them difficult. Is it a catch-22? I don't think so.

Reflection offers at least one way out, and it's a way available to us all. Through reflection, we can make our tacit knowledge explicit and begin to internalize a different set of assumptions about reading, writing, and learning and about our work, students, and ourselves. In fact, Berger and Luckmann claim that "'better knowledge' of myself

requires reflection" (29). To find out "what I am"—to identify the
constructs, beliefs, and assumptions that shape me so that I can begin
to transform them—"requires that I stop, arrest the continuous spon-
taneity of my experience, and deliberately turn my attention back
upon myself. What is more, such reflection about myself is typically
occasioned by the attitude toward me that *the other* exhibits. It is
typically a 'mirror' response to attitudes of the other" (29–30). As
teachers, we have no shortage of mirrors. Our students, both individually and collectively, can serve as catalysts for the kind of reflection
that enables us to pose questions and construct new concepts. But is
the time and energy required for such reflection worthwhile?

My own answer is yes. The more I reflect and internalize a different view of what being a teacher means, the easier it becomes to enact
the theories I hold. As a teacher, I am energized both by the greater
sense of congruity between what I believe and what I do and by the
rich context for my own thinking and learning that is created when
I enact constructivist theories. And, because those theories are more
consonant with the emerging values of the new age than those I
internalized as a child, the benefits extend to other areas of my life,
making it easier to cope with changes in the larger social context. Just
as the challenges inherent in teaching writing today reverberate with
those of living in a transitional era, so do the rewards.

Notes

1. All references to Toffler in the text come from *The Third Wave*, originally
published in 1980 and now considered the middle volume of his extensively
researched trilogy on social change. Although these volumes, published ten
years apart, highlight the same seventy-five-year period (from the mid 1950s
to 2025), each focuses on a different dimension of change: *Future Shock* on
the process of change and its effects; *The Third Wave* on directions of change;
and *Powershift* "on the crucially changed role of knowledge in relationship to
power" (xx). In each work, Toffler probes a wide range of institutions in
countries throughout the world, which may be why, in part, his work continues to be so frequently translated and published abroad (within a year of
its release, *Powershift* was being published in more than twenty countries,
including, for instance, Brazil, Bulgaria, China, Malaysia, and Turkey). *The
Third Wave*, based on ten years of wide-ranging research, offers a particularly
powerful lens for examining change because the directions and principles
Toffler identified in it have become increasingly visible.

2. These interpretative frameworks, of course, not only differ from one

another in important ways, but theorists within any one framework differ from one another as, for instance, Steven Mailloux's categorization of reader-response critics suggests.

3. Although *Literature as Exploration* is now in its fourth edition, the second edition did not appear until 1968. In a recent essay ("Retrospect"), Rosenblatt tries to correct the notion that her work "has 'finally' received recognition" by noting that in 1938 it received "a surprisingly wide favorable response" (101). She acknowledges that traditional formalist views and methods prevailed in the years following, but she stresses continuity, saying that her work and that of other progressive educators continued to influence some: "No matter what elitist ideas dominated in the universities, there have always been teachers, I have found, who understand the need for a new approach" (102).

4. When I refer to constructivist theories in the rest of this chapter, I am using the term in the very broad sense established in this section describing changes in our theories of reading, writing, and learning. Although I do not again reiterate the broad sense in which I use *constructivist* here, I alternate my use of "constructivist theories" with "current theories" as a gentle reminder.

5. The current semester when this was drafted was Fall 1991.

Works Cited

Bartholomae, David. "Released into Language: Errors, Expectations, and the Legacy of Mina Shaughnessy." *The Territory of Language: Linguistics, Stylistics, and the Teaching of Composition.* Ed. Donald McQuade. Rev. and enl. ed. of *Linguistics, Stylistics, and the Teaching of Composition.* 1979. Carbondale: Southern Illinois UP, 1986. 65–88.

Bennett, William J. *The De-Valuing of America: The Fight for Our Culture and Our Children.* New York: Summit, 1992.

Berger, Peter L., and Thomas Luckmann. *The Social Construction of Reality: A Treatise in the Sociology of Knowledge.* 1966. New York: Anchor, 1967.

Bruner, Jerome. *Actual Minds, Possible Worlds.* Cambridge, MA: Harvard UP, 1986.

———. *On Knowing: Essays for the Left Hand.* 1962. Expanded ed. 1979. Cambridge, MA: Belknap P of Harvard UP, 1979.

Emig, Janet. *The Composing Processes of Twelfth Graders.* Urbana: NCTE, 1971.

———. "Writing as a Mode of Learning." *College Composition and Communication* 28 (May 1977): 122–28.

Faulkner, Claude W. *Writing Good Prose: A Simple, Structural Approach.* New York: Scribner's, 1961.

———. *Writing Good Sentences: A Functional Approach to Sentence Structure, Grammar, and Punctuation.* Rev. ed. New York: Scribner's, 1957.

38   *Jane Peterson*

Freire, Paulo. *Pedagogy of the Oppressed*. Trans. Myra Bergman Ramos. 1968. New York: Continuum, 1984.

Hirsch, E. D. *Cultural Literacy: What Every American Needs to Know*. Boston: Houghton, 1987.

Lloyd-Jones, Richard, and Andrea A. Lunsford, eds. *The English Coalition Conference: Democracy Through Language*. Urbana: NCTE and MLA, 1989.

Luria, A. R. *Cognitive Development: Its Cultural and Social Foundations*. 1974. Trans. Martin Lopez-Morillas and Lynn Sulotaroff. Ed. Michael Cole. Cambridge, MA: Harvard UP, 1979.

Mailloux, Steven. "The Turns of Reader-Response Criticism." *Conversations: Contemporary Critical Theory and the Teaching of Literature*. Ed. Charles Moran and Elizabeth Penfield. Urbana: NCTE, 1990. 38–54.

Moran, Charles, and Elizabeth Penfield, eds. Introduction. *Conversations: Contemporary Critical Theory and the Teaching of Literature*. Urbana: NCTE, 1990.

Perl, Sondra. "A Look at Basic Writers in the Process of Composing." *Basic Writing: Essays for Teachers, Researchers, and Administrators*. Ed. Lawrence Kasden and Daniel Hoeber. Urbana: NCTE, 1980. 13–32.

Peterson, Jane. "Valuing Teaching: Assumptions, Problems, and Possibilities." *College Composition and Communication* 42 (February 1991): 25–35.

Polanyi, Michael. *Personal Knowledge: Towards a Post- Critical Philosophy*. 1958. Corrected ed. 1962. Chicago: U of Chicago P, 1962.

Rose, Mike. "The Language of Exclusion: Writing Instruction at the University." *College English* 47 (1985): 341–59.

Rosenblatt, Louise. *Literature as Exploration*. 1938. 4th ed. New York: MLA, 1983.

———. "Retrospect." *Transactions with Literature: A Fifty-Year Perspective*. Ed. Edmund J. Farrell and James R. Squire. Urbana: NCTE, 1990. 97–107.

Scholes, Robert. *Textual Power: Literary Theory and the Teaching of English*. New Haven: Yale UP, 1985.

Shaughnessy, Mina P. *Errors and Expectations: A Guide for the Teacher of Basic Writing*. New York: Oxford UP, 1977.

Toffler, Alvin. *Future Shock*. New York: Bantam, 1971.

———. *Powershift: Knowledge, Wealth, and Violence at the Edge of the 21st Century*. New York: Bantam, 1991.

———. *The Third Wave*. New York: Bantam, 1981.

Tompkins, Jane. "Pedagogy of the Distressed." *College English* 52 (1990): 653–60.

Vygotsky, L. S. *Mind in Society: The Development of Higher Psychological Processes*. 1974. Ed. and trans. Michael Cole et al. Cambridge, MA: Harvard UP, 1978.

———. *Thought and Language*. Ed. and trans. Eugenia Hanfmann and Gertrude Vakar. Cambridge, MA: MIT P, 1962.

Yankelovich, Daniel, and John Immerwahr. [no title] *Work in the 21st Century:*

An Anthology of Writings on the Changing World of Work. Ed. American Society for Personnel Administration. Alexandria, VA: American Society for Personnel Administration, 1984. 11–23.

Zaleznik, Abraham. An Introduction. *Work in the 21st Century: An Anthology of Writings on the Changing World of Work*. Ed. American Society for Personnel Administration. Alexandria, VA: American Society for Personnel Administration, 1984.

2

Reflections on Empirical

Research: Examining Some Ties

Between Theory and Action

Anne J. Herrington

Janet Emig often tells of Don Graves's saying about "theory" that you can't get out of bed without one. I understand him to be saying that theory is not just a formal cluster of abstract ideas distinct from us; it is within us and our actions. Whether we are aware of it or not, some theory—or belief—guides even our everyday actions, including our actions as teachers and as researchers. We may grow into some of these actions without much reflection or awareness of alternatives and the beliefs about writing, learning, and reality underlying them. The assumption underlying this collection is that we should stop and reflect on our actions, trying to identify the beliefs that guide us and reflect critically on them in light of alternatives. That reflection may reaffirm our commitment to how we have been acting or it may lead us to change. Regardless, if we engage in such reflection, we will be more likely to actually make choices and have a fuller understanding of our reasons for doing so.

I have approached this chapter with that aim in mind. For myself,

I have used the process of working on it as an occasion for a reflexive exploration of myself as a researcher, examining my own research practices and assumptions in relation to alternatives and trying to understand the consequences of each for the findings that result from a study. My hope is that the essay will encourage similar reflections for others, whether initiating their own investigations or reading the research of others.

While I believe that we should engage in such critical reflection for our own personal growth, we also have a professional obligation to do so. Those of us engaged in research are attempting to create a certain reality of classroom life and schooling, a reality we want others to accept as valid. Moreover, in most cases, through our research accounts, we are trying to affect—either directly or indirectly—decisions about teaching. For this reason alone, it is important that researchers and readers of research understand more about the assumptions and research practices that shape those studies.

For many of us, examining these assumptions means starting to ask new questions from the ones we have been accustomed to ask as researchers and readers of research. We have been used to asking questions like the following:

- What do I want to focus on—what guiding question?
- What and who will be my sources of information and the methods of obtaining it?
- How will I analyze and interpret the information?

Corresponding to these questions are criteria by which we as researchers and readers are accustomed to assess research: For example, is the research question focused enough? Is a sound rationale provided? Do the sources of information and methods of obtaining it answer the questions asked? Do the methods of obtaining information avoid distorting what is being studied? Do the methods of analysis and interpretation seem valid and reliable?

While these questions are useful for "getting us out of bed"— getting on with research and even evaluating it in some measure— they are not adequate for examining the assumptions behind our actions, specifically fundamental assumptions about reality, knowing, and values that influence the problems and questions that are posed, the views and voices that are represented, and the perceived purposes and audiences for research.

To examine those assumptions entails asking what for many of us is a new set of questions:

- Whose views are included in a research study and by whom are they represented? More generally, what are participants' roles throughout a study?
- In what ways do researchers recognize their own roles in shaping research findings?
- In what ways do researchers recognize the function of ideology and, more generally, values in research studies?

The chapter proceeds by examining each question in turn. The development of each section reflects my own process of inquiry, moving back and forth between theory and practice. Each section opens with a basic theoretical assumption that frames the discussion. I then explore how that assumption is interpreted differently by various approaches, examining connections between abstract assumptions, practices, and research findings. Because this is a chapter, not a book, I have been selective, choosing approaches and theories that seem right now to be challenging more established ones and that present the strongest challenges to my own practices.

To ground my self-reflections as I worked on the chapter, I reexamined my first formal research study, a study of writing in two undergraduate chemical engineering classrooms, conducted for my PhD dissertation in 1982–83 ("Writing"). As I worked on the chapter, this study provided me something concrete against which to consider the implications of alternative assumptions and practices. I have included some of my reflections on this study because it also provides a clear contrast to some of the alternatives I discuss.

I also chose to review this study because when I was doing it, I was not very aware of the assumptions implicit in the practices I chose. I had grown into them just as I had grown into many teaching practices—influenced by my past experiences, my graduate faculty and studies, and my personal inclinations. In this respect, I suspect that I am like most other people: by disposition, past experiences, and present encounters, we are inclined toward a certain general way of inquiry whether that be historical, personal introspection, experimental research, contextual, or other. As will become evident as you read further, I was and remain inclined toward studies of writing in context, trying to understand people's actions and perceptions. That general way of inquiry fits with the kinds of questions that interest me, specifically questions of how writing is used by students and teachers in school. It also fits with my own sense of a type of work I find satisfying: working with people and hearing how they experience their situations and what they value. In other words, my allegiance to this general approach is not based on a distanced, intellectually articulated decision; it is based on my own preferences and intuitive sense. For me, no amount of critical reflection is likely to change this general inclination, although such reflection helps me understand its merits and limitations in relation to alternative approaches.

Further, acknowledging a personal inclination to a *general* way of inquiry does not mean that we cannot step back, critically scrutinize, and even revise our *particular* practices and beliefs. It is in this spirit of critical reflection that I revisited my earlier study and composed this chapter.

Whose Views Are Included and by Whom Are They Represented?

It is a commonplace to accept that our understandings of everyday activities are shaped by each of our perspectives and vary among us, even when we participate in the same activity. The same holds for research. People participating in a given setting—for instance, students and teachers in a classroom—and people observing it are likely to have a number of different understandings of the meaning of participants' actions and, for instance, purposes for classroom activities. Those different understandings will be shaped by—among other things—people's roles, aims, and vantage points in the immediate setting as well as their prior experiences, class, gender, race, and values. In other words, different individuals are likely to **construct** different understandings of the "reality" of the setting; it is in that sense that reality can be said to be constituted by **multiple realities** (Lincoln and Guba 83–84; Doheny-Farina and Odell 507–10; Brodkey, *Academic* 100–106). For example, in one of the chemical engineering classrooms that I studied, I found that while teachers intended for writing assignments to serve as a means for students to explore their ideas, the students viewed the writings as a means of demonstrating their knowledge to the teachers. Neither view could be said to be any more real than the other, but had I failed to interview both the teachers and students, I would not have learned of this discrepancy in their views, one that indicated that the writings were not serving their intended educational purpose.

It is important to ask not only whose understandings are included but also who is selecting the understandings to be included and who is actually constructing them into an account that presents the "reality" or knowledge that arises from the study. Implicit in these questions is a link between research—even qualitative research in one's own classroom—and the distribution of authority. Yvonna Lincoln underscores this link when she asks rhetorically, "*Whose* knowledge is legitimized, whose findings become a part of the official record, [and] who is permitted to speak for others" (503). In other words, whose reality(s) get included and by whom? Who will be the researcher? Who the participants?

Usually, the researcher role is assumed by a university-trained and university-based researcher, like me. The participants—those being studied—are most often teachers and/or students. Advocates of teacher-research—as distinct from university-based research—challenge this relationship, saying that university-based researchers do not adequately speak for those they study, specifically teachers. As Cochran-Smith and Lytle argue, university-based researchers are often concerned with different questions than are the teachers in the classrooms they are studying and they do not adequately include teachers in the generation of knowledge. For this reason, Cochran-Smith and Lytle advocate that classroom teachers take on the role of researcher so that they are empowered to investigate questions of concern to them and speak for themselves. Still, the same questions of roles and authority relations pertain for teacher research. This research could easily replicate a parallel set of power relations, just with different players—the teachers being the researchers who control the study and the students being the objects of study. If we, as teachers, are conducting studies of our own classrooms, are students' views represented and who is representing them? Who is speaking for whom?

One way to answer these questions—and to understand some of the implications of the choices made—is to view participant involvement on a continuum of little to great involvement in a study. At one end of the continuum, participants play a relatively passive role in comparison to the researcher; at the other end, they are more actively involved with the researcher in the design and implementation of a study.

Participants play the most passive role in interpretative studies where the researcher-interpreter is the one to construct the knowledge that arises from the study. For instance, in *The Social Uses of Writing*, Tom Fox, identifying his approach with interpretative, critical ethnography, constructs case studies of three students from one of his classes by interpreting their writings from the class. He "reads" these texts to show the influence of the students' social identities—specifically gender, class, and race—on their language use. Fox is the sole one to construct the reality that arises from the study. His approach is in the tradition of hermeneutic studies of texts by literary scholars. In this case, his students' writings are the texts to be interpreted instead of, say, the writings of Toni Morrison. The students, as authors of those texts, do not also interpret them. As with others who espouse a hermeneutic approach (North; Clark and Doheny-Farina), Fox recognizes his interpretations as constructions—his interpretations of the texts of these individual students—and does not claim for them any wider generalizability. It is for readers—primarily teachers—to decide if these interpretations seem to "fit" their context. Readers are also invited to offer alternative explanations.[1]

Most ethnographic research attempts to involve the participants more, aiming to include in the study not only participants' texts but also their understandings of those texts. Still, the participants' role remains relatively passive, limited to offering information—being the "informants"—and serving in some way to validate emerging interpretations. The assumption is that the researcher will, through the analysis, interpretation, and writing of the account, take care to represent the multiple realities of the participants or informants. My own analytic study of the two chemical engineering classes is a case in point. My aim was to identify and report the views of the students and teachers in those classes. Although participants' views were my primary source of information as provided through surveys and extensive interviews, I—an outside researcher—was the one in charge: I posed the research questions in advance and decided on a conceptual framework from rhetorical theory to use to analyze the two classes. It was that theoretical framework that guided my selection and classification of information from the participants and their writing, using such categories as audience, purpose, issue, and types of appeals. In some instances, I used quantitative methods to examine differences between the two classrooms. Because I believed that in order to be valid my work had to make sense to the teachers and students in the study, I also checked out my scheme for analyzing texts with one of the teachers and, in final interviews, discussed a number of my provisional conclusions with participants, asking them whether they seemed valid or not ("Writing" 338).

Participants have also had relatively little involvement even in ethnographic studies of writing that have been more inductive and fully qualitative than my study of the chemical engineering classrooms (e.g., Doheny-Farina, "Case Study"; Odell; Herrington, "Composing"). Still, in contrast to my more deductive approach, these studies do more to try to avoid fitting participants' views into the researchers' own lens or interpretative structure. For instance, while Doheny-Farina began his study with a general research interest identified, he did not define the specific research questions until he had spent some time in the two settings he was studying. Further, he did not specify a theoretical framework in advance to use to interpret findings. Instead, he worked inductively to try to identify issues and themes that he saw operating within each context, using more open-ended and inductive research approaches (e.g., informal, less structured interviews; inductive approaches to analysis; Doheny-Farina and Odell). The assumption is that through these means he would be more likely to identify the participants' understandings from those participants' frames of reference.

Researchers, such as Lincoln and Guba, who advocate a "naturalistic" research approach depart from the approaches I have just described in their conception of the researcher's role. While the researcher is still the one in charge, Lincoln and Guba depict the ideal researcher as a neutral medium who fully brackets her own prior beliefs in order to be fully responsive to the situation being studied and to transmit the participants' views without distortion. To this end, they argue for a more fully inductive approach where neither the research design nor the guiding theory is defined in advance; each is to emerge during the process of inquiry. They argue that "no *a priori* theory could possibly encompass the multiple realities that are likely to be encountered," so the researcher "wishes to enter his transactions with respondents as neutrally as possible" (41). "Wishes" and "as possible" are the operant words in that quote. While such neutrality may be an aim, it cannot be attained. To assume that any one of us could view a situation free of any theoretical frame—any personal construct of values and beliefs—is to aspire to a positivist myth of an "objective," neutrality of mind. The best we can do when we begin a research study is to try to acknowledge our frame of reference and try as best we can to listen to and include the perspectives of others, most important, those participating in a study.[2]

This aim leads other researchers to include participants more actively in research studies, taking even more strongly the theoretical claim that reality is multiple and constructed. The methodological implication is that any attempt to understand the constructions of individuals requires a more reciprocal relation with those individuals, involving them *throughout* the inquiry—not just using them as a source of information but also to "negotiate meanings and interpretations" and to verify working hypotheses (Lincoln and Guba 41).

For instance, many researchers who identify themselves with a feminist methodology argue that knowledge should be constructed through a more collaborative relationship with those being studied (Harding 8). In contrast to the inductive, theoretically neutral approach that Lincoln and Guba advocate as the ideal, much feminist research is guided by an acknowledged theoretical perspective that shapes the research right from the start. Patti Lather stresses this aspect of a feminist methodology and demonstrates it in her own research, which has an explicit ideological and transformative aim. As Lather writes, echoing the aim of much other feminist research, "the overt goal of feminist research . . . is to correct both the invisibility and distortion of female experience in ways relevant to ending women's unequal social position" ("Feminist" 54). Lather acknowledges the tension existing between a collaborative approach she advocates and the a priori theory she endorses. For researchers to deal with this tension, she advocates that they be candid in identifying their guiding theoretical assumptions and take pains to avoid rigidly imposing them on those participating in a research study. To that end, she also advocates methods that are standard for other naturalistic research (e.g., triangulation) and a "maximal approach to reciprocity" ("Research" 264). By the latter phrase, she means a reciprocal relationship between "researcher" and "participants"whereby participants are involved not only in gathering information but also in "the interpretation of the descriptive data [and] construction of empirically grounded theory" (264).

It is not just researchers who identify themselves with feminist approaches who have argued for and begun conducting studies that involve participants more fully in the research. Increased participation and more reciprocal researcher-participant relationships are evident, for example, in Denny Taylor and Catherine Dorsey-Gaines's ethnography of literacy among inner-city families, *Growing Up Literate: Learning from Inner-City Families*. The research questions that evolved as their study progressed cast the participants not simply as passive objects of study but as active agents who, with the researchers, shaped the findings. For example, instead of asking "What social forces have shaped the families' lives?" Taylor and Dorsey-Gaines ask "How have the families helped us understand the social, political, and economic forces that shape their lives? What have the families taught us about literacy?" (xviii).

Family members' active participation is also evident in specific ways throughout the study. Participants were involved in collecting information (e.g., children bringing home their schoolwork, and all family members saving a full range of the family's writing, reading materials, and even children's drawings). Throughout the study, the researchers discussed their inferences and hypotheses with participants. Further, the researchers shared drafts of their final written account with participants in order to "include their interpretations and comments in the final text" (202, 222). In some instances, the researchers also reciprocated by trying to help families, especially in trying to make contacts with social service agencies (for instance, to obtain housing and to obtain an independent psychological evaluation of one child).

All of these actions served to minimize the distance between researchers and participants and to increase the trust these families had in the researchers. For instance, the families seemed willing to share quite sensitive family problems and personal writings that might otherwise have been kept from researchers. As a consequence, I believe we, as readers, gain more insight into the social and institutional forces that shape these families' lives, including their access to learning. We learn of an adolescent boy who has been physically abused by a teacher and the school's subsequent attempts to classify him as emotionally disturbed. What we see in this instance is the powerlessness of economically disadvantaged children and their parents and the power of institutions (as used by individuals within those institutions) to work against them. As with *Ways With Words* (Heath), we also see beyond fragmentary glimpses to a more inclusive view of literacy practices (e.g., children's drawings as linked to their emerging literacy, personal expressive writing by family members—poetry, an autobiography written by a dying mother for her daughter). What emerges is a picture of these inner-city families as functioning families,

as users of language for personal and public purposes, and as struggling to survive against a myriad of social, economic, and political
forces.

Other recent studies of writing move to even fuller involvement
by participants—leveling the distinction between researcher and participants so that they function together as a research team. This sharing
extends beyond checking in with those being studied, to sharing on
a more equal footing all aspects of the research, from framing the
originating questions to writing the research account. We see this
collaboration to some degree in a recent study by McCarthy and
Fishman. When they began their project, it was envisioned to be a
study of one of Fishman's college philosophy classes, with McCarthy
as the outside researcher and Fishman as one of the insider "informants" as well as a collaborator in the research. From the outset, the
plan was to give Fishman place in the final account to "tell his story."
However, once the study began, McCarthy and Fishman discovered
that giving "informant-collaborators" an equal voice also involves giving them the "opportunity to pursue their own questions, generate
their own data, and formulate their own conclusions" ("Text" 10).[3]
Essentially it means sharing authority with them. In the published
account of their research ("Boundary"), they explain that they shared
in interpreting much of the data but also that they divided the research
with each pursuing the issue of interest to each individual. They
report their results in "three voices": first, Fishman reporting on his
findings, then McCarthy on hers, and then both on their research
collaboration.[4] Students from Fishman's class also participated in the
study but in a more passive role, not as "informant-collaborators."

In another recent study, "Cross-Curricular Underlife," by Anderson et al., students play a much more active role. Indeed, six of the
seven researchers were undergraduate students, the seventh, a college
English professor. Instead of the professor's assuming the role of
researcher interviewing the six students, they all acted as researchers,
with each student deciding on the issues he or she would focus on
in observations of his and her classes. Their general purpose was to
investigate how students and teachers used language and valued
specific language interactions in their courses across the curriculum.
As readers of their account, we receive each individual's—the students' and teacher's—"realities" unfiltered by any other's. Indeed,
much like McCarthy's and Fishman's accounts, their written account
is a series of distinct reports preceded by a brief opening which they

coauthored. McCarthy and Fishman characterize this approach as a "sequential informant/researcher narrative" ("Text"4). In this study, we also see one of the possible limitations of this approach: a lack of focus. At the outset of their account, Anderson et al. report on a common finding that academic literacy was "an independent competitive action through language" (12). Unfortunately, since each student was interested in different issues (e.g., other students' ways of learning, teachers' influences on uses of language), there was little consistent tracing out of this claim across all of their classes. Instead of having multiple perspectives on one or two of the issues, we are presented with individual perspectives on different issues.

Still, their study and McCarthy and Fishman's suggest the value of continuing to experiment with participatory approaches. To me, the promise of such approaches lies in the discussion and negotiation that would be required among all participants if a study were to be a genuinely shared enterprise with people working together to achieve an agreed-upon end. Such discussion and negotiation would seem to help forestall early closure on a research focus, bring more perspectives into the interpretation of research information, and encourage more examination of possible differences among the languages participants use, specifically what those differences might reflect about how people construct a given "reality."

Given these various assumptions about participants' roles in creating the reality that emerges from a research study, how do I reflect on my earlier study in the chemical engineering classes? How might I have proceeded differently and to what consequence if I had taken a different approach? For instance, how might I have involved the participants more actively in the shaping of the research and the interpretations? For one thing, assuming that I still wished to shape the inquiry according to an a priori theory that I felt to be valid—in this case, rhetorical theory—I might have explicitly explained the rhetorical framework I was using—audience, purpose, issue, writer role—and made that a subject of discussion: Did that seem like a reasonable way to consider that context? Was I shaping their views in a way that seemed distorted to them? While I still believe the construction I developed was valid and useful as one way to interpret the context for writing in those classrooms, I also recognize that I may have screened out viewpoints from the students and teachers that could have been equally important to understanding the function of writing in those classrooms. To establish an even more collaborative relationship, I might have worked with participants right from the start to define the questions or problems to focus on and worked more inductively to try to understand the two classroom settings from their frame of reference. For example, in a first interview, I might have asked the students about their prior experiences with writing in school: for example, their perceptions of functions and conditions for writing in specific classes; differences between these classes that struck them as significant; questions, problems, or conflicts they had with writing in these classes. I would have asked the faculty similar questions. I would then have used information from these interviews to shape the research questions and identify topics to pursue in subsequent interviews regarding the two classes I was studying. Further, I might have made every effort to provide them with drafts of my written account of the research and offered them the opportunity to respond and include their responses in the final text. Or I might have tried to work with them to compose a final account that they had a more direct role in authoring. Had I done some or all of these things, the resulting study would have explored some different or, at the very least, additional issues and, as a consequence, come to different "findings."

I do not say that to suggest that full collaboration between researcher and participants is the only valid way of constructing knowledge. I certainly have learned a good deal from studies where participants have a relatively passive role, for instance, where the researcher identifies the research questions in advance or interprets a situation from the perspective of a particular theoretical framework. My concern is that as a research community, we have opted too exclusively for such studies, specifically those where university-based researchers control the study and create the knowledge, while others—teachers and, even more so, students—are spoken about and spoken for. Whether we are conducting a study in our own classes or in another, if our aim is to understand and represent the experiences of others, we need to involve them more centrally in shaping that knowledge. The degree and ways in which we do that will vary, but the choice should be a reasoned and principled one made with an awareness of alternatives. Granted, unless participants participate as equals in writing the account of a study, the "researcher"—or whoever writes the account—is still the central one to construct the knowledge. Still, that does not negate the possibility of involving participants more—rather than less—in creating that knowledge.

In What Ways Do Researchers Recognize
Their Roles in Shaping Research Findings?

Implicit in this question is an affirmative answer to a prior one: Does the researcher shape the reality that is created through a research study? In an essay advocating a phenomenological approach to research, Knoblauch and Brannon refer to Heisenberg's "principle of indeterminacy," that "the act of seeing . . . has a *material* effect on what is observed, altering it in the very process of focusing on it" (17). They quote Heisenberg's statement stressing the "subjective element in the description of atomic events, since the measuring device has been constructed by the observer, and we have to remember that what we observe is not nature itself but nature exposed to our method of questioning" (Heisenberg 57 in Knoblauch and Brannon 18). In other words, whether the instruments we are using are carefully calibrated machines or solely our own minds, through the act of using them, we are altering and shaping what we attempt to observe. What we call "data" are not nature itself; they are our constructions, shaped by the questions we ask and the interpretative instruments we use.

I think it is fair to say that most researchers accept these basic assumptions and, as a consequence, affirm that critical reflection is central to the research process in order to heighten one's awareness of how one's self and one's research decisions shape what is seen. In *Ethnography: Principles in Practice*, Hammersley and Atkinson stress that reflexivity is one of the distinguishing characteristics of any scientific inquiry, including ethnography: "There is an obligation placed upon practitioners to scrutinize systematically the methodology by which findings, their own and those of others, were produced, and, in particular, to consider how the activities of the researcher may have shaped those findings" (236).

In many published accounts of contextual studies of writing, reflexivity is evident in explanations of the methodological precautions taken to guard against the limited and fallible nature of a researcher relying on commonsense reasoning alone or working alone. However, the focus is on method, not the researcher's own attributes and interests. For instance, the assumption underlying many analytic, quantitative studies is that if accepted procedures are carefully followed the researcher will be able to conduct the analysis and interpretation in an impartial manner. In other words, the influence of the researcher can be limited to the initial design of the study and the development of the analytic instruments. Essentially, such studies try to compensate for what might be idiosyncratic or biased interpretations by using measures that attempt to minimize the amount and level of interpretation (e.g., questionnaires that can be machine-scored, multiple readers to analyze writings and calculations of reader reliability).

My study of the chemical engineering classes offers an example of an analytic study that proceeded this way. For the analysis, I set up an analytic framework to be used to classify interview comments according to rhetorical concepts of audience, writer's *ethos*, and purpose. Once I developed this framework and a scoring guide, I used other readers to classify the comments, calculating their percentage of agreement as an indication of the reliability of their judgments. This procedure was meant to insure two things: for myself as the researcher, that the findings would be arrived at inductively through the independent agreement of two people not so invested in the study as I; and for the readers, that those findings had been arrived at systematically and not impressionistically. To apply Brodkey's explanation of analytic approaches to my methods, I can say that the assumption behind them was that the researcher's "bias"—my *constructive* role—would be minimized by the analytic methods adopted so that the researcher would be representing the views of those being studied, within the interpretative frame chosen (*Academic* 82–90).

Qualitative studies that rely on the researcher's mind as the instrument of interpretation have also traditionally tried to control for "observer effects," recognizing that the researcher's presence and manner can influence the actions and comments of those being studied. They do so, for instance, by extended periods of observation, talking with participants multiple times and in various situations, using nondirective interview techniques, and drawing on multiple sources of information (Doheny-Farina and Odell).

In contrast to analytic, quantitative studies, though, qualitative studies do not try to minimize the researcher's central role as the instrument of analysis and interpretation. Instead, the effort is to insure that the researcher considers the broadest possible range of views in the process of interpretation—not to control out the researcher's view but to broaden it and insure that in selecting a particular approach or interpretation, the researcher has considered it in light of alternatives. So, for instance, researchers are advised to draw on multiple theoretical perspectives to try out different ways of interpreting research data and to test out emerging interpretations by trying to apply them to new cases (Hammersley and Atkinson 174–206; see also Doheny-Farina and Odell's discussion of triangulation, 508–9). Lather argues that reflexivity is especially important for studies guided by an a priori theory so that a researcher avoids rigidly imposing a theoretical framework on a situation that is open to counter interpretations ("Research").

The approaches I have discussed focus on research decisions and activities. Other researchers, including those advocating feminist and critical ethnographic approaches, stress that the researcher's own personal history, attributes, and assumptions should be included as part of the "data" for a study. They argue further that reflexivity extends from reflecting on how one's own values, gender, class, and culture shape research to including that reflection in the published account of the research. In "On Critical Ethnography," Simon and Dippo urge that "we need to recognize our own implication in the production of data and thus must begin to include ourselves (our own practices and their social and historical basis) in our analyses of the situations we study" (200–201).

Similarly, in identifying a central characteristic of a feminist methodology, Harding writes that it "locates the researcher in the same critical plane as the overt subject matter" ("Introduction" 7–8). Harding stresses that not only is it a researcher's responsibility to reflect on how her or his personal characteristics and attitudes might influence a study but also to present those characteristics and attitudes to readers as part of the "data" they have for reading and assessing a study. She explains:

> This does not mean that the first half of a research report should engage in soul searching (though a little soul searching by researchers now and then can't be all bad!). Instead, as we will see, we are often explicitly told by the researchers what her/his gender, race, class, culture is, and sometimes how she/he suspects this has shaped the research project—though of course we are free to arrive at contrary hypotheses about the influence of the researcher's presence on her/his analysis. Thus, the researcher appears to us not as an invisible, anonymous voice of authority, but as a real, historical individual with concrete, specific desires and interests. (9)

Harding's point is one all researchers should heed, not just those who identify themselves with particular feminist or critical ethnographic approaches.[5]

   This sort of reflexivity and public accounting has not been apparent in much composition research, although it should be. My study
of the chemical engineering classes is a case in point. For instance,
in my written account of the study in *Research in the Teaching of English*,
I did not identify myself explicitly—my "social and historical biases,"
to the degree that I know them—nor my gender, race, class, culture
and how any of these factors might have shaped the study. Does that
make any difference for readers? Clearly, my "biases" or views are
apparent from my naming of research approaches and theories that
guided my study, from the kinds of questions I asked and didn't ask,
from the interpretative frame I used and, implicitly, the ones I didn't
use, and also from my acknowledgment of the people who "offered
me guidance throughout the study." In retrospect, what else might
I have said that would have placed me on the same plane as the
research? I am a white, Anglo-American female, the first generation
in my lower middle-class family to attend college. My father was a
largely self-taught mechanical engineer who learned by working with
a college-educated mentor. For him, learning the skills of engineering
was personally and professionally rewarding. Also, my prior teaching
experiences included working with colleagues to develop a writing-
across-the-curriculum program grounded on the assumption that writing is a valuable medium for learning. I can't say for sure how that
sort of autobiographical information would have led readers to read
my study differently. It certainly would have *located* the research differently, explicitly connecting it with my personal experiences and helping make evident that choices I made in the study and my general
acceptance of the goals of the two courses were influenced by my
personal history and not solely, as may be implied by the absence of
such references, guided by detached "objective" reasoning. Equally
as important, if I had reflected on these possible connections during
the study, I might have achieved more insight into how I was position-
ing myself in relation to the study I was conducting: in retrospect, I
believe I was predisposed to view engineering education positively
and to assume that writing did serve positive functions for learning
in those classes beyond demonstration of knowledge for purposes of
evaluation. Recognizing these predispositions at the time may have
helped me to examine them critically through my own thinking and
discussions with participants. Those examinations might have included pursuing the relative importance of writing in relation to other
class activities, the values embedded in the writing these students

were doing, and the authority relations between students, teachers, and knowledge operating in the course.

While it is difficult for me to speculate further on my own earlier study, as a reader of studies that acknowledge the researcher's personal presence, I can see what is to be gained by such reflexivity in the written account. For instance, in *The Social Uses of Writing: Politics and Pedagogy*, Tom Fox opens with a chapter that situates his study in his personal context, trying to make explicit to us how the study arises from his teaching experiences, his graduate studies, and his family background and politics. For instance, he tells us that his family was politically active, stressing to him "the responsibility of enacting one's political values in everyday life" (4). That information helps me, as a reader, understand some of the sources of the "activist pedagogy" (13) Fox advocates in his book, his identification with critical ethnographers, and his interpretation of his students' experiences.

Some element of reflexivity is also evident in the narrative accounts written by some teachers of research studies they have conducted in their own classrooms and with their students. For instance, a number of the accounts in Goswami and Stillman's *Reclaiming the Classroom: Teacher Research as an Agency for Change* open with statements by the researchers (the teachers) explaining the experiences, feelings, and/or interests—often classroom connected—that led them to conduct the studies they report on. One "letter" included in the volume— written by Gail Martin about a project in process—is a reflection on what she, as a non-Arapaho teacher, learned about differences between her own and her Arapaho students' cultural views of written language by talking to and listening to them and other Arapahos.

Reflection on the connection between personal history and present beliefs is also evident in McCarthy and Fishman's account of their collaborative study where they discuss how their own different educational experiences likely influenced their differing perspectives on a concept central to their study, student initiation to academic fields. That is, McCarthy, who felt positive about how teachers had introduced her to disciplinary methods and languages, viewed initiation positively as learning disciplinary ways; Fishman, who felt he had been silenced by the language and conventions he was expected to take on as a student, had a less positive view of "disciplinary initiation" as an aim for his classes, choosing instead to stress "development of student voices" ("Boundary" 60–61).By including themselves to some degree as subjects of inquiry, McCarthy and Fishman in no way undermine their study nor acknowledge a "limitation" of it. Instead, their self-reflection and public accounting contributes to the study: it leads them to consider these personal influences as an aspect of the study to take into account when they shaped their findings. For readers, it explains the basis in personal history for the positions each had taken. Further, it illuminates how abstract aims (e.g., "initiation") are defined variously depending on how they are enacted and experienced in specific classroom situations.

Recently, it would seem that some critics of ethnography have been questioning how possible it is for researchers to represent at all the views of others, given that their accounts will always be partial and committed, influenced by their background, class, gender, race, and the discursive tradition from which they write (Clifford and Marcus). Others criticize the positivist assumptions of objectivity that they see embedded in some accounts of ethnographic research (Herndl). To acknowledge that our methods of seeing and our personal histories shape how and what we see does not make our efforts meaningless. Nor should it lead us to reject practices aimed at trying, for instance, to elicit multiple perspectives on a situation. It should lead us to being more reflexive about our methods and the ways our own histories and values connect with our research. It should also lead us to try to unmask the masked researcher in our published accounts, documenting for readers our own understandings of personal factors that may contribute to the conduct and findings of a study—recognizing that these understandings, too, are partial and constructed.

As I have tried to make clear in this section, it is possible to recognize these influences and still proceed with good faith inquiries that attempt to provide accounts that participants and readers will find valid.[6] That is, we can still acknowledge our "situatedness" while simultaneously trying, as Brodkey writes, "to understand others on their own terms" (*Academic* 100; see also Mascia-Lees, Sharpe, and Cohen).

In What Ways Do Researchers Recognize the Function of Ideology and Values in Research Studies?

John Schilb concludes his essay "Ideology and Composition" saying, "I discovered that people interested in examining the ideologies of composition and people interested in empirical research aren't reading each other's work" (29). According to Schilb, to study ideology is to study the "political ramifications of all discourse" (22). Studying the ideology of composition would entail examining the sociopolitical assumptions that are embedded in and conveyed through composition scholarship—specifically assumptions about the relations of individuals to institutions and "how institutions attempt to shape human identities" (26).

Schilb takes the lack of contact between these two groups—those interested in ideology and those in research—as a sign of the power struggle between them, concluding that one consequence is that "the interplay between them will be left unilluminated" (29). I think he is right in his conclusion. My aim in this section is to examine this interplay between ideology and research a bit. In doing so, I am accepting an assumption that ideology and, more generally, values are implicated in *all* research, whether researchers acknowledge those relations or not.

Some researchers question that basic assumption. This view and the challenge to it is evident in an exchange over a research study conducted by Michael Graves and colleagues, "Some Characteristics of Memorable Expository Writing: Effects of Revisions by Writers with Different Backgrounds." For their study, Graves et al. asked three pairs of writers to rewrite two passages from high school history texts to try to make them more "comprehensible and memorable" (242). One of the passages focused on the United States' involvement in the Vietnam War. It was titled "Communists Threaten South Vietnam." The revisions included changes aimed to increase "clarity, coherence, and emphasis" (248) and, for one pair, changes to make the text more "exciting, vivid, rich in human drama" (249).

In a subsequent issue of *Research in the Teaching of English* where the original study appeared, John Reiff criticized the study on two grounds. The first ground was the ideological framework embedded in the textbook passage Graves and colleagues used for the study, Reiff's feeling that the passage functioned to "confirm an ideology of present and future American military and political domination" (104). The second ground was what Reiff sees as their narrow definition of the problem of "comprehension" and, implicitly, their limited view of the aim of education. According to Reiff, Graves et al. reduce comprehension to passive recall of information: the research problem being how to improve reader comprehension by refining the sorts of textual features that enhance recall. Reiff's view is that comprehension should be defined more broadly to include "the ability to think critically" (106). Given this aim, he is especially critical of texts that present history as unproblematic, as a single view, instead of showing multiple views and the way historical knowledge itself is a construction. And of research that defines learning so narrowly.

In their response to Reiff, Graves and Slater focus on his ideological critique, dismissing it as rankling and narrow-minded: "It is ironic that Reiff—whose major complaint is that the passages we used present a single point of view when they should have presented alternative views—sees it as his place to tell others what to study" (108). In other words, while Reiff purports to call for multiple points of view, he is actually calling for one view and one doctrinaire approach to research.

While Graves and Slater are right to resist any call for a single, doctrinaire approach, there is another aspect of Reiff's critique that can't be dismissed so simply. He is calling for Graves et al. and others to be more aware of the ideology implicit in the way a research problem is framed, the methods used, and the larger social and political context of their research. Graves et al. deny the relevance of this aspect of Reiff's critique or fail to recognize it, saying "the question of the appropriate content for textbooks is largely a political question rather than an empirical one" (107). In other words, they imply that empirical research is not political. That view is evident as well in the closing comments in their account of their study when they claim that "a huge volume of research and theory will be needed to establish a science capable of fully describing the nature of effective texts" ("Some" 258). It is this view precisely that Reiff and others are criticizing, arguing that "science" is not value-neutral and is not free of ideology. My point here is not to argue that researchers—Graves et al. or others—should adopt a particular ideology. It is simply that they should acknowledge that ideologies and values are embedded in research and that these connections should be open to debate just as are research methods and findings.[7]

Increasingly, scholars in the physical and biological sciences as well as in the human sciences recognize this interrelationship, seeing inquiry as value-bound in multiple ways—including, for example, research inquiries into gender and racial characteristics, molecular biology, and education.[8] In *Naturalistic Inquiry*, Lincoln and Guba identify at least four ways that inquiry is value-bound. It is influenced by

> *inquirer* values as expressed in the choice of a problem . . . and the framing, bounding, and focusing of that problem; . . . by the choice of the *paradigm* that guides the investigation into the problem; . . . by the

choice of the *substantive theory* utilized to guide the collection and analysis
of data and in the interpretation of findings; . . . by the values that inhere
in the *context*.(38)

Clearly, one aspect of Reiff's critique was the framing of the
problem in the Graves et al. study. As Harding writes, "The questions
that are asked—and, more significantly, those that are not asked—
are at least as determinative of the adequacy of our total picture as
are any answers that we can discover" (7).

To my mind, that is a valid critique to offer. For instance, my
earlier study of the chemical engineering classes could be examined
for the way I framed the problem and the ideology implicit in it. For
example, I did not take the assumptions embedded in the discourse
as a "problem" to be investigated or critiqued. That is, I presented
without any comment the overriding value in the Process Design
course—meant to simulate industry—that feasibility and profitability
were the sole criteria for evaluating a design. In general, I accepted
the values and authority of industry and school and the assumption
that students were to learn the ways of these institutions. I make
these acknowledgments now not to disavow the study for what it did
accomplish nor to imply that there existed a simple, uniform set of
educational-industrial values to be endorsed as a whole or rejected.
Still, I do feel my inquiry was limited by my failure to try more
rigorously to identify and decide on my position regarding the range
of particular ideological values operating in the setting.

No research study can be so broad as to encompass all possible
perspectives and ways of framing questions. Still, as a researcher, it
is important for me to hear critiques from other perspectives and to
consider alternatives: What didn't I see that I might have had I framed
my study differently? How do others view the relation of my study
to a larger educational, political, cultural context? As a reader of other
research, I need also to question the values implicit in a study and
try to consider alternative perspectives as a way for me to understand
and assess what I am reading. What values am I buying into if I accept
this study and the knowledge it puts forward for me to accept?

The interplay between research and ideology is more obvious in
research that is overtly ideological in aim, making "issues of hegem-
ony, resistance, subjectivity, and power" the focus of study (Schilb
27). This overt ideological aim is evident in much feminist research.
As Lather writes, "To do feminist research is to put the social construc-

tion of gender at the center of one's inquiry. . . . Through the questions that feminism poses and the absences it locates, feminism argues the centrality of gender in the shaping of our consciousness, skills, and institutions as well as in the distribution of power and privilege" ("Feminist" 571). More specifically, a feminist methodology is fueled by an ideological assumption that women have been suppressed and their experience distorted by male-centered approaches. Flynn writes that "women's perspectives have been suppressed, silenced, marginalized, written out of what counts as authoritative knowledge. . . . Men become the standard against which women are judged" (425).

Guided by this assumption, Flynn makes women's experiences the center of her study, exploring whether males and females "represent the world in a similar fashion" in their writing (431). She does so with the overt aim of challenging us in composition to reexamine critically theories of writing that make no gender distinctions, feeling that "our models of the composing process are quite possibly better suited to describing men's ways of composing than to describing women's" (432). To interpret the writing, she draws on the theory and research of such feminist scholars as Belenky and her colleagues, Chodorow, and Gilligan.

In another study, Mary Kupiec Cayton focuses on women and writing blocks, finding that extant theory and research on writing apprehension/writing blocks do not adequately account for factors that cause women to experience writing blocks. She concludes that "any assessment of factors involved in the writing process that purports to be gender-neutral runs the risk of obscuring the ways in which certain writing contexts may be more fraught with peril and internal contradictions for women than for men" (334). For instance, she found a concern for "voice" to be an obstacle for many women, but it was "not merely a pragmatic one of reaching the audience they desired; more often, it involved a question of identity, and how much control they had over language in the face of discourse communities that they often experienced as hostile to their self-definitions" (334).

Like feminist methodologies, critical hermeneutic and ethnographic research originates with an a priori assumption about social inequities. As Simon and Dippo state in "On Critical Ethnographic Work," "The interest that defines critical ethnographic work is both pedagogical and political. It is linked to our assessment of our own society as inequitably structured and dominated by a hegemonic culture that suppresses a consideration and understanding of why things are the way they are and what must be done for things to be otherwise" (196). By implication, then, it "supports transformative as well as interpretive concerns" (195). Given this grounding theory, critical ethnography focuses on social practices—viewing individual practices as manifestations of those practices—and attempts to understand those practices in relation to the culture, specifically institutions and material conditions that define class and power structures.

A critical ethnographic approach is evident in Thomas Fox's *The Social Uses of Writing: Politics and Pedagogy*. Fox specifically identifies his approach with Simon and Dippo's and distinguishes it from ethnography as practiced by Shirley Brice Heath or Clifford Geertz. Fox writes that his aim is not only "understanding and interpretation" but also "cultural change" (34), in the sense of using research overtly as a way of intervening to change oppressive social and political structures. Further, the conceptual frame shaping his research locates it with other critical approaches: "The stratification of our society along gender, class, and racial lines serves as the governing problematic that informs the analysis of student language and classroom contexts" (19). This conceptual frame shapes the classroom approach he describes in the book and his hermeneutic interpretation of the three case studies he presents. Clearly, his aim is transformative: through his work, he hopes to convince teachers to adopt a particular interpretative approach, one that "should be shaped by our most urgent problem in education and society, which is now the continuing inability for education to work democratically" (110).

The transformative purpose espoused by critical ethnographers and feminists like Fox, Simon and Dippo, and Harding raises questions about the intended audiences for research: If the aim of research is not only to document and interpret but also to change what researchers see to be oppressive conditions, then researchers have to reassess their notion of the audiences for whom they are doing their research.

According to Simon and Dippo, instead of thinking of an academic research community as their primary audience, researchers have to "enter the public sphere" and "contribute to the critique and transformation of unjust and disabling forms of moral regulation and material distribution" (198). To do so requires that one direct research to the public being studied by the research, not just to an academic community of other researchers.

Feminist methodology stresses the same commitment to those involved in a study. Harding writes that "the goal of this inquiry is to provide for women explanations of social phenomena that they want and need, rather than providing for welfare departments, manufacturers, advertisers, psychiatrists, the medical establishment, or the judicial system answers to questions that they have" (8). Harding is not simply restating that the inquiry will focus on women's experiences; she is saying that the participants in a study will be the primary audience.

Mascia-Lees and colleagues make a similar point in "The Postmodernist Turn in Anthropology: Cautions from a Feminist Perspective." In distinguishing a feminist approach from other postmodern approaches to ethnography—such as that depicted by Clifford—Mascia-Lees et al. are critical of ethnographic research in anthropology that is intended primarily for other scholars instead of the groups being studied. Acknowledging the political nature of feminist research, they stress the importance of researchers' asking "for whom they write" and state that "feminist research is more closely aligned with applied anthropology, whose practitioners also often derive their questions from and apply their methods to the solution of problems defined by the people being studied, than with new ethnographers. Applied anthropologists frequently function as 'power brokers' translating between the subordinate, disenfranchised group and the dominant class or power" (23–24).

Citing this same essay, David Bleich, in "Sexism in Academic Styles of Learning," raises a question about the aim and audience of all research. Posing this question to encompass any research academics do, he wonders

> what it would be to change the axioms of academic work: to orient this work according to the needs of the (oppressed) group that is being studied. To extend this principle is to adopt the idea of socially generous research in all fields, that is, research that self-consciously contributes to a social constituency that it can help, enable, or empower. This means examining why we are doing research to begin with, who we are really writing for, and how we are going to learn from our students instead of enslaving them, just as scientists will learn from nature without enslaving it. (240)

In calling for "socially generous research," Bleich is asking us to consider our obligations as researchers to those people who participate in our studies—including students—and the broader educational community and society, asking us to consider what we are contributing to others and how: Whose questions are we answering? To whom are we reporting and how? How is our research being used? Our decisions about such questions represent one way in which values are embedded in research. Further, we need not accept a particular ideology and need not pursue a particular line of research. We should, however, accept that ideological views are implicit in all of our work. Finally, recognizing the connection between ideology and our role as researchers in shaping research findings, we need to try to articulate and examine our own values, backgrounds, and present involvements to try to bring to our awareness and readers how they may shape the meaning we are making throughout a research inquiry. Because the "data" we select and make some sort of meaning of are shaped by those personal factors, being "accountable to the data" requires such self-examination. Being accountable to others requires examining our social conscience.

Closing Reflections

I have heard colleagues say that as a profession we in English and composition studies are too consumed with self-questioning and theorizing. Along that line, you could be thinking right now that "the over-analyzed and theorized research study never gets begun." We could get so taken up with questioning ourselves and our actions that we never act at all. I certainly don't advocate such all-consuming questioning and abstract reflecting. Still, I want to press the alternative claim that "the under-examined research study should not be begun." As Linda Flower has written, "It is time for the systematic and self-questioning stance that goes with theoretical explanations—whether we are explaining a historical event, an experimental or observational study, or an approach to teaching" (286). As I've worked on this project, I've tried to maintain that systematic and self-questioning stance as I reflected on my actions as a researcher, trying to clarify my beliefs and links between them and research practice.

While we cannot get inside ourselves as neutral observers to identify fully the beliefs that guide our actions, we can get some perspective on them, locating them in relation to others and in relation to theoretical assumptions about knowing and values. To do so need not require detailed technical or theoretical knowledge of various research methodologies. At base, it requires what Peter Elbow calls a "theoretical stance," trying to get at the premises implicit in actions.

Elbow is talking primarily about a theoretical stance toward teaching. Here I extend it to our inquiries. If we are to be conscious about our acts as "meaning makers," we need to aim to become more aware of "our tacit knowledge-in-practice." Drawing on Polanyi, Elbow emphasizes that our success in this self-reflection "usually depends on respecting and trusting practice for a while and afterward interrogating it as a rich source for new theory" (87). It also calls for a commitment to listening to other perspectives—granting that they may be equally plausible as the one to which we are committed—and trying to understand the premises underlying them. That self-reflection and openminded dialogue and questioning with others are healthy not only for a community but also for individuals within it.

Notes

1. Advocating a hermeneutic approach in composition studies, North stresses that it does not assume a single, approachable reality. He writes, "Indeed, the nature of reality, like all other matters, is subject to debate among holders of the full range of individual perceptions/constructions of reality, so that truth is sought *intersubjectively*. It follows, then, that hermeneutical knowledge . . . accumulates *dialectically*" (255). That is, it emerges from the dialectical exchange among members of a scholarly community through the interplay among multiple ways of interpreting a set of texts. That set of texts may be a sample of student writings—the texts for Fox's study—or as in the studies by North and Clark and Doheny-Farina, writings and transcripts of interviews. That dialectical exchange is evident in the exchange of views over Clark and Doheny-Farina's article "Public Discourse and Personal Expression." See Jarratt; Lunsford and Ede; Clark and Doheny-Farina, "On the Other Hand." Although none of these scholars mentions this possibility, it would seem plausible that members of the community being studied might also be involved in the dialectical exchange.

2. It is not my purpose in this essay to discuss research methods in detail. I refer readers to such works as Doheny-Farina and Odell; Lincoln and Guba; Hammersley and Atkinson; and the research studies and critiques of research cited in this chapter.

3. Their experience reinforces the claim made by Cochran-Smith and Lytle that the questions on the mind of a researcher outside of a setting may not match those of a person—in this case, a teacher—within that setting. For another example of a study conducted by a team of researchers that included teachers within classrooms being studied and writing researchers, see Walvoord and McCarthy.

4. These experiments with heteroglossic texts bring to the fore the ques-

tion of whose discourse is authorized to speak for others, to put their realities into words. Related to that question is one about how researchers construct their authority in their written accounts. For discussion of these questions and critiques of ethnographic writing from the perspective of rhetorical and contemporary narrative theories, see, for example, Clifford, "Allegory" and *Predicament* 21–54; Brodkey, *Academic* 82–107 and "Writing" 70–74, and Herndl. Herndl argues that ethnographic discourse—like other established genres—is "embedded in a tissue of material and historical conditions," including the discourse conventions maintained by existing institutions and research groups (326–27). See also Pratt. Doheny-Farina calls for researchers to be more reflexive and candid in acknowledging the rhetorical decisions they make, including the roles they create for themselves to adapt to their audiences. He contends that these audiences that "may exert pressure on a researcher" include disciplinary colleagues, participants in a study, and "our bosses"—department chairs, college deans, and evaluation committees ("Research" 17–18).

5. This attempt to account for and report personal factors that might influence the analysis should not be confused with the personal accounts of fieldwork written by some anthropologists that are completely separate from their formal ethnographic accounts of that work. Indeed, Harding and Simon and Dippo would reject as fallacious the distinction between researcher as person and researcher as scientist that such a separation of personal and research accounts suggests. See also Pratt.

6. For different research approaches, the meaning of validity and methods for obtaining it vary, but all recognize the aim of trying to be accountable to the situation being studied, whether that validity be judged by readers of research or people in the situation being studied. For discussions of validity from various perspectives, see, for instance, Lincoln and Guba 289–331, discussing naturalistic inquiry; Hammersley and Atkinson 184–85, discussing ethnography, 195–98; Lather "Research," discussing transformative research shaped by explicit ideological views; Mishler, and Connelly and Clandinin, discussing narrative inquiries; Cochran-Smith and Lytle, discussing teacher-research.

7. A similar exchange has taken place over a study conducted by Berkenkotter, Huckin, and Ackerman. It is a case study of a graduate student as he adjusts to the conventions of research and writing in a particular PhD program in rhetoric. Schilb used the published account of this study in his article on ideology and composition to demonstrate how "composition scholarship can itself purvey ideologies." His claim is that "it serves as a case study of how certain political questions can get dodged in the effort to legitimate a certain research paradigm and a certain institution embodying it" (22). In two subsequent articles, Berkenkotter has defended the study, charging Schilb with trying to put a particular ideological view on the situation—one that did

not match with their data ("Paradigm")—and with failing to understand an empirical approach to inquiry ("Legacy" 79–80). As with Graves and Slater, it is appropriate for Berkenkotter to resist the imposition of a particular ideological view. Still, she, like they, seems to subscribe to a view that research—at least, data—is neutral. In both articles, she speaks of the necessity of being "accountable to the data" as if "data" were empirical realities, not already shaped by the researcher. In retrospect, that influence is particularly evident with this study since, as Berkenkotter acknowledges in one of the articles, the subject of the case study is one of the researchers, John Ackerman ("Paradigm" 161). In the original research account published in 1988, this information is withheld from readers. Indeed, the case study student is identified only with the pseudonym "Nate." In presenting the research account, the authors convey an air of detachment as if their different positions—e.g., Huckin as a faculty member in the department being studied, Ackerman as the graduate student being studied—did not figure in their formation of the research questions or collection and analysis of the "data." Had they acknowledged Ackerman's position throughout, their study may have offered even more insights into the dynamic of an individual student trying to find his way of operating in a new institutional setting as that dynamic is viewed from a number of perspectives. At the least, they would have been honest with readers.

8. Spanier reviews biological research that perpetuates socially constructed views of gender differences (for example, attributing males' superior performance in tests of mathematical ability to hormones and brain structure). Reviewing similar research to show how socially constructed views of gender have shaped research on sex differences, Bleier points out that "this sensitivity of science to social events and values is nothing new" (147). She reminds readers of biological research in the nineteenth and early twentieth centuries that concluded that nonwhite races were mentally inferior (148). Spanier, Keller, and the Biology and Gender Study Group—among others—also discuss the way in which socially constructed values have shaped research in molecular biology.

Works Cited

Anderson, Worth, et al. "Cross-Curricular Underlife: A Collaborative Report on Ways with Academic Words." *College Composition and Communication* 41 (February 1990): 11–36.

Berkenkotter, Carol. "The Legacy of Positivism in Empirical Composition Research." *Journal of Advanced Composition* 9 (1989): 69–82.

———. "Paradigm Debates, Turf Wars, and the Conduct of Sociocognitive Inquiry in Composition." *College Composition and Communication* 42 (May 1991): 151–69.

Berkenkotter, Carol, Thomas N. Huckin, and John Ackerman. "Conventions,

Conversations, and the Writer: Case Study of a Student in a Rhetoric Ph.D. Program." *Research in the Teaching of English* 22 (1988): 9–44.

Biology and Gender Study Group. "The Importance of Feminist Critique for Contemporary Cell Biology." *Feminism and Science.* Ed. N. Tuana. Bloomington: Indiana UP, 1989. 172–87.

Bleich, David. "Sexism in Academic Styles of Learning." *Journal of Advanced Composition* 10 (1990): 231–48.

Bleier, Ruth. "Sex Differences Research: Science or Belief?" *Feminist Approaches to Science.* Ed. R. Bleier. New York: Pergamon, 1986. 147–64.

Brodkey, Linda. *Academic Writing as Social Practice.* Philadelphia: Temple UP, 1987.

———. "Writing Critical Ethnographic Narratives." *Anthropology and Education Quarterly* 18 (1987): 67–76.

Cayton, Mary Kupiec. "What Happens When Things Go Wrong: Women and Writing Blocks." *Journal of Advanced Composition* 10 (1990): 321–37.

Clark, Gregory, and Stephen Doheny-Farina."On the Other Hand: Response of Lunsford/Ede and Jarratt." *Written Communication* 8 (January 1991): 120–24.

———. "Public Discourse and Personal Expression." *Written Communication.* 7 (October 1990): 456–81.

Clifford, James. "On Ethnographic Allegory." *Writing Culture: The Poetics and Politics of Ethnography.* Ed. J. Clifford and G. E. Marcus. Berkeley: U of California P, 1986. 98–121.

———. *The Predicament of Culture: Twentieth-Century Ethnography, Literature, and Art.* Cambridge, MA: Harvard UP, 1988. 21–54.

Clifford, James, and George Marcus, eds. *Writing Culture: The Poetics and Politics of Ethnography.* Berkeley: U of California P, 1986.

Cochran-Smith, Marilyn, and Susan L. Lytle. "Research on Teaching and Teacher Research: The Issues That Divide." *Educational Researcher* 19 (1990): 2–11.

Connelly, F. Michael, and D. Jean Clandinin. "Stories of Experience and Narrative Inquiry." *Educational Researcher* 19 (1990): 2–14.

Doheny-Farina, Stephen. "A Case Study of One Adult Writing in Academic and Nonacademic Discourse Communities." *Worlds of Writing.* Ed. C. Matalene. New York: Random, 1989. 17–42.

———. "Research as Rhetoric: Confronting the Methodological and Ethical Problems of Research on Writing in Nonacademic Settings." *Research on Writing in Non-Academic Settings.* Ed. R. Spilka. Carbondale: Southern Illinois UP, forthcoming.

Doheny-Farina, Stephen, and Lee Odell. "Ethnographic Research on Writing." *Writing in Nonacademic Settings.* Ed. L. Odell and D. Goswami. New York: Guilford, 1985. 503–35.

Elbow, Peter. *What Is English?* Urbana, IL: NCTE, 1990.

Flower, Linda. "Cognition, Context, and Theory Building." *College Composition and Communication* 40 (October 1989): 282–311.

Flynn, Elizabeth. "Composing as a Woman." *College Composition and Communication* 39 (1988): 423–35.

Fox, Thomas. *The Social Uses of Writing: Politics and Pedagogy*. Norwood, NJ: Ablex, 1990.

Geertz, Clifford. *The Interpretation of Cultures*. New York: Basic Books, 1973.

Goswami, Dixie, and Peter R. Stillman, eds. *Reclaiming the Classroom: Teacher Research as an Agency for Change*. Upper Montclair, NJ: Boynton/Cook, 1987.

Graves, Donald H. "Research Update: A New Look at Writing Research." *Language Arts* 57 (1980): 913–19.

Graves, Michael F., and Wayne H. Slater. "On Knowing What You're Doing and Telling Others What To Do: A Reply to Reiff's Rankling Response." *Research in the Teaching of English* 24 (1990): 107–8.

Graves, Michael F., et al."Some Characteristics of Memorable Expository Writing: Effects of Revisions by Writers with Different Backgrounds." *Research in the Teaching of English* 22 (1988): 242–65.

Hammersley, Martyn, and Paul Atkinson. *Ethnography: Principles in Practice*. New York: Tavistock, 1983.

Harding, Sandra. "Introduction: Is There a Feminist Method?" and "Conclusion: Epistemological Questions." *Feminism and Methodology*. Ed. Sandra Harding. Bloomington: Indiana UP, 1987.

Heath, Shirley Brice. *Ways with Words: Language, Life, and Work in Communities and Classrooms*. New York: Cambridge UP, 1983.

Herndl, Carl G. "Writing Ethnography: Representation, Rhetoric, and Institutional Practices." *College English* 53 (March 1991): 320–32.

Herrington, Anne J. "Composing One's Self in a Discipline: Students' and Teachers' Negotiations." *Constructing Rhetorical Education*. Ed. M. Secor and D. Charney. Carbondale: Southern Illinois UP, 1992. 91–115.

———. "Writing in Academic Settings: A Study of the Contexts for Writing in Two College Chemical Engineering Courses." *Research in the Teaching of English* 19 (1985): 331–61.

Jarratt, Susan. "On the Other Hand: Comments on Clark and Doheny-Farina." *Written Communication* 8 (January 1991): 117–20.

Keller, Evelyn Fox. *Reflections on Gender and Science*. New Haven, CT: Yale UP, 1985.

Knoblauch, C. H., and L. C. Brannon. "Knowing Our Knowledge: A Phenomenological Basis for Teacher Research." *Audits of Meaning: A Festschrift in Honor of Ann E. Berthoff*. Ed. Louise Z. Smith. Portsmouth, NH: Heinemann-Boynton/Cook, 1988. 17–28.

Lather, Patti. "Feminist Perspectives on Empowering Research Methodologies." *Women's Studies International Forum* 11 (1988): 569–81.

————. "Research as Praxis." *Harvard Educational Review* 56 (1986): 257–77.

Lincoln, Yvonna. "Campbell's Retrospective and a Constructivist's Perspective." *Harvard Educational Review* 60 (1990): 501–4.

Lincoln, Yvonna, and Egon Guba. *Naturalistic Inquiry.* Beverly Hills, CA: Sage, 1985.

Lunsford, Andrea, and Lisa Ede. "On the Other Hand: Comments on Clark and Doheny-Farina." *Written Communication* 8 (January 1991): 114–17.

McCarthy, Lucille, and Stephen Fishman. "Boundary Conversations: Conflicting Ways of Knowing in Philosophy and Interdisciplinary Research." *Research in the Teaching of English* 25 (1991): 419–68.

————. "A Text for Many Voices: Representing Diversity in Reports of Naturalistic Research." Ms., Dept. of English, U of Maryland-Baltimore County, 1991.

Mascia-Lees, Frances, Patricia Sharpe, and Colleen Ballerion Cohen. "The Postmodernist Turn in Anthropology: Cautions from a Feminist Perspective." *Signs* 15 (1989): 7–33.

Mishler, Elliot. "Validation in Inquiry-Guided Research: The Role of Exemplars in Narrative Studies." *Harvard Educational Review* 60 (1990): 415–42.

North, Stephen M. "Writing in a Philosophy Class: Three Case Studies." *Research in the Teaching of English* 20 (1986): 225–62.

Odell, Lee. "Beyond the Text: Relations Between Writing and Social Context." *Writing in Nonacademic Settings.* Ed. L. Odell and D. Goswami. New York: Guilford, 1985. 249–80.

Pratt, Mary Louise. "Fieldwork in Common Places." *Writing Culture: The Poetics and Politics of Ethnography.* Ed. J. Clifford and G. Marcus. Berkeley: U of California P, 1986: 27–50.

Reiff, John. "Remembering Things Past: A Critique of Narrow Revision." *Research in the Teaching of English* 24 (1990): 101–6.

Schilb, John. "Ideology and Composition Scholarship." *Journal of Advanced Composition* 8 (1988): 22–29.

Simon, Roger I., and Donald Dippo. "On Critical Ethnographic Work." *Anthropology and Education Quarterly* 17 (1986): 195–202.

Spanier, Bonnie. "Encountering the Biological Sciences: Ideology, Language, and Learning." *Research and Scholarship on Writing, Teaching, and Learning in the Disciplines.* Ed. A. Herrington and C. Moran. New York: MLA, 1992. 193–212.

Taylor, Denny, and Catherine Dorsey-Gaines. *Growing Up Literate: Learning from Inner-City Families.* Portsmouth, NH: Heinemann, 1988.

Walvoord, Barbara, and Lucille McCarthy. *Thinking and Writing in College: A Naturalistic Study of Students in Four Disciplines.* Urbana, IL: NCTE, 1990.

3

Writing in the Content

Areas: Some Theoretical

Complexities

David Kaufer and Richard Young

In 1985 Carnegie Mellon University began to rethink its program in undergraduate education, a process that included, as a central issue, rethinking the writing program. Our long-term goal was, in the words of Preston Covey, the vice provost and supervisor of the project, "integrating writing across domains and disciplines in affordable ways that appreciably enhance disciplinary and collaborative learning" (2). By 1988 several initiatives had been taken, drawing on ideas associated with the writing-across-the-curriculum (WAC) movement. These initiatives included a research project on the use of primary-trait scoring in peer evaluation, a writing-fellow program echoing the one at Brown, and collaborations with faculty members in various disciplines intended to introduce write-to-learn techniques into their teaching. As projects with limited objectives, the initiatives were reasonably successful. However, they did not add up to a coherent and unified program, and they provided neither an easy route nor a warrant for moving from the small-scale projects to a large-scale

71

educational program. We began to wonder seriously whether even the accumulated experience of the WAC movement provided such routes or warrants. Our skepticism was partly the result of the many constraints under which we were operating. We needed to develop a program that would demonstrably improve education in an environment where there were no compelling incentives for faculty to focus on the quality of their teaching. We needed a program that was conceptually unified while remaining sensitive to the distinctive features of the educational environment. Finally, we needed a program that would require no more time, energy, or money than we were sure would be available from year to year. We were especially apprehensive about what would happen when our start-up grant and the enthusiasm of the start-up faculty were both depleted.

David Russell's historical research on the numerous cross-disciplinary writing programs throughout the past century in this country was particularly worrisome. Of the many programs Russell describes, all started with an air of excitement and optimism, some were heralded, many endured for a time, but none appears to have survived. History did not seem to be on our side. Moreover, though we found much to admire in other WAC programs, we found none that we thought we should imitate. A strong program, we were convinced, must be shaped to the peculiarities of its environment; hence, no program is likely to be a good model for other programs, since all academic environments differ, often substantially.

These considerations discouraged us from starting a university-wide project and convinced us to set up a small-scale pilot project that would provide a laboratory for developing and testing ideas and for finding out what did and didn't work and what were reasonable expectations about costs and benefits in our own institutional context. It made little sense to launch a large-scale project with captive participants and limited resources if we could not make something interesting and useful happen on a small scale, where we had willing participants and ample resources. We began with some simple assumptions, summed up by Covey in his comment that

> an important premise of our pilot effort is that exploiting writing for improving learning in a discipline is (a) part-and-parcel of improving one's teaching generally and (b) naturally integral to teaching one's discipline. Our project is a "proof of concept" of the notion that this can and should be done—like the improvement of teaching generally—by

affordable incremental efforts assimilated into one's normal teaching duties and activities, not by grandiose leaps requiring extraordinary compensation. (3)

The discussion that follows describes what has happened so far in the pilot project and reflects on the implications of those events. The project was intended, in part at least, to answer a number of practical questions about the design and implementation of writing programs outside the English Department, and it did that, though not always as we had anticipated. One surprising outcome of the project has been the number of exceedingly difficult theoretical questions that it raised. These cluster in two broad categories: (1) questions about writing and content and (2) questions about the nature of expertise in unfamiliar settings and about how people acquire it.

Writing and Content

Inquiry into the relationship between writing and content can quickly provoke a wide array of questions: for example, questions about the relationship between learning to write and learning a subject or, more fundamentally, about the relationship between language and meaning, assuming we interpret "writing" to include language practices generally. Since first-language learners learn language and meanings concurrently, we might ask what role learning the language practices of a specialized discipline plays in learning the discipline's specialized meanings. There are other related questions, less basic, perhaps, but of more immediate interest to designers of writing programs in the content areas: What is content knowledge? What is writing knowledge? Are they the same or different? If different, how? If interactive, how?

These are difficult questions. They become more difficult still when we begin confronting the second category of questions about the conditions under which content expertise and writing expertise are best acquired. Can and should both kinds of knowledge be taught by the content teacher? By the writing teacher? Is there a principled division of labor? And, finally, what is the nature of rhetorical expertise and how does it relate to subject matter expertise?

We soon learned that we cannot rely on subject-matter experts for help with answers. The writing education of many such experts is a glimmer of light at the periphery of their own intellectual awakening, pale in comparison with what they learned in their own disciplines. And insofar as the subject-matter expert may genuinely recognize the importance of writing, it tends to be a recognition of the importance of language practices in the speciality, practices that the subject-matter expert does not associate with the writing expert or writing courses in English departments. Even though the content teacher may value good reading and writing skills, it usually falls to the writing expert to make the case for writing instruction in specialized subjects and, to add to the difficulty, to make the case prospectively—that is, to speak to the legitimacy and logistics of writing instruction in the content areas without the benefit of much, if any, direct experience in those areas and, because of this, without good models of expert performance and the insight they can yield. Neither the subject-matter expert nor the writing expert is likely to be expert in writing in specialized areas—that is, "expert" in the sense of having *both* an ability to carry out successfully the rhetorical tasks associated with a subject-matter discipline and an understanding of and ability to articulate the reasons for the success.

Writing in the content areas and developing writing programs in the content areas are enterprises saturated with theory or, if not theory, assumptions about writing and the teaching of writing that perform many of the functions of theory. In this essay we want to use the pilot project to suggest such theoretical issues, which are often implicit in statements and practices of the participants; the project also serves to ground the issues in the immediate experiences of university life. Interestingly enough, many of these issues align themselves on different sides of long-standing questions in the history of rhetoric, especially, as we have noted, the question of how rhetorical knowledge and content knowledge relate to one another and the question of rhetorical competence in the disciplines. The remainder of this section explores three related theoretical dichotomies that we confronted in the pilot project.

Language/Content Dichotomies

The pilot project began as a collaboration of Linda Kauffman, a scientist who teaches the Biology Department's required two-semester laboratory course for undergraduates; Lili Velez, a doctoral student in the English Department's rhetoric program; and Richard Young, a professor of rhetoric in the English Department.[1] The lab course seemed to all three to be an appropriate focus of attention because it is designed as a kind of doorway into the profession. It is part of a program designed primarily to produce research biologists headed for PhD or MD/PhD programs. A small percentage of students, particularly those who switched into biology in midstream, seek positions as research technicians in labs in order to prepare for PhD programs; some want to become researchers for companies like DuPont and Dow. No matter what their goals, when students enter the course they are biology majors; when they leave they are expected to be biologists. At the inception of the pilot project, Kauffman, Velez, and Young agreed that this particular course would offer a good opportunity to investigate and influence language practices in a particular discipline.

Their strategy for collaboration was based on the seemingly reasonable assumption that Velez and Young were the experts in rhetoric and Kauffman, the expert in biology. Velez and Young also brought another assumption to their interaction with Kauffman, though both are a bit embarrassed by it now. They had begun working with Kauffman rather like missionaries bringing the Word to unbelievers. Here, for example, are notes made by Young at one of their early meetings:

> I asked L[inda] if it would be possible and productive to think of her course as one in which students learn how to make arguments for members of the biological community. I had John Ziman's *Public Knowledge* in mind and some of the recent work in WAC on language behavior and acculturation in disciplinary communities, not to mention a long preoccupation with argument both as discourse form and as a kind of behavior that encourages the formation of communities and their maintenance. I thought the answer from L[inda] would be "yes, that's an interesting way to think about the discipline of biology"; and, of course, from there it's only a step to affirming the importance of rhetoric in biology, something that I have been trying to get her to do but had been finding various resistances. In particular, I want her to see formal features of discourse as involved with meaning, but she tends to treat rhetorical matters as strictly formal, readily separable from meaning, and hence relatively unimportant—a view shared by virtually all her students.

> Her answer was a very emphatic "no." I leaned over to Lili and said that I was beginning to feel a certain strangeness. And she replied, "Richard, exuberances and deficiencies" [a reference to Ortega y Gasset's discussion of the difficulties of translating from one language community to another— we always add something that wasn't there in the original, i.e., exuberances, and we always miss something that was, i.e., deficiencies].

For one thing, L[inda] said, "argument" sounds too "confrontational" and "unscientific." How about, she said, "presentation" rather than "argument"?

The assumption underlying Kauffman's comments appears to be that issues of language are separate or at least separable from issues of thought. Her rejection of argument in favor of presentation seemed to Young to imply that biological thinking is done not during the process of writing but prior to it, that in science the real "argument" is to be found in the design and execution of the experiment. When the experiment is finished, one writes it up, "presents" it in written form.

What became apparent here, as well as elsewhere in their conversations, was the quite different investment each had in words in their shared vocabulary, in words like "argument" and "presentation." For Young, "argument" was not only communication but an epistemic activity involving invention, exploration, and organization of ideas; and his preference for characterizing scientific communication as argument, as opposed to presentation, suggested the contentiousness of intellectual communities within which knowledge is developed and the corrigibility of knowledge. For Kauffman, "argument" had the more common meaning of combative discourse. For Young, "presentation" was an activity of display that resulted after the hard thinking was over. However, as Young and Velez later came to understand, "presentation" for Kauffman was an epistemic activity through which a scientist organizes small moments of scientific activity into more connected lines of thinking. "Presentation" for her was a literate activity, and, while it can be seen as a persuasive form, it persuaded in a quiet way by satisfying criteria of accuracy and completeness. But it also became apparent that her students' "presentations" often fit Young's stereotype better than Kauffman's richer understanding. Since they were not being cued to language as a problem-solving tool, often a problematic one, Kaufmann's students were not discouraged from making sharp and unproductive dichotomies between language and thought. (For an analogous situation in engineering education, see J. R. Kalmbach's "The Laboratory Reports of Engineering Students: A Case Study.")

Such unproductive dichotomies are associated with one of our oldest and most familiar traditions in writing instruction. We talk about language being the clothes of thought, about putting our thoughts into words, about not saying what we mean, about having good ideas but not being able to express them, and so on. "In the eyes of many teachers," observe Slevin, Fort, and O'Connor, the developers of Georgetown University's WAC program,

> the ultimate goal for student writing is to make the writing, to some extent, "unimportant." What teachers want in "good" writing is unobtrusive, transparent prose that does not get in the way of the perception of the truths being written about. . . . Fundamental to this view is the separability of "writing" from content and the assumption that there is neutral prose. Such an attitude is common, perhaps a defining characteristic of most academics' views of writing. (11)

We might call any approach to writing that separates issues of language from issues of content and from the context in which it is used "dualistic." Dualistic theories of style—in which matters of language are separable from matters of content—are at least as old as Aristotelian rhetoric, where invention and style were separate rhetorical arts; Aristotelian rhetoric helped one discover not only what to say but how to say it. However, the conception of rhetoric as a discipline concerned only with style and presentation is more recent, dating from the work of Peter Ramus in the sixteenth century. Ramus separated the traditional art of invention from the other arts of rhetoric and assigned it to dialectic, that is, an art of formal reasoning. As Walter Ong observes, Ramus subsumed content learning under the arts of invention and dialectic; he left it to rhetoric "to make the whole appealing by decorating or ornamenting it with suitable figures of speech and suitable delivery" (161). In his classroom practice, Ramus had students analyze texts from the perspective of various subject matters and rely on rhetoric only for help in the linguistic presentation of their analyses (163).

In the rhetorical tradition of Ramus, the separability of language and content is the *fundamental premise*. When it is the basis for writing instruction, we will call it "writing with no content in particular" (henceforth, the tradition of Writing-WNCP). The tradition of Writing-WNCP, based on Ramism, has dominated the thinking of most English departments and the university community in general. It has encouraged the establishment of separate courses in freshmen composition and the splitting off of writing from the rest of what is taught and learned in the academy. Composition courses tend to focus on language, epitomized in the ubiquitous handbooks on mechanics, usage, style, and the paragraph; the rest of the academy focuses on content, for which language is only a vehicle.

Separating issues of language from content should not be taken to imply that content has no place in the Writing-WNCP tradition. It does have a role—albeit an instrumental rather than an intrinsic one. Although attention to content in this teaching tradition is a practical necessity, it is a relatively peripheral issue. The function of content in the tradition of Writing-WNCP follows from contingent premises about what is required to learn to write. These premises are familiar dictums about writing:

1. Writing must be about something.
2. Teachers and students must share some knowledge about the subject of writing.
3. Learning to write requires textual models.

Such dictums furnish reasons for introducing content in writing courses and for the way it is used.

In the tradition of Writing-WNCP, it is assumed that pretty much the *same* skills of writing will develop no matter what content is chosen. The content is specific (the double helix, euthanasia, *Huckleberry Finn*, what I did last summer, etc.), but the language skills taught and learned are generic. The *Harbrace Handbook* and the like are standard across English composition courses, at least if we can judge from sales; but readers, case books, fictional texts, and so on, vary widely and unpredictably. Because, as the saying goes, one "can't write writing," some content is always necessary to practice writing, but almost any content will do. Consequently, there is no fixed subject matter for freshman composition, though particular composition courses are free to claim their own subject matters. We might add that in the pedagogy that has been developed in the Writing-WNCP tradition, the content chosen to write about in the writing class tends to be dictated not by the demands of a discipline but by what is presumed to be of interest to students, the assumption being that students write best about things that interest them.

We do not want to be misunderstood here as assailing the pedagogy and textbooks in freshmen composition. Clearly, there are many fine composition texts and much imaginative and effective teaching in the Ramist tradition. And there are also texts used in freshman composition courses that, at least by implication, repudiate the Ramist split by offering students help in the creation of meaning. We are simply calling attention to some characteristics of texts and methods that function within the Writing-WNCP tradition.

In the tradition of Writing-WNCP, nothing of substance rides on the distinction between *content* and *subject matter*. A subject matter, as we will use the term, consists of a content that has been discussed in recurring and public rhetorical situations. "What I did last summer" can be a content, but it is unlikely to be a subject matter. Because subject matters have publicly shared histories and have usually been analyzed from the perspective of abstract writings called "theory," a writer who tackles a subject matter (the Civil War, rhetoric, Romantic poetry, biology) must first engage in learning this history and theory and sifting through relevant information to the extent necessary for credibility. Science education tends to disregard information about the history of science but nonetheless requires students to learn a network of densely related and shared information that has accumulated as part of the "achievements" of the scientific field. In both humanities and scientific education, a subject matter presents to the student a formidable challenge requiring a steep learning curve. However, within the tradition of Writing-WNCP this kind of subject-matter learning tends to be a distracting and dispensable constraint on learning to write. Hence, while there is no principled difference between subject matters and contents when one is learning to write in the tradition of Writing-WNCP, the tradition nonetheless expresses a *practical* preference for having students deal with contents that do not require so much time and effort to learn—lest instruction in writing be compromised.

Accordingly, the emphasis in the tradition of Writing-WNCP is on personal expression in interpersonal rhetorical transactions. In a survey of forty-eight leading composition teachers who were asked to nominate their "best" student papers (later anthologized in 1985 in William Coles and James Vopat's *What Makes Writing Good?*), all but four nominated examples that fit into the genres of "personal expression," "narrative," or "autobiography" (Faigley). Some of the most heralded teachers of writing, for example, Macrory and Elbow, encourage students to write out of immediate experience. The fact that content for writing can be so cleanly divorced from publicly defined subject matters underscores the practical and marginal role, relatively speaking, of content in the tradition of Writing-WNCP.

Faced with the subtle Ramist assumptions of Kauffman's students, Velez and Young became convinced that they needed to make some interventions in Kauffman's class that would show students the generative and inventive capacities of language. Young wanted to introduce into the course one of the characteristic techniques of WAC pedagogy, the journal, and he asked Kauffman whether students already were required to keep some sort of journal or notebook in the course. In true missionary fashion, he was trying to introduce new practices by grafting them on similar but already well-established ones. When she said that her students were required to keep a record of their lab work in a notebook, Young suggested that the functions of the notebook be expanded to include what the WAC literature associates with the epistemic uses of language (e.g., Fulwiler; Kalmbach; Selfe and Arbabi). These include using the journal as a place to identify and explicate problems as they arise in the student's thinking and as a way for students to keep a written record of their transactions with teachers.

Kauffman's reply was dismaying. She said that while the suggestion was not unreasonable, the lab notebooks of professional researchers are often used in patent applications and in product litigation and hence are controlled by strict conventions. Her students' notebooks had to be string bound; the pages had to be numbered before they were written on; ink had to be used, not pencil; and lines had to be drawn through any blank space at the end of pages—all this so that no undetectable alterations could be made after the original entries. Since Kauffman was trying to teach her students how to behave like professional biologists, Young's suggestion, no matter how useful it seemed to him, was simply inappropriate. The problem was not that keeping journals in Kauffman's class was necessarily a bad idea; even if the students had to keep two separate journals for different pedagogical purposes, it might well be a profitable activity. The problem for Young and Velez was that they began to think that they did not know enough about practices in the biology class to make useful suggestions.

Method/Content Dichotomies

Two quite different approaches are discernible in the educational movement that goes by the name *writing across the curriculum*. The first approach (e.g., Flynn and Jones) is based on the notion that writing is an epistemic activity and seeks to introduce generic languaging activities (e.g., the journal and collaborative learning) into educational environments of any kind. The second approach (e.g., Williams and Colomb) seeks to identify, systematize, and teach the rhetorical practices of particular disciplinary communities. In the first approach, the same teaching methods are assumed to be equally appropriate and equally effective in any disciplinary community. It implies a dichotomy between pedagogical method and content somewhat analogous to the dichotomy between language and content noted earlier in the discussion of Writing-WNCP. As Slevin et al. note,

> With regard to the teaching of writing, then, we distinguish between the concept of writing across the curriculum and the concept of writing within disciplines. In the former, writing across the curriculum, we look for general practices, common procedures for teaching writing that will work in all sorts of courses; so our attention here will be on generalizations about the writing process, learning, and cognitive growth.

In the second approach, writing within disciplines, the separation of method and content is never an issue because writing assignments are dictated by the specific rhetorical practices of the community. For example, in a journal Kauffman kept on her teaching, she wrote,

> During lecture today I made a small writing assignment that students should turn in a week later at the next lecture. The assignment was, for those students in the Monday class that would, on Friday, complete Experiment III, to plot the turbidity of the culture, as requested in the report section of Experiment III and then to describe the resulting curve. This was to be completed in five or six sentences, since as I said in Appendix I, more words did not convey more meaning. . . . Since the material that they were writing would be an integral part of their final report, this exercise was not a "ghost" or "dry" effort. (Sept. 7, 1988)

At the inception of the pilot project, Velez and Young had been taking the first approach to WAC and not paying much attention to the second. This was apparent in their efforts to introduce journal-keeping into the biology class and in their lack of any effort to learn about education in biology. When Kauffman rejected the proposal to expand the functions of the lab notebooks, Velez and Young realized that they were outsiders, strangers in a strange land, so to speak, and that they needed to find a more appropriate strategy to guide their activities in the project; as it turned out, this required moving from the generalist-epistemic approach to a more discipline-oriented approach.

They realized that they needed to learn a great deal more about language practices in biology before they could be useful to Kauffman and before they could hope to introduce useful changes that would persist in her class. As Velez now recalls, both she and Young had been talking too much. But this was understandable, she says, because neither she nor Young had known what to listen for. She further recalls this moment as the point at which she started to immerse herself in biology materials, thinking that if she was going to help redesign a course, she had better first know something about the course. Metaphorically speaking, Velez and Young abandoned their role of WAC missionaries and became something like anthropologists investigating the culture of academic biology.

Clifford Geertz defines the culture of a people as an "ensemble of texts, themselves ensembles, which the anthropologist strains to read over the shoulders of those to whom they properly belong" (129). Velez and Young began reading "over the shoulders" of those to whom the texts properly belong, both literally and figuratively. They began to collect information about practices in Kauffman's course, using surveys, tape-recorded interviews with Kauffman and students, taking notes on what went on in lectures and labs, and assembling sets of syllabi, assignments, and student reports. Their immediate goal was a deep, if narrow, knowledge of language practices in the lab course as a reflection of broader disciplinary practices and the rhetoric underlying those practices.

Writing with a Specific Content

Thus far we have been characterizing a particular tradition in writing instruction (i.e., Writing-WNCP), a tradition that has dictated many of the distinctive features of composition instruction in English departments in this country and that many in other disciplines invoke when thinking about writing instruction. When Kauffman talked about writing and writing instruction, she appeared to be drawing on this tradition. But when she talked about teaching biology and the language practices of biologists, another conception of writing seemed to be invoked—what we might call "writing with a specific content" (Writing-WSC). In this second tradition of writing instruction, content serves more than the sort of instrumental function discussed earlier.

As we have noted, Writing-WNCP is a dualistic conception of writing and writing instruction, in which language forms and content are seen as separable; in contrast, this second conception (WSC) is monistic. If we try to tease out the underlying assumptions of this conception we get something like the following:

1. A language act is a composite of form and meaning.
2. Subject matter constrains writing, that is, it is not simply a passive environment.
3. Subject matter makes a significant difference in the particular writing skills that get learned.

Given these assumptions, neither the student nor the teacher can afford an indifference to subject matter any more than they can afford, in a traditional writing course, an indifference to the principles of writing being taught. To teach the subject matter of a discipline is, in effect, to simultaneously teach languaging about the discipline; and, perhaps also true, to teach languaging in the discipline is to teach the subject matter of the discipline.

In one of the interviews Velez had with a student, trying to discover the sources of the student's knowledge about the rhetoric of biology, she asked the student (Bill) about his work in other courses:

B[ill]: The next year, though, I plan on taking . . . two classes in the spring which are graduate-level courses. The whole theme is to read [a report] and discuss it . . . be able to critique them. . . . You know, if what you see is wrong with that approach, [the] conclusions, [the] capabilities of their methods from the data, results. . . .

B: And essentially it's just like a round table. People sit there, they've read them, give their ideas. . . . We've done that a little bit in the classes this semester . . . where he had a paper that he wanted everyone to read. Everybody read it, and myself and somebody else, one other person . . . talked about, which makes you kind of feel pretty stupid because if no one else wants to say anything . . . whereas in graduate courses that's what you're really wanted [to do].

LV: Do you think that the situation of those round table classes are comparable to the kinds of the discussion you might have at a lab meeting? Were you looking for research procedures . . . ?

B: Our lab meetings, you have a lab meeting followed by a journal article. Lab meeting people come in and discuss the results . . . where to go next, what everyone thinks . . . . And then after we do have a journal [club] where somebody's read a paper and he gets up and essentially outlines it, and starts discussing it, and people, if they have questions they'll ask you, and if they have thoughts, so, it's not quite a round table discussion. . . .

LV: Is that a function of your group . . . ?

B: Uh-huh, well it's essentially, it forces people not to get hooked into just [one way of thinking], it keeps their eyes open so they're not ignorant of what's going on. And sometimes you're forced to read a section of the paper that you're not comfortable with, so you have to go back and read it. Now the previous papers, you get a feel for it.

The focus of such critical activity, Kauffman has observed, is on the relation of the method to the data and the conclusions drawn from the data. But it seems apparent that one important way biology students learn the rhetorical practices of their discipline is by discussing the accuracy, completeness, coherence, and relevance of information of scientific reports. Unfortunately, we do not know much about this kind of learning.

Informal Learning in Writing-WSC

Part of the acculturation process in a discipline is learning to control its characteristic language practices. When writing is taught in the Writing-WSC tradition or, perhaps more accurately, if writing is taught rather than learned through practice, care is likely to be taken to explain just how the subject matter of the discipline shapes language behavior. In the Writing-WNCP tradition, writing is usually taught formally; explicit instruction is provided in its various features. In contrast, as Velez's interview with the student suggests, in Writing-WSC learning the linguistic and rhetorical practices of a field is an informal process and is supposed to take care of itself, no matter how important the teacher regards the practices.

Because of the loose coupling they tend to perceive between formal writing instruction and their own capacities to write as members of a field, many content experts believe that writing ability in their discipline is essentially a maturational skill, something gradually inferred from practice while learning the subject matter. Many who hold the maturation hypothesis lump writing with the many abilities that must be acquired in the struggle for initiation, as part of the unspoken dues-paying that goes into any worthwhile rite of entry. But for all its intuitive appeal, the experts' maturational hypothesis is seriously confounded. For it may be that experts who give voice to it constitute a self-selected population who managed, through tenacity, practice, or some heroic act of intervention from their mentors or peers, to overcome an inadequate formal training in writing. Analogously, there may well be populations who managed to learn the subject matter of a field to some acceptable level but who nonetheless were denied further education or entry because of inadequate training in writing. However, members of this population are seldom around to lend their dissenting voices. (Kauffman notes that Darwin had a term for this process.) Such excluded populations would call into question the maturational hypothesis that says, "In time everyone can learn, more or less, to write in their chosen subject matter."

As we have already seen, the informality of rhetorical education in the Writing-WSC tradition seemed to be apparent in Bill's comments. It is also apparent in one of the interviews where Kauffman, Velez, and Young were discussing introductions in scientific reports, how students learn to write them in biology, and what might be done to improve student performance:

> L[inda]: So I think if we do this as a more directive exercise, considering that our goal is to focus on introductions. . . .

> Y: You might . . . say, look, this isn't just a pedagogical exercise. [There are] values [for the professional biologist in this]. Outlining or summarizing is a powerful heuristic. . . .

> L: Well and not only that but these kids are looking forward to writing papers for other classes . . . in their upper level courses. [In] many cases their grades depend on them writing a good paper on the research topic of their choice. And these kinds of skills [rhetorical skills having to do with scientific articles that enable them] . . . to read them effectively, summarize them effectively, write them up effectively, and find them in the library are things which they're expected to be able to do, *and I, for the life of me don't know how they learn how. I really don't* . . . [italics added].

An English teacher working out of dualist assumptions might suggest that Kauffman doesn't know how they acquire their rhetorical knowledge because she isn't the one who teaches them. However, the students themselves cast some doubt on this explanation, for they tend not to see English as relevant to their work in biology. In a survey of the students early on in the pilot project, one of them responded to the question of whether there were subjects that did not contribute to their progress as biologists as follows: "Spanish. English (though necessary, it was not helpful)." Although similar attitudes have been reported in other studies (e.g., Kalmbach), one should be careful not to make too much of comments such as this one, since not many students responded that way and since they also criticized courses in biology.

Theoretical Consistency and Practice

Since the assumptions of Writing-WSC seem on their face thoroughly incompatible with those of Writing-WNCP, one would expect an intense theoretical battle in composition pedagogy between proponents of each tradition. But this is far from the case. While some clearly see an intellectual divide, many teachers move freely across these frameworks as if there were no inconsistency between them. They act as if the frameworks represented a de facto curricular division (between, for example, freshman writing and advanced disciplinary writing) rather than a fundamental intellectual difference about the acquisition of writing skill; as if one set of learning assumptions made sense for freshmen and a wholly different and incompatible set made sense for upperclassmen. Notice that Kauffman appears to hold both positions. When she is talking about writing and writing instruction, she seems to dichotomize linguistic form and content. But when she is talking about practices in biology and the teaching of biology, language practices are inextricably linked to the discipline.

Why do many see no necessary theoretical barriers to moving eclectically between seemingly incompatible sets of assumptions? At least part of the answer may be that one motive for offering writing instruction in content courses is practical rather than theoretical. Many writing teachers and content specialists alike are concerned with the poor ability of students to write in particular subject matters, particularly academic subjects. Even though they continue to subscribe to the learning assumptions of Writing-WNCP, they realize that for the sake of helping students in their academic subjects and their careers it is best to alter conventional practices. Becoming more conscious of the need to teach writing in the subject matters with which students have difficulty, they incorporate contents associated with disciplinary learning directly into writing courses. The result has been the familiar upper-level technical writing and business writing courses and, more recently, WAC courses taught by English teachers in which students from the various disciplines write about the subject matters of their disciplines (Kinneavy 16–17; Hamilton). These steps can be taken without violating the assumptions of Writing-WNCP; to put it another way, they do not necessarily require adopting the premises of Writing-WSC. They may be simply practical responses to particular language difficulties.

A similar tendency to ignore theoretical inconsistencies and their pedagogical implications is apparent in the way writing teachers have approached dualist and monist theories of style. In "The Problem of Style" Louis Milic notes that "no inconsistency seems to be felt by those who hold those essentially inimical opinions, perhaps by reason of the minor importance usually attached to theories of style since any compromise offering pragmatic satisfaction makes theoretical consistency unnecessary" (277). It is not at all clear that a theoretically consistent pedagogy is necessarily preferable to an eclectic pedagogy that is effective in solving immediate problems. It seems reasonable for the teacher of writing to prefer pragmatic effectiveness to theoretical consistency, particularly when the adequacy of available theories is often questionable.

A disadvantage of pragmatic eclecticism, at least an uncritical eclecticism, is that one thereby forgoes the heuristic and critical power that theories, even in their present state of development, can offer the teacher-scholar who is trying to examine existing programs or develop more effective ones. Furthermore, unless one tries to hold practice to certain standards of theoretical consistency, one is likely to perpetuate the kinds of misunderstandings that beset Young and Kauffman when they exchanged innocent-sounding words like "argument" and "presentation." For both, "argument" and "presentation" were not isolated dictionary entries, but theoretical terms within elaborate theoretical frameworks. Our vocabulary about writing is already highly "theorized"; if we do not take the time to understand the ways in which this is so, our discussions about writing are likely to have little impact on our practice. And our practice will remain piecemeal, ad hoc, and unaccountable.

Learning Writing and Content Together: Acquiring Expertise

In the fall semester of 1990, Velez was hired by the Biology Department to continue and expand the work with Kauffman. A year later they gave a progress report on the project at the one of the Teaching

Center's luncheon forums; Kauffman, remarking on her perceptions of the project, noted that she had initially thought the project would "enhance the students' learning to write reports, i.e., to communicate their discipline," but that she has come to see it as learning how to use "writing to learn the intellectual tasks of the discipline." We get some insight into how this change of perception came about from answers Kauffman and Velez gave to two questions: How has the collaboration worked? What has been done?

1. First, we had to learn how to talk to each other: the goals, language, and assumptions we have are not the same. Hours of classroom observations clarified the logic and focus of biology.
2. We had to identify what student assignments already in place might be served better by a different "process."
3. We had to dissect assignments to identify what students were supposed to learn. In the process we clarified where they had difficulties. We often found there were multiple tasks or goals within a single assignment.
4. By separating multiple tasks or goals from each other, we could redesign assignments so that they more clearly served only one of those goals. We could then set up a series of smaller assignments or activities to build experience or understanding progressively.
6. We promote practice and experience rather than testing.
7. We emphasize both the separate tasks and their integration, but at different stages in the series. For example, in the first semester, the emphasis in lab report requirements might be on good graphic and tabular presentation of data and correct analysis of these data, while in the second semester the task expands to include writing good introductions to the reports.

The project, which continues, has a double purpose—to provide opportunities for developing and testing ideas about writing in the content areas and to position us for initiating a more comprehensive program. As a model for program development throughout the university, it is open to question, since the commitment of time and dollars has been too great to be duplicated on a large scale. On the other hand, if we judge it by its educational outcomes, it has been very successful. The amount and diversity of writing in the biology courses has increased substantially, and the purposes to which it is put are more varied; for example, a substantial amount of writing is now done whose goal is not communication or knowledge testing but learning.

And as an exercise in exploratory research it has been invaluable. We have, as we have suggested, learned much about contextual constraints on pedagogical methods, about language practices in another disciplinary community, about tacitly held assumptions and their consequences, and about the conditions for effective interaction across disciplinary communities. And we have become much more aware of how much research must be done in order to understand the tangled assumptions that drive WAC programs in their various forms and how much must be done in order to make effective use of this understanding in the development of more adequate writing programs.

Tangled Assumptions about Expertise

The uncertain and tentative interactions between Velez and Young on the one hand and Kauffman on the other arose, in part at least, because of the uncertain and tentative locus of expertise. Velez and Young began their work with Kauffman on the assumption that they were the experts in writing who *had* the Word and she was the expert in biology who *needed* the Word. It was up to Kauffman to make use of what they brought her. Kauffman, for her part, did not question Velez and Young's expertise but assumed from the start that their expertise would accommodate her own expertise in biology. When all three soon recognized that no easy accommodation could be made, there was a perceived vacuum of power and authority. Who should be teaching whom? Since Velez and Young had placed themselves in the role of consultants, they resolved that it was up to them to learn more about Kauffman's expertise. They came to believe that the sought-after expertise lay with Kauffman and that they were there simply to help Kauffman gain greater access to its rhetorical dimension. However, as they continued to interact with Kauffman, it became apparent to all that Kauffman was not simply relying on Velez and Young to remind her of what she already knew about writing in biology. Velez and Young were learning more about relevant features of biology education, and Kauffman was learning more about writing. Despite their mutual efforts to pinpoint the locus of expertise, the more they interacted the less well defined the center of expertise seemed to become.

This course of events, which we believe is not peculiar to the circumstances we have described, makes WAC a cruel temptress. From a distance, developing a WAC program appears not only to be a highly desirable task but also to be a relatively simple one, in part because the division of expertise seems so clear. Subject-matter experts have a problem fostering language skills in their students. Who else to solve it but experts in writing? Up close, however, the boundaries demarcating expertise become more blurred and problematic.

The uncertain distribution of expertise between the writing teacher and the subject-matter teacher may be a consequence of unrefined dichotomies not only in the WAC movement but, more broadly, in our understanding of writing as well. Dualists, as we have noted, separate language and content, leaving the relationship between them unaddressed. Within this school of thought, the division of expertise between the writing expert and the subject-matter expert remains neatly—but usually too simply—demarcated. Monists try to resolve the problematic relationship between language and content by denying their separability. We can see the insistence on fusion in John Middleton Murray's remark that "style is not an isolable quality of writing; it is writing itself" (quoted in Milic 281). Here language and content are seen as identical: to study the one is to study the other. Thus, thoroughgoing monists are likely to have difficulty accommodating the concept of writing expert, if we define writing expert as the dualist does, that is, as one concerned exclusively with the language of discourse. What is needed, we suggest, are more sustained efforts to refine our understanding of these definitions and dichotomies, regardless of whether our refinements lead to a resolution of the matter. In this concluding section, we wish to review some contributions to such refinements in an attempt to understand experiences in the pilot project and, more generally, writing programs in the content areas.

Work relevant to understanding the relation of linguistic form and content has been carried out in a variety of disciplines and under a variety of names. The relationship itself produces a whole family of dichotomies, their common denominator being language: language and content, language and thinking, language and cognition, language and method, language and meaning, and so on. Still another dichotomy that must be considered as we explore language practices in the content disciplines is that between generic problem-solving strategies and practices unique to particular kinds of problems and contexts. In each case, the question arises as to the role of language in specialized performances that go beyond the exemplification of linguistic skill alone.

Models of Expertise

The General Skills Model. One literature that speaks to many of these dichotomies and, in particular, to the one between general articulable strategies and skills unique to particular contexts and data has been that of cognitive psychologists, especially those with a long-standing interest in modeling expert knowledge on computers or at least on the basis of a mechanistic model of mind. In the 1950s and early 1960s, a widely held view among cognitive psychologists (e.g., Newell and Simon) was that expertise is a matter of controlling general strategies that are useful in any subject area.[2] Polya's influential work found that experts in mathematics rely on a battery of strategies (e.g., decomposing a problem, making diagrams, examining special cases) that are in no way unique to mathematics. In the late 1950s, Newell, Shaw, and Simon developed a computer program called the "General Problem-Solver" that could solve problems in a variety of domains through a common set of general strategies involving the monitoring of goals along with monitoring the extent to which certain actions move one toward or away from these goals. While there is no necessary connection between an expert's reliance on these general strategies and the expert's ability or need to *articulate* them as part of his or her intellectual activity, it should be clear that general strategies (e.g., keep a list of your goals and monitor your actions toward them) are, in principle, easier to articulate and teach than are skills whose formulation requires substantial contextual information.

When Velez and Young first approached Kauffman, they were relying on a simple division of expertise implied by these formulations. That is to say, Velez and Young assumed they had a battery of general strategies to offer Kauffman and that these general strategies, configurable to any subject matter concerns, would do no violence to Kauffman's practices. However, as Young and Velez came to realize, they were, if not totally wrong, at least not right enough, and for the same reasons that the aforementioned model of expertise has been called into question.

Perkins and Salomon note that the model of expertise that assumes generality across domains fell out of favor in the early 1970s for three reasons. First, studies of expert performance in chess suggested that experts seem to rely more on noticing and recognizing patterns on the chessboard than on applying general strategies. According to Perkins and Salomon, a person who applies a strategy can report (or, in principle, be induced to report) the whys and wherefores of doing what he or she is doing. However, they note that studies of expertise in chess found that experts are more inclined to reason in terms of highly contextualized configurations (e.g., "I move my bishop from square A to B whenever my bishop is in square A while my knight is in square C and my opponent's bishop is in square D") than in terms of general strategies applied to chess (e.g., "If I closely monitor my goals and the success of my actions toward achieving them, I increase my chances of overall success" or, even more specifically, "control the center").

The second reason models favoring general articulable skills fell out of favor came to light in another battery of studies in which a computer programmed with local knowledge in a subject area performed more impressively *in that area* than a computer equipped only with general strategies. Simply put, a computer with some mathematical knowledge will solve math problems better than a computer with only general strategies that can be applied to math; a computer with some chess knowledge will solve chess problems better than a computer with only general strategies that can be applied to chess.

Finally, a third set of studies revealed that expertise in one area or in one form of a problem does not necessarily transfer to other subjects or problems. These results are of a piece with the common observation among writing teachers that expertise in one genre of writing does not guarantee expertise in another. Being a superb technical writer does not make one a great poet, and vice versa.

The common implication of these studies is that the subject area and the context in which it is presented are both vital to a theory of expertise. The power of this contextualist view of expertise came home to Velez and Young when they were initially confronted with the limitations of their own expertise. Nonetheless, the recognition of contextualism was a hard one for them to accept because they understood that Kauffman had all along been looking to *their* expertise. This put Velez and Young in the strange position of having to claim their ability to understand Kauffman's rhetorical expertise as being the expertise they could bring to Kauffman. The claim was both strange and strained for Velez and Young but no less for Kauffman because at times she wanted to disavow the very expertise (i.e., the art of writing biology) on which Velez and Young claimed their own depended. Recall, for example, Kauffman's remark about how her students learned to write in the discipline: "I don't know how they learn it. I really don't." From a belief in expertise as general strategies that Velez and Young could bring to biology, all three came to embrace an entirely different image of expertise, one which deeply embedded the expertise of "writing biology" in Kauffman's subject matter and in the context in which she wanted to present it.

The Contextualist Model. The contextualist view of expertise they then embraced had already been for some time an important theoretical framework for writing in the content areas. Advocates of this movement, spurred on by the writings of Richard Rorty, argue that to learn how to write is to learn the local contexts in which discourse communities acquire knowledge. Rorty (48) has argued against the existence of universals that exist independent of local situations and the local vocabularies used to describe them. He has described disciplines as islands of historically contingent vocabularies (75) that must be traveled on their own terms. Expressions across islands may overlap, but the overlap represents no overarching "generality." It merely represents the same historical contingency that exists on any single island. Young and Velez's impulse to drop the missionary attitude and become anthropologists was very much a Rortian impulse.

This impulse and the contextualist conception of rhetorical ability that it implies require some clarification. First, it may seem that contextualism is incompatible with training that passes as "general" or "generic." But this is not necessarily the case. Contextualists can concede that some skills of writing (e.g., skill in spelling, grammar, usage) are transcontextual and can be taught with very light references to content and context—even though, in principle, they would deny that these skills are or ever can be strictly "decontextualized" or "content-free." Second, while contextualism is currently a strong force in the WAC movement, it is not the only force. Many WAC advocates, for example, seem to retain the Ramian split between form and content, believing that students should simply get more writing practice in their content courses as a way of fostering a kind of generalized literacy. Even those for whom writing knowledge and content knowledge are a problem-free duality will grant the benefits of practice, no matter what the content or context. Hence, encouraging writing practice in a particular disciplinary context does not necessarily imply a contextualist position.

Were the contextualist position the end of the story, we would expect Velez and Young to have helped Kauffman gain access to and solidify what she knew all along about writing biology. In such a case the flow of new knowledge would have been mostly one-way, with Kauffman changing Velez and Young far more than they changed her. That is, Velez and Young would have learned a great deal that was new to them about the rhetoric of biology, but Kauffman would only come to understand better what it was she already knew. After all, the native normally changes the anthropologist; not the other way around. As contextualists, all Velez and Young could want or expect to do is define what it means to "write biology" and to study the expert's, that is, Kauffman's, practices in order to crystalize for her the rhetorical definitions, principles, and procedures that she was already using.

The story doesn't have this ending, however. In fact, the story is still unfolding. Yet it is already clear that the ending foreshadowed by contextualism is not wholly supported by the events of the project. Velez and Young's interaction with Kauffman has led to Kauffman's becoming more sensitive to rhetorical principles and practices, both within biology and without. While investigating Kauffman's expertise, Velez and Young have convinced Kauffman that their own expertise has relevance to her work as a biologist and a teacher of biology.

The Interactionist Model. The changes in the unfolding story between Velez, Young, and Kauffman seem related to changes now taking place in current theories of expertise. The contextual view of expertise is being supplanted by newer, synthetic theories that argue that expertise relies on a complex and so far unspecified interaction between context knowledge and general strategies that are in principle articulable and teachable. The basis for these synthetic theories of expertise is in experimental studies showing that experts benefit from general strategies when they enter new and unfamiliar areas of study. For example, Clement found that experts in physics resort to general strategies (e.g., analogy, goal-monitoring, exploring extreme cases) when they work on problems in areas of physics that are unfamiliar. Schoenfeld found that general strategies can significantly improve performance in mathematics when the strategies are taught in conjunction with the context. Salomon and Perkins found that skills in one context are likely to transfer to another if learners get the chance to practice the skill extensively and across a variety of contexts or if they are made mindful of the applicability in new contexts of skills already in their possession.

These recent theories of expertise—which we might call "interactionist"—seem more descriptive of what Kauffman, Velez, and Young actually experienced in their collaboration. More than generalist or contextualist theories, these theories are able to account for the shifting back and forth of the locus of expertise between the two rhetoric experts and the expert in biology. They also adumbrate the shifts that any student might experience in seeking to combine subject-matter expertise with expertise in writing for a particular disciplinary community. Thus, a fundamental question of WAC pedagogy is how to engender in student writers both these kinds of expertise and the ability to relate them. Drawing from interactionist theories of expertise, Michael Carter has sought to do this. Carter sees expertise in writing as including both local and general knowledge, and he relies heavily on the literature that views general strategies as stepping-stones to localized expertise or, to change the metaphor, as bootstraps by which a writer can pull himself or herself to a fuller and more detailed understanding of how to work within specific disciplinary domains. Such general strategies become, with practice, increasingly streamlined, routinized, and contextualized.

Carter's approach to expertise in writing does not subvert either dualist or contextualist assumptions; instead, it houses them within what Carter hopes to be a single unified theory. One set of assumptions, he argues, is useful for thinking about writing before a subject-matter has been entered; an entirely different set of assumptions comes to play upon entry into a subject-matter domain and a disciplinary community. An attractive feature of his argument is that it tends to confirm the status quo, in which English departments provide instruction in generic strategies and knowledge, and the content areas provide instruction in local language practices; in effect, his version of interactionist theory justifies the current division between freshman composition and upper-division writing courses. Since it provides a theoretical justification for the present situation, it does not call for major disruptions in current institutional structures and educational practices, which might well for practical reasons disqualify the theory from serious consideration.

A difficulty with his argument, however, is that it overlooks the discontent that helped to shape WAC programs in the first place—that is, the uneasy perception shared by many that the writing taught in freshman English programs is not sufficient for and is not easily adapted by student writers entering specific content areas. Were both freshman writing and subject-based writing working elements of a single theory and a single coherent educational process, as Carter suggests, it would be difficult to explain why the transition between them is not smooth. Had Velez and Young perceived that biology students were merely extending freshman principles of writing within the biology course, they would have seen no problem with writing in the biology major. Had Kauffman perceived that biology students were localizing their rhetorical knowledge to biology in appropriate ways, she might not have collaborated with Velez and Young.

A second literature that has proved useful in refining the relationship between generalist knowledge and particular subject matters is that on reflective practice, since it provides another rationale quite different from Carter's for valuing both insider and outsider knowledge. Theorists interested in reflective practice tend to center their focus on the expert's unusual ability to reflect upon a problem even in the process of solving it. A central voice in the literature on reflective practice has been that of Donald Schon, who characterizes the professions and the sciences throughout the first half of this century as having slighted the importance of reflection in technical practice. He calls the ideology that has slighted reflection *technical rationality*. Technical rationality, according to Schon, consists only of "instrumental" problem-solving; it assumes that the role of the practitioner is to apply knowledge without needing to reflect upon it or adjust it in any significant way to the peculiarities of a local context; it assumes that there is no indigenous theory of practice (21–34). Schon argues that since the 1960s both the general public and the professions themselves have become increasingly aware that practice often implicates many areas of specialization and exposes uncertainties in existing theory:

> When professionals consider what road to build, for example, they deal usually with a complex and ill-defined situation in which geographic, topological, financial, economic, and political issues are all mixed together. Once they have somehow decided what road to build and go on to consider how best to build it, they may have a problem they can solve by the application of available techniques; but when the road they have built leads unexpectedly to the destruction of a neighborhood, they may find themselves again in a situation of uncertainty. (40)

Schon argues that a good practitioner relies heavily on what he calls knowledge-in-action, that is, knowledge about what we are doing. But this knowledge is often inadequate to the problem at hand and must be supplemented by what Schon calls reflection-in-action, which is our ability to think about and think through the consequences and implications of what we are doing as we are doing it (54). Studying architects, psychotherapists, engineers, agronomists, and economists, Schon found that all make significant use of reflection-in-practice when they run into situations of unanticipated complexity, uncertainty, or instability, situations, according to Schon, that occur all the time in professional life but which are seldom recognized as having a distinctive character:

> Although reflection-in-action is an extraordinary process, it is not a rare event. Indeed, for some reflective practitioners it is the core of practice. Nevertheless, because professionalism is still mainly identified with technical expertise, reflection-in-action is not generally accepted—even by those who do it—as a legitimate form of professional knowing. (69)

It is too strong a claim to associate reflection-in-action solely with linguistic skills. Musicians and baseball pitchers rely on reflection-in-action according to Schon but do not necessarily reflect in words. "We need not suppose that they [musicians] reflect-in-action in the medium of words. More likely, they reflect through a 'feel for the music' which is not unlike the pitcher's 'feel for the ball' " (56).

However, there is no doubt that many reflective practices are linguistic. Much of reflection-in-action involves setting the problem that needs to be solved. And problem-setting, according to Schon, includes the linguistic activities of naming the components of the problem and framing the context in which they will be attended to. "Problem setting is a process in which, interactively, we *name* the things to which we will attend and *frame* the context in which we will attend to them" (40). Schon found, for example, that designers often rely on talking to others in order to monitor their drawing (80), that they have an extensive vocabulary dealing with function, cost, scale, materials, and so on that they keep coming back to as they work and rework their technical sketches (96). In an observation related to Schon's, Kauffman points out an interesting difference between the work environments in the English Department and the Biology Department at Carnegie Mellon, a difference that may reflect not only different styles of research but different reflective practices. In the English Department each faculty member has an individual office; thus, each is isolated from the others. In the Biology Department the architectural layout is designed to encourage continual collaborative interaction between the faculty leader and members of the research project team.

A clear implication of Schon's theory is to blur the boundaries between insider and outsider knowledge since a reflective practitioner must constantly "get outside" his or her own context in order to understand it better. And what better way to get outside one's own context than to make use of the perceptions of people who are already on the outside. Consequently, Schon argues that a reflective practitioner should have an entirely different relationship to a client than a professional committed to the notion of the technical expert. Schon contends that a reflective practitioner has every reason to discourage a passive client and to encourage the client to form a working partnership with him or her (302). In many respects, this is the relationship that formed between Kauffman on the one hand and Velez and Young on the other. Early on, they defined their relationship according to the value of the distinctive specialties they brought to one another. Each was a specialist to the other and each was, at one time or another, a client. As time went on, the value of what they supposedly knew as specialists began to wane. The value of what they knew and could bring to each other as outsiders, as nonexperts, began to grow. Velez and Young began to recognize that Kauffman's outside (allegedly naive) perspective about writing enhanced their own specialized understanding. Kauffman began to recognize that Velez and Young's outside (allegedly naive) perspective about biology, or perhaps more accurately the teaching of biology, could enhance her own. Who knew what and who was the client for whom became less important issues. Both sides had a common mission of deciding what biology students needed to know about uses of language, and both sides became more reflective in their practice, making the "sides" themselves less distinct.

Reflective theories of practice based on Schon's model have been used in a number of contexts. For example, Fischer, McCall, and Morch have been working on a computer environment to teach graphic designers reflection-in-action by integrating a sketching environment with a verbal reasoning component that allows them to reflect on what they are doing in language as they are doing it. The computer is not itself reflective but is designed to help students augment their own reflective processes. Reflective theories of practice have been incorporated into writing research as well, partly in an attempt to refine the relationship between rhetorical knowledge and subject-matter knowledge in writing. Bereiter, Scardamalia, and Steinbach ("Teachability"; "Fostering") report that expert writers negotiate two very different *problem spaces* as they write. They call one space the *content space*, the other, the *rhetorical space*:

> We may conceive of composition planning as taking place in two types of problem spaces. One type, the *content space,* is made up of knowledge states that may be broadly characterized as beliefs. It is the kind of space in which one works out opinions, makes moral decisions, generates inferences about matters of fact, formulates causal explanations, and so on. Content spaces thus have wide use in daily life and are by no means limited to composition planning.
>
> The other type of problem space, the *rhetorical space,* is specifically tied to text production. The knowledge states to be found in this kind of space are *mental representations of actual or intended text*—representations that may be at various levels of abstraction from verbatim representation to representation of main ideas and global intentions. ("Fostering" 302)

If dualist views of writing were true, these spaces could work in parallel with little or no conflict and with an easy return from one space to another. But Bereiter and Scardamalia report that novice writers have a great deal of difficulty moving effortlessly back and forth between these spaces. They report that novices tend to start in the content space (i.e., find something to say), transfer this information to the rhetorical space (i.e., put the idea in the paper), but often show little capacity for evaluating the results on the page and re-working them once again within the content space. "The . . . novice possesses [i.e., internalizes] productions for transferring information from the content space to the rhetorical space, but lacks productions for the return trip" (304). This observation explains for Bereiter and Scardamalia why the papers of student writers invariably reflect their initial thinking but also why student writers are so seldom able to use their papers, their written expression, to turn back on and refine that thinking. It is the use of language to "turn back on" and reshape one's thinking that Bereiter and Scardamalia associate with the "reflective" process in writing: "Our contention is that this interaction between the two problem spaces constitutes the essence of reflection in writing" (302).

Kauffman had vast experience teaching biology, but she had little structured practice guiding a student's biology-based reasoning from the vantage of the student's oral or written language. If writing is seen as the presentation of prior findings in the laboratory, a view

Kauffman expressed early in the pilot project, reflection in writing tends to be discouraged. Information is transferred from the content space, but there is no return trip. Kalmbach reports a similar situation in a case study of engineering students at Michigan Technological University:

> Students in this case study apparently didn't value lab reports because their reports were written without any meaningful context. They reported procedures and results but didn't have to use those results in any sort of problem-solving. . . .
>
> . . . students left MTU valuing writing, but not valuing writing as a way to do better engineering. They understood the value and importance of communication skills, but they didn't appear to see the connections between writing and engineering. (181–82)

Clearly, biological reasoning does not depend entirely on the reflective processes of the writer. But some does, and it has become a challenge for Kauffman, Velez, and Young to determine what kind of learning in biology is most likely produced from such a stance. The challenge extends to anyone seeking to develop the pedagogical uses of what in the WAC movement has come to be called "writing to learn."

Working with the concept of reflective expertise, Geisler has been developing a reflective model of practice for ethical philosophers. Observing a specific group of experts in the process of writing in extended naturalistic settings has allowed Geisler to refine Bereiter and Scardamalia's original distinction of a content space and a rhetorical space. For example, she has found that the ethical philosophers she observed had to work across three problem spaces: one that contains information about abstract concepts in ethical philosophy (e.g., justice, paternalism, freedom), one that contains information about specific narrated cases (e.g., "Suppose a person, call her Jones, goes to . . .") used to illustrate and test the applicability of concepts in the first space, and finally a space in which a linear argument is laid out on paper. Although she found that experts can "reflect-in-action" by testing the consequences of their work in a space for work in the other spaces, she also found that even experts commonly get stuck, lose their place, and must do a great deal of backtracking before they finally finish a paper satisfying, even minimally, the goals of each space.

Working with children writing about everyday experiences, Bereiter, Scardamalia, and Steinbach ("Teachability"; "Fostering") have held out the hope—with some justification—that many reflective practices of expert writers could be directly taught to students in the form of facilitating prompts. But Geisler's results, drawn from experts working in subject matters, suggest that, at least for college-age adults working in their majors, expert behavior is not so easily distilled into strategies for teaching. Velez and Young found that whatever rhetorical skills of reflection Kauffman brought into the biology class, they were not usually skills that she could bring into the classroom as explicit, fully articulated rhetorical strategies. They were habitual skills embedded in particulars and of sufficient complexity to discourage the idea that practitioners, working by themselves, are the best at bringing to the surface the rhetorical secrets of their discipline.

Velez and Young's initial encounter with what the "journal" meant in biology exemplifies what can happen when a writing teacher is eager to teach a method before he or she is willing to study it. They had supposed that the "journal" is or could be used as an instrument for exploring for ideas across a variety of subject matters. They had assumed that the argument for its utility and appropriateness was based on a number of impediments to learning commonly experienced by students: the students' often negative attitudes toward writing, the need for them to develop their rhetorical skills by writing at regular intervals, their difficulty in thinking through an idea without the aid of writing, and, perhaps, their tendency to ignore or lose unobtrusive but potentially significant experiences by failing to write them down when they occur. Kauffman, however, related the "journal" to an entirely different set of practices and assumptions. She saw the journal as a means for preserving the information yielded by laboratory processes and as a rhetorical instrument for demonstrating that scientific practices and values had been observed scrupulously (note, for example, the prohibition against altering observations and methods after the fact).

Significantly, the different interpretations brought to the "journal" by Velez and Young, on the one hand, and Kauffman, on the other, led to an interaction that produced changes on both sides. It seemed to sensitize Velez and Young to the fact that certain genres, methods, and motivating concepts (the importance of frequent writing, of writing to preserve experiences, of writing to motivate writing) so familiar to the English teacher may have no obvious correlates in writing practices in another discipline. The needs that prompt particular rhetorical practices in one discipline may be handled differently in another, assuming that corresponding rhetorical practices exist at all. Young and Velez learned that important rhetorical situations in biology are created, in part, by having students read what are thought to be exciting findings from the literature and by confronting students in the lab with provocative anomalies that make no sense without a thoughtful explanation behind them. These experiences suggest that a distinction needs to be drawn between rhetorical situations that are articulated and codified and those that are not. The rhetorical situations of the specialized disciplines are not always codified, and when they are not, specialists in rhetoric need to sensitize themselves to these situations and help the subject-matter expert codify them. Young and Velez became sensitized to look for what, at the beginning, they did not know was there to be found.

At the same time, the interaction seemed to sensitize Kauffman to the existence of general writing strategies and to the written forms, practices, and reasons behind them. Kauffman came to believe that writing is more than the last and, relatively speaking, less important step in a research project; it is an activity to be valued, studied, practiced, and motivated. And from that perception comes the ability and willingness to create places in the classroom for other rhetorical practices and purposes.

As we have said, from a distance, developing a WAC program seems a rather straightforward task because the division of expertise seems so abundantly clear. Up close, however, the standard solutions seem inadequate to the theoretical problems that remain for the most part unclear. Improved theories of expertise, some relying on the computer as metaphor, some on the notion of reflection, are only now beginning to help us understand the problems better. It will take much more theoretical and empirical refinement before we have shaped our ignorance into something other than good intentions, faith, and a call for further research. The pressing issue now, as always, has been to understand the elusive relationship between language practices, on the one hand, and meaning and knowledge, on the other, a relationship that for the most part remains a mystery. All the while, at the level of administration and practice, the invitation to develop writing programs in the content areas is an open invitation to engage in cross-cultural communication and collaboration. Neither the writing teacher nor the content teacher can select the role of anthropologist or native. Both must play both roles. Both must be willing to travel.

Notes

1. We want to thank Linda Roman Kauffman and Lili Velez for their help with this essay. Their work in the pilot project, of course, made the paper possible. But they have also been generous in their criticisms of the paper itself, particularly in pointing out our misperceptions of events in the project, a kind of criticism that only those who have been intimately involved with it and thought carefully about it can give.

2. We are heavily indebted throughout this section to D. N. Perkins and Gavriel Salomon's comprehensive and detailed survey of the literature on expertise in "Are Cognitive Skills Context-Bound?" and refer our readers to it for references instantiating the various positions in the controversy.

Works Cited

Bereiter, Carl, and Marlene Scardamalia. "Fostering Reflective Processes." *The Psychology of Written Composition*. Hillsdale, NJ: Lawrence Erlbaum, 1987. 299–317.

Bereiter, Carl, Marlene Scardamalia, and Rosanne Steinbach. "Teachability of Reflective Processes in Written Composition." *Cognitive Science* 8 (1984): 173–90.

Carter, Michael. "The Idea of Expertise: An Exploration of Cognitive and Social Dimensions of Writing." *College Composition and Communication* 41.3 (1990): 265–86.

Clement, John. "Analogical Reasoning Patterns in Expert Problem Solving." *Proc. of the Fourth Annual Conference of the Cognitive Science Society*. Ann Arbor: U of Michigan, 1982.

Covey, Preston. *Outline of a Pilot WAC/Writing-To-Learn Project*. Pittsburgh, PA: Carnegie Mellon U, 1988.

Faigley, Lester. "Judging Writing, Judging Selves." *College Composition and Communication* 40.4 (1989): 395–412.

Fischer, Gerhard, Raymond McCall, and Anders Morch. *JANUS: Integrating Hypertext with a Knowledge-based Design Environment*. Hypertext '89. Pittsburgh, PA: ACM, 1989.

Flynn, Elizabeth A., and Robert W. Jones. "Michigan Technological University." *Programs That Work: Models and Methods for Writing Across the Curriculum*. Ed. Toby Fulwiler and Art Young. Portsmouth, NH: Boynton/Cook, 1990.

Fulwiler, Toby. "The Personal Connection: Journal Writing across the Curriculum." *Language Connections: Writing and Reading Across the Curriculum*. Urbana, Illinois: NCTE, 1982.

Geertz, Clifford. "Deep Play: Notes on the Balinese Cockfight." *Daedalus* 101.1 (1972): 1–38.

Geisler, Cheryl. "Exploring Academic Literacy: An Experiment in Composing." *College Composition and Communication* 41.1 (1992): 39–54.

Hamilton, David. "Interdisciplinary Writing." *College English* 41.7 (1980): 780–96.

Kalmbach, James. "The Laboratory Reports of Engineering Students: A Case Study." *Writing Across the Disciplines: Research into Practice*. Ed. Art Young and Toby Fulwiler. Upper Montclair, NJ: Boynton/Cook, 1986.

Kauffman, Linda, and Lili Velez. *Taking Writing Across the Curriculum: Off the Drawing Board and into the Laboratory*. Pittsburgh, PA: Teaching Center, Carnegie Mellon U, 1991.

Kinneavy, James L. "Writing Across the Curriculum." *ADE Bulletin* 76 (1983): 14–24.

Milic, Louis. "The Problem of Style." *Contemporary Rhetoric: A Conceptual Background with Readings*. Ed. W. Ross Winterowd. New York: Harcourt, 1975. 271–95.

Newell, Alan, J. C. Shaw, and Herbert A. Simon. "Report on a General Problem-Solving Program." *Proc. of the International Conference on Information Processing*. Ed. Walter R. Reitman. Paris: UNESCO, 1960.

Newell, Alan, and Herbert A. Simon. *Human Problem Solving*. Englewood Cliffs, NJ: Prentice-Hall, 1972.

Ong, Walter J. *Rhetoric, Romance, and Technology: Studies in the Interaction of Expression and Culture*. Ithaca, NY: Cornell UP, 1971.

Perkins, D. N., and Gavriel Salomon. "Are Cognitive Skills Context-Bound?" *Educational Researcher* Jan.-Feb. (1989): 16–25.

Polya, G. *How to Solve It: A New Aspect of Mathematical Method*. 2nd ed. Garden City, NY: Doubleday, 1957.

Rorty, Richard. *Contingency, Irony, and Solidarity*. Cambridge: Cambridge UP, 1989.

Russell, David R. *Writing in the Academic Disciplines, 1870–1990: A Curricular History*. Carbondale: Southern Illinois UP, 1991.

Salomon, G., and D. N. Perkins. "Transfer of Cognitive Skills from Programming: When and How?" *Journal of Educational Computing Research* 3 (1987): 149–69.

Schoenfeld, A. H. "Measures of Problem-Solving Performance and of Problem-Solving Instruction." *Journal for Research in Mathematics Education* 13.1 (1982): 31–49.

Schon, Donald A. *The Reflective Practitioner: How Professionals Think in Action*. New York: Basic Books, 1983.

Selfe, Cynthia L., and Freydoon Arbabi. "Writing to Learn: Engineering Student Journals." *Engineering Education* 74 (1983): 86–90.

Slevin, James, Keith Fort, and Patricia E. O'Conner. "Georgetown University." *Programs That Work: Models and Methods for Writing Across the Curriculum*. Ed. Toby Fulwiler and Art Young. Portsmouth, NH: Boynton/Cook, 1990.

Williams, Joseph M., and Gregory G. Colomb. "The University of Chicago." *Programs That Work: Models and Methods for Writing Across the Curriculum*. Ed. Toby Fulwiler and Art Young. Portsmouth, NH: Boynton/Cook, 1990.

4

Rethinking the Sense of the Past:

The Essay as Legacy

of the Epigram

Shirley Brice Heath

In American education, the essay has become the vehicle through which teachers expect students to display knowledge and to argue a single point or hypothesis. High school requirements, college entrance examinations, and freshman English courses use the essay or composition as the proving ground of students' abilities to organize, think clearly, and argue persuasively in written form to a central point—prerequisites for acceptable performance in academic institutions. The essay becomes the examination form—the gatekeeping mechanism within individual courses as well as at critical stages of passage through secondary schools and into college.

How did this come about? How did our current understanding of the essay evolve? And what have we lost through this evolution? My argument in this chapter is that our current notion of the essay is a twisting and diminishing of two genres—the epigram and the literary essay. I trace briefly the history of these two genres, showing how we have lost sight of their richness and power—especially their links to oral traditions. We have reduced these genres to a form of writing, the school essay, that excludes many of our current students from the educational process.

Reflecting on How to Look at What We Do

Primary within New Historicism is the assumption that all discursive acts are embedded within our social practice and material production.[1] That is, our every utterance is surrounded by habituated—often institutionally driven—ways of interacting with each other and with the goods that our work creates and that we wish to own and control. Thus, as we attempt to reveal, critique, or oppose our social and material practices, we must use the very tools and texts we wish to unmask because we are caught up in those practices we try to expose as politically and materially motivated. We are the fish in the proverbial fishbowl, unable to see and to challenge the environment about us, for it is that which sustains us and through which we come to our discourse and our ideologies.

Proponents of New Historicism further assume that the separation of literary and nonliterary texts is not possible and that no forms of discourse, whether descriptive, imaginative, or legislative, reveal unalterable truths.

Some New Historicists would follow these assumptions to the nihilist position of saying that scholars or critics cannot then stand within the practices they examine while at the same time they expose the supports of these practices. More would, however, be content to take up the cautions of New Historicism and urge such examinations along with a keen awareness that research—as well as those habits and artifacts under study—exists within the context of institutional goals, material practices, and ideological pursuits.

It is from this latter perspective within New Historicism that I pursue the current examination of the essay as it has come to be used in composition classes. I ask here not only the questions noted above, but I try to prod teachers and theorists of composition alike to ask further: Who is being excluded by the practices that currently surround the essay, and what might the effects of this exclusion be? Of particular attention here is the extent to which the functions and expectations of certain other genres have merged into the essay and fed a readiness to use it as academic gatekeeping tool. I also ask whether the legacy of such functions and expectations is what we would choose for today's increasingly diverse student population. These learners are preparing for adulthood in a world of work and public services that differs radically from that of the centuries in which our expectations of the essay originated.

Scholars have asked such questions more for the preferred academic genres for *reading*—scientific reports, canonized literature, and textbooks—than for the most commonly requested forms of *writing* in academic study—compositions and essays. The failure to consider this key genre of writing in schools, its evolution, and possible sources is particularly curious, since most reformers of education have agreed that the essay as defined in school bears little relation to writing needs of adults in either their employment or lives as ordinary citizens. Moreover, the school essay, often reduced to formulaic prescriptions for a five-paragraph version, bears little relationship to the canonized forms of literary essays students read as models: those by writers such as Francis Bacon, Charles Lamb, Ralph Waldo Emerson, or even contemporary essayists such as Joan Didion, William Gass, and Annie Dillard.

As we approach the end of the twentieth century, much of the theory and research on writing in academic institutions focuses on ways to shift the contexts of writing rather than on any fundamental need to question the forms of writing. Essential reforms center on ways to teach writing by providing collaborative learning occasions and authentic audiences, as well as adequate time to draft, revise, and edit compositions and essays.[2] These proposals for specific classroom practices, as well as psychological and anthropological theories, such as L. S. Vygotsky's activity theory and various social construction perspectives, dwell much more on mental and social processes in the making and receiving of texts than on the features of those texts themselves. They also give little attention to the contexts that gave rise to current expectations of the internal features of these texts (such as conciseness, clarity, brevity, and straightforward reasoning). No doubt, this resistance to examining *texts as texts* or their prior *contexts* came about in part from poststructuralist challenges to the objectivity of *texts* or the empirical wisdom of confining the term *text* to only the actual physical evidences of writing. In addition, the examination of *texts as texts* may remind many composition teachers of what they viewed as the sterility of "practical stylist" or other formalist practices that entered composition instruction in the 1940s.

From Epigram to Essay

The specific focus in this chapter will be the examination of how the text form of the school essay came to be seen as a window to a writer's thinking capabilities. What were the presuppositions that contributed to the evolution of a highly stable normative estimation of the form's power to say something definitive about the intelligence of the writer? We will consider the reshaping of the oral epigram into the preferred written form of the essay in academic settings. Since the English Renaissance, the earlier form of the epigram has come to epitomize in the academic essay key evidence of a writer's ability to move from an initial premise through supporting evidence to a well-argued point. Examination of the history of the epigram and its immersion within the borders of the academic essay tells much about ways in which formal education institutions came to reify logical argumentation in the Cartesian approach to testing propositions to demonstrate an objective truth.

Though English definitions of *epigram* are by no means uniform, most agree that it bears key features: a central point, expressed with compression and conciseness, but with balance, simplicity, and, preferably, some turn of thought or expression that is seen as witty and wise. English definitions of the epigram differ from early Greek prescriptions that called for a very short poem "summing up as though in a memorial inscription what it is desired to make permanently memorable in a single action or situation. It must have the compression and conciseness of a real inscription, and in proportion to the smallness of its bulk must be highly finished, evenly balanced, simple, and lucid" (Mackail 4). One of the oldest forms of written poetry in Western art, the epigram was originally orally composed and then inscribed—or chiseled—onto monuments or statues as epitaphs or epithets.

Epigram as Social Commentary

However, in the first century under Nero and Domitian, the Latin epigrammatist Marcus Valerius Martialis, known in English as "Martial," set the model of the form that has remained most prominently associated with the genre.[3] Central to Martial's epigrams was a style and form that ensured a final point, an antithesis achieved through a witty turn of thought that built from the prior elements of exposition.

Martial's epigrams won him considerable favor and fame among rich patrons of Rome. Based on his close observations of human nature in both low and high life, his poems also offered central contrasts between politics and morality, pompous claims and harsh realities.

> Diaulus, recently physician,
> Has set up now as a mortician:
> No change, though, in the clients' condition.

> Asia and Europe each provide a grave
> For Pompey's sons, and he himself lies under
> Egypt, if grave he can be said to have.
> Or is the world his tomb? There'd be no wonder
> In that: one monument would be too small
> To house so huge, so ruinous a fall.

> If an epigram takes up a page, you skip it:
> Art counts for nothing, you prefer the snippet.
> The markets have been ransacked for you, reader,
> Rich fare—and you want canapes instead!
> I'm not concerned with the fastidious feeder:
> Give me the man who likes his basic bread.
> (Translations by Michie 27, 95, 145)

Somewhat socially marginal, Martial was not Roman but Spanish; he had no political position in Rome and depended on favors from the powerful and often brutal emperors Nero and Domitian to sstain his life as a poet. To keep the favor of rich patrons and to maintain some germ of integrity, Martial focused on the trivial matters of everyday life and poked fun at topics safely away from the fundamental wrongs of Roman society. He never satirized real people, even under pseud-onyms, and he never wrote out of spite (Michie 14–15). His somewhat bohemian life in both Rome and occasionally in a house in the prov-inces brought Martial into contact with people of all classes and back-grounds, and he did not exclude the ways of these from his writings.

Martial developed the epigram as a literary art that appeared to cover trifles but also offered a pointed remark on a single action or situation. Many of his epigrams touched on friendship, sentiment, pathos, and the preference for a pastoral setting for the good life; others were satirical or ironic and dealt with the spectacles of food, drink, and gifts that he thought marked the hypocrisy of the seekers of profit and fame in all classes of society. The structure of Martial's epigrams usually consisted of exposition and conclusion, with occasional epigrams containing a transition from one of these to the other. For those consisting only of exposition and conclusion, Martial included either statement and comment, statement and question, or question and answer. However, most of his epigrams also included a transition from exposition to conclusion, usually by statement, transition question, and answering conclusion. Direct address and direct quotations frequently appeared in his epigrams.

The epigram, enthusiastically revived in the sixteenth and early seventeenth centuries, drew considerable attention because of its flexibility. Writers of this period of classical revival experimented with the form until Ben Jonson tried to establish once and for all the form as Classical and the purpose as didactic.[4] It is this legacy of literary wit and wisdom encapsuled in exposition, transition, and conclusion, with a central didactic point, that came to the "theme" or school essay of later centuries. Central in this influence was the two-part frame of the epigram: the preparation or expectation and the point or explanation. Closely linked with these matters of formal structure was the fact that the epigram was analogous in its two parts to the original object and its inscription: the first part (or occasionally the title) set the object or situation; the second inscribed the point on the first. By the seventeenth century, epigrams usually carried titles, and the majority of these were "To ———" or "On ———." [5]

The story of the sources available to the epigrammatists of the sixteenth century and the background of the debates of that century over the epigram's proper form and purpose are too long and convoluted to include here. However, throughout the century, numerous forms and functions—vernacular and classical, poetic and prosaic, satirical and morally authoritative, secular and religious—confused its generic status. Poets wrote epigrams of primarily two types—as humorous nugatory commentaries and as serious moral counsel. By the end of the sixteenth century, those that were satirical, jesting, and popular, and sometimes obscene and erotic, seemed to be in greatest favor, and the form seemed to be remaining decidedly vernacular—a weapon of the common people for critiquing those in favor. In public inns and taverns, customers wrote epigrams on walls and counters, their purpose usually to ridicule or poke fun at "idle persons," "flatterers," and individuals whose manners, conceits, or fashions drew censure. An anonymous writer wrote of the form in 1588 (represented here in the original and inconsistent spelling):

> Therefore the poet devised a prety fashioned poeme short and sweete (as we are wont to say) and called it *Epigramma* in which every mery conceited man might without any long studie or tedious ambage, make his frend sport, and anger his foe, and give a prettie nip, or shew a sharpe conceit in few verses: for this *Epigramme* is but an inscription or writting made as it were upon a table, or in a windowe, or upon the wall or mantell of a chimney in some place of common resort, where it was allowed every man might come or be sitting to chat and prate. . . . Afterward the same came to be put in paper and in bookes. (Puttenham 54)[6]

The epigram was a form of street wisdom that was both spoken lore and written artifact from those who enjoyed humor and had a somewhat rough spirit. It worked in the interest of characterizing what it is to be human.

Epigram as Academic Exercise

Since the epigram had such a rich vernacular history, how did it come to be a form for "long studie" and to be "put in paper and in bookes"? And what were those intermediate steps that brought it by the nineteenth century to be the mini-model of the central features desired in the school essay? How did its late sixteenth-century reliance on direct observation, oral wit, and personal commentary get lost in the school essay's demand for information, literary sources, facts, and premises leading to a conclusion?

In the early decades of the seventeenth century, idealistic and high-flown forms of the epigram emerged as preferred, and their influence was felt in the lyric, pastoral, sonnet, and madrigal. In 1615, with publication of Ben Jonson's *Epigrammes.I. Booke*, a determined focus and form set the sense of the epigram for the coming centuries. Jonson elevated the epigram by claiming to model it on Classical examples, asserting that such emulations would ensure that its purposes be moral and critical, its goals to praise excellence and satirize foolishness, corruption, and greed. Jonson was careful, however, to disassociate himself from those epigrams of Martial that might be considered "profane and base." Jonson wrote his epigrams to be spoken and chose to focus on their didactic purpose and to insist on balance, conciseness, wit, and wisdom in the form.

Shortly after Jonson's publication, the *point* of the epigram came to have a fixed label of its own; the *Oxford English Dictionary* places the first usage of this meaning of *point* in 1643. Yet, as early as the first decades of the sixteenth century, epigrams had been accepted for their authoritative advice as well as their satirical thrust and had thus laid the groundwork for the later association of *point* with import and authority.

Through the Middle Ages and into the Renaissance, written epigrams preserved from the Classical era had served as models of writing for schoolboys, and many poets had prefaced their collections with apologies for writing in such a "youthful amateur genre" (Crane 158). Students translated Greek and Latin epigrams and composed their own, and writers such as Erasmus both wrote epigrams and recommended their merits for serious study, noting their usefulness as one of the "most effective methods of proof" (I, 258). Promotion of Classical ties and the need for both moral critique and a central authoritative point set the frame for its later support by those who urged its usefulness as a teaching device and as a model of "proper" thinking. Rhetorical teachings in the Renaissance stressed "sententiousness" to emphasize that epigrams need not end in a turn or twist of thought but could go straight to the "sentence" to end with an emphatic summary of materials already presented in the form (Hudson, *The Epigram* 4).[7]

The first direct connection between epigrams and essays came in 1597 when Francis Bacon's first *Essays* appeared. These consisted "essentially of detached aphorisms [or epigrams] on particular topics" (Vickers 74).[8] Their basis was empirical—rooted in observations of life that could be usefully reapplied—and their topics concerned with the study of human society, of humans as social and political beings. These brief writings surrounding epigrams became the short prose works known since Bacon as "essays" in the English-speaking world.

This early generic extension of epigram into essay became a primary pattern of literature in the seventeenth century: "The diction, the brisk rhythm of short word-groups, the surprising complex turns of thought, the 'points,' and the fondness for a certain unexpected brevity" (Fowler 201) came to mark the essay as epigrammatic.[9] However, it was primarily the formal features of the epigram that remained—along with some remnants of its earlier role as commentary on everyday life. Lost were its oral primacy among those often marginal to society's rich and powerful and its serious commentary about apparent trifles or playthings of those who held power.

The writing of epigrams that imitated Classical forms but omitted their earlier functions and performers had a firm place in English academic life by the seventeenth century, and it would continue its influence on judgments of the school essay or "theme" into the nineteenth century. Numerous accounts of particular schools, tutors, and scholars describe the extent to which the composition of Latin epigrams held favor as a common exercise in rhetoric. Young scholars were to write both themes *and* epigrams; advice given about the two was often the same: they were to display grace and to have some point.[10] For both themes and epigrams, a proverb or phrase (often called "the theme") provided the prompt from which the writer composed written words of exposition, transition, and conclusion. Writing on proverbs became especially popular as assignments by tutors and schoolmasters who believed that epigrams challenged schoolboys to paraphrase poets or orators, vary sentences in numerous ways, collect witty phrases from Classical authors, and learn how to make a point about important patterns in human life.[11]

By the late nineteenth century, writing themes that bore an epigrammatic quality became the favored exercise by which to test students' abilities to make a point concisely, conclusively, and with careful diction. Topics of these themes were reminiscent of those of epigrams: "on beauty," "on goodness," "on honor," "of studies," "of friendship," and the like. Classical epigrams on such topics often became the epigraphs of written compositions. Here the *epigram*, now termed *epigraph*, gave evidence of a young writer's literateness, as well as knowledge of a form closely associated with matters Greek and Latin. Moreover, it illustrated in miniature the form and the point of the essay that followed it. Bacon, in *The Advancement of Learning*, had said of the relation of aphorisms or epigrams to essays: "[They] do invite men to inquire further" (173).

Into school essays or compositions came features that had earlier marked the epigram ("intellectual, rhetorical, and conscious, addressed to stir in the hearer an approval of art" [Schelling, quoted in Hudson, *The Epigram* 16]). Previous titles of "theme" or "composition" often became synonymous with "essay," presumably because this genre presented itself as a brief prose model appropriate for classroom reading since it required no specialized expertise or base of information for its understanding. Like the epigram in school so often *written* upon a proverb, an *oral* form, the essay on familiar everyday topics of conversation became, in effect, "a writing over the voice; by embedding a culturally specific scheme on a vaguer form of oral wisdom" (Manley 261). Wisdom regarding everyday life—often woven into storytellers' tales, folk proverbs, and other oral forms—moved into permanent written forms, such as the essay. The essay of the schoolroom came to be identified as a high form of rhetoric designed to display or persuade and intended for a particular effect upon audience.[12]

From their reading of Classical literature, students collected in their copybooks or commonplace books epigrams and other brief pieces that they might later use as epigraphs for their compositions. Both the self-taught and those with tutors committed these to memory, ready for quick retrieval into their writing and as models for creating their own. Copying in commonplace books filled hours of study that included much intense memorization and imitation by students.[13] Such bits of wit and wisdom opened academic essays with great frequency throughout the seventeenth and eighteenth centuries in Great Britain, and well into the late nineteenth and early twentieth centuries in the United States.

Closely linked with reading literature—especially the Classics— were these copybooks in which readers could capture the "point" of their reading for later incorporation into their own writings. Some students devoted their copybooks to particular aspects of human experience, such as friendship, and composed their own epigrams, poems, or brief prose passages to include in their works.[14] These formed the seeds of the required daily themes or essays in nineteenth-century colleges, but they also served those who were excluded from formal education. By far, the largest proportion of copybooks preserved in the United States are those written by women, many of whom used the tidbits of literary knowledge recorded there to enliven their conversations.[15] Segments most frequently chosen were those that summed up in brief form clever observations and witticisms suggestive of profound thoughts to motivate the good life.

Use of the epigram marked a single individual's abilities in "wit and wisdom" through the representation of a point with a didactic thrust in a brief statement of marked literary language. Though British writers after Jonson did not themselves dwell on the form as authors of the sixteenth and early seventeenth centuries had done, the epigram remained as a prized written encapsulation of knowledge. Within education, oral examinations predominated until the beginning of the nineteenth century in both Great Britain and the United States, and the ability to weave epigrams into one's performance enhanced estimations of the scholar and proved argumentative abilities. But while the term *epigram* and its ties to Classical learning, schoolboy exercises, and high didactic purpose slipped out of conscious memory of generations of students, the essence of its form remained in academic life. Essays that moved from exposition through transition to a concluding point proved the abilities of its writers in logical reasoning, argumentation, and organization. Academic institutions had not only picked the essay's carcass clean and left only sun-bleached bones, but they had also assigned it a gatekeeping role that excluded its earliest functions of satiric commentary on power and wealth by those marginal to the societal mainstream.

Were the history of the twisting and diminishing of the epigram to be capsuled, it would go something like this. From the Classical era through the seventeenth century, socially marginal figures, such as Martial, and later those who frequented public taverns and eating halls, developed expertise in both oral and written delivery of these forms. Bits of dialogue, quick witticisms, and rapid turns of thought marked epigrams delivered by those observing from the outside and only occasionally allowed into the higher reaches of society. Epigrammatists carried a doubleness of vision that could bring the satiric bite, the concise wit, and the wise observation to the epigram. Though intent on turning the epigram's content to higher purposes than its vernacular proponents had intended, Ben Jonson drew from the spoken word and wrote his epigrams for oral delivery as well as written recapitulation in schoolboys' copybooks.

Over the years, the epigram, once both oral and written and best performed by those outside the upper levels of society, came to penetrate in its form (exposition and conclusion with a sentence or point) the ethos and standard of written composition in academic institutions. Into the school essay as the testing exercise for students came key features of the epigram that overshadowed the literary history of the forms and functions of the essay itself.

Gatekeeping

In the United States, English composition emerged as a gatekeeping mechanism for immigrants and the increasing portion of working-class students attempting to make their way into secondary and higher education at the end of the nineteenth century. Remnants of Greek and Latin or Classical forms slipped away, but the importance of "making a point," "proving a point," "leading up to a point," and so forth transferred into expectations for the school essay. The school essay stood as the external evidence of one's capacity to organize thought, to be logical, and to think in an orderly and predictable fashion; *the point* became the ultimate focus for judgment of the merit of any composition. Without a dependence on extensive "book learning," the essay and the topics that prompted it in classrooms ostensibly invited all to participate equally. But as the rules of its presentation and the equation of its organization with processes of orderly thinking became more and more firmly imposed, it excluded those whose patterns of social organization, habits of making decisions, and ways of arguing were collaborative and encompassing of nonabsolute truths or final points.[16]

At issue was something more than formal requirements of a written form. Central in expectations of the school essay was the view that propositions or premises could be proven true through a series of logical steps of reasoning by the Cartesian method—moving from doubt through proof to certitude. Such principles and practices ran counter to the expectations of groups whose fundamental traditions were not grounded in formal schooling, written authorities, and performance of solitary achievements. The primarily oral rhetorical practices of these groups—story-swapping, retelling of myths, proverbs, folktales, and witty nuggets of conversation—worked instead with probable truths. Speakers often argued their points from personal or socially established convictions that furnished motives for action and contributed to the growth of *sensus communis*.[17] Perceptions of a shared background, as well as the power of metaphorical learning (seeing the case or situation at hand as similar to previous ones), enabled members of such groups to understand imaginative wide-ranging arguments that formulated such similarities. Both audience and orators share images, sayings, and examples that carry listeners forward not in a linear progression, but in relational terms that offer plays of meanings—connotations, allusions, and other figures of speech shared by the community, though with some peculiar to individuals and derived from their own empirical observations or experiences. Keenly important to *sensus communis* is a "feel" for or affective relationship to the language of the community that can move the group to action.[18]

These approaches to the display of knowledge, its logical alignment behind a single point or truth, and to the roles of affect and action in public uses of language contrasted sharply with those of the school. Academic norms required that writers working as solitary displayers of their knowledge from written authorities portray their reason and logic through a linear progression toward a centered point. Reflecting the assertive and confident leadership of the writer, words on the paper were to impel the reader to follow the thinking of the writer and thus arrive at the common point of the composition. Neither specific actions nor creation of a sense of community was the customary goal of such writing.

The Literary Essay

For skeptics who might wonder whether it was not academics but essayists through the centuries who incorporated the epigram's form and linear prescriptions of argumentation, a brief account of the history of the literary essay is necessary. These essayists held the form close to a style that bore contrails of the oral—spontaneous breaks in the flow of thought, quick give-and-take idea exchanges, and insertions of everyday incidents or knowledge bits. Beginning with publication of his *Essays or Counsells, Civill and Morall* in 1597 (with enlarged reprints in 1614 and 1625),[19] Bacon described his writings as "brief notes," "dispersed meditations," and emphasized the role of direct experience rather than "studied" postures in his essays. Bacon appears to have intended his *essay* to be an "experiment" or "trying"—a process of thinking that could be an alternative to the step-by-step "scientific method" of moving from hypothesis to conclusion. He often included (particularly in his revisions in 1625) several aphorisms, many metaphoric and open to multiple interpretations. Bacon termed the distinctions he saw between the display of knowledge appropriate for the sciences and for the humanities as conflicts between "the magistral" (scientific) and the "initiative" (humanistic) and linked the essay to the latter for its possibilities of creative exploration.

Bacon began a tradition that has remained: essayists almost invariably describe the literary or scientific essay by its brevity, openness, reliance on personal observations, and rambling experimental nature.

Many of these essayists have explicated what the essay is *not*. It does not move to a single unified point or argument; it values a multiplicity of voices and perspectives that lets readers see a mind at work. The essay draws heavily from oral forms (conversation, aphorisms) and does not purport to be a formal demonstration of knowledge or logic. It is neither centered in a desire to demonstrate a single truth nor committed to the recitation of facts; it reveals human experiences and uses these to explore and try ideas.

A survey of over fifteen hundred essays and writings on the essay published between 1800 and 1950 reveals no exceptions in the pattern of defining the essay by its openness—to oral forms, other genres, and outcomes.[20] Ironically, the essay is sometimes termed a "nongenre," though essayists claim many genres work together to make it identifiable as its own genre. Some have described its art as that of "liberationist artifice":

> Neither a deterministic game nor a set of verbal gestures, an essay deploys power freely. It is discourse as discourse, discursivity as such, textuality untrammeled by generic boundedness. . . . An essay's unprogrammatic identity is freedom to sport negations, to disorient, to play, to abnegate the self by constructing a voice out of ceaseless discourse the very drift of which is to disclose what becomes as its contradictions and diversities destroy what seems to be. (Snyder 150)

Writers of and on the essay have since the sixteenth century noted the extent to which it must include other genres—not because these taken together add up to a formal inclusive genre, but because these genres create the epistemological point of the essay—to watch minds at work through a necessary multiplicity of voices.[21]

Ralph Waldo Emerson named just some of the genres the essay can hold: "philosophy, ethics, divinity, criticism, poetry, humor, fun, mimicry, anecdotes, jokes, ventriloquism. All the breadth & versatility of the most liberal conversation, highest lowest personal local topics, all are permitted, and all may be combined" (Emerson, *Journals* vii, 224). In this July 1839 journal entry, he speaks of his expectations for the lecture, a form he was soon to find disappointing and to replace with the essay. In the essay, Emerson finds a way to provide personal communication—a revelation of himself debating and weighing serious intellectual topics with an openness that allows others to enter the dialogue.

William H. Gass has described this prose as resembling talk: "the tall tale, the loud spiel, or the sermon's moral prod; often it has the gentle swing of slow and sober reflection, the laudatory march of patriotic speech, or the unspoken assumptions of private conversation" (33). Essays contain narratives as problem-solving nuggets, aphorisms that assert intellectual force, witty asides that flirt with impudence, and revelations and responses across dissenting, agreeing voices within the writer's personae and in mock engagement with the reader's as well. The essay, like the told story, is meant to be experienced (relived from prior conversational experiences), not just heard or read. Just as Walter Benjamin tells us that "all great storytellers have in common the freedom with which they move up and down the rungs of their experience as a ladder" (102), so the essayist as sometime storyteller has the same freedom. Neither a unitary voice nor closure of argument is expected of the essay.

What do essayists say about the context that enables them to produce the essay? Bacon, as well as Michel de Montaigne, the French essayist, wrote much about the fact that their essays were conceived in leisure. Evoking conversation among friends, unpressured times for listening and reflecting, their essays were to offer what quiet times of reading and talking among friends might give—tidbits of thoughts and germs of ideas to carry away from such leisurely encounters. Bacon, under the constraint of being a philosopher-scientist in need of support, took care in the dedicatory epistle to the 1612 edition of his *Essays or Counsells, Civill and Morall* to note:

> To write just treatises requireth leisure in the writer, and leisure in the reader; and therefore are not so fit, neither in regard of your Highness's princely affairs, nor in regard of my continual services. Which is the cause that hath made me choose to write certain brief notes, set down rather significantly than curiously, which I have called *Essays*. (8)

Bacon used his brief notes to reveal how curiosity should be played out in observation and experience. He reversed the general principle by which writers used their pens to illustrate a preestablished doctrine rather than to reveal their observations and experiences. Bacon wanted his essays to allow the dialogue of reader and writer, as well as that of those conflicting internal voices of the writer engaged in the *trying* of ideas through the essay.

From Bacon forward, with a consistency of agreement rarely found in the history of English literature, writers such as Addison,

Steele, Hazlitt, Carlyle, Macaulay, Emerson, Stevenson, Belloc, Chesterton, Priestley, Woolf, Krutch, Huxley, Adorno, Lukacs, White, Gass, and Hardwick have agreed on the contexts and expectations of the essay. Its brevity, variety, conversational quality, and opposition to any strict ordering or predictable and methodical system of prose presentation appear again and again in the writings of essayists. Many essayists mention also the essay's ways of leading the reader to see how the mind of the writer sets forth an idea, reflects on it, turns it to a new angle, reflects then on this new twist, and then steps back to view the process. The essay invites readers to do the same and to take up a part in the conversation or the trying out of ideas—but without challenge or the immediate pull of worldly concerns or needs. Virginia Woolf said of the modern essay: " The principle which controls it [the essay] is simply that it should give pleasure; the desire which impels us when we take it from the shelf is simply to receive pleasure. Everything in an essay must be subdued to that end. . . . The essay must lap us about and draw its curtain across the world" (211). Behind the form lies the goal of the piece—to invite, even promote, exploration of ideas. Charles Lamb so believed that essays were prefatory for the reader that, after writing a preface for one of his editions, he redrew it, notifying his publisher that indeed all of the essays were prefaces—initiations—openings.

Though essayists have differed on the extent to which they advocate the insertion of the person or the role of the principle of pleasure in essays, they concur on the need for the reader to hear speaking voices of different minds within the form. Some claim that the *voice* of the essay is its primary distinguishing mark, as it cuts across affiliations with other forms ranging from Machiavellian discourse to philosophical treatise (Snyder 151).[22] Aphorisms, witticisms, portions of dialogue, brief narratives, quick series of statements and counterstatements, wry asides, and extensive name-dropping (as though conversationalists were chatting about neighbors down the street) mark essays. Semantic reversals, changes of key (to irony, for example), and shifts of tempo are marked by attribution through personal pronouns of the first and second or third persons, but more often, this tension is revealed through the use of adversatives (*however, but, nevertheless,* etc.) and concessives (*despite, even if,* and so forth).

Some essayists have spoken as though once the writer is into the writing, the essay takes on a life of its own—much as conversations do—one idea provoking, extending, or denying the next in a series of twists and turns that bear little or no evidence of prior planning.

> Essays are aggressive even if the mind from which they come is fair, humane, and when it is to the point, disinterested. (Hardwick xiv)

> [The essay] denies any primeval givens . . . refuses any definition of its concepts . . . takes the anti-systematic impulse into its own procedure . . . [and] urges the reciprocal interaction of its concepts in the process of intellectual experience. (Adorno 159–60)

> The energy of the essay, like the energy of life, is always in danger of dissipation. Pages lie in unsorted heaps, full of notions which have not been extended to their complete reach. Somewhere in those piles, inferences may lie quiet now like a powerful figure hidden in clay, but where are the shaping hands, the steady intent, the attention? (Gass 35)

Emerson foreshadowed many of these points when he argued that conversation and the essay's attempt to imitate it captured something of the "ordinary" in the human bent toward curiosity. Humans seek answers to matters deep and trivial often out of curiosity. When speakers explore these answers in conversation, they do not expect to emulate the erudite, but instead to hold these issues for exploration through their own experiences and ideas. To be sure, literary essays through the centuries have included epigrams from others or statements appropriate for epigrammatic extraction, but such expressions have appeared not as the summative challenge of a single argumentative voice, but as the contradictory aside or the opening challenge of counter voices that make themselves heard to the essayist displaying the meanderings of the mind at work.

For Emerson, a central issue was how people expressed their questions about morality, and he felt that, unlike earlier civilizations that acknowledged such debates only among philosophers, Americans could hear such debates wherever ordinary men and women might engage in conversation at leisure. Those households most privileged on these occasions were not those of the more educated.

> In every family of ordinary advantages in the middle ranks of life the great questions of morality are discussed with freedom and intelligence, introduced as matters of speculation but as having foundations of certainty like any other science. In the lowest orders of the people the

occurrences of the day are debated, the prudence or folly of politicians and private conduct examined, and all with a reference to know the principles of ethical science. ("Two Unpublished" 73)

Emerson saw these occasions as connected with the recollections of childhood and with the domestic arrangements of every household. Essays, continuing the goals of such household conversations and perpetuated by self-renewing desire, could penetrate where treatises would never enter. For both the reader and the writer of essays, the attraction rested in the way in which "intentional action, directed inward, becomes aware of the tension and rhythm that drives it forward. . . . What stands out, then, is not a map or portrait of the 'deeper' self, finally deciphered, but rather the tireless subject who, knowing nothing, is engaged in a never-ending investigation of himself" (Starobinski 227).

These investigations come from a will to know and through multiple explorations within personal observation and reflection, as well as conversations with friends and colleagues. Often, though not necessarily, literary reading enters as prompt, comment, or example in such investigations. Ironically, the essayist is most often free to write only by knowing and valuing direct sources of experience and having a sense of the boundaries and limits of human ways of accumulating and testing knowledge. Essayists strive to gain expressiveness not by following expected genre boundaries or processes of knowing, but by exercising freedoms: "freedoms illicit in the minds of some readers, freedoms not so much exercised as seized over the border" (Hardwick xiv).

The Challenge

Michel Foucault tells us: "People know what they do; frequently they know why they do what they do; but what they don't know is what what they do does." In the case of the essay, it is clear *what* the essay as redefined in academic use does is exclude. It excludes collaborative voices at leisure in the freedom to think and explore ideas; it excludes those whose habits of argument and uses of ideas as prompts to action depend on explorations of alternatives. It excludes genres associated for the young and unschooled with oral language— narratives, quick asides of witty observation, brief question-answer dyads that challenge but do not drive to a single truth. Folkloric and linguistic studies of aphorisms, riddles, narratives of fact and fiction, as well as special forms of conversation, such as gossip, illustrate the ways in which the processes of thinking revealed in these oral forms move in a kind of crab-wise walk, seemingly lost in the mazes of argument. Terms used to describe such forms of talk echo those used to describe essays: prefatory, without conclusion; filled with quotations of direct speech, loosely linked ideas, twists of opposition; and overlapping with simultaneous streams of talk.

We are compelled to ask about the effect on creativity, the pursuit of alternative answers, and the power of collaborative thinking in academic life, when the central form used to judge students' academic abilities closes off so many of these possibilities. The paradox is that only at the highest forms of academic pursuit—graduate education and research projects, particularly in the sciences—do creative possibilities enter academic study with great frequency and then primarily in oral forms in seminars or research project meetings. If creativity and an ability to weigh alternatives stand as desirable academic goals, then writing pedagogy should not reject the contexts and texts that reflect the workings of the mind—tension-filled and conflictual, acceptable to the problem-solving power of narrative, affectively and cognitively engaging, and unappropriated by fixed interpretations. But a theory of writing pedagogy that would incorporate these views must rest on a rhetorically oriented theory of human thought and human community deriving from oral praxis. It is this orality, combined with acceptance of observation and experience, that permits the play of the ancient epigram and the literary essay, and their moves away from the power of single authorities or final truths. In the spirited exchanges of "oral cultures" and within the literary essay often used as models in classrooms, there is no way to "prove" one's intelligence or linkage to intelligent others through elaborate systems of citation. The force and thus the central intelligence of the piece has to be in the multiple voices of the writer expressing his or her experiences reflected in the range of genres drawn from everyday discourses. Literary, nonliterary, and oral texts circulate in interdependence, heavily influenced by the position, marginal or central, of both institutions and individual observers, writers, or speakers.

But these forms challenge writing instructors in ways for which their own training and professional positions do not prepare them. "Teacher training" orients classroom instructors to see themselves and the texts they choose as central authorities; assessment and accountability demand "right" answers and examine students with questions and problems to which only one "correct" answer may be given. Moreover, if the interdependence of accomplishment with oral genres, twists and turns of thought, and collaborative exchange were to be rewarded in classrooms, then we would need to acknowledge the abilities of many students from cultures and backgrounds not previously privileged in academic situations. These students challenge classroom use of only "authoritative texts," the display of knowledge only in written forms of solitary achievement, and single standards of judgment of what is an acceptable essay. Secondary-level English teachers as well as college writing instructors teach the way they have been taught; thus these challenges represent threats to their positions, bases of knowledge, and forms of practice. Hence, we and they perpetuate the goals of academic institutions to exclude those who do not conform to the reshaped and redefined genres and modes of knowledge display that derive from a twisting of purpose, form, and expectations of the epigram and the essay. When we are forced to see the history of these texts and their contexts, we must see ourselves as part of the politics of the academy that work to protect its own and those most like the professionals who have traditionally dominated its institutions.

As New Historicists consistently warn, even in "exposing" the embeddedness of forms, norms, and myths about class, gender, or cultural exclusions, we remain ourselves caught in "society's dominant currencies, money and prestige," as well as particular possessions of social assets and particular sexualities (Greenblatt 1). Even those practices that may purport to be disinterested or "objective," such as some of those in this chapter, have some intention of maximizing certain kinds of symbolic profit. Thus, the works of art, the genres, discussed here, as well as this chapter itself and the volume that contains it, resulted from negotiations between writers and speakers of only certain classes and backgrounds. All write and judge out of a communally shared repertoire of conventions and within the institutionalized practices of not only editorship patterns but also publishing and marketing practices.

As we recognize the multiple mirroring effect of this kind of acknowledgment, we should not then just direct our attention merely to the forms or histories "out there" but to our own as well. We need to attend to the texts we encounter and to the assumptions we may unwittingly bring to these texts and our uses and productions of them in our classrooms. Here we must look more to *texts*, not as autonomous artifacts, but as open interwoven forms backed by belief systems and highly interdependent with both oral and written channels. In addition, we must acknowledge that when belief systems are taken up as institutional rules and practices, these beliefs can claim genres as fixed and absolute artifacts. Our attention in these reflections has centered on migrations of genres, non-genres, and sub-genres, rather than on tendencies to center on hierarchies, dichotomies, and single or universally applicable outcomes. However, the practices of institutions in all these realms work to reinforce standard expectations—especially in formal schooling—of only certain genres rendered usually only in written form.

We may also consider some of the ways that bureaucratic practices, ideals of gender and family relations, and perceptions of "natural" ways of communicating become blindly accepted as neutral or benign. Dichotomies of canonization (male/female, citizen/noncitizen, indigenous/intruder, literary/nonliterary) pile upon central divisions in composition that alienate, falsify, and relegate. Such delusionary tactics prevent our looking beyond labels and lists to acknowledge actual text features and gradations, crossovers, and reversibles in the belief systems that support these.

But through our examinations of others then and now, and of ourselves, we can bear in mind a caution issued long ago by Saint Augustine: "Discussing words with words is as entangled as interlocking and rubbing the fingers with the fingers, in which case it may scarcely be distinguished, except by the one himself who does it, which fingers itch and which give aid to the itching" (372). To move beyond being engrossed in looking only at "words with words," we can promote and pursue intense examination of contexts and of shifting valuations across situations. We may profit in our learning if we expand our consideration of types of discourse and knowledge sources for oral and written discursive practices and their institutions. The theme of this work, and of this chapter, carries the possibility of acknowledging the potential for enslavement (and the resultant creation of new majority/minority distinctions) of practices and institutions conceived in goals of liberation and freedom.

Notes

1. The term *New Historicism* was introduced by Stephen Greenblatt in the introduction to a special volume of *Genre* in 1982 and later renamed by him "the poetics of culture." Neither term carries precise definition, but the

general thrust of those scholars who embrace either is to draw from interdisciplinary approaches as they consider the sources and original contexts of the texts from which they generate current historical treatments. Past and current institutional forces—especially money and prestige—that promote particular interpretations and actions come in for considerable attention by New Historicists. An accessible overview of the various meanings and representations of New Historicism appears in the introduction to Veeser. With regard to the history of writing instruction in formal educational institutions, several historians not identified with New Historicism have also encouraged reexaminations and reconsiderations of the power that goes with the teaching of composition. For example, Berlin (91–92) has reminded us: "Most students . . . learn what we teach them. For this reason, it is important to be aware of what we are teaching, in all its implications. The way we teach writing behavior, whether we will it or not, causes reverberations in all features of a student's private and social behavior."

2. Histories of English (especially those of American college departments) have similarly focused primarily on methods and materials for the teaching of literature and rhetoric (as both oratory and writing); see Berlin and Ohmann. Studies of the rise of composition and its relegation to a preparatory role for the work of writing throughout college center on the social and institutional conditions that gave rise to such writing instruction; for treatments of the weaknesses of these approaches and their relationship to a tendency to reify "traditional rhetoric" as a unified ideal, see Hudson, "Field," and Miller.

3. Though Martial is generally credited as establishing the form in Latin, scholars who have considered the influence of the epigram on sixteenth- and seventeenth-century English writers also point out the epigrammatic qualities of the *distiches* of Cato the Elder (also known as Cato the Censor for his austerity, strictness of character, and severe moral posture) written in the third century BC. Though these are hexameter distiches usually printed as continuous verse and not poems in the usual epigrammatic meter and brief forms, their serious purpose and moral tone strongly influenced early English Humanists who wrote epigrams, such as Sir Thomas More and the Protestant Robert Crowley. See Whipple and Crane for somewhat conflicting views on the question of the relative influence of purpose and form from Classical Writers on English Humanists in the century before Ben Jonson.

4. For discussion of the role of Ben Jonson in turning poets away from the tendency of late sixteenth-century poets to use the epigram for "trifles" toward more serious purposes, see Coiro, Part II. Whipple describes these poets who preceded Jonson and elaborates on their relations with satire, punning, bawdy living, and jests; Crane argues for a more balanced perspective to recognize some sixteenth-century poets as convinced of the moral authority of the epigram as was Jonson.

5. For example, in Richard Dutton's edition of Ben Jonson's *Epigrams*,

only 2 of the 133 epigrams carry an "Of ————" title, and these are "Of Death" and "Of Life and Death," topics that presumably cannot be explained to any satisfactory conclusive point. Manley characterizes the epigram of Renaissance London as reflecting: "first, an impulse to define the indefinite or fix the elusive in formulas; and second, an impulse to *be* definitive by inscribing that formula literally or metaphorically 'on' the matter defined" (259–60).

6. Though the work from which this quotation comes, *The Arte of English Poesie*, is often referred to as "anonymous," scholars generally agree that it was written by George Puttenham, a sixteenth-century little-known poet. The work is, however, acclaimed as perhaps the most ambitious and comprehensive piece of Elizabethan criticism. The book makes a central point of justifying poetry as the expression of social and individual needs and examines poetry in its oral and written forms as a way to link experiences across classes and circumstances.

7. See Hudson's *Epigram in the English Renaissance*, especially chapter 1, for extensive discussion of the mutability of the form but the persistence of its "pointed" nature.

8. Links between the aphorism and epigram are many, and the two forms are often used interchangeably; see, for example, Auden and Kronenberger. A major difference in their origins stems from the fact that epigrams were composed with the idea that they would be inscribed or written on objects, while aphorisms were both spoken and written in the Classical era as general maxims or principles on matters of medicine, law, and general rules of life. Aphorisms have tended to carry more general purposes and remained after the seventeenth century more in the consciousness of the general public than did epigrams, which retained their prominence in academic circles. However, both have received respect for their power to state principles, to display authoritative judgments, and to offer concise, well-formed, witty commentaries on general rules of life. Both also have some hidden meaning to be discovered as well as a hint of didactic purpose. For a discussion of the origins of the aphorism and its influence on Bacon's prose, see Vickers, chapter 3.

9. For various literary periods after the seventeenth century, Fowler (especially chapter 11) discusses the various reasons why certain features of the epigram (or epistle, or treatise) might have been favored for incorporation into that which was regarded as "essayistic."

10. The most comprehensive examination of the epigram in English schools and colleges is in a chapter only partially complete in *The Epigram in the English Renaissance* (Hudson). This study was cut short by the author's untimely death when he had written only three and a half chapters of a book projected to include some twenty chapters. See also Foster Watson's study *The English Grammar Schools to 1660* for discussion of the sense in which the understanding of grammar interacted with writing assignments that involved the epigram.

11. In an examination of the relative roles of imitation and discovery in the Renaissance, Greene argues that the writing of epigrams served both as a teaching device and as commonsense practice for good writing.

12. Relevant to this shift is the history of rhetoric and its various definitions and interpretations in English schools from the time of the Renaissance. One matter seems clear: agreement on rhetoric did not exist among either schoolmasters or literary figures. See, for example, a letter by Erasmus on "the rhetorical art," reprinted in Woodward 124. By the eighteenth century, self-acclaimed rhetoricians often exhibited authoritative postures analogous to those of late twentieth-century literary theorists: strongly held and fiercely argued positions that helped ensure attention to their works by publishers and English educators.

13. For discussion of commonplace books and their roles in shaping choices of themes and patterns of discourse, see Gernes. It is possible to trace through commonplace books the consistency of choices of themes that persisted for school essays: friendship, charity, travel, death, seasonal changes, etc. See, for example, Repplier on "the album amicorum." It is also the case that epigrams, because of their written form, contributed to a sense of stability and security; their form offered more system than those of the narrative, list, or ballad. See Manley for further discussion of the power of the epigrammatic to offer a sense of order, selection, and articulation.

14. The largest collection of such copybooks in the United States is housed in the John Hays Library at Brown University. See Gernes for discussion of the importance of these, both for those admitted to academic institutions and those excluded, such as women.

15. Many observers who wrote of conversation in the nineteenth century often noted the ability of unschooled women to inject brief epigrammatic literary points in their talk. For discussion of women as conversationalists and similarities between their preparation and that of essay writers, see Heath, "Women."

16. The strong equation by the end of the nineteenth century of "proper" school essays as evidence of good character, predictable citizenship, and logical thinking is reviewed in Heath, "Toward." The extent to which such behaviors correlated with principles of scientific management and expectations of docile follow-the-orders workers is covered in Calhoun.

17. Perhaps the best coverage of such principles of rhetorical theory and practice comes from Giambattista Vico who first used the term *sensus communis* to refer to both the language and life of a community. These ideas were developed in an oration Vico gave to the faculty and students of the University of Naples in 1708—*De nostri temporis studiorum ratione*. For an analysis of his rhetorical theory in opposition to that of Descartes, see Schaefer.

18. Numerous descriptions of the sense of community, language, and argument or persuasion in groups of widely varying cultures echo these points. See, for example, Gumperz and Hymes. In addition to the many

studies done by anthropologists, current cross-cultural communication guides to achieving consensus among Japanese executives also describe similar principles of rhetoric and views of alternative approaches to "the truth."

19. Though discussion here will center only on English essayists, Michel de Montaigne, in his *Essais* published in 1580, made points similar to those recounted here by Bacon. In his opening "To the Reader," Montaigne emphasized the "simple, natural, ordinary fashion, without straining or artifice" that he offered. It is probably the case that Montaigne chose *essai* with the original Latin meaning of *exagium*, meaning "exact weighing," and later by extension, "examination," "ordeal," and "trial." Montaigne's motto in his publications appeared beneath a pair of scales.

20. For a full description of these sources, see Heath, "Women."

21. For further analysis of the writings of essayists on the essay and the heteroglossic nature of the form, see Klaus, Heath, "The Essay," and essays in the collections of Butrym and Good.

22. Wertsch offers a useful discussion on "voices of the mind"—a concept that seems closely akin to the ideas that essayists have put forward to portray the ways in which the voices within essays show the workings of the mind of the writer.

Works Cited

Adorno, T. W. "The Essay as Form." Trans. Bob Hullot-Kentor and Frederick Will. *New German Critique* 32 (Spring-Summer, 1984): 151–71.

Auden, W. H., and Louis Kronenberger. Foreword. *Aphorisms*. Middlesex: Penguin, 1962. vii–viii.

Augustine, Saint. *Basic Writings of Saint Augustine*. Vol. 1. New York: Random, 1948.

Bacon, Francis. *The Advancement of Learning*. Athlone Renaissance Library. London: Athlone Press, 1975.

———. *Essays*. Intro. Michael J. Hawkins. London: J. M. Dent, 1972.

———. *The Essays or Counsels*. Intro. Melville B. Anderson. Chicago: A. C. McClurg, 1900.

Benjamin, Walter. *Illuminations*. Ed. Hannah Arendt. New York: Schocken, 1969.

Berlin, James. *Rhetoric and Reality: Writing Instruction in American Colleges, 1900–1985*. Carbondale: Southern Illinois UP, 1987.

Butrym, Alexander, ed. *Essays on the Essay: Redefining the Genre*. Athens: University of Georgia P, 1989.

Calhoun, Daniel. *The Intelligence of a People*. Princeton: Princeton UP, 1973.

Coiro, Ann Baynes. *Robert Herrick's Hesperides and the Epigram Book Tradition*. Baltimore, MD: Johns Hopkins UP, 1988.

Crane, Mary Thomas. "*Intret Cato*: Authority and the Epigram." *Renaissance*

Genres: Essays on Theory, History, and Interpretation. Ed. Barbara Kiefer Lewalski. Cambridge, MA: Harvard UP, 1986. 158–89.

Emerson, Ralph Waldo. *The Journals and Miscellaneous Notebooks of Ralph Waldo Emerson.* Ed. William Gilman. Boston: Harvard UP, 1960–77.

———. *Two Unpublished Essays: The Character of Socrates and the Present States of Ethical Philosophy.* Boston: Lamson, Wolffe, 1896.

Erasmus. *The Collected Works of Erasmus.* Vols. I, II. Trans. R. A. B. Mynors and D. F. S. Thompson. Toronto: U of Toronto P, 1974.

Fowler, Alastair. *Kinds of Literature: An Introduction to the Theory of Genres and Modes.* Cambridge, MA: Harvard UP, 1982.

Gass, William H. "Emerson and the Essay." *Habitations of the Word.* New York: Simon and Schuster, 1985. 9–50.

Gernes, Todd Steven. "Emblems of the Heart and Mind: The Rhyme and Reason of the Album Amicorum in Nineteenth-Century America." Paper given at American Antiquarian Society, 14 August 1990.

Good, Graham. *The Observing Self: Rediscovering the Essay.* London: Routledge, 1988.

Graff, Harvey J. *The Legacies of Literacy: Continuities and Contradictions in Western Culture and Society.* Bloomington: Indiana UP, 1987.

Greenblatt, Stephen. "Towards a Poetics of Culture." Ed. Aram Veeser. *The New Historicism.* New York: Routledge, 1989. 1–14.

Greene, Thomas M. *The Light in Troy: Imitation and Discovery in Renaissance Poetry.* New Haven: Yale UP, 1982.

Gumperz, John J., and Dell Hymes. Eds. *Directions in Sociolinguistics: The Ethnography of Communication.* New York: Holt, 1972.

Hardwick, Elizabeth. Introduction. *Best American Essays 1986.* New York: Ticknor and Fields, 1986. xiii–xxi.

Heath, Shirley Brice. "The Essay in English: Readers and Writers in Dialogue." Ed. Michael Macovski. *Textual Voice, Vocative Texts: Dialogue, Linguistics, and Literature.* New York: Oxford, forthcoming.

———. "Toward an Ethnohistory of Writing in American Education." Ed. Marcia Farr Whiteman. *The Nature, Development, and Teaching of Written Communication.* Vol. 1 of *Variation in Writing: Functional and Linguistic-Cultural Differences.* Hillsdale, NJ: Lawrence Erlbaum Assoc. 25–46.

———. "Women in Conversation: Covert Models in American Language Ideology." Ed. Robert Cooper and Bernard Spolsky. *Language, Society, and Thought.* Berlin: Walter de Gruyter, 1990. 202–22.

Hudson, Hoyt Hopewell. *The Epigram in the English Renaissance.* Princeton: Princeton UP, 1947.

———. "The Field of Rhetoric." *Quarterly Journal of Speech Education* 9 (1923): 167–80.

Jonson, Ben. *Epigrams and the Forest.* Ed. Richard Dutton. Manchester: Carcanet, 1984.

Klaus, Carl H. "Montaigne on His Essays: Toward a Poetics of the Self." *The Iowa Review*, forthcoming.

Mackail, J. W. Ed. *Select Epigrams from the Greek Anthology*. London: Longmans, Green, 1890.

Manley, Lawrence. "Proverbs, Epigrams, and Urbanity in Renaissance London." *English Literary Renaissance* 15 (1985): 247–76.

Martialis, Marcus Valerius. *The Epigrams of Martial*. Ed. James Michie. London: Hart-Davis MacGibbon, 1972.

Miller, Susan. *Textual Carnivals: The Politics of Composition*. Carbondale: Southern Illinois UP, 1991.

Montaigne, Michel de. *The Complete Works of Montaigne*. Trans. Donald M. Frame. Stanford: Stanford UP, 1957.

Ohmann, Richard. *English in America*. New York: Oxford UP, 1976.

Puttenham, George. *The Arte of English Poesie*. Ed. Gladys Willcock and Alice Walker. Cambridge: Cambridge UP, 1936.

Repplier, Agnes. "The Album Amicorum." *A Happy Half-Century*. Boston: Houghton Mifflin, 1908. 234–49.

Schaefer, John D. "The Use and Misuse of Giambattista Vico: Rhetoric, Orality, and Theories of Discourse." Ed. H. Aram Veeser. *The New Historicism*. New York: Routledge, 1989. 89–101.

Snyder, John. *Prospects of Power: Tragedy, Satire, the Essay, and the Theory of Genre*. Lexington: U of Kentucky P, 1991.

Starobinski, Jean. *Montaigne in Motion*. Trans. Arthur Goldhammer. Chicago: U of Chicago P, 1985.

Veeser, H. Aram. Introduction. *The New Historicism*. New York: Routledge, 1989.

Vickers, Brian. *Francis Bacon and Renaissance Prose*. Cambridge: Cambridge UP, 1968.

Watson, Foster. *The English Grammar Schools to 1660*. Cambridge: Cambridge UP, 1908.

Wertsch, James V. *Voices of the Mind: A Sociocultural Approach to Mediated Action*. Cambridge, MA: Harvard UP, 1991.

Whipple, T. K. *Martial and the English Epigram from Sir Thomas Wyatt to Ben Jonson*. Vol. 10 of *Publications in Modern Philology*. Berkeley: U of California P, 1925. 279–414.

Woodward, W. H. *Desiderius Erasmus Concerning the Aim and Method of Education*. Cambridge: Cambridge UP, 1904.

Woolf, Virginia. "The Modern Essay." *The Common Reader*. Intro. by Andrew McNeillie. First Series. New York: Harcourt, 1984. 211–22.

5

Rethinking Diversity:

Axes of Difference

in the Writing Classroom

Beverly J. Moss and Keith Walters

Few issues on campus in recent memory have sparked the debate, argument, and some would contend uncivil behavior by students and faculty that have accompanied the topic of diversity. From our perspective, the topic represents the latest attempt to deal with long-standing issues—many would say problems—in the academy and the larger society. Yet given the social, economic, and political contexts in which the topic has been raised, it represents far more than a trendy relabeling of another problem that simply will not go away. As citizens and educators, we are faced with the fact that large numbers of students—mostly African Americans, Hispanics, Native Americans, Appalachians, and other poor Americans of European roots—are not succeeding in our schools and universities or in the workplace. At the same time, these institutions have begun to confront a major demographic shift in the populations they serve, the ultimate result of which is that no single ethnic group will constitute the majority of Americans: instead, the majority will soon be composed of various groups of ethnic minorities that have traditionally been underrepresented in these same institutions.

Although many would reduce discussions of diversity to questions of the changing demographics of this society and issues of ethnicity and social class, we contend that a serious analysis of diversity in American writing classrooms encompasses far more. Especially in higher education, for example, one finds a growing number of international students, immigrants, and Americans for whom English is not a first language. Representing a number of cultural traditions and language backgrounds, these students are often simultaneously mastering both the English language and the preferred ways of structuring information and arguments in the academic discourse of this culture. In fact, the class composed uniquely of native speakers of English is a thing of the past in many institutions. Similarly, classes in which everyone is the same age—eighteen to twenty-two—are increasingly rare. Instead, one finds students of many ages who are attempting to integrate a college education with professional and family responsibilities. Although we as educators are quick to pay attention to these changes in process, we sometimes overlook the fact that a generation or two ago, the ratio of females to males in most classrooms would have been quite different from what it is today or what it may become in the future. In considering issues of diversity, then, one should probably ask about the extent to which the presence of males in previously all-female institutions or females in all-male or predominantly male institutions might have an impact on classroom dynamics. Finally, one must acknowledge the population of gay, lesbian, and bisexual students who have always been there, usually silently and invisibly, but present nonetheless. As we seek to demonstrate in this essay, each of these axes of difference has ramifications for what occurs or might occur in writing classes.

At least since earlier this century when large-scale standardized examinations began to play a major role in American education, schools and universities in this country have operated largely as if diversity did not matter. Despite what a great deal of scholarly research has revealed and what our common sense teaches us, we as teachers often continue to evaluate ourselves and our students as if there were a single, appropriate way of using language and of being literate in this culture. As reading specialist Frank Smith has pointed out, educators and the public have accepted a purely psychological model of literacy. In other words, literacy is considered a property of individuals who are seen only as individuals and never as members of groups. It is likewise perceived to be a cognitive operation that is invariant across the species; consequently, whatever social aspects literacy might have are taken to be largely epiphenomenal and therefore unin- teresting. In addition to accepting a psychological model of literacy, educators and the public have, we contend, been willing to accept an especially narrow view of language upon which to base their model of literacy. In doing so, we as teachers have assumed that "if reading and writing are analyzed into component elements of basic skills and knowledge which are presented and rehearsed under appropriate conditions of incentive and reinforcement, then every relevant factor has been attended to" (viii). Although some of our willingness to ignore diversity can be traced to trends in psychology, psychometrics, and educational theory in general, some of it—as well as at least part of the popularity of the trends in these disciplines—seems to derive from a societal need to deal with differences by making all people appear alike. Some individuals interpret this process as encourage- ment or pressure to conform; others, however, see it as a relentless effort to silence and dismiss those who are different from some ideal or idealized majority.

Regardless of how members of our society perceive or react to what seems to be this societal need, we as classroom teachers (and especially classroom teachers of writing) cannot deny the inadequacies of past and current ways of dealing with diversity, nor can we escape the future challenge it represents. How we deal or fail to deal with issues of linguistic and cultural diversity in our own classrooms reveals much about our identity as individuals and as members of the many social groups of which we are or have been a part. It likewise reveals much of what we perceive teaching and learning to be about, that is, what we think the proper role of a teacher is and how he or she should think about, plan for, and judge the value of what goes on in his or her classroom.

In this essay, we try to grapple with what we have learned in trying to deal with some of these issues in our own teaching. We do not see ourselves as experts, but as practitioners struggling to find ways to use the diversity present in every classroom as a resource in responsible, thoughtful, and productive ways. Rather than offering answers, we are looking for ways of thinking about these issues that cause us to reflect critically and analytically on our own practice, that lead us to be willing to risk altering the ways we have traditionally taught, and that help us decide how to evaluate our actions as we seek fresh alternatives to this newest version of a persistent problem. Consequently, we resist offering checklists that one can tick off, believing that he or she has dealt adequately with diversity. Similarly, we will try to avoid suggesting classroom activities that may assuage our pangs of guilt while ignoring larger, recalcitrant issues relating to diversity.

In short, we are concerned in this essay with rethinking many of our own fundamental assumptions, both those into which we were socialized as students and those that we were encouraged to accept during our training to be teachers. Crucially, however, we believe that *all* teachers *and* students are implicated in dealing responsibly with diversity. In other words, issues of diversity are not simply issues that cause us to think about how we—if, for example, we are heterosexual males of European extraction hailing from middle-class backgrounds—teach everyone else or how we—if, for example, we are "different" in some way—learn. Rather, they are issues that challenge us to give great thought to who we are, why we use language and literacy as we do in our professional and private lives, and what roles language and literacy play in the construction of our identity as well as the identities of those we believe to be similar to and different from us—inside and outside the classroom.

To examine these issues, we consider diversity from three perspectives. First, we consider diversity and how we teach. Specifically, we examine how thinking about teaching as a speech event forces us to admit that no strategy or practice in the classroom is neutral; rather, every strategy or practice assumes, encourages, or values certain ways of using language and literacy while simultaneously discouraging others or evaluating them negatively. Second, we consider what we teach; here, we focus narrowly on the issue of Standard English for several reasons. Significantly, in the minds of many writers, educators, and citizens, especially those who reduce diversity to the issue of our country's shifting demographics, the major challenge of diversity is getting "those people" to use Standard English. Moreover, the issues of Standard English and its teaching have been of long-standing concern and debate among teachers of writing. Finally, and most important, we contend that because language is the medium through which writing instruction takes place, teachers of writing should examine thoroughly their own assumptions about language—and especially Standard English—because of the many ways in which these assumptions influence interactions with students and their texts. We will seek to demonstrate that the models of language upon which most current practice is based are likely to be woefully inadequate for meeting the challenges of diversity of particular kinds.

Following our discussion of what we teach, we turn our attention to whom we teach and comment on several axes of difference that are likely to have an impact on teaching and learning in any classroom although we, as teachers, may not have given them a great deal of systematic thought in the past. First, as a parallel to and extension of our discussion of language, we examine in some detail the issue of patterns of home literacy and language use. Recent research has demonstrated that the more the conventions for using language and literacy in a community differ from those assumed or rewarded by the academy, the greater the likelihood that students from the community will have difficulty at school. Thus, this research often reminds us that our notions about what it means to be literate are generally quite parochial, usually limited to middle-class—and, more specifically, academic—ways of using language and literacy. Additionally, we examine other axes of difference—first language (when it is other than English), age, sex or gender, and sexual orientation—that have received less attention in the literature, sketching the kinds of issues these sorts of difference might raise for teachers and students.

Finally, we conclude the essay by reflecting on who we are as individuals who happen to be teachers, arguing that any adequate response to diversity requires that we rethink our authority in the classroom and consequently renegotiate the relationship between teachers and learners there. Such divisions in our subject are artificial, but they offer us a starting point for examining ways in which we have often unknowingly tended to ignore the kinds of difference increasingly found in all classrooms.

Diversity and How We Teach

One can approach teaching from many perspectives. One can see it as transferring information, coaching (or something akin to it), or assuming the role of master craftsperson in a process of apprenticeship. Similarly, but perhaps less obviously, one can think about teaching as a speech event, an activity or aspects of an activity "directly governed by rules or norms for the use of speech" (Hymes 52). From this sociolinguistic perspective, teaching involves participants—minimally, a teacher and students, although assistants, observers, or visitors may be part of the event. Likewise, it involves rules for speaking or remaining silent as well as norms for evaluating both linguistic and nonlinguistic behavior. As is usually the case with social phenomena, the rules and norms usually go unstated: they are assumed to be shared and are noted only when violated.

From this perspective, the focus of teaching, even the teaching of writing, becomes spoken language and the ways in which spoken language is used for a host of purposes: to convey information about written texts and writing in general, to design and make assignments, to set up appointments, to talk to students about their texts, or to interact with students as fellow human beings through greetings, leave-takings, and the paying and receiving of compliments. Thus, a discussion of how we teach focuses our attention on the very complex, unfolding world of the pedagogical conversation,[1] whether in the classroom, the office, the hallway, or some other setting, in which we can never be sure that our norms or motives for interacting will automatically be shared by our interlocutors.

When any particular interaction with a student or students does not go well from our point of view—when a class does not pay attention, when a student behaves in what we believe to be a surly fashion, when we cannot understand why an especially bright student refuses to speak up in class—we might respond by claiming that whatever problems exist belong to the student or students who do not share our assumptions. In the past, such a claim was usually considered appropriate. Today, however, such a response seems less and less acceptable, logical, or fair. Increasingly, we are learning to ask questions about misunderstandings between teachers and students and coming to realize that many axes of difference can interfere with what at one level seems like such a simple task: helping students develop the skills they already have in order to progress as writers and thinkers.

Last year, Keith had a problem involving a Pakistani-American student who clearly had different rules from those that Keith expected for asking questions of the teacher. For instance, in class discussion, the student sometimes asked what he believed to be an information question and received what Keith believed to be an adequate reply. Then, when asking a follow-up question, the student began by restating the assumption that led to the original question as if to reconstruct his position and perhaps to rehearse all of the steps of argumentation in whatever was being discussed. Perceiving that the student had ignored (or at least failed to acknowledge) the answer that he had just given the student, Keith believed that his authority was being baldly challenged. From discussions with the student, Keith knew that the student perceived his own behavior to be neither overly insistent nor rude, yet given Keith's own assumptions about questions and how they should be asked in the classroom, Keith perceived the behavior to be rude and even belligerent. Did the student have a problem because Keith and some of his other professors perceived that he challenged them to an excessive degree in class? Did Keith have a problem because his assumptions were not shared by all of his students? Or did the student and his teachers share a problem because they seem to be operating with different assumptions about the rules and norms for the use of speech in classroom settings? What are the consequences of assigning the "problem" to the student or teacher alone, or to the student and his teachers?

Similar questions arise for Beverly and other teachers with respect to issues of age difference in the classroom. Although many teachers lament that they and their eighteen- and nineteen-year-old undergraduates inhabit different worlds, we rarely examine seriously the role of age differences as a source of misunderstanding in the classroom. Beverly, because she looks as young as some of her undergraduates and is younger than many of her graduate students, finds herself in the position of dealing with possible conflicts resulting from age differences. She frequently finds herself questioning how she deals with older students who, Beverly feels, at times seem to challenge her authority in the classroom. Yet, these older students appear to think they treat her the way they treat all of their professors. Are there assumptions that members of our culture make about cross-age face-to-face interaction that might lead to misunderstandings between a younger professor and an older student or an older professor and a younger student?

The sorts of misunderstandings related to assumptions about language and language use extend far beyond students' asking questions in what teachers might feel are inappropriate ways or differences of age between teacher and student. In fact, almost all former Peace Corps volunteers who served as teachers can relate stories about how they initially (at least) failed because they did not know how to do something as simple as taking attendance. The details vary from country to country and culture to culture but include, for example, gaffes like not making students stand at attention outside the classroom and await permission to come in, as is the custom in many former French colonies and other countries; using first and last names, rather than title and last name or only first name; or not making "calling the roll" a clearly delineated part of the class period, preferring instead simply to scan the classroom for absences. When volunteers in foreign countries took attendance "the American way," their students quite understandably assumed that the volunteers were not competent teachers and consequently did not take them seriously. The stories of returned Peace Corps volunteers remind us that issues of language use and diversity within or across cultures can be great, often involving small things that have great consequences. If a teacher cannot get through the first five minutes of class when attendance is being taken in a way that students find acceptable, he or she probably will not be effective for the other fifty minutes of the period. In other words, the kinds of differences we wish to consider are not limited to formal teaching of lessons; instead, they involve all aspects of language use in teaching including how teachers organize and divide up class time, how they signal the transition from one part of the lesson to another, how they ask questions of students, and how they interpret, evaluate, and respond to students' responses and behaviors.

Sarah Michaels and Susan Philips are two researchers who have examined the nature of misunderstandings that can occur between teachers and students from different cultural and linguistic backgrounds. In the first grade class that she studied, Michaels found that the black children were more likely to be interrupted and "corrected" by the white teacher than were the white children during sharing-time (sometimes referred to as "Show and Tell," when first graders shared stories with their classmates while all sat on a rug at the front of the classroom). An analysis of the discourse patterns used by black and white children during sharing time revealed that the white children's discourse patterns, labeled topic-centered, more closely matched those of the white teacher and more closely resembled an academic notion of a narrative than did those of the black children. Yet the black children's discourse patterns—moving from one event to another and assuming that context or listeners' knowledge would establish connections among these events—were the norm in their home communities, where to be explicit about the links between episodes of a narrative is to insult the listener by assuming that he or she is not intelligent or interested enough to deduce the connections. The well-meaning teacher assumed that the black children did not know how to tell stories properly and sought to "help" them by interjecting questions as they talked. At least some of the black students, however, perceived these questions as frustrating interruptions. As Michaels clearly demonstrates, sharing-time is not just about telling stories—the characterization that both teacher and students might initially offer; rather, it is really about a student's co-narrating a story with the teacher, who, through questions and comments, creates a scaffolding of sorts that the student, through responses, fills in. When teacher and student share this schema for storytelling and for teacher/student interaction, the stories are acceptable to the teacher—and by extension the academy. But when teacher and student begin with different notions of what a good story is or how one co-narrates a story with a social superior, the mismatch may well have grave repercussions for not only sharing-time but later instruction and achievement in speaking and writing as well.[2]

Working in the Warm Springs Indian community, Philips found that the cultural expectations brought into the classroom by Anglos were very often in direct conflict with rules for communicative behavior native to the reservation community. Like others who have worked in Native American communities, she found that the preferred response patterns of the Indian children did not match the patterns of white, middle-class students and were often unacceptable to the non-Indian teachers. Because, for example, the Native American children would not respond to direct questions and sought to avoid going to the blackboard, the Anglo teachers perceived the students to be uncooperative or unintelligent. As Philips pointed out, what the teachers did not understand (and therefore could not appreciate) was that in this Native American community, as in many, direct questions are rarely posed because the person who tries to answer but answers incorrectly loses face. Similarly, individuals in this community are rarely forced into public situations—like going to the blackboard—in which they could fail before their peers and superiors or in which they might be forced as individuals to excel, thereby distinguishing themselves from other members of the group. Rather than seeking to demonstrate individual competence or mastery—so much a goal of mainstream schooling—these students were much happier working in groups with no appointed leader or "helping" the teacher solve a problem. Thus, Philips concluded that "in the structuring of attention, and in the regulation of talk, there are differences between Anglos and Warm Springs Indians that result in miscommunication between students and teacher in the Indian classrooms" (127). Certainly, research such as that of Michaels and Philips has encouraged us to see that no methodology or pedagogy is culture free or culture neutral.

The discussion of the research of Michaels and Philips raises questions about assumptions relating to teaching method, on the one hand, and linguistic and cultural differences, on the other. If we as teachers accept, as these researchers suggest, that no pedagogy is free of assumptions about how to use language appropriately, then we are led to examine whatever teaching techniques we might use, whether these might be labeled traditional or alternative, from the perspective of what they presuppose about how language is or should be used. For example, we know little about the consequences or implications of currently popular alternatives like collaborative learning, networked classrooms, or small-group activities, especially when we acknowledge that an increasingly diverse student population brings with it increasingly heterogeneous assumptions about how to interact appropriately through language.

Traditionally, teachers at the college and university level have favored the lecture method as a teaching tool, and those who teach large classes may feel they need to rely on a classroom format that involves the teacher holding the floor and speaking all (or nearly all) of the time. In such cases, the goal is transmitting a body of knowledge organized and presented (some might say broadcast) by the teacher. Writing teachers, however, have long held such lecture methods in disdain, arguing instead for small-group activities or discussions that students participated in or led. Of course, organizing classroom time so that students talk to the teacher or to one another represents a shift in goal: the focus is no longer the monologic transmission of knowledge but creating (or, more accurately, cocreating) it through dialogue or polylogue. These methods are not without controversy. They are not value free; rather, they entail assumptions about using spoken and written language that may not be shared by everyone who enters the classroom door.

As demonstrated in the following sections, "Diversity and What We Teach" and "Diversity and Whom We Teach," teachers of writing, like all educators, find themselves in a fix. Unhappy with the lecture method that informed most of our own educations and all too acquainted with its limitations for many students, we seek alternative methods of teaching and interacting with students. Yet we understand little about the ways in which various teaching techniques or methods constrain or shape students' possibilities for displaying knowledge (cf. Freeman; Janda; Sperling; and Walters " 'It's Like Playing

Password' "). In his research on classroom interaction, Hugh Mehan has pointed out that the competent student must not only possess the requisite information, but he or she must also display it in an acceptable fashion. With respect to diversity, it is this issue of display, the complex problem of finding acceptable packaging, that we believe to be especially crucial. In a very important sense, each display of knowledge is a possible locus—a point in real time and social space—at which diversity may play itself out before our eyes. Keith's Pakistani-American student is exceedingly bright, yet he risks receiving poor evaluations because he and his teacher have different notions about how student questions should be packaged and about a host of other behaviors that constitute the teacher/student relationship.

How can we allow Keith's student to display knowledge or ask questions in a way that both he and Keith find useful? We see one of the most formidable tasks for educators striving for inclusive class-rooms to be that of valuing and using the diverse ways of knowledge-making that students from various populations bring to the classroom. Much of our discussion and much of the research we will cite suggests that different communities make knowledge in various ways, value different kinds of knowledge, and display or package their knowledge in ways not commonly valued in the academy. Developing appro-priate methods of evaluation, then, will be challenging, but the alter-native seems increasingly untenable. If our understanding of diversity suggests that students from some backgrounds create knowledge in ways different from traditional academic ways, then it stands to reason that they will best be able to show their knowledge in forms that may contrast with traditional forms. Perhaps we should consider allowing students to display their knowledge in ways that permit them to demonstrate their expertise even if these displays have not tradition-ally been used in the academy while continuing to help students learn how to display knowledge in the ways traditionally valued by educational institutions.

In an effort to meet this challenge, Beverly makes a point in all of her classes of having at least three different types of assignments for evaluation—singly authored writing assignments, collaboratively authored assignments, and singular or collaborative oral presenta-tions—as well as, in some cases, visually presented assignments that might include videotapes, paintings, and so on. The philosophy be-hind this variety of assignments is that students come from varied cultural and linguistic backgrounds that may prefer different ways of displaying knowledge and value different uses of the spoken and written language. By asking students to complete several kinds of assignments, Beverly hopes that every student will be successful in displaying his or her knowledge using at least one of these formats. She also believes that students gain important experience as they are required to display knowledge in several ways and challenged to work in formats that might not be their chosen ones. Thus, Beverly's students complete a large number of writing assignments, especially in her writing classes, but her approach acknowledges that the traditional singly authored essay is not the only way to display knowledge or even to work on the many requisite skills necessary to improve one's writing.

How Beverly integrates these assignments into a course can perhaps best be seen by looking at the work she requires of students in her "Introduction to African-American Literature." When she first looked at the syllabi a previous professor had used for this survey course, Beverly found that the only method of evaluation in the course had been the objective exam. The assumption behind such an approach seems to be that students best display knowledge by giving back to the teacher what he or she has given them. In contrast, Beverly assigns group oral reports on the most difficult readings; singly authored critical essays on particular works; research-based single-student oral reports requiring annotated bibliographies on relevant historical, cultural, and biographical information; and exams that include both objective and essay questions. Our goal here is not to highlight Beverly's teaching; instead, it is to point out that if we are committed to broadening our repertoire of pedagogical strategies and widening our methods of sampling and evaluating student ability, knowledge, and achievement, we can begin in our own classrooms, usually without waiting for administratively sanctioned curricular change.

From our perspective, how we teach—our assumptions as well as our actions—reflect the extent to which we accommodate diversity, whether we use it as an integral part of learning, merely acknowledge it, or, perhaps, at worst, teach to an ideal student who may bear little resemblance to those who actually occupy the seats in our classrooms.

Diversity and What We Teach

Teachers of writing at the college and university level are teachers of language and of advanced literacy skills. In this section, we deal with a basic part of what we teach, language and, more particularly, Standard English as it relates to other varieties of English. In a very real sense, our discussion of what we teach spills over into the next section, "Diversity and Whom We Teach," in which we consider the related but broader topic of home literacies and language use as they sometimes contrast with what Ron Scollon and Suzanne Scollon term the *essayist literacy* of the academy. Although the topics of language and literacy are closely related, we have chosen to separate them in order to highlight the constellations of issues surrounding each. As noted in the introduction, we see the topic of language as a very important one because our assumptions about language ultimately influence nearly everything we say and do. Certainly, nearly all of the spoken or written language that is produced in the context of writing classes is in some sense language about how to use written language effectively. Equally important, because writing teachers insist that students use Standard English, it is important for teachers to have as rich as possible an understanding of that variety and the nature of standard languages in general.

In classrooms, and especially classrooms in which English or writing is taught, the picture of language that informs much of the talk and probably all of the writing is a simple one: there are many varieties of English, but only one variety—Standard English—is appropriate for the talk and writing in academic contexts. If the picture represented no more than this simple statement, it would not be especially problematic. But the picture is more complex. In fact, it looks something like figure 5.1.

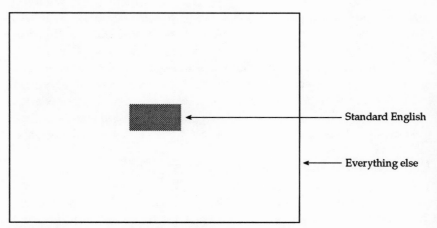

Figure 5.1. The view of language promulgated by schools.

It is the nature of both the smaller box and the larger area surrounding it that concerns us. First, let us examine how the notion of Standard English operates in the classroom. If asked to define what Standard English is, most students and many teachers would reply that it is "good grammar" or "correct language that doesn't break any rules"— characterizations they learned from teachers and textbooks. There would be no comment about where this variety of language came from, who makes up the rules, or where we might find them.

Those with some training in linguistics might say something about the difference between descriptive and prescriptive approaches to language. A descriptive approach, one that considered language as it is, would be praised for any number of reasons, while a prescriptive one, which focuses on how language should be, would be damned because it is arbitrary, illogical, and downright undemocratic. Armed with what they learned in their linguistics courses, these students and teachers might also note that people cannot or should not make judgments about speakers' intellectual abilities on the basis of the way they speak. Soon, however, those with training in linguistics have little to add, leaving us with little insight into what Standard English is or how to deal with it and other varieties of English in classrooms.

In fact, defining what the standard is and is not constitutes a very complex task because we are dealing with several notions of the standard at once. In one instance, we might think of the *descriptive standard*, the variety of American English that corresponds to the definitions of standard languages that most sociolinguistsand language planners might give. Such definitions usually note that a standard variety is the one used by people with social, political, and economic power and influence—"a dialect with an army and a navy," as some put it. It is also the variety taught to native and nonnative speakers of the language and used in the various media in its spoken and written forms.

Such a descriptive standard is much broader than the *prescriptive standard*, which corresponds to the written variety the rules of which are inscribed in handbooks of the sort that are used in writing classes. Most of the marks that are made in the margins of student papers— frag, dm, split inf., diction—represent efforts to get students to respect, use, and internalize the rules of this prescriptive standard. Of course, handbooks differ, and pronouncements about usage change. Most important, careful readers frequently find "violations" of these prescriptive rules in the speaking of the socially, politically, and economically powerful and in such written texts as *The New York Times*, textbooks, and professional journals. In other words, teachers of writing ultimately must acknowledge that these speakers and writers do not seem to be following the sets of rules inscribed in the handbooks used in our classes. Additionally, those of us with prescriptivist tendencies should acknowledge that many of the students who currently suffer our marginal comments are soon likely to wield far more economic, social, or political power than we ever will; consequently, their speaking and writing will help determine the descriptive standard for the coming generation. In earlier periods when our profession sought to acknowledge and deal with linguistic diversity, considerations such as these were frequently marshaled by those trained in linguistics in order to argue against the existence of something called Standard English. For example, these sorts of arguments favored prominently in the discussions and debates surrounding the "Students' Right to Their Own Language" statement issued in 1976.

In addition to the descriptive and prescriptive standards, we also find what we might term the *perceived standard*, that is, what speakers and writers believe Standard English to be. Here, we find such myths as "Never start a sentence with *and*," and "Never end a sentence with a preposition," as well as patterns of conscious analysis that lead writers to mispunctuate dependent clauses beginning with "whereas" or "which is to say" as if they were sentences. Thus, the perceived standard is what language users, whether students, graduates, or teachers, ultimately invoke when evaluating their own language and that of others or when called upon to justify their judgments or behaviors. For many speakers, this perceived standard contains inconsistencies or logical contradictions. Some speakers scrupulously insist on the subjunctive following "if" in *irrealis* constructions about the present ("If I were she, I would return it" or even "If I were her") but use the conditional, rather than the past perfect, following "if" in utterances and sentences about the past ("If I would have been born in China, I would speak Chinese"), despite the canons of prescriptive usage. Others pride themselves on never using object pronouns in subject position but use subject pronouns in object position ("That matter is between Paige and I") or use reflexive pronouns when object pronouns would suffice ("They offered Naima and myself promotions").

Interestingly and importantly, part of this perceived standard, for many, is the belief that whatever they do or say represents the standard language or something closely akin to it. In other words, speakers or writers who use constructions like the examples from the last paragraph in their speaking and writing sincerely believe that they are using Standard English. (In fact, they may evaluate negatively or attempt to correct speakers or writers who, in fact, follow the prescriptive rules of the language.) From a purely *descriptive* point of view and especially one that acknowledges variation, language users who employ the structures illustrated in the previous paragraph, particularly if they are well educated, are probably correct: the behavior of their group becomes the descriptive standard, regardless of what teachers and newspaper columnists say. Protestations of conservative language users to the contrary, for example, *impact* has become a verb for most educated speakers and writers. Assuming (or attempting to enforce) a prescriptive notion of the standard, however, the Mr. or Ms. Fidditches among us will continue to mark or correct such "errors."

Because a component of the *perceived standard* involves judging the behavior of the self and the other, whatever is different from one's own behavior becomes part of that "everything else" in figure 5.1 for nearly all speakers and writers—teachers of writing included. In that larger area of figure 5.1, unsavory things like regional, social, and ethnic dialects exist along with all of the "ill's," "un's," and "non's," of the society: illiteracy, illegitimacy, unemployment, underachievement, and nonstandard language. In these cases, "different from the standard" really means "inferior" because what is being judged is not simply language but a host of personal and cultural attributes that members of the society associate with varieties of language and, by extension, their users. It is not acceptable for most Americans to label someone inferior because of his or her skin color; far more acceptable, however, is the sort of claim made by a white American on *The Oprah Winfrey Show* during a discussion of Black English when he asserted that the use of "good English," which he assumed he spoke and wrote, to be a question of self-discipline. In his eyes, speakers of Black English simply lacked self-discipline—because their speech did not resemble his. This speaker, like most, clearly associates the use of what he perceives to be Standard English with particular moral virtues. His comments remind us that the issues involved in discussions of standard language extend far beyond the question of the nature of Standard English as a linguistic variety.

Obviously, the model of language in figure 5.1 leaves us poised to ignore diversity, for those who speak anything resembling the varieties of American English used by the middle class will locate themselves inside the "Standard English" box—often complaining sheepishly that they don't know any grammar—while simultaneously locating those whose language differs from theirs—members of what have traditionally been ethnic minorities as well as those from working-class and poorer communities—in the vast uncharted "everything else."

These "everything else" speakers, by virtue of their experience growing up and getting an education in this culture, have often learned that the variety of language they use is "bad" or "wrong." Never have they heard that their native dialect is rule-governed and hence systematic, nor have they been helped to see the nature of the situation they find themselves in as they are expected to be able to shift between the language of school and that of the community. Rather, they have been encouraged (or commanded) to give up the language of the home and embrace the language of the school instead. Accompanying these exhortations are promises of social mobility and a better life, promises that often mock the reality of these students' daily experiences.

Additionally, by the time anyone becomes a teacher, he or she places himself or herself in the "standard" box, regardless of class or region of origin. Those who have changed social class during their lifetime may have worked hard to modify their language so as to be able to pass as speakers (even near native speakers) of the variety enshrined in what they believe to be the confines of that smaller box— a fact that may lead them to be especially critical of those whose language cannot be so circumscribed.

The view of language put forth in figure 5.1 is far too simple to be of much use in understanding the kinds of choices our students as language users are faced with as they seek to succeed in our classes. As our discussion has demonstrated, figure 5.1 certainly fails to acknowledge the obvious fact that there is variability even within what is usually termed *Standard English*. More specifically, it in no way represents the fact that educated Americans are far more tolerant of a speaker's maintaining his or her native regional accent while speaking Standard English than they are of his or her retaining grammatical features of a regional dialect when speaking or writing. It is fine to sound like a Southerner, a New Yorker, or a Californian, as long as one sounds educated—that is, as long as one's "grammar" stays within the range acceptable to speakers of Standard English. Equally important, the figure does not capture other observations that any speaker of English who has lived in this country for any length of time realizes:

as one goes up the social ladder, one finds less variation among dialects. In other words, it is from lesser-educated individuals that one most frequently hears forms labeled nonstandard. In contrast, the more that people become educated, the more likely they are to have learned to bleach their speech and writing of markers that reveal their native regional and social dialect, especially if these dialects are considered nonstandard by society at large. Such a commonsense observation is, of course, an admission that access to Standard English is related to issues of social class and social mobility. Figure 5.2 seeks to capture these generalizations.

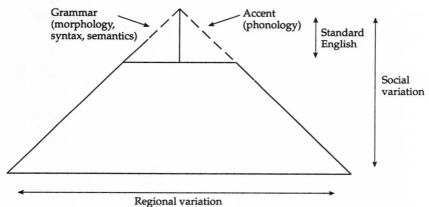

Figure 5.2. One view of the relationship between regional and social variation in American English. Ethnic varieties are not included. Adapted from Trudgill 188.

In this figure, we see regional and social dialects converging toward a standard variety that is, itself, characterized by some variability. The standard variety is less fixed in terms of accent (i.e., pronunciation) than in terms of grammar. Importantly, like all graphic representations of knowledge, figure 5.2 permits us to see generalizations that we might otherwise have missed. We can, for example, begin to locate individuals within this triangle, mapping the range of styles along which they might shift. For example, the style-shifting abilities of people who grew up speaking a strongly stigmatized regional and social variety of American English but who now speak Standard English might be represented by a very long line reaching from the lower part of the triangle to near its apex. On the other hand, the style-shifting of someone who grew up in a middle-class community might be represented by a much shorter line, beginning near the triangle's apex of Standard English and just crossing the line into Standard English. In other words, with this figure, we are able to see that students coming from different backgrounds are faced with different challenges as they seek to master and use Standard English.

Furthermore, this figure permits us to begin thinking about Standard American English in comparative perspective. If we were to draw triangles for British and Australian English, for example, we would find figures that differ from figure 5.2 in crucial ways. The triangle for British English would be much larger, both broader and deeper. Because of the age of the country, its settlement history as well as the history of English, and the nature of its social system, we find far more varied and pronounced regional and social dialects in Britain than in the United States. Additionally, we find a far more focused standard for pronunciation—RP (or Received Pronunciation), which most Americans think of as BBC English—than we find in the United States. Although the pronunciation of Standard British English is highly constrained, we find a narrow range of variation in the grammar there as we do in the United States. In contrast, the triangle for Australia would be much smaller. A much younger country, Australia boasts little regional or social variation, although this situation has begun to change with recent waves of immigrants for whom English is not a first language. Interestingly, Australian English has two standards for pronunciation, an older one based on British English, preferred by the older generation, and a newer, emerging one based on the local Australian accent, preferred by younger speakers.[3] This comparative perspective reminds us that when we speak about Standard English in our classes, we really mean Standard American English and that the linguistic situation in this country differs in important ways from that of other countries in which English is the most frequently used language.

Consequently, a representation of the relationship between Standard English and other varieties of English like the one found in figure 5.2 contains much information that, on the one hand, most speakers of American English know and realize at some level but, on the other, does not seem to influence most of their discussions of Standard English. It offers a richer representation than figure 5.1, which seems to represent more about the society's linguistic ideology than about its actual linguistic situation, by providing information that may be able to help us appreciate why some students have more difficulty with mastery of Standard English than others.

As the legend for figure 5.2 notes, ethnic dialects are not included in that figure. The presence of ethnic dialects certainly complicates a representation like figure 5.2. Considering them carefully, however, may help us understand the particular problems faced by speakers of these varieties. Here, let us examine that family of varieties of American English usually referred to as Black English or African-American English, asking what sorts of factors influence its use and the likelihood that a speaker of African-American English will have difficulty using Standard English. From figure 5.2, we saw that speakers of stigmatized regional and social dialects have, literally, a longer way to go as they move from their native variety to Standard English. Of course, the same is true for speakers of Black English. Their ability to style shift from African-American English toward Standard English will depend on their life circumstances. Speakers who live, work, and relax in communities where African-American English is the most commonly used variety of American English will probably be most comfortable using that variety. On the other hand, African Americans who live, work, and relax in communities where Black English is rarely or never used may not even be able to speak Black English. Their native variety of American English may be one that is close to the regional and social variety of the community in which they live, work, and relax. Most African Americans will find themselves somewhere between these two extremes. This situation is illustrated in figure 5.3.

Figure 5.3 illustrates the likely relationship between an African American's access to and interaction with members of what John Baugh has termed "the Black vernacular street culture," on the one hand, and, non–African Americans, on the other, as they influence the speaker's use of Black English, Standard English, or something that combines features of the two. From this figure, we see that a person's integration into an African-American speech community in the various domains of his or her life will play a large role in exposure to and probable use of Black English and other varieties of American English. Like figure 5.2, this figure suggests generalizations other than those on which it is based. For most African Americans, for example, the degree of integration into the African-American community changes across the lifespan as does their linguistic behavior, a

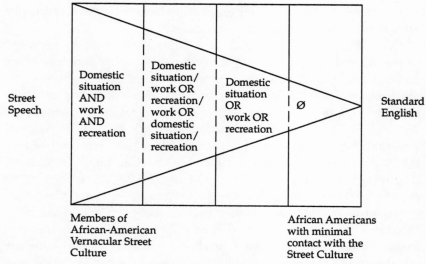

Figure 5.3. African Americans in their speech communities. Representation of the relationship between degree of integration into the vernacular street culture and use of Black English. Adapted from Baugh 218, and Baugh, personal communication.

fact this figure can help us appreciate the consequences of. Interestingly, for example, a number of African-American students at the University of Texas at Austin who come from racially integrated, middle-class communities and who attended public high schools in Texas report that they are exposed to and use Black English more now that they are at UT than at any previous time in their lives. Because African Americans constitute a very small minority at UT and because they perceive that the university is hostile to their presence, they turn to other African Americans for support and hence spend a great deal of time in the presence of African Americans from a variety of social backgrounds. Thus, some African-American students who grew up not speaking Black English make a conscious effort to acquire and use it while at UT in order to be accepted as members of the African-American community there. Extrapolating from figure 5.3, we can also begin to get a clear picture of the kinds of forces that are likely to influence the linguistic behavior of speakers of highly stigmatized social or regional dialects across their lifetimes.

In a very real sense, figures 5.2 and 5.3 contain little new information, but they present important "facts" about language and, more particularly, the relationship between the standard variety and other varieties in visual form. Importantly, both figures acknowledge the nature of the socially related linguistic variation reflecting the diversity of our culture and its history in the view of reality that they put forth. Perhaps the most interesting observation to be made about these figures is their foreignness. Even though most readers of this article will have had courses about language and linguistics, even though they consider themselves teachers of language and literacy skills, they will likely find thinking about language in these ways, visualizing it in its social context, a new experience. For Keith, as a linguist, this fact is evidence that most of us who teach have not been encouraged or forced to think seriously or systematically about the nature of standard language or Standard English, in particular, or the possible relationships between the standard we teach and the varieties of language students bring to class with them.

At this point, readers may complain that they are not teaching a course about American dialects or Black English but trying to get students of all races and backgrounds to become better writers. Necessarily, however, writing teachers talk about language and its use a great deal of the time, and most of their comments on student papers represent efforts to persuade students to develop certain kinds of strategies for using written language in particular ways in particular contexts. All of this talk about writing is based on some sort of model— however implicit, however inchoate, however unexamined—of language and the relationship of the standard to other varieties. And the less accurate and less rich the model of language that informs a teacher's comments and commentary, the more likely his or her students will not reach everyone's goal: mastery of Standard English for use when it is appropriate. Talking about "correct" or "incorrect," for example, assumes one model of language; talking about "appropriate" and "inappropriate" in this or that context assumes a very different model. Over the years, Keith has discovered in his own teaching that replacing a model of language based on correctness with one based on appropriateness is a very challenging task because it forces him to think constantly about *why* a particular usage should be labeled inappropriate or appropriate in a given context. Marking things "wrong" is much simpler than thinking seriously about context and appropriateness, but the consequences of the former view—figure 5.1 and the practice such a view inspires—seem to be overwhelmingly negative. Certainly, if we, as writing teachers, talked about language as if diversity were an integral part of it—if we admitted that the standard language itself continues to change and that the notion of standard is itself problematic—we would have to move away from the view of language presented in figure 5.1, the view that we so easily (and naturally) fall back on unless we have spent a great deal of time examining our own assumptions and educating ourselves about the nature of language.

A potentially useful alternative approach to the view of language represented by figure 5.1 is represented by the work of R. B. Le Page and Andrée Tabouret-Keller, who spent over a decade looking at language and identity in several of the creole-speaking communities of Central America and the Caribbean. In accounting for how individuals make choices about language and identity, these researchers begin with the following hypothesis: "The individual creates for himself the patterns of his linguistic behaviour so as to resemble those of the group or groups with which from time to time he wishes to be identified or so as to be unlike those from whom he wishes to be distinguished" (181). In other words, linguistic choices made by individuals are acts of identity, ways of being in the world. Consequently, to ask or require individuals to change their language is to ask or require them to change their identity. Certainly, many of our students come to us expressly for tools that they believe will help them realize an identity they imagine for themselves. Yet, as Le Page and Tabouret-Keller acknowledge, not everyone is successful in his or her efforts to use language as do the members of the group(s) to which they wish to belong. In fact, Le Page and Tabouret-Keller attach four riders or conditions to their hypothesis:

> We can only behave according to the behavioural patterns of groups we find it desirable to identify with to the extent that:
> (1) we can identify the groups
> (2) we have both adequate access to the groups and ability to analyse their behavioural patterns
> (3) the motivation to join the groups is sufficiently powerful, and is either reinforced or reversed by feedback from the groups
> (4) we have the ability to modify our behaviour. (182)

Each of these riders plays a role in how language is used in school and in the choices that students are faced with. As the first rider notes, language users, in this case, students, must be able to identify the groups to which they belong. For middle-class students, this choice may seem moot, unless, like the middle-class African Americans at UT, they wish to be accepted in several groups simultaneously: ultimately, most of us do. The choices for students who are not middle class—those most likely to speak stigmatized social, regional, or ethnic dialects—is quite different. Through its focus on "correctness" and the eradication of "bad grammar" (i.e., regional, social, and ethnic varieties of American English), school has traditionally offered such students a forced choice between the language of the home community and the standard variety of the school rather than a "both/and" choice that would encourage the student to develop language skills appropriate for each context, a problem to which we will return when we discuss home literacy and language use.

Rider two notes that individuals must have access to the varieties of language they wish or need to master as well as the ability to analyze those varieties. As figure 5.3 demonstrates, students from a community where a stigmatized variety of American English is commonly used are likely to have far less access to Standard English in their daily, face-to-face interactions than are middle-class classmates. Le Page and Tabouret-Keller also acknowledge that individuals will differ in their ability to analyze and use the patterns of the variety that is not their native variety, in this case, Standard English. At least since the time of Mina Shaughnessy, teachers of writing have learned to think in terms of patterns of error rather than innumerable random mistakes. Such patterns of error result not from stupidity or laziness, but from misanalysis, and, as rider four might suggest, the ability to use a nonnative variety of any language consistently so as to internalize it varies from individual to individual.

Rider three is especially important for teachers, because it reminds them that their behavior can play a great role in providing feedback to and motivation for the student. Crucially, however, a major issue in this case becomes "Is the student motivated to become someone who uses language as I do, that is, someone like me?"[4] Teachers who hold attitudes about language like those represented in figure 5.1 are quite unlikely to be accepted as models worthy of emulation by students who speak natively a stigmatized social, regional, or ethnic dialect.

In this section, we have tried to outline productive ways of thinking about one of the major things that we teach—language and specifically the standard language. Rejecting the society's ideology about the nature of Standard English, we have provided alternative ways of representing the relationship between the standard variety and other varieties of English. These representations mesh nicely with the hypothesis and riders of Le Page and Tabouret-Keller, who see all uses of language as acts of identity and hence the task of the language user, throughout his or her lifetime, as matching language with context of use in an appropriate fashion so as to be granted membership in particular groups. For us, such a view of language and human behavior—one that attempts to describe what speakers and writers do as they use language strategically to create and maintain individual and group identities—is far more likely to help us value and appreciate linguistic diversity in its many forms than a view of language that *ab initio* labels some varieties and users of language deficient.

Diversity and Whom We Teach

At least since the time of Aristotle, teachers of rhetoric have taught their students that one persuades different audiences in different ways and that the successful rhetor knows a great deal about the characteristics of his or her listeners. As our student audience becomes increasingly diverse, we as writing teachers need to consider the possible axes of difference we may encounter in our classroom and our potential responses to these kinds of difference. In this section, we look at several axes of difference that our experience has led us to conclude influence the ways various segments of our increasingly diverse student population respond in the writing class. These variables include language and literacy practices of the home community, first language, age, sex or gender, and sexual orientation.

Home Literacies and Language Use

Although some thinkers like E. D. Hirsch, Jr., argue for a monolithic approach to issues of literacy, language, and knowledge (cf. Walters, "Whose Culture?"), we find such an approach seriously lacking when we consider the challenges we face in the classroom or the challenges our students face during their lives as they become part of an increasingly interdependent world economy. At the heart of this monolithic approach is the notion that only one kind of literacy—academic literacy—exists. In contrast, we argue that academic literacy is but one of many literacies, albeit a powerful and important one. Associated with this literacy (as with all others) is a particular belief system, which includes beliefs about how language—oral and written—should be learned and used. Even though the notion of academic literacy has been most closely associated with school literacy, it has also become the standard for judging literacy and language practices outside of school.

What has largely been ignored until recently is the fact that academic literacy is not universal but tied very closely to middle-class values and attitudes about language use. Our schools and, therefore, our classrooms perpetuate these values and attitudes. In a recent paper, "Writing in Education," Keith has linked ways of using spoken and written language in school contexts with what Scollon and Scollon label "essayist literacy," which "involves the ability to read and write material that is decontextualized, high in the proportion of new information to old information, and internally logical. The relation of the text to the situation is deemphasized and a reading 'public' or at least a partially unknown audience is assumed, and therefore both readership and authorship are fictionalized" ("Literacy as Focused Interaction" 26). Scollon and Scollon and others have contended that this notion of literacy is narrow and limited at least partly because it ignores as well as silences other kinds of literacies prevalent in non-mainstream, non-middle-class, and mostly non-white communities. Deborah Brandt (1990), for example, argues that "it is only middle-class children who can sustain themselves in their transition to school by clinging to language customs of family and community; this same process for others is called context-dependence, the dangerous source of certain failure" (109).

It is easy to see why schools in this culture and around the world succeed admirably in the task of educating children from middle-class backgrounds: they arrive at school bringing with them the very assumptions about using language and literacy that the school seeks to inculcate and most frequently rewards. The greater challenge—and one we have yet to meet in this country—involves those who arrive with expectations that are no less rational, no less systematic, no less grounded in social practice, but that differ from those assumed by the school. Thus far, however, schools have had little room for difference, preferring a pedagogy that has often guaranteed near exclusion for many of the very groups most in need of assistance.

One of the many ways to help us rethink our traditional ways of thinking about language and literacy is to consider work in such fields as anthropology, sociolinguistics, and education about linguistically and culturally diverse populations. Although a quick survey of a few of these studies provides teachers with information about the linguistic and cultural backgrounds of particular groups of students, it more importantly suggests the kinds of issues teachers might begin considering when thinking about issues of diversity in the classroom. Thus, examining studies on a variety of kinds of difference may be able to help us train ourselves to think about what dealing with difference might really mean. We begin with the topic of home literacy and language practices for several reasons.[5] First, it has received a great deal of attention in the research literature, and as the number of detailed descriptions of literacy, literate behavior, and conventions associated with the use of oral and written language across communities and cultures grows, our understanding of the nature of literacy deepens. Second, perhaps more than any other body of literature, these studies, because of their reliance on the ethnographic technique of "thick description," may cause us to reflect critically on our own practices, seeing them in their own cultural contexts.

Probably the best-known research in this tradition is Shirley Brice Heath's work, which has challenged many teachers to ask questions about the literacy and language practices in the home communities of their students. From Heath, we learn about functions and uses of literacy in three Piedmont Carolina communities in the late 1970s. Heath concludes that

> the patterns of language use of the children of Roadville [a blue-collar white community] and Trackton [a blue-collar black community] before they go to school stand in sharp contrast to each other and to those of the youngsters from [middle-class] townspeople families. Though parents in all three communities want to "get ahead," their constructions of the social activities the children must engage in for access to language, oral or written, vary greatly. The sequence of habits Trackton children develop in learning language, telling stories, making metaphors, and seeing patterns across items and events do not fit the developmental patterns of either linguistic or cognitive growth reported in the research literature on mainstream children. Roadville children, on the other hand, seem to have developed many of the cognitive and linguistic patterns equated with readiness for school, yet they seem not to move outward from these basics to the integrative types of skills necessary for sustained academic success. (343)

Like Heath, Scollon and Scollon also point out differences between a non-mainstream group's practices, the Athabaskan, a group of Native Americans, in Alaska, and mainstream practices. For example, as they grow up, Athabaskan children are taught not to take the initiative in speaking to a person they do not know. Scollon and Scollon note that "where the relationship of the communicants is unknown [in face-to-face interaction] . . . the Athabaskan prefer silence" (*Narrative* 53). Yet, in mainstream schools, these students are expected to write to an unknown audience on a consistent basis, a practice that conflicts with the norms governing interaction in their home community. Using examples like this one, Scollon and Scollon conclude that "where the interethnic communication patterns produce social conflict between [Athabaskan and non-Athabaskan] speakers, these same patterns produce internal conflict for an Athabaskan writer." Continuing, they contend that "it is this internal conflict that explains much of the problem of native literacy programs as well as problems with English literacy in the public school systems of Alaska and Canada" (53). The examples from the work of Heath and that of Scollon and Scollon should remind us of the potential for conflict between home community patterns for using language and literacy and those of the school. Although some students may be relatively successful in moving between the two, that success often comes at a great price as these students seek to create identities that will allow them to belong to the communities of both home and school. Traditionally, however, school has set up a false dichotomy, forcing non-mainstream students to choose one—the "correctness" of the school and its practices—or the other—the "ignorance" of native and natural ways of using language and literacy (Walters, "Whose Culture?").

Among the barriers we as teachers face in understanding, learning about, and then building upon the growing diversity in our classrooms is a lack of information about groups to which we do not natively belong. Important complicating factors are the myths and false information—which we often treat as fact—that we have about the practices of those who are different from the mainstream "ideal" student. For example, the ethnographic work of Denney Taylor and Catherine Dorsey-Gaines focuses on several poor black families of Shay Avenue in an urban New Jersey city. In their work, rather than finding the urban black families that do not value education—seemingly ubiquitous in television specials and newspaper special reports—we find families with strengths and weaknesses, doing the best they can to survive while providing educational opportunities for their children. Rather than seeing culturally deprived families in which there is no literacy, we find "active members in a print community in which literacy is used for a wide variety of social, technical, and aesthetic purposes, for a wide variety of audiences, and in a variety of situations" (200). In fact, the researchers remind their readers that the parallels between the Shay Avenue families and Heath's middle-class townspeople are in many respects "far more striking than the differences" (200). Yet, as the passage from Heath cited above makes unequivocally clear, the shared goal of families in many communities—ensuring a better life for their children—does not entail using spoken or written language in ways that the school expects, supports, encourages, or rewards. From our perspective, ethnographic research about the patterns of language and literacy use across communities can become the basis for building bridges between home communities and schools, a necessary step if educators are to move from being merely curious about linguistic and cultural diversity to using such diversity as a resource.[6]

Beverly's own research (Moss 1988), an ethnographically oriented study of literacy in African-American worship services in Chicago, grew out of her desire to build such bridges between the academic and home communities of African-American students. From her own experience, she knew that a great deal of literate behavior took place in black churches among the very people who were often labeled illiterate by schools and other institutions and that schools seemed to be unable to capitalize on the kinds of literacy and literate behavior used in black churches and black homes. In conducting her fieldwork, Beverly learned a great deal about the kinds of texts and literacy people are exposed to as they grow up in this community; she also observed that the nature of the major literacy events in this community differ markedly from that of the major literacy events in school. Additionally, although she found some literacy practices that are similar to those in the academy, the function and uses of these events and the values attached to those practices are complicated and probably unique to the African-American church. One of the more interesting and complex literate texts, for example, was the church bulletin. In most churches, bulletins include the order of service and a few church-related announcements. Generally, they are printed on two to three 8½-by-11-inch sheets folded in half to comprise four to six pages of information. In the largest church that Beverly observed, however, the Sunday bulletin averaged fifteen letter-sized pages with print on both the front and back of each sheet. In addition to the traditional order of worship and church-related announcements, the bulletin of this church also included advertisements for apartments and jobs, information about upcoming plays and concerts, and community-related news as well as statements, memos, and essays from the minister. The texts written by the minister covered a range of topics, but their general function was protest. For example, one memo called for a boycott of Colgate-Palmolive products because the company was marketing a new product, Sambo toothpaste, the name of which carried negative connotations for African Americans. Another piece stated the minister's position against apartheid and P. W. Botha. A third memo railed against a local Chicago politician.

Clearly, this text fulfills the traditional roles of church bulletins in that it provides information about the day's service and related announcements. We can safely assume that the creators of such a large bulletin believe that members of the congregation have certain kinds of literacy skills that lead them to do far more than merely receive information. In fact, the text is used to connect the congregation to the church community, the local African-American community, the city, the nation, and the world. It is also a text that introduces people to and engages them in political debates. It is sometimes a document of protest. Finally, this voluminous text, read from front to back by most congregants, signals to us that print literacy is an integral part of what has traditionally been mislabeled and reduced to an oral culture. Many of our African-American students have probably been exposed to this type of multifunctional literate text. Yet, because we know little about the language and literacy practices of students from home communities like these, we remain ignorant about this complex use of a written text, the skills they might bring to our classrooms, or the ways in which we might be able to build upon their knowledge and skills.[7]

If we understand that African-American churches have historically been the community institution that African Americans have looked to not only for spiritual guidance but also for information and for models of how to use language, then we begin to appreciate the influence of this institution on language use in the community. We can recognize that the participant structures—the interweaving of text and talk during the service, the dialogic quality of the sermon, the seamlessness of the service—are the norm for interaction in the African-American community. Yet, the behaviors that are appropriate in this community setting are usually anything but appropriate outside this setting, largely because outsiders know so little about what goes on in this community that they devalue its practices. Hence, a potential resource in the classroom is lost.

In our discussion of home language and literacy practices, we have sought to demonstrate that ways in which the culture the student brings to the classroom may have a profound influence on his or her behavior there. If we as teachers of writing are to do any more than scratch their heads and comment "Well, the problem must have something to do with the kid's background," that is, if we are to build any sorts of bridges between the kinds of knowledge about language and literacy students bring to the classroom and the expectations of the academy, a necessary first step is learning a great deal about those kinds of knowledge. Perhaps the best way to learn about those kinds of knowledge is to examine available ethnographic research on literacy across communities (e.g., Moss, *Literacy Across Communities*). Such research can provide important information about particular communities, but more important, it can help us as teachers develop a healthy respect for differences in this area and a useful perspective for considering the problems experienced by our own students.

First Language

Certainly, a major change in writing classrooms across the country over the last few decades has been the decrease in the number of classrooms made up uniquely of native speakers of English. Consequently, teachers, even those with extensive training and experience in teaching composition to native speakers, find themselves faced with new kinds of problems at many levels. Although a growing body of research deals with many of these issues, we have little understanding of the range of topics that are relevant. A tendency of many teachers is to belabor the point that speakers of certain languages have special problems with articles or the use of the perfect tenses. These code-related problems can, on the one hand, be dealt with through the help of an editor or native-speaker friend; on the other hand, research shows that certain patterns of error often become fossilized and can be corrected only with the greatest effort. Thus, although we do not wish to minimize the importance of mastering the code itself, we contend that many teachers fall prey to a developmental fallacy: the student must get the surface features of the code perfect before advancing to "larger" issues. From our perspective, focusing on patterns of fossilized errors may not be a teacher's or student's best use of time or energy. Consequently, our concerns here are those that relate to issues of rhetoric: how to develop and arrange arguments in order to persuade readers; how to select and organize material to support arguments; how to use logical, ethical, and pathetic appeals appropriately.

Those with experience in this field can attest that native signers of American Sign Language, Spanish-dominant Hispanics who have been reared in the United States, Nigerian students who have been educated largely in British and West African English, and North Africans schooled in Arabic and French who began to study English in high school share some problems when learning to write academic prose in English but differ dramatically in other respects. Certainly, native language matters a great deal; also of great importance, however, is the system of education in which one is trained, as well as the rhetorical tradition associated with that system of education and the language or languages it employs—factors often ignored, even in the literature on what is often termed cross-cultural rhetoric.[8]

Equally problematic in our efforts to understand the relevant issues has been the very poor understanding we have of how our own language, system of education, and rhetorical tradition interact, a point clearly related to our earlier discussion of home literacy and language practices. Particularly telling, but not at all uncharacteristic, is an example from an early (but often reprinted) study of cross-cultural rhetoric in which Robert Kaplan hypothesized about the preferred paragraph structure, which he unfortunately associated with "thought patterns," used by writers with various native languages.[9] The diagrams along with the immediately preceding and following sentences of text are reproduced in figure 5.4:

Superficially, the movement of the various paragraphs discussed above may be graphically represented in the following manner:

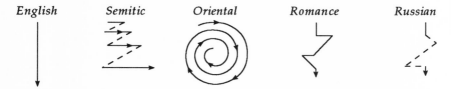

| English | Semitic | Oriental | Romance | Russian |

Much more detailed and more accurate descriptions are required before any meaningful contrastive system can be elaborated.

Figure 5.4. The "doodles" from Kaplan's original article on cross-cultural rhetoric and ESL composition (14–15).

Ostensibly, the diagrams, or "doodles" as they are sometimes called in the literature, represent the preferred paragraph structure of writers from different language backgrounds. When Keith presented this diagram to a group of Tunisian teachers of English, it was greeted with gales of laughter; one teacher commented, "We [i.e., speakers of Arabic] write in a straight line; it is you people who do all of those funny things." Here, again, we see evidence of the human tendency to believe that the ways of doing things that seem natural for us— whether we are concerned with organizing a paragraph, constructing a sentence, participating in a class discussion, or interpreting a text— are somehow the simplest or most natural. Anything that deviates from that way is to be seen as somehow deviant.

As the research cited in note 8 reminds readers, Kaplan's doodles are seriously flawed in significant and important ways, but his hypothesis—that writers from different cultural and linguistic backgrounds structure paragraphs differently—reflects a larger truth, namely, that individuals from different cultural and linguistic backgrounds do not necessarily share assumptions about how texts work. From his own study of Arabic, his experience teaching speakers of Arabic, and his reading of available research on the Arabic rhetorical tradition and the problems speakers of Arabic have when learning to write in English, Keith has learned some of the ways that Arabs and Americans are likely to differ when they construct, for example, an argumentative text. A native-speaker of Arabic reared in an Arab country and trained in the tradition of Arab rhetoric is likely to provide far more background information than an English-speaking American reared in the United States probably would. Often, the Arab will begin at a far more abstract level of generalization than the American is likely to. Keith remembers one Arab student's essay on families that began "All over the world and in many places, we find families." In addition to what seems to be the unnecessarily obvious generalization to the American academic reader, the pair of prepositional phrases in this opening sentence illustrates the extent to which repetition with variation is highly valued among speakers and writers of Arabic, at least partly because of the ways in which the morphology and semantics of the Arabic language interact, thereby providing linguistic resources simply not available to the English-language writer. Perhaps most important, however, might be the general notion that whereas persuasion in this country is ostensibly based on carefully amassing logical arguments for a position not already held by the hearer or reader, in the Arab tradition, persuasion is based on reminding the hearer or reader of some truth that he or she already shares with the speaker or writer, making way for a view of persuasion requiring logical, ethical, and pathetic appeals.[10]

Particularly important in discussions of these issues are the observations that cross-cultural and cross-linguistic differences exist and that they can create problems for members of either group who are trying to use the other language to persuade. For example, when Keith has attempted to write something in Arabic, he has had to work very hard to keep from falling back on what seemed like his perfectly good American strategies, which do not get him very far. What seemed like such an obvious, straight line to him was evaluated as being far too short and dotted by his Arab readers in much the same way that their English-language texts represent lines that are far too long, doubling back on themselves far too often. Thus, despite the inaccuracies it might contain, figure 5.4 reminds us that other cultures have conventionalized ways of selecting, organizing, and presenting information; even if we as researchers or classroom teachers have a very incomplete grasp of what those ways may be, we can begin to acknowledge the existence of differences and to realize that our preferred ways of structuring texts are themselves conventional, standing at the intersection of English as a linguistic system, the Western rhetorical tradition, the teaching of writing in American schools, and a host of other influences. Such a rethinking of our own position, such a decentering, reminds us again of the limitations of our own knowledge of our tradition and the traditions of others; it also demonstrates the need for models of teaching and learning based on mutual respect through collaboration and cooperation.

Age

In addition to the increase in the number of students from diverse ethnic backgrounds who will attend college in the coming years, the average age of students attending college will continue to rise, a tendency already clear in many schools. Consequently, no longer can we expect our first-year writing courses to be made up of eighteen- and nineteen-year-old students fresh out of high school. Our older students may include wives, husbands, single parents, military veterans, full-time workers, and part-timers of many sorts. These "nontraditional" older students bring life and work experiences into our classes that affect the way they value school and many of its practices. With these experiences come knowledge, expectations, and skills that we might not normally associate with the typical eighteen-year-old first-year student who may be away from home for the first time. Although we know of no research concerning the ways in which the presence of this population might affect the writing classroom, we know from personal experience that these students have different kinds of goals and different strategies for reaching them than their younger classmates. Beverly has noticed, for example, that older women returning to school often prefer to rely on their own life experiences and those of their friends rather than simply citing secondary sources when arguing a point. Beverly welcomes this source for authority and the concomitant personal narratives that are woven into otherwise academic papers, but she also recognizes that the academy traditionally values citations from scholarly works far more highly than it values narratives of personal experience. She has also observed that these older women's classmates are sometimes enthralled by the women's argumentative strategies; other times, however, they are baffled by them.

Similarly, as noted earlier, we, at least, find that many of these students are older than we are; consequently, patterns of face-to-face interaction shift as we find ourselves speaking with people who are our elders even though we may be their teachers and vested with the authority to evaluate their work and assign them grades. Additionally, for these students, responsibilities outside school often have to take priority over schoolwork. Recently, while Keith was working on this part of the essay, for example, a student in her fifties telephoned to say that her only sibling, a sister five years younger than she, had inoperable cancer; the student went on to say that she might be absent from class for several weeks. Similar tragedies also strike in the lives of traditional undergraduates, but they seem, to us, quite different in important ways. Consequently, we also believe that helping older students balance their schoolwork and personal lives will bring us new challenges. While we view the different perspectives that older students bring as resources, teaching them well will likely require that we rethink our notion of whom we teach and our assumptions about them. Having older students may ultimately affect our assignment-making, class discussions, and dynamics inside and outside the classroom just as having students from a variety of linguistic and ethnic backgrounds often does.

Sex/Gender

The last two decades have seen a great deal of research devoted to male and female differences in language use. With rare exception, researchers have assigned subject to categories according to biological sex (or, more accurately, apparent or reported biological sex), although their real interest has been gender, the complex set of cultural beliefs, norms, and behaviors associated with appropriate behavior for males and females or assumptions about the nature of masculinity and femininity. Even distinguishing between sex and gender in this fashion does not automatically make the relationship between sex, gender, and language transparent in any way. In "Language and Gender," Sally McConnell-Ginet, for example, distinguishes between (1) *gender deixis*, unknown in English but found in languages like Japanese in which males and females use different forms for the first-person pronoun, (2) *gender stereotypes* ("models 'of' "), (3) *gender norms* ("models 'for' "), and (4) *gender markers*, ways of using language associated with, but by no means exclusive to, members of one sex or the other (80–81). When researchers discuss sex- or gender-related patterns of language use in English, they are usually concerned with what McConnell-Ginet terms gender markers, although they often seem to rely heavily and unreflectively on gender stereotypes or gender norms, even in discussion and interpretation of empirical data.[11]

Among the most important findings to emerge from the research on sex- or gender-related patterns of language use in this society is the observation that males and females may well use language in different ways because they have different sorts of interactional goals (e.g., Tannen, *You Just Don't Understand*) and because they were socialized in different ways as children (e.g., Maltz and Borker). Male children tend to grow up playing in hierarchical groups, whereas female children seem to prefer to have a "best friend" who may change frequently. Researchers such as Penelope Eckert, who conducted ethnographic fieldwork in a Detroit high school as part of a study of linguistic variation and language change in progress, points out that the reputation of male adolescents seems to depend on what they do, but the reputation of female adolescents seems to depend on "the whole woman": "Girls in high school are more socially constrained than boys. Not only do they monitor their own behavior and that of others more closely, but they maintain more rigid social boundaries" ("The Whole Woman" 258).

Given these differences in life experience and perception of the self and the Other (as well as the self in contrast to the Other), should we be surprised that females and males might use language in different ways to different ends? Females, it appears, are often concerned with watching the group interaction and paying attention to both what is said and how it is said—the affective dimensions of the interaction. Borrowing Eckert's language, in general, females seem to monitor carefully the interactions in which they are involved in ways that most males do not. Based on these sorts of observations, Pamela Fishman has contended that most, if not all, of the "shitwork" in interactions falls to females. Males, on the other hand, appear to be less attuned to the affective aspects of messages. As Deborah Tannen ("Teachers' Classroom Strategies") points out, in class discussions, for example, males may feel it is their responsibility to contribute by speaking, even if they seem to dominate, whereas females may see their responsibility as being sure that they do not speak too often lest others not have the opportunity.

Not surprisingly, researchers investigating language and sex or gender frequently talk about issues of power. From this perspective, males often seem to believe it is their right to speak in most situations as often as they have what they consider an important contribution while females may not feel that way. In many contexts—classrooms, professional gatherings, and university meetings, for example—we have observed issues of language, sex or gender, and power interact. For historical reasons, the most senior group of participants in such gatherings and meetings, for example, is nearly all male; in contrast, the junior groups are more balanced in terms of sex. During most discussions, the senior group, which happens to be male, holds the floor for the majority of the time. Some junior members, mostly male, interject themselves into the discussion, but females—regardless of rank—hold the floor far less than one might predict based on the percentage of female participants alone. We contend that the members of the senior group, who are male, if interviewed, would state that anyone could claim the floor and speak. If, however, we interviewed members of the junior group or any of the women, we believe that although they might state that anyone could claim the floor, they would also acknowledge that they did not feel comfortable or able to do so. On occasion, we have observed moderators invite comment from the junior groups, the females, or other groups who had not, for whatever reason, spoken. Such attempts are sometimes greeted with grumblings of censorship from the senior males, but we believe the situation to be more complex: what we are all involved in is the complex interaction of language, sex or gender, and power to which, because of our own socialization, we may well be blind. Similar situations occur and recur in our classrooms.

In "Teachers' Classroom Strategies Should Recognize That Men and Women Use Language Differently," Tannen reminds university professors that such differences in using language have implications for what happens in the classroom. Professors who rely uniquely on one style of interaction should not be surprised to find that males or females as a group may be uncomfortable—or perhaps even alienated—by what occurs or fails to occur. Because large-group discussions are in many ways "public" forums, males may feel more comfortable contributing to them than females; similarly, males may be more comfortable than females with interactions that resemble debate or argument. Yet, as earlier research (Hall and Sandler as well as references cited in Kramerae et al.) reminds us, both male and female teachers tend to give male students more eye contact and verbal feedback than their female counterparts; similarly, teachers tend to reward uses of language that resemble "essayist literacy" as discussed above, practices that some have associated with male ways of using language (cf. Tannen's discussion of Ong's *Fighting for Life* in "Teachers' Classroom Strategies"). For example, one study demonstrated that even in a graduate seminar devoted to feminist approaches to the works of a female novelist and taught by an avowed feminist, the female professor attended to and reinforced the verbal comments and nonverbal behaviors of the male members of the class, even though they made up a small proportion of the class, far more than she did those of the female students (Lopez). Similarly, Keith was among the examiners for the oral examination of a bright female graduate student who nearly failed her exam, not because she did not know the material, but because she did not, as he puts it, "speak in paragraphs." Her interactional style was one that more or less resembled the ways of interacting some writers associate with women's communication. In other words, she did not seize and keep the floor, nor did she take combative positions. She did not lace her comments with frequent references to the research literature, which she obviously knew. Instead, she behaved as if the examiners and she were colleagues engaged in a friendly—rather than an academic—conversation in which everyone might be expected to speak a similar amount of time with no single person holding the floor for long periods of time.

Such studies and observations are sometimes seen as indictments of the particular teacher whose behavior is analyzed or evidence of a societal conspiracy to silence females or to eradicate certain styles of interaction. Yet, as researchers such as Tannen remind us, sex and gender interact with culturally influenced conversational style and individual personality in complex ways. Our point in discussing this body of research is to remind ourselves and our readers that sex or, perhaps more accurately, interactional styles traditionally associated with male and female socialization in this culture constitute one additional axis of diversity that is likely to manifest itself in the classroom. Related work such as that of Cynthia Selfe and Paul Meyer, on the one hand, and Elizabeth Flynn, on the other, on the behavior of female writers and readers reminds us again of how much we have to learn about the ways that sex and gender may influence the production or comprehension of written language.

Sexual Orientation

We know very little about the ways in which sexual orientation can be an issue in educational settings or more specifically writing classes. First, as Sarah Sloane, in "Invisible Diversity: Gay and Lesbian Students Writing Our Way into the Academy," reminds us, "the gay and lesbian community . . . comprises a unique minority because, to a large extent, members can choose whether or not to reveal their minority status." Because of societal homophobia and the fear it inspires in individual lesbians, gay males, and bisexuals, few should be surprised that many members of this group choose not to reveal their sexual orientation, especially when one considers the possible negative consequences of doing so. Additionally, we must acknowledge that there is little encouragement for students to be honest about these issues in the classroom. Certainly, any bisexual, lesbian, or gay student can attest to the absence of representation (except perhaps negative ones) of his or her life experience in the reading assigned for most courses. Keith remembers many courses he had as a student in which the fact that a particular writer was not a heterosexual went unacknowledged—even though, years later, he realized it could have a direct bearing on interpretations of the text. Gay, lesbian, or bisexual students can also quickly point out the assumed heterosexuality of classrooms: in choosing examples or relating past experiences, teachers and students nearly always assume when speaking that everyone present is heterosexual—to do otherwise is to open oneself to great suspicion or even censure. Yet teachers who have been influenced even marginally by reader-response or feminist theories of reading or by social constructionist epistemologies must logically acknowledge that because the life experiences of lesbian, bisexual, or gay students differ in significant ways from those of their strictly heterosexual classmates, their responses to the texts they are asked to read or construct may differ. Investigating these differences is made all the more complex because college represents a time when many students are first dealing with these issues for themselves and because various institutions of our society including the university are being challenged to rethink their public and private stances on these issues.

Despite these difficulties, we can point to the findings of some research and speculate about other potential areas of interest. Sloane interviewed several gay and lesbian students at a large Midwestern university. On the basis of her research, she reminds teachers that assignments in writing classes, especially highly personal writing assignments, can put lesbian and gay students in a difficult position, leading them to engage in what she terms "omission," the silencing of parts of experience that they fear may not be safe to reveal, and "transformation," which might include such strategies as "pronoun laundering" to disguise the sex of the participants involved in an event. Examples of such assignments might include garden-variety essay topics that require students to construct texts about trying to meet someone in a bar, about what they consider important in a marriage partner or the kind of family they wish to have, or about the most difficult problem they have in dealing with their parents or roommates. Deciding how to respond honestly to such assignments for gay, lesbian, and bisexual students is likely to be a different sort of choice than it is for heterosexual students, something that most professors probably have not considered.

Sloane, for example, discusses the case of a gay male student who simply quit attending a communications course because of a writing assignment he was given. His professor announced that everyone would be required to write an essay on a topic chosen by the class. Following a discussion, class members decided by majority vote to write about AIDS, despite this student's protestations. Because he could not sort out all of the private and public, emotional and intellectual issues surrounding the topic, he stopped going to class and failed the course. What, we might imagine, did the student see as his options: Reveal his sexual orientation and risk derision in class or perhaps violent retaliation outside of class? Keep quiet and pretend to be

heterosexual? Engage in or at least not speak out against the gay
bashing that so often accompanies discussions of AIDS? Sloane also
discusses the experiences of a lesbian student, making the interesting
observation that as the content of the student's texts increasingly
discussed issues relating to lesbianism, the professor's comments
moved from content to issues of form and correctness. Our goal in
discussing this issue is certainly not to label any subject matter off
limits. Rather, it is to remind readers that topics of discussion or
writing assignments may force students to make decisions we can
scarcely imagine and to remind them that because of society's attitudes
about the sexes, gender roles, and sexuality, the experiences of bisexuals, lesbians, and gay males as members of groups are not uniform—
although all share the fact that they are not heterosexual or at least
not uniquely so.[12] From one point of view, the problem does not lie
with particular topics or with gay, lesbian, or bisexual students; rather,
the source of the problem is a homophobic society that stigmatizes
the open acknowledgment of certain kinds of affection, relationships,
or commitments between human beings of the same sex.

Similarly, if teachers want bisexual, lesbian, or gay students in
their classrooms to feel comfortable talking about issues related to
their life experience—and we acknowledge that many teachers do
not—those who do will have to let these students know that it is safe
to do so. The best strategies here probably do not include announcing
to the class that these students may talk about "their issues"; rather,
it will likely involve including their issues in texts assigned or giving
hypothetical examples involving them. For example, in an undergraduate course that Keith taught about language in the African-American
community, one of a dozen or so possible topics included on a handout
about course projects including a topic about the language use of gay
and lesbian African Americans. One student in the class of thirty-five
chose to investigate language-use in the black gay community. As
time approached for oral class reports, he came to Keith very concerned about the repercussions of revealing the true topic of his project
and, by implication, his sexual orientation to his classmates. During
the report, he engaged in some omission and transformation—with
Keith's blessing. Depending on their assumptions about how issues
of sexual orientation should be addressed in the classroom, readers
may criticize Keith from any of a number of perspectives; at the time,
however, the agreement he and the student negotiated seemed to
represent the best of the apparent alternatives.

Even though the student was not comfortable making a completely honest oral report about his project, he was very glad that he had done the project and that he had had the opportunity to relate information from course material to his life experience. In fact, he has used the text as a writing sample in his application to graduate programs. The seeming contradictions of this student's behavior should serve to remind us as teachers of the complexity and the very individual, personal nature of dealing with issues surrounding sexual orientation.

In our discussion of whom we teach, we have considered a number of particular axes of difference for several reasons. First, we want to report on the ways in which we have come to see difference as important in our own teaching. Second, we wish to acknowledge the resources that we are aware of for those who grapple with these axes of difference in teaching diverse populations. Third, we hope that the paucity of literature on some topics will act as impetus for additional research. Finally, we trust that with a beginning such as this one, we can set into motion new dialogues about issues of difference, dialogues that will help us see the limitations of our own perspectives as we continue to examine our own practice. At the same time, we issue some very strong words of caution. Obviously, the easily labeled variables we have discussed do not show up in disembodied form in our classrooms. Instead, we teach individuals who may differ from their teacher along several of these axes at once. These variables are in no sense additive: to be a first-generation Asian-American lesbian is not to be merely "native language other than English + Asian-American + female + lesbian." It represents a particular way of being in the world—in this society at this time—that is similar to and different from the ways of being in the world of others who are different. Similarly, although understanding the cultural and linguistic backgrounds of our students provides teachers with great insight, we must constantly recognize that not all students from a particular cultural background are alike. Not all African Americans are alike. Not all women or Native Americans are alike. Not all bisexual, lesbian, or gay students are alike just as not all straight white males—dead or alive—are alike. Assuming that we should treat all members of a particular group the same is just as dangerous as not recognizing the differences between groups. As the example of Keith and his African-American student who worked on the issue of gay language reminds us, teachers and students who are similar in some way because society has labeled them different will often negotiate their response to such labeling in complex, contrasting ways.

Many times what emerges from efforts to deal with diversity is a well meaning but, we believe, errant notion that recognizing and building upon diversity means developing separate pedagogies for each group—the "right" way to teach African-American students, Native Americans, women, and so on. We find such a move troubling. For example, following the work of Sarah Michaels on what she has characterized as ethnic differences in narrative style, many educators seem now tempted to assume that all (and only) African-American children use a topic-associative discourse style and that all (and only) white children use a topic-centered discourse style. We fear the day may have already arrived when students in education programs are given charts contrasting these two ways of constructing and using narratives with one column labeled black and the other labeled white. If so, the black or white child coming into a classroom for the first time will not be an individual; instead, regardless of social class background or prior life or school experience, he or she will be labeled "topic associator" or a "topic centerer" before uttering a word. For us, the desire or need to put students into fixed categories or to lock them into our neat little boxes based on ethnicity, sex, age, first language, sexual orientation, or some other sociodemographic variable is as irresponsible as denying that diversity exists in our classrooms.

Diversity and Who We Are: Rethinking Authority in Our Classrooms

Thus far, we have concentrated on diversity among students, who they are, what they know, and what they bring to the classroom. Yet, no discussion of diversity would be complete without a consideration of the teacher, who, we contend, is always more than simply a conduit of information. Every teacher who reads this text is an individual of a particular social class, age, sex, sexual orientation, and ethnic and social background. It is our belief that these axes of difference matter in the classroom and that they influence how all of us have learned and how we now teach in ways we can probably never understand. When we seek to understand the significance of these kinds of difference, we find ourselves confronting issues of authority, its origin, and its manifestations in the classroom.

Sometimes, the significance of one or more of these axes of difference in relation to authority is both evident and salient. Most of us, for example, would be surprised to find a male teaching a course entitled "Introduction to Women's Studies," a reaction that should remind us of our assumptions about who is most likely or most suited to teach certain subjects. When, for example, Keith began teaching an undergraduate course about the structure, history, and use of Black English, he was immediately faced with issues of authority. A few minutes into the course on the first day of class the first time he taught the course, a Hispanic female asked about his "background." Certain facts—that he is a sociolinguist familiar with the relevant research literature, that he had grown up in the South and taught in sub–Saharan Africa, that he had worked with many African-American students—were not obvious in the way that his ethnicity is.

Before the course began and even now as he continues to teach the course, he is concerned about students' reaction to the fact that he is not African-American; from the audible gasps when he walks into the classroom on the first day of the semester, he realizes that at least some of his students are surprised by his ethnicity. Although some might argue that Keith's worries are a misplaced waste of time, he believes he needs to acknowledge openly in class that many of the students in the class have had far more direct, varied, and prolonged experience in African-American speech communities than he has. He thinks that he has little or no right to talk about what it is like to live in such a community, and he certainly knows that he cannot play the dozens or signify. Consequently, he finds that he spends some time considering what he can and cannot offer his students, what the limits of his knowledge and experience are, and how he can find ways of teaching that might build on the knowledge and experience that he and all of the students—African Americans, Hispanics, and Anglos (as the world has traditionally been divided in Texas)—bring to the classroom.

The course, described in some respects in "Language as Social Fabric: Ties That Bind and Separate" (AFR320/LIN325), includes developing ways of interacting in class that seem native to no one but comfortable, perhaps, for everyone. Keith has noticed that at some point in the semester, usually about halfway through as the course content shifts from the linguistic structure of Black English to its use in African-American speech communities, the nature of classroom interaction shifts as well. Students begin speaking up more often in class, often without raising their hands, and rather than responding to the teacher, they may respond to one another. In other words, the role of the teacher has shifted from dispenser of knowledge to manager or facilitator of discussion among students with very different life experiences and often very different responses to assigned readings. What becomes important is far more than merely negotiating who knows what; it also includes how students and teacher draw on their knowledge and contribute in different ways to class discussion. One of the tasks for all involved is learning how to talk about subjects that have traditionally not been part of the curriculum and drawing on kinds of knowledge often ignored in the process of formal education, wedding knowledge gained from everyday life to the ideas and theories of scholars in the field.

Certainly, Beverly faces different issues than does Keith. Almost every time that she walks into an undergraduate English course (other than one with "African-American" in the title), students are surprised to see her, an African-American woman, stand before the class. Because she teaches at a university that attracts large numbers of white students from rural or suburban areas, many of her students, especially the first-quarter freshmen, have never had or even seen an African-American teacher. Most of what they know or think they know about African Americans comes from the media, and much of that is negative. Once many of these students get over the shock of finding out that she is the professor, many of them start to question her authority. She is asked many times if she has a PhD, where she went to school, and how old she is. And often she is challenged by students in ways that she doubts a white male or even a white female would be.[13] She remembers the day that someone observed her Freshman Honors Composition class and commented afterwards that the all white class seemed uncomfortable with a black teacher. She also recalls that in one of the evaluations of an introductory literature and composition class, a student complained that Beverly had focused too much on "that minority literature" when less than twenty percent of the writers read in the course were people of color, a percentage Beverly sees as low when one considers the demographics of the English-speaking world. She wonders if the student would have complained about the syllabus had the teacher not been a woman of color. Many times when Beverly attempts to design a class in which she and the students negotiate or share authority, the students never perceive her as having any authority to begin with. She sees part of her task as teacher as helping students see that her being an African-American woman adds a positive dimension to their classroom experience as their presence contributes to her life experience. Yet she knows that students must be educated to rethink their views on diversity in the classroom (including diversity in front of the class) in the same way that teachers must be.

When an American of British heritage teaches a course about Black English, issues of power and authority quickly come to the fore. When an African-American woman or other people of color teach anything other than Black English or African-American literature, issues of power and authority quickly come to the fore. We contend, however, that these issues are inherent in all acts of teaching and learning and that they manifest themselves in myriad ways in all classrooms. We likewise believe that all of us need to continue thinking about these issues with respect to the teaching we do. At the same time, we do not believe we can or should tell others how to negotiate issues of authority in their classrooms. We can only point to our current understanding of our experiences, share what we think we have learned from them, and challenge others to do the same.

Traditionally, the notion of teaching culturally and linguistically diverse populations within one institution, one classroom, has often resulted in the question, "What am I supposed to do with them?" (The "them," of course, refers to those who have not been represented in large numbers in our university writing classes, and the "I" is someone whose ancestors hail most recently from Europe.) This panicked approach has traditionally been dealt with by the scholarly community through a growing numbers of conferences and publications (much like this one) on the topic. A similar attitude prevailed in the 1960s, when the advent of open admissions served as impetus for such work as Shaughnessy's *Errors and Expectations* and sometime later David Bartholomae's "Inventing the University." What this body of scholarship and most of our teaching experience have encouraged us to do is to rethink our definition of "student." We now acknowledge that there is no monolithic student; there are students who come to the classroom from various communities and bring with them much of the baggage, positive and negative, of those communities as well as their own individual idiosyncracies and agendas. They also bring into the classroom their own discourse patterns, reflecting community values and worldviews. Sometimes these patterns and values match those of the teacher and others in the academic institutions; sometimes they do not. The mismatches and the ways in which teachers and those who design curricula respond to them call attention to how sensitive or insensitive we are to issues of linguistic and cultural diversity. Because we have operated for so long with an "ideal student" mentality that has not only failed to acknowledge difference but also been philosophically and ideologically opposed to building upon whatever difference might have grudgingly been acknowledged, reeducating ourselves to serve our diverse student populations represents a major task.

It is easy to see why we as teachers, even teachers of writing, have long wished to ignore diversity. Acknowledging difference, examining it, and finding creative ways to build upon it—to make it the cornerstone of individual and corporate philosophies of educational theory and classroom practice—require that we see ourselves, our beliefs, and even our actions, from a new perspective, one that forces us, as Clifford Geertz has put it, to see ourselves among others. Our preferred way of using language and of being literate becomes a way among ways rather than the single, correct way; it is appropriate in some contexts and useless in others. What seem like natural or logical ways of presenting information or evaluating knowledge no longer stand alone as the only possible alternatives or even the most expedient ones.

In *On Christian Doctrine*, a major work on teaching in the Western rhetorical canon, Saint Augustine, writing about the treatment of the Scriptures, reminds us of two things all effective teachers must have: "a way of discovering those things which are to be understood and a way of teaching what [they] have learned" (7). In this essay, we have tried to point to ways in which we personally have been challenged as we seek to discover a way of teaching what we have learned when we acknowledge and attempt to build upon the diversity we believe to exist in all classrooms. We have come to realize that dealing with diversity in these ways has led us to change not only how we teach but also our understanding of what constitutes "those things which are to be understood" in the first place. Throughout this process, we find ourselves having to rethink—that is, renegotiate—our authority and, consequently, our role and our practice in the classroom and in the larger professional arena. We have come to see these sites as places where we should assume far less common ground than we traditionally have and where we realize we probably have more to learn than we do to teach or at least a great deal to learn as we teach. These are lessons all good teachers have no doubt known since long before the time of Augustine. The need to relearn them and to think about them in new and deeper ways constitutes, we believe, a challenge of tremendous proportion, one that, if met, has the potential of changing what it means to teach and learn in this society in important, positive ways. Augustine also warns readers against "those who boast when they have learned the rules of valid inference as if they had learned the truth of propositions" (70). We trust we have followed the rules of valid inference. We profess to know little about the truth of propositions.

Notes

1. We use "conversation" metaphorically to include, as implied above, a variety of teacher/student interactions ranging from classroom lectures during which a teacher may speak to a group of students, receiving little direct verbal feedback, to conversations between student and teacher on the telephone or in the office to electronic exchanges between two or more parties, one of whom is the teacher. To varying degrees, all of these kinds of interactions are based on patterns associated with face-to-face two-party conversations; as the literature on language in the classroom reminds us, these categories of interactions also differ crucially from one another and from "everyday conversation" in ways that are not at all transparent.

2. Michaels's work clearly shows that the black students are quite aware of the differences between their narrative style and that of the teacher. In "Deena's Story: The Discourse of the Other," Beth Daniell argues that Deena's refusal to adopt the teacher's preferred strategies lest she forfeit her own identity and autonomy constitutes an act of resistance. Deena's refusal can also be read in light of the work of Le Page and Tabouret-Keller, described later in this essay.

3. For information on the situation in Britain, see the works of Dick Leith and Peter Trudgill. For information on Australia, see Barbara Horvath's research. As figure 5.2 indicates, the idea for representing the relationship between standard varieties and other varieties of English within an English-speaking country comes from Trudgill.

4. As ethnographic research on high schools (e.g., Penelope Eckert's *Jocks and Burnouts*) and universities (e.g., Michael Moffatt's *Coming of Age in New Jersey*) reminds us, far more is at stake than providing a model of "correctness." In fact, Eckert's study makes clear that many students will define themselves in opposition to the norms of the educational institution so as to rebel or create a sense of individuality. Not surprisingly, language is a common medium of resistance, as discussed in note 2.

5. Following practice in this body of literature, we use the term *home* to include not merely the house in which a child grows up but the communities of which he or she is a member. Consequently, when writing about home literacy or literacy in the home community (in constrast to literacy practices at school), a researcher might describe the uses of reading and writing in such varied contexts as a particular home, formal institutions such as the church or organizations like Boy Scouts or Girl Scouts, and informal, spontaneous organizations such as short-lived, same-sex neighborhood "clubs" that elementary-aged children often create for themselves.

6. For an especially interesting exchange on the possible limits of ethnographic research in effecting educational change, see the paper by Cazden ("Can Ethnographic Research Go Beyond the Status Quo?"), Kleinfeld's response ("First Do No Harm"), and the comments on this exchange by Amsbury, Barnhardt, Bishop, Chandler, Greenbaum and Greenbaum, Grubis, Harrison, and Stearns as well as the final statements of Kleinfeld ("Some of My Best Friends") and Cazden ("Response").

7. Valerie Balester's unpublished dissertation examines some of the ways in which the rhetorical practices of the African-American community and especially the African-American church influence the writing of students familiar with these traditions.

8. For recent research on this subject, see Arndt, Kroll (especially the articles by Silva, Krapels, Hamp-Lyons, Eisterhold, and Friedlander), and Leki as well as a forthcoming volume edited by Butler, Guerra, and Severino.

9. For a recent review of the complex issues involved in thinking about the relationship between thought and language, see the essay by Hill; on the not-so-hidden assumptions about the relationship between language, logic, and literacy that permeate much thinking in this culture, see Walters's essays ("Language, Logic, and Literacy" and "Whose Culture? Whose Literacy?").

10. Of course, exceptions to this generalization are plentiful. Advertising in this country rarely focuses uniquely on logical appeals alone; in fact, Keith would contend that an interesting part of Western rhetoric (or at least Western rhetoric as instantiated in most freshman texts) is its pretending that only logical appeals matter. In some ways, the task of the Arab rhetor might be compared to that of many Christian ministers, especially Fundamentalist ones, who, even in their efforts to save souls, often do so by reminding the lost ones of the Truth that, at some level, they are assumed already to know. Many of these issues are treated in a book by Barbara Johnstone and an unpublished manuscript by Keith ("On Written Persuasive Discourse").

11. A major intellectual problem for this field of research—like all fields involving axes of difference—is determining the extent to which its findings represent actual accounts or explanations of phenomena rather than reifications of cultural categories, stereotypes, or norms.

12. Likewise, as teachers who raise any of a number of topics—racism,

sexism, classism, homophobia—know, the consequences of attempting to deal with these topics raises new sets of questions that our training or experiences have left us poorly equipped to think through or evaluate. Many of us can relate stories about attempts—ours or those of colleagues—that have not gone as we had hoped; at the same time, we feel compelled to seek ways of openly incorporating these issues into course material rather than allowing them to remain palpably hidden.

13. Interestingly, in his course about Black English, Keith wonders if his students—African-American and non-African-American—do not question the data he presents in class (often from published research) in ways they might not if he were black.

Works Cited

AFR 320/LN 325. "Language as Social Fabric: Ties That Bind and Separate." *Writing Instructor* 10.3 (1991): 149–58.

Amsbury, Clifton. "The Problem of Simplicity." *Anthropology and Education Quarterly* 15 (1984): 168–69.

Arndt, Valerie. "Six Writers in Search of Texts: A Protocol-Based Study of L1 and L2 Writing." *ELT Journal* 41 (1987): 257–67.

Augustine, Saint. *On Christian Doctrine.* Trans. D. W. Robertson, Jr. Indianapolis: Bobbs-Merrill, 1978.

Balester, Valerie M. "The Social Construction of *Ethos*: A Study of the Spoken and Written Discourse of Two Black College Students." Diss. U of Texas at Austin, 1989.

Barnhardt, Ray. "Anthropology Needs No Apology." *Anthropology and Education Quarterly* 15 (1984): 179–80.

Bartholomae, David. "Inventing the University." *When a Writer Can't Write.* Ed. Mike Rose. New York: Guildford, 1985. 134–65.

Baugh, John. *Black Street Speech: Its History, Structure, and Survival.* Austin: U of Texas P, 1983.

Bishop, Ralph J. "Educational Failure and the Status Quo." *Anthropology and Education Quarterly* 15 (1984): 167–68.

Brandt, Deborah. *Literacy as Involvement: The Acts of Writers, Readers, and Texts.* Carbondale: Southern Illinois UP, 1990.

Butler, Johnnella E., Juan Guerra, and Carol Severino, eds. *Writing in Multicultural Settings.* New York: MLA, in preparation.

Cazden, Courtney. "Can Ethnographic Research Go Beyond the Status Quo?" *Anthropology and Education Quarterly* 14 (1983): 33–41.

———. "Response." *Anthropology and Education Quarterly* 15 (1984): 184–85.

Chandler, Joan M. "Education Equals Change." *Anthropology and Education Quarterly* 15 (1984): 176–78.

Daniell, Beth. "Deena's Story: The Discourse of the Other." *Gender, Composi-*

tion, and the Academy. Ed. Deborah H. Holdstein. New York: MLA, in press.

Eckert, Penelope. *Jocks and Burnouts: Social Categories and Identity in the High School.* New York: Teachers College Press, 1989.

——. "The Whole Woman: Sex and Gender Differences in Variation." *Language Variation and Change* 1 (1989): 245–67.

Eisterhold, Joan Carson. "Reading-Writing Connections: Toward a Description for Second Language Learners." Kroll 88–101.

Fishman, Pamela M. "Interaction: The Work Women Do." Thorne, Kramerae, and Henley 89–101.

Flynn, Elizabeth. "Gender and Reading." *Gender and Reading: Essays on Readers, Texts, and Contexts.* Ed. Elizabeth Flynn and Patrocinio Schwieckart. Baltimore: Johns Hopkins UP, 1986. 267–88.

Freeman, Sarah, ed. *The Acquisition of Written Language: Revision and Response.* Norwood, NJ: Ablex.

Friedlander, Alexander. "Composing in English: Effects of a First Language on Writing in English as a Second Language." Kroll 109–25.

Geertz, Clifford. *Local Knowledge: Further Essays in the Interpretive Anthropology,* New York: Basic Books, 1983.

Greenbaum, Susan D., and Paul E. Greenbaum. "Integrating Ethnographic and Quantitative Research: A Reply to Kleinfield with Implications for American Indian Self-Determination." *Anthropology and Education Quarterly* 15 (1984): 171–73.

Grubis, Steve. "A Teacher Perspective." *Anthropology and Education Quarterly* 15 (1984): 178–79.

Hall, Roberta M., and Bernice R. Sandler. "A Chilly Climate in the Classroom." *Beyond Sex Roles.* 2nd ed. Ed. Alice G. Sargent. St. Paul, MN: West Publishing, 1985. 503–10.

Hamp-Lyons, Liz. "Second Language Writing: Assessment Issues." Kroll 69–87.

Harrison, Barbara. "Training for Cross-Cultural Teaching." *Anthropology and Education Quarterly* 15 (1984): 169–70.

Heath, Shirley Brice. *Ways with Words: Language, Life and Work in Communities and Classrooms.* Cambridge: Cambridge UP, 1983.

Hill, Jane. "Language, Culture, and World View." Newmeyer 14–36.

Hirsh, E. D., Jr., *Cultural Literacy: What Every American Needs to Know.* Boston: Houghton, 1987.

Horvath, Barbara. *Variation in Australian English: The Sociolects of Sydney.* Cambridge: Cambridge UP, 1985.

Hymes, Dell. "Models of the Interaction of Language and Social Life." *Directions in Socio-Linguistics: The Ethnography of Communication.* Ed. John G. Gumperz and Dell Hymes. New York: Hold, 1972. 35–71.

Janda, Mary Ann. "Collaboration in a Traditional Classroom Environment." *Written Communication* 7 (1990): 291–315.

Johnstone, Barbara. *Repetition in Arabic Discourse: Paradigms, Syntagms, and the Ecology of Language*. Amsterdam: John Benjamins, 1991.

Kaplan, Robert. "Cultural Thought Patterns in Intercultural Education." *Language Learning* 16, 1–2 (1966):1–20.

Kleinfeld, Judith. "First Do No Harm: A Reply to Courtney Cazden." *Anthropology and Education Quarterly* 14 (1983): 282–87.

———. "Some of My Best Friends Are Anthropologists." *Anthropology and Education Quarterly* 15 (1984): 180–84.

Kramerae, Cheris, Barrie Thorne, and Nancy Henley. "Sex Similarities and Differences in Language, Speech, and Nonverbal Communication: An Annotated Bibliography." Thorne, Kramerae, and Henley 151–331.

Krapels, Alexandra Rowe. "An Overview of Second Language Writing Process Research." Kroll 37–56.

Kroll, Barbara, ed. *Second Language Writing: Resource Insights from the Classroom*. Cambridge: Cambridge UP, 1990.

Leith, Dick. *A Social History of English*. London: Routledge and Kegan Paul, 1982.

Leki, Ilona. "Twenty-Five Years of Contrastive Rhetoric: Text Analysis and Writing Pedagogies." *TESOL Quarterly* 25 (1991): 123–44.

Le Page, R. B., and Andrée Tabouret-Keller. *Acts of Identity: Creole-Based Approaches to Language and Ethnicity*. Cambridge: Cambridge UP, 1985.

Lopez, Veronica. " 'Can We Talk Now, or Is This a Good Time?': A Cross-Sex Conversation Analysis in the Feminist Classroom." Unpublished paper, Ohio State University, Columbus, 1989.

McConnell-Ginet, Sally. "Language and Gender." Newmeyer 75–99.

Maltz, Daniel, and Ruth Borker. "A Cultural Approach to Male-Female Miscommunication." *Language and Social Identity*. Ed. John J. Gumperz. Cambridge: Cambridge UP, 1982. 196–216.

Mehan, Hugh. "The Competent Student." *Working Paper #69*. Austin, TX: Southwest Educational Development Laboratory, 1979.

Michaels, Sarah. "Sharing Time: Children's Narrative Styles and Differential Access to Literacy." *Language in Society*. 10 (1981): 423–42.

Moffatt, Michael. *Coming of Age in New Jersey: College and American Culture*. New Brunswick, NJ: Rutgers UP, 1989.

Moss, Beverly J. "The Black Sermon as a Literacy Event." Diss. U of Illinois at Chicago, 1988.

———. ed. *Literacy Across Communities*. Cresskill, NJ: Hampton Press, in press.

Newmeyer, Frederick, ed. *Language: The Socio-Cultural Matrix*. Vol. 4 of *Linguistics: The Cambridge Survey*. Cambridge: Cambridge UP, 1988.

184 *Beverly J. Moss and Keith Walters*

Ong, Walter. *Fighting for Life: Contest, Sexuality, and Consciousness*. Ithaca, NY: Cornell UP, 1981.

The Oprah Winfrey Show, Exec. prod. Debra DiMaio. Dir. Jim McPharlin. With Bernadette Anderson, Ronnie Carter, Gary D., Thomas Kochman, Geneva Smitherman, and Bonnie Thompson. NBC. WXAN, Austin, TX. 19 Nov. 1987.

Philips, Susan U. *The Invisible Culture: Communication in Classroom and Community on the Warm Springs Indian Reservation*. New York: Longman, 1983.

Scollon, Ron, and Suzanne B. K. Scollon. "Literacy as Focused Interaction." *Quarterly Newsletter of the Laboratory of Comparative Human Cognition*. 2.2 (1986): 26–29.

———. *Narrative, Literacy and Face in Interethnic Communication*. Norwood, NJ: Ablex, 1981.

Selfe, Cynthia, and Paul Meyer. "Testing Claims for On-Line Conferences." *Written Communication* 8 (1991): 163–92.

Shaughnessy, Mina. *Errors and Expectations*. New York: Oxford UP, 1977.

Silva, Tony. "Second Language Composition Instruction: Developments, Issues, and Directions in ESL." Kroll 11–23.

Sloane, Sarah. "Invisible Diversity: Gay and Lesbian Students Writing Our Way into the Academy." *Writing Ourselves into the Story*. Ed. Laura Fontaine and Susan Hunter. Southern Illinois UP, in press.

Smith, Frank. Introduction. *Awakening to Literacy*. Ed. Hillel Goelman, Antoinette Oberg, and Frank Smith. Exeter: Heinemann, 1984. v–xv.

Sperling, Melanie. "Dialogues of Deliberation: Conversation in the Teacher-Student Writing Conference." *Written Communication* 8 (1991): 131–62.

Stearns, Robert D. "Beyond an Emic View of Anthropologists and Anthropology: An Alaskan Perspective." *Anthropology and Education Quarterly* 15 (1984): 174–76.

Students' Right to Their Own Language. Urbana, IL: NCTE, 1976.

Tannen, Deborah. "Teachers' Classroom Strategies Should Recognize That Men and Women Use Language Differently." *Chronicle of Higher Education* 19 June 1991: B1, B3.

———. *You Just Don't Understand: Women and Men in Conversation*. New York: Morrow, 1990.

Taylor, Denney, and Catherine Dorsey-Gaines. *Growing Up Literate*. Portsmouth, NH: Heinemann-Boynton/Cook, 1990.

Thorne, Barrie, Cheris Kramerae, and Nancy Henley, eds. *Language, Gender and Society*. Cambridge, MA: Newbury, 1975.

Trudgill, Peter. "Stnadard and Non-Standard Dialects of English in the United Kingdom: Attitudes and Policies." *On Dialect: Social and Geographical Perspectives*. New York: New York UP, 1983. 186–200.

Walters, Keith. " 'It's Like Playing Password, Right?': Socratic Questioning and Questioning at School." *Texas Linguistics Forum* 24 (1984): 157–88.

———. "Language, Logic, and Literacy." *The Right to Literacy*. Ed. Andrea A. Lunsford, Helene Moglen, and James Slevin. New York: MLA, 1990. 173–88.

———. "On Written Persuasive Discourse in Arabic and English." Unpublished essay, University of Texas at Austin, 1987.

———. "Whose Culture? Whose Literacy?" *Diversity as Resource in the Classroom: Redefining Cultural Literacy*. Ed. Denise Murray. Alexandria, VA: TESOL, in press.

———. "Writing in Education." *Writing and Its Uses/Schrift and Schriftlichkeit*. Ed. Harmut Gunther and Otto Ludwig. Berlin: Walter de Gruyter, in press.

6

The Education of At-Risk Students

Sally Hampton

Most Americans are aware that our schools often have relatively little success in educating students who are poor, members of racial/ethnic minorities, and/or speakers of a first language other than English. Although some of these students live in rural areas, most of them live in the inner cities. School people have many different labels for this group of students. All the labels have the potential for being offensive and insensitive and for shaping a reductive view of the situation that is probably part of the problem, including *at-risk*, the label I will use in this chapter to describe students who are not expected to succeed academically.

Many people assume that at-risk students will not be successful academically because of those very factors that serve to classify them at-risk, reasoning that for "these kids" life is so hard that it is no wonder they don't do well in school. Studies coming from today's classrooms, however, including teacher-researcher studies, offer convincing evidence that in classrooms where teachers are willing to depart from the conventional wisdom about at-risk learners, students struggling with poverty, violence, and other realities of contemporary life can, in fact, succeed academically. Consequently, it seems likely that obstacles to school success for at-risk students are not rooted in factors existing out of school but, rather, in the conventional wisdom governing most at-risk schooling. It seems, further, that programs established to empower those students most in need of help have actually denied them access to the development of literate behaviors that underlie success in all academic areas. In other words, this country's schools and most of the programs designed to help at-risk youth present almost impenetrable barriers to their success.

Studies in cognitive psychology contend that the conventional wisdom governing at-risk education reflects a vision of teaching and learning that today is largely discredited for mainstream learners. Yet this vision still governs the education of at-risk learners both because it has been institutionalized and because, even where it has been challenged, there are beliefs—often tacitly held—that at-risk children need something different if they are to succeed as readers and writers.

We are not likely to improve the chances of at-risk students to succeed academically until we examine the assumptions we currently hold about their needs and abilities, consider how those assumptions led to flawed educational practices, and enact new practices and assessment procedures based on what we know about what works and what does not work.

Current Practice, Current Assumptions

In its effort to educate at-risk students, the American school system has built its programs around research that grew out of the compensatory education movement, that educational effort designed to make up for things that some children (poor/minority children) do not have but that the school assumes most children should have. This research, most of it done during the 1960s and 1970s, suggests that poor students lack the drive and motivation of the middle class; are not learning oriented; have difficulty using Standard English to express feelings and ideas; and speak a restricted language that leaves them less able to handle abstractions and complex conceptualizations than middle-class students.

Other studies done during this same period report that the poor are concrete rather than abstract thinkers; depend on real-life rather than symbolic experience; speak non–Standard English; are impatient listeners; prefer quick gratification; have low self-esteem; and are angry and mistrustful of mainstream people. It is important to point out that this research concentrates exclusively on what poor/minority children do *not* know and how these deficiencies influence their performance in school. In short, what the research says is that poor/minority students are ill-suited to the kinds of knowing and ways of displaying knowledge that schools require, especially when schools are organized around traditional guidelines.

These research findings of the 1960s and 1970s have led to the development of a curriculum designed to remedy "deficits" in non-mainstream students, rather than deficits in the ways schools structure learning. Rexford Brown tells us that the curriculum based on this research favors a low-level, atomized, concrete approach to developing basic skills, an approach both highly reductive and artificial. The at-risk curriculum, according to Brown, has been "stripped of richness and context and made fundamentally meaningless, which is to say unabsorbable by normal people, except through memorization, whose effects last only for a few hours or days" (140).

A number of scholars point out that undergirding the at-risk curriculum is a range of assumptions, none of which stands up to careful analysis. Michael Knapp and Brenda Turnbull, in *Better Schooling for the Children of Poverty: Alternatives to Conventional Wisdom*, list the following as the basis for the at-risk curriculum:

- At-risk students begin schooling with serious deficiencies in language, knowledge, and skills which arise out of a disadvantaged background; therefore, emphasis should be placed on what the learner does not know and at-risk students' learning should be defined by low expectations;
- Learning proceeds from simple to complex, from concrete to abstract; therefore, the curriculum should be focused—at least initially—on development of certain discrete basic skills;
- The most efficient form of instruction is needed to help at-risk students master basic skills; therefore, instruction should be teacher-centered, direct instruction;
- It is essential to make the most efficient use of time and to control any and all discipline problems [slow learners may be disruptive because they will be frustrated with academic learning experiences]; therefore, classroom management should be rigid and should emphasize specific student behaviors; and
- In the interest of efficiency and for [teachers'] convenience, students should be grouped according to ability or achievement.

Each of these assumptions has created a view of instruction for at-risk learners; and instructional practice, once institutionalized, is rarely questioned. To the extent that the assumptions underlying at-risk programs go unexamined, they become increasingly more difficult to change. Instead, they are reinforced and reconfirmed in the next generation of programs that they inspire.

Let us examine each of these assumptions in turn.

Student Deficiencies

One might assume that the notion that certain students begin school with a disadvantage might logically lead to the creation of a curriculum that would first value whatever strengths these students do come with and then routinely engage students in experiences that would further enable them. Not so. Educators recognize increasingly that not all students come to school with the same kinds of knowledge, the same language habits, or the same strategies for learning. Nonetheless, schools are set up to recognize and value only particular ways of displaying knowledge. Further, schools acknowledge only certain well-defined teacher and learner roles and assume that certain information is shared by all. Consequently, students from minority cultures or from economically disadvantaged circumstances are often automatically labeled academically at-risk. Conventional wisdom has held that these students are somehow deficit learners because their social and/ or economic circumstances have given them a start in life that does not prepare them to function well in school. Conventional wisdom locates the problem in the learner and his or her background and discounts completely whatever resources and language experiences shape the knowledge of these non-mainstream learners.

Michael Cole provides an excellent example of how students can come to be labeled deficit learners when awareness of their specific cultural content is not taken into consideration. In *The Cultural Context of Learning and Thinking* Cole describes his work with the Kpelle tribe of Liberia (Cole et al.). Children from this tribe who were sent to Western-style schools had a great deal of difficulty learning mathematics. Rather than assuming that they were all slow or mathematically deficient, Cole investigated the rules governing Kpelle speech and logic. He discovered that the Kpelle's failure to demonstrate certain cognitive processes necessary for success in mathematics was tied to these students' need for a culturally relevant setting to be present before the skills could be demonstrated. In other words, Cole determined that with the Kpelle, the skills were available—they were not deficit learners—but for some reason traditional academic contexts did not trigger their use. So, for example, some Kpelle children were adept at measuring rice but not at measuring distance. Some could not memorize a multiplication table but could recite precise statistics of major league sports teams and players. Cole's work is cross-cultural and is certainly applicable to cultural minorities in American schools.

Similarly, Glynda Hull and Mike Rose have shown how social and cultural factors might make it appear that a student is unable to do other kinds of academic work (Hull et al.). They tell of one student from a non-mainstream background whose reading of a particular poem seemed somewhat off the mark. The poem tells about a young girl outfitted in garments purchased from the Sears catalog. Mainstream readers would likely infer from the allusion to the Sears catalog that the girl in this poem comes from a family of lower income level, and they might also be expected to appreciate the irony of the "girl fulfilling her romantic dreams via Sears and Roebuck" (Hull et al. 10). On the other hand, the non-mainstream reader in Mike Rose's class viewed Sears and Roebuck merchandise as "affordable" and "economical" and so "practical" and "desirable." Consequently, this reader made different assumptions about the girl's economic background and most certainly missed any irony the poet might have intended. The non-mainstream reader's background, then, created a different understanding of the poem's imagery, but that is not to say that the non-mainstream learner lacked the skills necessary to interpret poetry and, hence, needed to be placed in basic classes.

If we do not consider non-mainstream learners within their social and cultural contexts, we may assume that they are indeed deficient and, therefore, come to expect only very low levels of achievement from them. Such low expectations make it routine for teachers to evaluate students merely on their ability to obey instructions or to follow correctly the steps in a procedure. These expectations lead teachers to articulate goals that, according to Jeannie Oakes, are typical of the low-prestige knowledge addressed by the basics curriculum: developing respect, promoting growth in life skills, developing more mature behavior, fostering business-oriented skills, teaching how to fill out forms, creating an understanding of personal hygiene, developing the ability to follow directions, fostering the ability to formulate realistic goals, and developing socialization skills. These expectations reflect a view of learning that serves students who are capable of only very modest intellectual achievement and result in a very impoverished set of teaching acts that Martin Haberman says constitute the core functions of urban teaching: giving information, asking questions, giving directions, making assignments, monitoring seatwork, reviewing assignments, giving tests, reviewing tests, assigning homework, reviewing homework, settling disputes, punishing noncompliance, marking papers, and giving grades (292). Oakes points out that students who are controlled by such teaching acts and only have access to low-prestige knowledge are denied access to other educationally and socially important work that entails abstract thinking, meaning making, and problem solving. Without access to these high-prestige learning processes, at-risk students are restricted to a marginalized existence not only while they are in school but after school as well.

A Sequence of Discrete Skills

Another assumption underlying the education of at-risk students is that learning proceeds from simple to complex, from concrete to abstract. This assumption has resulted in content being broken into a fixed sequence of discrete skills, beginning with the simplest (the basics) and moving toward the more complex (higher-order skills). According to Knapp and Turnbull, instruction typically emphasizes mastery of these skills by linear progression through the sequence. In reading, for example, children learn sound/letter correlations through an intensified phonics program that might feature endless numbers of workbook pages (or computer drills), then read lists of words out of context, work up to sentences, and finally work with whole pieces of text. In math, students memorize multiplication tables before they attempt series of paper-and-pencil multiplication problems before they tackle practical problems involving multiplication. In writing, young children must first be able to control spelling before they can be allowed to generate whole stories. Older students in high school or college programs are often expected to drill on sentences before they attempt paragraph development. Let us consider how this spelling/writing issue plays out in a first grade classroom. In work done in conjunction with the development of the IBM Writing to Read programs, researchers determined that on average a student entering school has a working vocabulary of fifteen thousand words. And that, typically, by the end of first grade, students have mastered the spelling of ninety words; and we know that in first grade, students often write stories. If we require of first grade students that they use only words they can spell correctly, and if we then ask these same students to write a story, we can predict that those stories will be short and very, very simple. Even talented adults would be hard-pressed to develop any sort of complexity within a ninety-word limit, just as they would find it hard to maintain interest in a series of isolated syntactic exercises.

The notion that learning proceeds from simple to complex makes sense only if we ignore what Lauren Resnick calls the most important single message of modern research on the nature of thinking: even apparently elementary kinds of learning entail complex intellectual activity of the sort that is often labeled "higher order" thinking. Consequently, there is no basis for believing that learning proceeds from lower-level activities that require no independent thinking or judgment to higher-level ones that do. Further, there is no validity in drilling on the "basics" before engaging students in thinking and problem solving. In fact, cognitive research, according to Resnick, suggests that one source of major difficulty for young children may be the failure to cultivate among students thinking that is non-algorithmic, that is complex and yields multiple solutions, that involves nuanced judgments and the application of multiple criteria, that involves uncertainty and self-regulation and imposing meaning.

What's more, it is possible that the very art of drilling students on discrete skills is detrimental to their developing the capacity for complex thinking. This rote learning represented in conventional practice may actually be harming at-risk students rather than helping them. Medical research suggests that repetitive tasks do not stimulate the central cortex of the brain, that region where complex thinking takes place. Marcus Raichle reports that the flow of blood to the brain increases when a task is novel and requires conscious thought; it decreases in relation to degree of familiarity and repetitiveness of the task (Begley et al). What Raichle's work suggests is that by causing students to engage in routinized kinds of activities, we fail to develop their capacity for more complex thinking. Medical doctors using a PET scan are suggesting that there is physical evidence to show that rote is, indeed, almost mindless; it causes the brain not to have to think much. Hence, our conventional wisdom about the necessity of drill and practice on discrete skills has caused us to place real learning farther out of reach for the very students who need the most engagement.

Teacher-Centered Direct Instruction

A further assumption underlying the at-risk curriculum is the efficiency of direct instruction. A much-touted teaching method, direct instruction typically involves the following approaches: teacher-controlled instruction with much time given over to presenting the lesson and then monitoring students' work; extensive practice and feedback; carefully structured tasks that present content in small, manageable steps; and whole class instruction or homogeneous ability grouping.

Research shows direct instruction to be particularly well suited to basic skills acquisition, and studies indicate positive gains on achievement tests when direct instruction is employed. For example, students can be trained to recognize which word in a series begins with a consonant blend, one kind of skill typically measured on achievement tests. However, standardized tests are not an effective measure of the complex, multidimensional thinking fundamental to academic achievement. So the choice of direct instruction as the single teaching method is of doubtful merit.

In fact, direct instruction is highly problematic for a number of reasons. In the first place, when the teacher controls the learning and breaks tasks into small, manageable steps, explaining just how each step is to be done, students are required to do very little thinking. It is the teacher whose mind is at work; students are passive and not intellectually engaged simply because there is little left to think about. Next, the kinds of learning needed to address complex issues are not easily broken down into a series of small, manageable steps. The important questions, the fundamental concepts and themes, are large. They are messy to work through and so do not lend themselves easily to small, manageable increments. Another problem with direct instruction is that it causes students to easily become dependent on the teacher to structure and monitor their learning. When students have no ownership of the task and when they are not involved actively in making their own meaning, there is little chance that they will learn to become independent, resourceful learners.

Direct instruction is also problematical because it involves lecture and recitation to the exclusion of spontaneous talk and student meaning making. Lecture and recitation implies that the message that the student receives is the message that the teacher intends. It does not acknowledge that what students already know affects how they interpret new observations and how they accommodate new information. According to Howard Gardner, students come to school with serviceable theories of the physical world and the world of other people. These theories evolve as children struggle to make sense of their world; and to the extent that these theories serve the students well, they strongly affect new learning. Although what students "know" is often somewhat naive, fragmented, perhaps erroneous, this intuitive "knowing" can cause new learning to be rejected or altered significantly on a subconscious level. For example, Gardner tells us that students hold a number of common misconceptions about science. Since students have spent mental effort constructing these misconceptions and—more important—since the misconceptions do explain and predict various subsets of physical phenomena, students do not easily give up the misconceptions in favor of scientific concepts. For instance, students may have been told that the changing seasons of the year come to be as a function of the angle of the earth on its axis in relation to the plane of its orbit around the sun. But many times when students are questioned about seasonal change, they respond with the naive theory that seasons evolve as a result of the degree of proximity that Earth shares with the sun. They respond in this manner because they cannot give up the deeply held belief that temperature is strictly a function of distance from heating source. In essence, then, strongly held naive theories cause students to view events through the constraints of the naive theory or to make insignificant modifications to their theories in ways that fail to resolve the contradictions. Thus it is that when information is simply being transmitted, that is, delivered by lecture, and not acted upon, the teacher fails to discover erroneous preconceptions, and the student has no opportunity to alter or refine naive or intuitive theory.

Because the transmittal model guarantees large amounts of teacher talk, it inevitably leaves very little time for student talk. Yet we know that talk is a primary meaning-making activity. Roger Schank has pointed out that as individuals we have almost an intrinsic need to tell our stories and to respond (listen) to the stories of others. We learn from what happens to us and pass this knowledge on to others. The stories we tell form the context in which we embed what our experience has shown us to be true. Loss of time for student talk and for story is a critical flaw in typical at-risk programs. Those students for whom academic learning is often the most difficult should be guaranteed time to internalize what they know through talk and to create narratives that encapsulate their learnings and make recall an easier task.

All of this is to say that direct instruction is limiting in a variety of ways. It is not to say, however, that there is no place for explicit teaching that would provide for the acquisition of certain cognitive and linguistic capacities that many students may not bring to school because of limitations associated with poverty. According to Jere Brophy, while certain cognitive and linguistic capacities develop universally and automatically in all cultures and family environments, certain other capacities rely for their development on exposure to particular kinds of modeling and experience. Included among the latter is a variety of schemata, "scripts," and verbal mediation strategies associated with manipulating the kinds of formal codified knowledge that is emphasized in schools. Middle-class children are more likely than other children to learn these skills at home. For example, middle-class children usually begin school familiar with the process of reading and discussing the meaning of books so they are comfortable engaging in this activity in the classroom setting. Children not accustomed to this activity often lack well-developed scripts to provide for easily assimilating such reading activities. As a result, they must struggle to understand what the activities are about and how to respond appropriately to them.

Thus, if non-mainstream learners are not to be frustrated with such school activities, they will need explicit explanation of these activities. They will also need modeling of the processes appropriate to the activities and extensive scaffolding experiences. They will require time to reflect on how such activities relate to other activities and skills. These processes would no doubt require some elements associated with direct instruction because explicit attention would need to be given to developing the necessary cognitive and linguistic capacities. Lisa Delpit argues, for example, that some writing process classrooms—because they do not allow for explicit teaching—further disadvantage at-risk learners. She contends that non-mainstream students must be taught explicitly the content and verbal strategies necessary to be successful in the dominant culture. Delpit, however, is not arguing for a return to the fragmented low-level skills instruction associated with direct instruction. Her concerns are easily accommodated by the writing teacher who uses modeling, mini-lessons, and individualized or small group instruction within a writer's workshop format. Such a teacher does provide some very explicit teaching but does so within a context wherein learners are constructing meaning independently.

Classroom Management

Another fundamental assumption about at-risk instruction is predicated upon the belief that poverty/minority students are inherently disruptive and that what is needed, therefore, is a very rigid style of classroom management. This belief about at-risk students' potential for acting up might logically be well-founded, given the fact that in elementary and secondary schools they are restricted to seatwork for almost six hours a day and fed a curriculum of very boring, very repetitive learning tasks. Many times it is hard to imagine why these students do not embrace mayhem more often simply as a diversion.

In addition to discipline problems caused by a boring and repetitive curriculum, other problems may arise because of certain administrative policies that make it possible to label students with behavioral problems as slow learners and then place them in low-track classes—regardless of their academic aptitude. Pairing those who are at-risk because they may lack academic skills and/or aptitude with those who are low achievers because of disruptive behavior patterns creates an unstable classroom atmosphere wherein any teacher might well value establishing control over establishing an environment for learning. In fact, many teachers of at-risk students are so overwhelmed by problems resulting from this policy that they go beyond merely restricting student movement and talk and institute very controlling "discipline programs" that constrain students almost completely. Such programs often involve prominently posting lists of rules and punishment schedules. The resulting classroom atmosphere is both punitive and oppressive, leading one to assume that control and compliance lead the true agenda.

Even if there were no potential for disruptive behavior, teachers of at-risk students would probably use a very controlling, teacher-dominated system of classroom management because such a system meshes best with the kinds of low-level learning afforded at-risk students. In at-risk classrooms where there is virtually no inquiry, no group work, and no problem solving, the most efficient form of "organization" is teacher directed. Because at-risk students are fed a steady diet of busy work and work sheets, there is no occasion to implement the somewhat unpredictable classroom management systems required when students work with complex knowledge. In fact, in some at-risk classrooms the thinking is so reductive that low-level computer drill (electronic work books) has made the use of certified teachers almost unnecessary. Students are "managed" by placing them in front of computers. They are monitored by instructional aides or assistants who make certain that the students remain quiet and "on-task." Many administrators see this form of instruction and its unique classroom management (not teacher/student, but machine/student) as a highly efficient way of keeping students on-task while "freeing up" a class-room teacher for other duties. Such practice makes explicit that rigid classroom management is valued over sound instructional practice for at-risk students.

Ability Grouping

Perhaps the most damaging assumption underlying the at-risk curriculum is that students are best served when they are grouped with other students who share similar needs. Such grouping or tracking, so the conventional wisdom goes, allows teachers to match students with appropriate learning tasks and to provide an atmo-sphere that is supportive because all students share the same level of ability. Homogeneous classes, then, if the conventional wisdom holds true, offer promise to at-risk students. Yet the preponderance of the evidence finds no positive effect of tracking on educational attainment. Oakes summarizes the evidence as follows:

> [We] have virtually mountains of research evidence indicating that homo-geneous grouping doesn't consistently help anyone learn better. Over the past 60 years hundreds of studies have been conducted . . . [that] vary in their size and methodology. . . . The results differ in certain specifics, but one conclusion emerges clearly; no group of students has been found to benefit consistently from being in a homogeneous group. (7)

There are still further problems with tracking. First of all, tracking allows students to be identified and labeled in a very public way according to their perceived academic capabilities. Everyone in the school knows, for example, who goes to gifted and talented classes, who goes to Chapter I, who goes to learning resource rooms. Through tracking practices, certain students are forced to carry a certain stigma—a very public shame—whose emotional damage must be in-calculable. Second, tracking allows for students to be characterized in the minds of their teachers as having greater or lesser ability, and the research on the correlation between teacher expectations and learner achievement has made clear that when teachers expect much from students, that is to say, where there are high teacher expecta-tions, there is high student performance. Where there are low expecta-tions, there is poor student performance. Finally, when students are put in lower-track programs, they are offered a very different kind of education; they receive exposure to a very low-prestige kind of knowledge that will constrain their access to the kinds of knowledge necessary for serious academic work.

Pamela Keating and Jeannie Oakes point out that tracking may even retard the educational progress of students identified as average or slow. Certainly, the very act of assigning a student to a low track lowers that student's aspiration and self-esteem and fosters negative attitudes about school. In fact, so insidious are the effects of tracking that many educators are recommending that it be eliminated from this nation's schools. Essentially, this practice does little more than to offer a way to separate the disadvantaged from the mainstream, creating a two-tiered educational system that further disadvantages poverty/minority students while proclaiming to offer equal educational opportunity. Tracking may be the ultimate barrier to educating those students most in need of the best the education system has to offer.

New Assumptions, New Practices

If we are to be successful with at-risk learners, we must acknowledge that much of what we currently do does not—cannot—enable these students to acquire the knowledge and skills they need to succeed in school and function well in society.

We must recognize that these learners' ways of knowing come from vastly different home/family/community environments and that we must not devalue the diversity that students bring to the classroom. We must concede that a basic skills curriculum does not prepare students to think critically, and so we must begin to engage students in complicated real problems that will elicit complex thinking strategies. We must admit that direct instruction does not foster either complex thinking or independent learners and, hence, we must look to other instructional strategies that do not disadvantage children. And we must recognize that rigid classroom management systems work well only with very low-level learning so we must give up rigid classroom management practices in order to move to a more challenging curriculum. Finally, we must repudiate tracking if schools are ever to meet the needs of all children. To develop successful practices, we need to look outside schools—particularly at work done by at-risk students in community-based organizations.

When Shirley Brice Heath and Milbrey McLaughlin observed students engaged in community-based organizations, they found that the same students labeled *at-risk* in school were capable of very complex kinds of thinking outside of school. These same students were able to plan complicated projects (e.g., renovating an urban neighborhood), allocate time and determine who would be most able to accomplish various parts of the task at hand, perform complex mathematical computations, and persuade community agencies that they could, in fact, carry out the proposed project. In short, these students could do the sort of work they were never given the opportunity to do in school.

The successes documented by Heath and McLaughlin lead to a set of assumptions that differ radically from those underlying conventional programs for at-risk students. Heath and McLaughlin's work suggests we may assume that at-risk students:

1. value making immediate connections between academic concepts and real world application;
2. are challenged by ill-defined problems more closely aligned to those that people grapple with outside of school;
3. are capable of complex thinking and group effort sustained over long blocks of time;
4. respond well to agents and settings of learning that are not limited to classrooms and teachers;
5. value knowledge associated with the everyday life of people not traditionally associated with the school and school learning;
6. can engage in student-initiated, student-regulated tasks/projects.

All of this makes for a different kind of school experience and leads students far afield from formal academic learning. The Applied Learning Project in the Fort Worth, Texas, public schools is an effort to structure learning experiences for students in ways that acknowledge these assumptions. The project, only in its second year, involves over one hundred teachers across disciplines, grades one through twelve. Students in these teachers' classrooms routinely engage in both short-term (3–5 days) and long-term (spanning several months) projects— most of which they initiate themselves, all of which present a very different view of what schooling might look like.

For example, a class of ninth grade English students, several of whom are repeating ninth grade English for the second, third, and even fourth time, were asked to read *What Work Requires of Schools: A SCANS Report for America 2000*. Published by the Department of Labor, this document proposes that students must develop various high-level skills and competencies if they hope to be successful in the workplace. The ninth graders—all of whom eventually hope to join the work force—had a built-in interest in the document so they found the information particularly relevant. They were also somewhat reassured about what the Department of Labor identified as necessary skills and competencies. Most students said they could measure up to what work would require of them, whereas they were less certain that they would graduate from high school.

To insure the document's authenticity at the local level, the students interviewed area business people and asked what skills they required of entry-level workers. Local business people reinforced the need for the same kinds of skills and competencies outlined by the Department of Labor, and thus reassured, the students then created charts that displayed annotated lists of the SCANS competencies and skills. The charts, hung around the room, would—literally—keep in front of the students those things important for future employment. The students then began an audit of the ninth grade English curriculum and looked specifically for the inclusion of the competencies and skills that were articulated in SCANS. They found that the English curriculum encompassed many of the competencies outlined in the SCANS document but was weighted—they felt—too heavily in favor of literature.

Therefore, the students drafted a proposal suggesting that certain curriculum requirements be compressed and others expanded so that ninth graders could spend more time developing the foundation skills and competencies outlined by the Department of Labor. The students sent their curriculum recommendations to the directors of the school district's writing and secondary language arts programs. In order to insure that their recommendations for curriculum change not be ignored or patronized, the class also sent carbon copies of the document to those people who supervised the two program directors. This was a deliberate action to insure response, and it is a particularly significant act on the part of students traditionally marginalized by the educational system. It speaks both to the students' knowledge of systems (one of the SCANS competencies) and to their understanding of how to manipulate the school system to their own advantage.

As part of their recommendations for curriculum change, the students proposed a video about SCANS for all incoming freshmen and ninth grade English teachers. (Production costs for the video were paid out of monies secured through another proposal the students wrote.) The video would encourage freshmen students to develop the SCANS competencies and skills and would urge all ninth grade English teachers to include the SCANS report in the required reading for ninth grade English students. Development of this video is currently under way.

As a result of their work to date, the class has also been offered the opportunity to write a monograph about their experiences linking real world competencies and academic learning. The students plan to begin writing the monograph once the video's production is complete, and they have written a proposal to remain together for one more year in order to complete both the video and the monograph.

Fifth grade students assumed responsibility for an Applied Learning task that also requires a remarkable degree of competency: they organized a conference for young writers. This conference brought together elementary student writers and professional writers of children's literature. The intent of the conference was for the professional writers to confer with the elementary students about strategies for developing stories and polishing their writing. In addition to working with published authors, the students attended small break-out sessions directed by people who have expertise in writing. The fifth grade conference planners worked with a budget of $7,500 (monies secured through a grant) to cover honoraria and travel expenses for the keynote speakers, costs related to security precautions for the school building where the conference was held, refreshments for the conference participants, conference programs, and the like. All decisions related to the conference were made by these at-risk students, who also generated all correspondence and determined with whom to subcontract all services. This project involved many literacy acts: making phone calls, writing letters, designing conference programs, creating a schedule for conference small group sessions, advertising the event, organizing registration, designing registration forms, negotiating with airline reservationists and authors' agents, and answering on-the-spot questions at the conference itself. The conference attracted over fifteen hundred participants and came in under budget. The fifth graders created a manual that details all the tasks necessary to put on the conference; their intent is to pass the manual on to another group of students who will host next year's conference.

The learning associated with hosting the conference is impressive in itself, but equally impressive is what this project has meant to the class. The students have shown remarkable ingenuity—they have managed a significant amount of money, planning to use unexpended funds to cover the cost of a class end-of-year field trip. They are tremendously proud of having been trusted to run the conference, and they have worked hard to justify that trust. They have discovered class "experts," students who possess abilities not always recognized in traditional academic situations—and these students have been relied on routinely for their specific expertise (the good speller proofread letters/memos; the persuasive youngster negotiated with food vendors; the artistic youngster designed the program cover). The students have learned to work cooperatively because all decisions have been made by committee. Most important, then, youngsters—typical urban, inner-city students—have discovered that they can be successful, resourceful learners who can accomplish very demanding tasks. They speak freely and often about what they can do. They are seldom absent. They rarely present any discipline problems.

In a number of middle school classes, Applied Learning Project students are engaged in collecting, analyzing, and rewriting poorly written public documents and in creating new documents, ranging from simple instructions to complex policy statements. Students field-test and evaluate documents in order to experience what it means to write for real readers and to understand the consequences of writing. This Applied Learning effort provides a framework for working partnerships among young writers, business people, and the community and allows students to work directly with writing that affects their own lives and their communities.

For example, one eighth grade class is drawing upon local resources—including health department employees—to guide them in doing research on a variety of topics ranging from substance abuse to teenage alcoholism. These students plan to produce a series of brochures, one for each of the topics they investigate. The production of each document involves students in a range of research activities: reading general background information, studying charts and statistics, analyzing national trends, gathering data from local resources, interviewing informed sources. As students prepare the brochures, they work with people who have expertise in technical writing in order to understand effective principles of document design. Once the brochures are prepared, they will be field-tested in the school and in the community before they are revised and printed. The work these students are producing would typically be done in the public sector by professional writers or in the school system by central office staff.

Another group of middle school students is producing curriculum units. These units are intended for middle school students and would normally be written by the curriculum staff. Instead, students are doing all the research and writing the documents themselves. They research subjects as varied as the Colonial period (American history class), balancing equations (math class), and persuasive writing (English class) before writing these curriculum units. The students then field-test and refine their work before it goes in the district curriculum guide.

In all of the projects described thus far, students are acquiring academic skills and knowledge within a broader context. At the same time, these projects allow schoolwork to be valued by three different groups—students, parents, and teachers—all of whom often express dissatisfaction with the status quo. Students, especially those of lower socioeconomic status, many times see school as being irrelevant to the issues they routinely confront outside schools. Parents of these students share this view. For example, one parent asked school administrators what a haiku was and why his child had to spend six weeks learning how to write one. And teachers often voice their frustration with at-risk students' lack of knowledge that is commonplace among mainstream learners.

In the Applied Learning projects, students see the value of in-school knowledge since that knowledge is used to address particular issues or concerns of importance to the students. Parents at the same time are assured that their children are acquiring the kinds of knowledge and skills that will make these students employable or will enable them to continue their education. Teachers appreciate the academic rigor of the projects and recognize that the broader context for learning allows students to develop a frame of reference to draw upon in the future when specific rules may be forgotten but the memory of the projects is sufficient for reconstructing knowledge.

These Fort Worth efforts have merit for a number of reasons, perhaps the most important of which is the scale on which they have been initiated. The Fort Worth Independent School District is the twenty-fourth largest district in the country; it serves 71,000 students and employs 3,500 teachers. The Applied Learning Project is at the heart of the district's commitment to ensure that all students receive a worthwhile education. The project requires a massive staff development effort. Rigid disciplinary borders, "abstracted knowledge," and facts will have to give way to cross-curricular projects where knowledge is related to real problems and where students work in groups. In Fort Worth's case, such change has received support from local corporations as well as from the larger community, and the endorsement of these two groups reinforces the impetus for teacher change.

Another reason the Fort Worth effort is significant is that the district is building instruction around significant problems and issues that are important to students while it attempts to make explicit to students that the knowledge and skills they acquire in school prepare them to enter the workplace or institutions of higher learning. So, for example, a class of students may very well use a Department of Labor publication as the basis for evaluating the English curriculum; students may test the chemical composition of fertilizers used on the grounds around their high school and make subsequent recommendations to the district grounds and maintenance crew; and students may write and publish many of the documents that specify discipline policy, extracurricular activities, lunchroom rules, and so forth. Students learn skills in very meaningful contexts and engage in behaviors (e.g., working in groups, utilizing oral presentation techniques) that will contribute to their success whether they plan to go to work or to continue their education.

Finally, the Fort Worth project is significant because it helps students apply immediately what they learn. Typically students are told such things as "You will need to know this next year" or "You have to understand this when you get in high school." In short, application is usually deferred. What Fort Worth is trying to do is to make it possible for all students—at-risk students included—to make use of new knowledge as they learn it, thus reinforcing it and giving it credibility at the same time.

Roadblocks to Change

There exists terrible resistance to programs that are successful for at-risk students because such programs often are not part of our present cultural values about what school looks like. Actually, these cultural values about schooling are drawn from assumptions that no longer hold true, assumptions that arose from research done in settings that do not in any way resemble the schools we have today or the students who come to our schools—or their parents, their communities, or their values. There clearly is a mismatch between what was and what is and between current research, successful practice, and social notions of what will work, what students should learn, and what they should be able to do as a result of schooling. Yet even when the failure of accepted cultural notions is undeniable, forces are at work to maintain the old order.

School/Classroom Management

School management is typically rigid, bureaucratic, and top-down, designed to support the status quo. As Jane Peterson (this volume) points out, most schools are organized like factories of the Industrial Age, and they are characterized by lockstep, disconnected learning; arbitrary, discrete blocks of time; and a narrow view of learning. Often, teachers are required to record the number of minutes they spend on instruction in the various subject areas. They are further restricted by a standard lesson design that is most often very rigid and mechanical and by central office control of curriculum coverage, pacing, and assessment. Such mechanical, standardized practices fit well into the factory model of schooling. They do not, however, encourage the sort of learning associated with a broader view of knowledge. In fact, lesson plan design, coverage, pacing, and assessment all become less clearly defined when students are engaged in complex tasks that require them to work in more complicated ways. Although some teachers work hard to create a structure for complex learning situations, their classrooms may seem chaotic to an untrained eye, and they may be criticized for lack of control. On the other hand, as long as classrooms are quiet and students sit in desks doing something, many administrators, parents, and other teachers assume that learning is going on. Hence, many teachers play it safe and buy into low-level learning tasks with tight teacher control and much student seatwork.

Standardized Testing

Another reason not to change classroom practice grows out of the influence of standardized testing. Testing is at the very heart of curriculum in this country, and while tests are in place that masure rote kinds of learning, instruction focused on rote learning makes good sense. Although complex real-world tasks teach students to think critically, they do not necessarily prepare students to do well on standardized tests. Such tests typically require the learning of disconnected skills and information and do not afford students the opportunity to link concepts or make judgments. Therefore, any teacher who is held accountable for standardized test scores takes risks by engaging students in more challenging, integrated learning opportunities. For example, students in applied learning classrooms routinely generate whole pieces of text, revising for specificity, clarity, and elaboration. They proofread and make corrections in spelling, punctuation, capitalization, and usage. In short, they perform tasks real writers routinely do. Standardized testing formats, however, do not measure students on their ability to write and revise texts. Instead, students may be given examples of sentences that contain errors. Then students are asked not to make corrections, but to name—to label—the errors. Teachers held accountable for student performance on this kind of test item routinely spend four to six weeks "prepping" students on labeling activities. This is time taken away, of course, from real learning, but many teachers feel such prepping is essential, arguing that although the students may be capable of correcting the error, they may not necessarily be able to label it.

As long as student test scores are as critical as they are in most lower socioeconomic classrooms, it is chancy for teachers to do other than teach to the test. Often teacher evaluations—and sometimes pay—are directly related to test scores, making explicit the message about what is to be taught and how. There is a great deal of truth to the old adage that what gets tested gets taught.

School/Work Linkages

It is all well and good to say that efforts like the Applied Learning Project are valuable because they foster complex learning as they engage students in real-world applications. But "real-world applications" include the possibility of "work-world applications," for a variety of reasons, and linking education with work readiness serves as a red flag to many people.

For one thing, any concept of education that includes real-world or work-world linkages is problematic. Critics fear that when such linkages become a part of the educational agenda, learning will become too circumscribed by the values of the marketplace. This group of people fears the imposition of a curriculum that might, for example, slight literature and fine arts in order to accommodate subjects that translate more readily into the development of marketable skills. They believe absolutely in a liberal education that prepares people to think— but not necessarily to think about those things concerned with the world of work. It is difficult to take issue with those who defend students' right to a liberal education. What I am suggesting, however, is that the rigor and the inquiry that characterize liberal education can also characterize schooling that helps to link education to the world outside the classroom. Obviously, preparing students simply to work or to solve real-world problems must not become the sole goal of education, but neither must educators denigrate linkages between the classroom and the real world.

Another concern is that any change in the status quo represents a means of serving to perpetuate a two-track educational system: one track for those students who will go to college and another track that will prepare poor/minority students to do rudimentary, permanently low-level work. These people contend that poor/minority students, already oppressed by a capitalist society that has need of a permanent underclass, will be placed in the "new" program, which will in reality exist solely to prepare minorities for low-paying, entry-level positions.

This is a serious concern. Unless our society can create jobs that allow for advancement but do not require a college degree, the concern that education not focus on workplace competencies is absolutely valid. Although business people promise the development of "high performance workplaces" that offer advancement for any person who displays problem solving and creativity, most businesses are currently structured along very traditional line worker/management systems. To some extent we will simply have to trust that businesses will change. It is probable that this trust will be well-founded and that change will happen because "high performance workplaces" have been shown to be more competitive and more profitable than those organized in traditional ways. Therefore, there is some likelihood that if schools prepare students adequately to be successful in the work force, high performance workplaces will reward these students with responsibility and the possibility for advancement.

One final objection to school/workplace linkages is that a curriculum that fosters such linkages represents low-prestige knowledge or "vocational" education. This notion bears examining. For example, Stanford University, not an institution usually associated with either at-risk students or low-level learning, currently offers as an alternative to traditional composition courses, the Community Service Writing Project. This project affords students the opportunity to link academic knowledge and work done in a public or community service organization.

The Community Service Writing Project merges a core theory or theme, such as education, public service, or community, with an appropriate public service experience, perhaps a writing project for the service agency and/or a project in reflective writing in response to public service the student actually performs at the agency. This project fosters collaboration among students and the development of social and decision-making skills that are often an integral part of writing in both the business world and the academic community. Students write press releases, interviews, book reviews, newsletters, flyers, grant proposals, and anthologies of writings (oral histories and/or folk stories) by or about the population served by the organization. Students also elect to help at the agency in a capacity that may not involve writing. For example, they may choose to do research or tutoring. This program develops an awareness among students that writing for a real audience imposes particular constraints that are different from those constraints present with an academic audience. Students obviously benefit from engaging in alternatives that help them see the role of academic writing in comparison to writing for other reasons and audiences just as they benefit when they are encouraged to write about issues that concern them.

Teachers Assigned At-Risk Students

Of all the roadblocks associated with changing the instructional program of at-risk learners, however, perhaps the greatest is the quality of many of the teachers who serve this population. No one would dispute that many who teach at-risk students are outstanding teachers. These individuals teach at-risk students because they choose to work with this population, and they set an incredibly high standard of professionalism. Dedicated to helping those students who need good teachers the most, this group helps us see what is possible for at-risk students to achieve.

However, these remarkable teachers are relatively few in number for several reasons. For one thing inner-city districts—which have the largest numbers of at-risk students—as a whole have a very poor track record for attracting the best teachers. After all, teaching in the inner city is more difficult than teaching in the suburbs. The facilities and degree of support from parents and communities are often not comparable. Also, the pay scale in many inner-city districts does not match what suburbs can afford to pay their teachers. And there exists a greater possibility for violence associated with teaching in the inner-city schools. Much has been made of students who come to school carrying guns and knives, and while this practice is not restricted solely to inner-city students, the perception, at least, is that it is inner-city kids who most represent the threat of violence.

Another reason that at-risk students do not often have access to the best teachers grows out of inner-city teacher placement policies. Large urban districts routinely place new teachers and/or less competent teachers with those students most in need of good instruction. These placement practices are rooted in several traditions:

- rewarding the best teachers with the best teaching assignments (honors classes, gifted and talented classes) in a building;
- placing the weakest teachers in schools located in the poor and minority neighborhoods where parents are not likely to be critical of their performances; and
- assigning new, inexperienced teachers to the toughest schools because most vacancies exist in these schools even though these teachers will have less experience to draw upon.

Some school districts offer monetary incentives (termed *battle pay*) to teachers who volunteer to teach in low socioeconomic schools, but, increasingly, some of the best teachers are declining this inducement because they fear they cannot be successful in schools where students are held to almost impossibly high standards on achievement tests whose worth and bias they often question.

The result of these teacher placement policies is that many teachers who lack teaching experience or who do not feel empowered or challenged to implement a varied repertoire of teaching techniques are faced with working with students who desperately need the best instruction. Until districts place the best teachers in schools whose students need them most, what works with at-risk students will take place in a very few classrooms and not to the extent that schools can claim to be making a difference for students. Without the best teachers and administrators working with at-risk students, schools will continue to be responsible for being a major part of something that disadvantages large numbers of students and reinforces cycles of poverty and neglect.

That at-risk students continue to come to school at all is a wonder, given what schools often offer in the name of education. Many students give up on school completely: the Institute for the Study of At-

Risk Students estimates that one student in this country drops out of school every sixteen seconds, and studies show that the dropout profile is clearly established by the time a child reaches third grade (Davis and McCaul). Yet we know that these students are capable and that at-risk schools sometimes serve remarkable youngsters.

Several years ago an incident brought home to me the frustration urban children must have with in-school learning. I had been working with a group of children in a low socioeconomic status building and with one group of first graders in particular. One of these children, Chuck, could not be described in any way as being at-risk, though he was in a class with many students clearly described by that label. Chuck had proven to be gifted—a stunning writer capable of producing lengthy pieces of text both focused and complicated in their structure. Probably the text Chuck worked longest on (several weeks) was a book he wrote in honor of his dad's birthday. The book was titled *Wars In History of Amrica* [sic]. This was a ten-page, intricately illustrated text that traced American wars from our country's inception through Vietnam. Interwoven in this piece was an amazing amount of historical knowledge: a recounting of old-world predictions that Columbus's voyage would end in disaster; naming Washington and John Adams as early presidents; pointing out that our first flag had thirteen stars; pronouncing George Bush (Gorgbush) our forty-first president—even inserting the pledge of allegiance. Chuck wrote about what he knew, sometimes losing control of time shifts, always experimenting freely with spelling in order to make use of words he felt appropriate. For example, Chuck knows that

- AMIRCA is two senchrys old   (America is two centuries old);
- We have lots of dedly wepins   (We have lots of deadly weapons);
- Wen we get new wepons we bei-   (When we get new weapons we be-
  commor invisoble   come more invincible);
- Today we have meny simbols   (Today we have many symbols);
                                                          and
- Veietnom was a war and it caused (Vietnam was a war and it caused
  tragedy   tragedy).

His text even reveals mishearings—Chuck routinely refers to World War II as War War II. Nonetheless, the book gives testimony to the amazing degree of out-of-school knowing some students possess (Chuck's father was in the military) and calls us to task for the relatively bland curriculum we offer most children.

After Chuck finished writing *Wars In History of Amrica*, he began work on a text that he identified as a "school book." When asked what distinguishes a book as a schoolbook, he replied, "You know, its got units, not chapters." This second work parodies basal readers typical of those used with young children. Entitled *Cats*, the text provides striking contrast to the war book: *Cats* is marked by very simple vocabulary and the almost singsong rhythms of the basal reader ("and what do you thinch they wor fieting for? of cors the cat food. Thats it"). Chuck even uses tags to move readers through the text ("Now will go to the next unit. okayg. now torn the page. okayg lets get goin") and he provides a "looking back section" with very simple, very uninteresting questions ("how meny units or ther in this book?").

What is particularly interesting about Chuck and his classmates is that they all took seriously the book about war. Moreover, *everyone* realized that *Cats* was meant to be a joke. When even first grade children—including those whom school people traditionally classify as being at-risk—can become insiders to the extent that they recognize and ridicule what education proposes as worthy knowledge, we *must* reassess what we are doing.

Works Cited

Begley, Sharon, Lynda Wright, Vernon Church, and Mary Hager. "Mapping the Brain." *Newsweek* 20 April 1992: 66–70.

Brophy, Jere E. "Effective Schooling for Disadvantaged Students." *Better Schooling for the Children of Poverty: Alternatives to Conventional Wisdom.* Vol. 2. Ed. Michael S. Knapp and Patrick M. Shields. Menlo Park, CA: SRI, 1990.

Brown, Rexford G. *Schools of Thought.* San Francisco: Jossey-Bass, 1991.

Cole, Michael, John Gay, Joseph A. Glick, and Donald W. Sharp. *The Cultural Context of Learning and Thinking: An Exploration in Experimental Anthropology.* New York: Basic Books, 1971.

Davis, William E., and Edward J. McCaul. *At-Risk Children and Youth: A Crisis in Our Schools and Society.* Orono, ME: College of Education, U of Maine, 1990.

Delpit, Lisa D. "The Silenced Dialogue: Power and Pedagogy in Educating Other People's Children." *Harvard Educational Review* 58 (August 1988): 280–98.

Gardner, Howard. *The Unschooled Mind: How Children Think and How Schools Should Teach.* New York: Basic Books, 1991.

Haberman, Martin. "The Pedagogy of Poverty Versus Good Teaching." *Phi Delta Kappan* 72 (December 1991): 290–94.

Heath, Shirley Brice, and Milbrey Wallin McLaughlin. "A Child Resource Policy: Moving Beyond Dependence on School and Family." *Phi Delta Kappan* 72 (April 1991): 623–27.

Hull, Glynda, Mike Rose, Cynthia Greenleaf, and Brian Reilly. "Seeing the Promise of the Underprepared." *Quarterly* 13 (Winter 1991): 6–14.

"IBM Writing to Read—Teacher Training." IBM. Presentation. Fort Worth, TX, Fall 1986.

Keating, Pamela, and Jeannie Oakes. *Access to Knowledge: Breaking Down School Barriers to Learning*. Denver: ECS Distribution Center, 1988.

Knapp, Michael S., and Brenda J. Turnbull. *Better Schooling for the Children of Poverty: Alternatives to Conventional Wisdom*. U.S. Department of Education, Office of Planning, Budget, and Evaluation. Washington, DC: GPO, 1990.

Oakes, Jeannie. *Keeping Track: How Schools Structure Inequality*. New Haven: Yale UP, 1985.

Resnick, Lauren B. *Education and Learning to Think*. Washington, DC: National Academy, 1987.

Schank, Roger C. *Tell Me a Story: A New Look at Real and Artificial Memory*. New York: Scribner's, 1990.

United States Department of Labor. *What Work Requires of Schools: A SCANS Report for America 2000*. Washington, DC: GPO, 1991.

7

Strategy and *Surprise*

in the Making of Meaning

Lee Odell

Underlying this chapter is an assumption that appears frequently in discussions of composition theory: the most interesting,
the most challenging aspect of the composing process is the effort to
construct meaning. Whether writing about literature, personal experience, or data and theory from other disciplines, all of us—teachers
and students alike—have to make sense of things for ourselves. In
doing so, of course, we may collaborate with others, and we may
draw on experiences, values, and knowledge we share with others.
And our thinking is almost certain to be shaped by language we derive
from the various discourse communities we belong to. But finally, we
have to tell ourselves the significance of what we are reading, doing,
remembering, perceiving. We have to make our own meanings.

On this much, there seems to be general consensus. But how do
we and our students engage in this meaning-making process? What,
if anything, might we do to promote or guide this process? What
should we try to do? When we look to the literature of our field for
answers to these questions, we find anything but consensus. Consider, for example, some of the various admonitions one might derive
from recent discussions of theory, research, and pedagogy.

Plan what you want to say.	Forget about planning; let the writing take you where it will.
Become aware of what you are doing so that you can do it better.	Give up the notion that conscious awareness or choice has any part in what a fluent writer does.
Develop your analytic/rational abilities; learn an inquiry procedure or develop your own.	Rely on the spontaneous inventiveness that comes only through the act of writing, for rational thinking is not the source of insight or discovery.
Spend time examining your topic thoroughly, systematically.	Devote time to rituals or habits that create a state of mind in which insight is likely to occur.

Suggestions in the left-hand column are based on the view that significant parts of the meaning-making process involve strategies, thinking processes that can guide the way we try to make sense of any subject matter, whether abstract theory, statistical data, or personal memories, values, perceptions. Suggestions in the right-hand column reflect the view that important aspects of the meaning-making process are beyond our ability to control. This perspective emphasizes the importance of intuitive, unpredictable insights—what Donald Murray refers to as "surprise" ("Writing and Teaching") or what James Britton refers to as "spontaneous inventiveness" ("Shaping").

As far as I can tell, these two perspectives are complementary. They simply reflect different but interdependent aspects of a single, complex process. The use of strategy increases the chances of our arriving at the unexpected insights that constitute surprise; these insights, in turn, can lead us to refocus, redirect our conscious exploration of our subjects. Thus, without minimizing the importance of surprise, Murray (*Write to Learn*) can illustrate specific strategies writers can use to find a focus for their writing, develop a lead paragraph, assess an emerging draft, find an appropriate subject. For Murray, these strategies serve to enhance surprise, not preempt it. Speaking of his own development as a writer, Murray talks of learning "new tricks of my trade, new ways to allow language to extend my world, new ways to surprise myself with my writing" (267).[1]

Murray's view notwithstanding, representatives of each perspective have often minimized or explicitly rejected the other perspective. Consequently, I will review these perspectives and then suggest ways in which they are closely related rather than mutually exclusive. I will then consider a series of questions related to teaching: Should we be trying to teach students strategies for meaning making? If so, why? Which strategies? And how might we go about this work?

Strategy *Versus* Surprise

Those who emphasize the role of strategy in the meaning-making process assume that significant parts of the process entail relatively systematic patterns of mental (cognitive *and* affective) activity that can be made conscious and can be used in a variety of situations.[2] Taking this assumption to an extreme, Charles Bazerman expresses the hope that "by bringing unreflective practice to attention, we reassert conscious control over it" (15). This hope is based on Bazerman's belief that "writing improves through the intelligent choice of the linguistic resources in any situation; the more we understand how writing works, the more intelligently we can control our choices" (9).

From a different perspective, efforts to control the writing process are, at best, misguided. Representatives of this perspective—even those who might acknowledge the value of Murray's tricks of the trade—stress the importance of the spontaneous, unpredictable insights that arise through the very act of writing. They assume, in Elbow's words, that "writing is . . . a transaction with words whereby you *free* yourself from what you presently think, feel, and perceive" (*Writing Without Teachers* 15). Given this assumption, Elbow and others contend that conscious control is usually impossible and is frequently harmful.

Advocates of strategy and advocates of surprise have a long history of either attacking or simply ignoring the alternative point of view. Those who value surprise can be very critical of the view that there might be systematic elements in the meaning-making process. Britton, for example, emphasizes the importance of the process of "shaping at the point of utterance," the "moment-by-moment interpretive process" writers engage in while they are actually stringing words across a page or computer screen ("Shaping" 141). Britton is particularly insistent that this process of "spontaneous inventiveness" (139) does not entail conscious thought or planning.[3] By way of illustration, Britton cites a student's reflection on his own composing process:

"It just comes into your head, it's not like thinking, it's just there" ("Shaping" 141; see also Britton et al. 38–41).

This sort of explicit criticism does not often appear in more recent essays whose authors share Britton's perspective. Writers of these essays seem to assume that the strategy/surprise controversy has been resolved in favor of surprise and thus have relatively little to say about strategy. They concentrate, instead, on describing teaching practices (especially the use of informal, exploratory writing—journals and learning logs) designed to foster the spontaneous inventiveness Britton describes.[4]

All of these writers would surely accept the notion that informal, exploratory language promotes students' thinking and understanding. But only one of them, Toby Fulwiler, claims that journal writing entails identifiable "cognitive activities" (3) that might guide a writer's efforts at meaning making. And even Fulwiler does not give much attention to strategy, asserting that "it would be impossible to list here all the possible mental modes likely to be found in journal entries, as there would be virtually no limits to what a writer could try out" (3). In this assertion, Fulwiler does not explicitly criticize those who value strategy. Indeed, in asserting that the number of "mental modes" is almost limitless, Fulwiler effectively preempts debate with advocates of strategy. Given Fulwiler's claim, even the most industrious strategist would seem to have little prospect of finding some sort of system, some finite number of patterns in all this diverse activity. Who needs to criticize or debate when the other side appears to have no way to mount an alternative argument?

Those who take a more systematic approach to the meaning-making process are unlikely to make an explicit argument against the value of nonconscious, intuitive processes.[5] But despite their protestations to the contrary, they often seem to imply that the meaning-making process is essentially conscious and rational, even mechanistic. Those who have written most extensively about system have had little to say, in print, at least, about surprise. They may acknowledge that nonconscious processes are important or even that "trains of thought run through dark tunnels" (Theodore Reik, qtd. in Young, Becker, and Pike 71). But they typically concentrate on describing conscious aspects of the meaning-making process, seeming to suggest—through inattention rather than through explicit repudiation—that nonconscious processes are not terribly important. (One notable exception to this appears in the work of Gabrielle Rico, who, in *Writing the Natural Way*, presents a series of techniques intended to tap both the nonliteral, holistic powers of the mind as well as rational, linear thought.)

Unfortunately, this suggestion is reinforced by the terminology sometimes used by advocates of strategy. For example, in discussing systematic discovery procedures, Richard Young refers to the "codification of a particular sort of cognitive skill" ("Recent" 22). His point is simply that mental activity is not entirely random, idiosyncratic, or mysterious, and that we can identify habits of mind that may be useful to more than a single individual. But *codification* could suggest laws or general procedures that are to be followed without deviation. And for some, *cognitive* and *skill* may also be troublesome; the former term sometimes appears in contexts that make no allowance for affect or intuition, and the latter in contexts that emphasize drill on isolated behaviors that have no necessary relation to larger human purposes.

Strategy *and* Surprise

In light of the conflicts just described, it may seem pointless or misguided to look for some way to integrate strategy and surprise. As C. H. Knoblauch and Lil Brannon have argued, the effort to choose our theory piecemeal may lead to profound incongruities; we are better advised to respect the integrity of the theoretical systems we are concerned with. While I agree with Knoblauch and Brannon that we must not ignore or oversimplify differences between theoretical positions, I also agree with Britton that our theory must "remain close to the observed phenomena of teaching and learning" ("Theories"). As teachers and theorists, then, I think we need to be less concerned with adhering to a particular viewpoint than with developing a perspective that will allow us to work with the complexity of our own and our students' meaning-making processes.

Any such perspective will have to acknowledge the importance of surprise in the meaning-making process. When we talk or write— especially when we do so in an informal, exploratory manner—there is always the chance we will experience the spontaneous inventiveness Britton has described. Any effort to compose our thoughts can lead us to new, sometimes completely unexpected understandings of what we think or feel. Surprise, then, is a very real phenomenon, an important part of the meaning-making process.

But so is strategy. As David Perkins has argued, our most unex-

pected insights, our moments of "surprise," need not be attributed
to a visit from the Muse. Even if they are not predictable, such insights
are likely to occur in the context of relatively systematic activity that
sets the stage for moments of unpredictable insight. In some instances,
we may engage in this activity deliberately, perhaps by consciously
posing questions that seem likely to guide our thinking. But sometimes
our strategies may have become so familiar, so internalized that we
employ them without deliberate effort.[6] Moreover, even our most
spontaneous uses of language reflect strategies, patterns of mental
activity that can, to a useful degree, be understood and, when necessary, shaped by conscious effort. In the next several pages, I want to
illustrate these claims about strategy by drawing on current theory
about the relationship between language and thought and by analyzing some samples of classroom talk.

Language and Thought

The connections between language and thought can be so complex, powerful, and unpredictable that they can seem, to use Elbow's
term, "magic" (*WWP; WWT*). Elbow, of course, cautions against taking
the magic metaphor too literally (*WWP* 357). And Murray gives an
even more emphatic warning: "Writing isn't magic, but then magic
isn't magic either. Magicians know their craft, and writers must also
know their craft" (*Write* vii). But both Elbow and Murray give repeated
testimony to the power of language, to its ability to create surprise
and direct our thinking. If magic doesn't account for this power, what
does?

Part of the answer may be, as writers such as Janet Emig, Sabina
Thorne Johnson, and William Stafford would argue, that this power
derives from the interplay between the spontaneous use of language
and one's unconscious. Another part of the answer comes from theory
and research about connections between thought and language. In
essence, this work suggests that inherent in any use of language are
the processes of selection, generalization, and evocation, processes
that guide our efforts to construct meaning without letting us predict
just where those efforts will lead. Whether we are aware of them or
not, these processes are inherent in any use of language.

The process of selection is particularly emphasized in the work
of Kenneth Burke, who argues that our words constitute a set of
"terministic screens," filters that lead us to ignore some aspects of

our world and that color our interpretation of those aspects we attend to. Similarly, S. I. Hayakawa argues that language is like other instruments of observation: "languages select, and in selecting what they select, they omit what they do not select" (*Symbol* 133).

This selection process is a mixed blessing. We have to be able to restrict our attention. If we couldn't, we would be overwhelmed by a universe of thoughts, feelings, sensations, and memories, all of which would converge upon us at once, leaving us overwhelmed and helpless. But we run into trouble when our attention becomes too selective, when our terministic screens allow us to filter out information that might prove morally or intellectually unsettling. For example, we delude ourselves when we think of warfare only in terms of *antipersonnel devices* or *collateral damage* rather than in terms of *bombs, destroyed houses, dead civilians*.

In addition to selecting, language also generalizes. As L. S. Vygotsky has argued, "[a] word does not refer to a single object but to a group or to a class of objects. Each word is therefore already a generalization" (*Language* 5). If we are to have a usable language, we cannot have a separate word for every phenomenon we encounter or for each of the meanings each phenomenon has when it appears in different contexts.[7] Consequently, any given word cannot refer solely to the object we are observing, the specific emotion we are experiencing, the specific concept we are trying to articulate. Instead, it has to apply to a variety of objects existing in a variety of contexts, none of which are exactly the same. If I say *cat* or *orange* or *small* or *doze* or *affection*, I may be intending to describe the animal that is resting its head against my computer keyboard while I am trying to type. But none of these words applies uniquely to this specific animal; instead, they refer to types of characteristics that this particular cat may share with people or objects or other cats. Any word, then, entails some element of generalizing, implying that a given idea, feeling, perception, object is in some ways similar to other phenomena to which we apply the same language.

Beyond its power to select and generalize, language also has the power to evoke the wide range of contexts in which we have experienced a given word. According to Vygotsky, each of these contexts gives the word a slightly different *sense*; that is, each context entails its own set of "psychological events"—concepts, feelings, perceptions. Consequently, when we think or write or speak a given word, we, in effect, plug ourselves into a psychological network that allows us to juxtapose a great range of psychological events, and any of these juxtapositions may surprise us and redirect our thinking.

For Vygotsky, the power to surprise is especially characteristic of what he refers to as "inner speech," speech that is intended "for oneself" and that is both cryptic and psychologically rich. This inner speech is likely to seem "disconnected and incomplete" (*Mind* 139), since it often takes the form of sentences that have no explicitly stated grammatical subjects. Moreover, Vygotsky claims, it contains words that are so "saturated with sense" (*Mind* 148) that their full import may be clear only to the person who speaks them.

This "saturated" quality and the power to surprise are not found exclusively in inner speech. To a greater or lesser degree, all language is psychologically rich, all words are given shades of meaning by the various contexts in which we have heard them used, and all words have the power to evoke those contexts. This characteristic of language accounts for puns, in which a word usually encountered in one context appears in a different context. (Linguist Kenneth Pike cites this example: "Even worse than raining cats and dogs is hailing taxis" [131].) And, of course, it can lead to misunderstanding and even apparent lapses in reasoning. People can talk past each other partly because the contexts a given word evokes for one individual or group are different from the contexts evoked for another individual or group.

A relatively innocuous example of this last point: A middle school teacher wanted her students to become more sensitive to the assumptions they brought to language, so she asked them to write a response to the question, "Do they have a July 4th in England?" One student wrote: "No, they don't. I know because my family and I were in London last summer." Other students agreed, not because they assumed that Britain and the United States operated on different calendars, but because, as they mentioned in a class discussion of the teacher's question, they were thinking of July 4th in the context of American independence from England.

The evocative power of language, combined with its generalizing power, plays a large role in creativity. Any time we use a word, we imply that what we are referring to is in some important way like some other thing (idea, object, feeling, etc.). Further, each evoked context may give us a fresh perspective on the *sense* of a word, and in evoking different contexts, a given word may lead us to surprise ourselves by making unexpected connections among apparently different concepts, feelings, or perceptions.

It may be, as Britton and others have argued, that this sort of surprise is more likely to happen when we are able to use language playfully, spontaneously.[8] But there is always the potential for any given word or group of words to evoke the *sense(s)* associated with any context and for that context to evoke—in Vygotsky's phrase "flow into" (*Mind* 147)—still other contexts, other *senses*. Once the flow is set in motion, there is, literally, no telling where it may lead.

The processes of selecting, generalizing, and evoking usually occur quickly and spontaneously. Yet these processes do constitute strategies, ways of examining and reflecting upon ideas, perceptions, feelings, memories. We may choose to engage in these strategies consciously; indeed, we may need to, if only to check on the tacit assumptions that are directing (and sometimes misdirecting) our efforts to create meaning. But whether we use them deliberately or intuitively, these strategies are inherent in language and, thus, they are as unavoidable as they are unpredictable.

Classroom Discourse

Another perspective on strategy comes from what may seem an unlikely source: a discussion in which a class of tenth graders (cited by Massialas and Zevin 98–103) are trying to identify a historical artifact, a small statue of a Sumerian priest. These students have been labeled by their school district as "low average" in ability (the mean IQ score for the class is 91), and they have had little previous experience with this sort of work. Nonetheless, they successfully identify the object, displaying in the process some useful strategies for examining and making sense of unfamiliar information.

After the statuette is passed around the class and students take about fifteen minutes to examine it, the discussion begins as follows:

Teacher.	What do you think this is?
Gary.	A Buddha.
Ivan.	A girl who lost her hair?
Ken.	It's not a girl but a man. Have a closer look.
Gary.	A Buddhist monk.
Ivan.	Is it Chinese? Aztec? Mayan?
Michael.	The Rolling Stones!
Cynthia.	His ears don't match.

Mary Ann.	And his head is lopsided.
Carla.	One eye is lower than the other.
Ivan.	It's a Chinese god.
Michael.	It's an Egyptian god.
Gary.	Some guy struck his father and they cut his hands off.
Mary Ann.	Does it say anything on the bottom?
Bill.	Made in Japan!
Michael.	It looks like a god.
Bill.	It's a slave from Egypt.
Gary.	It looks like a monk.
Paulette.	It's a surgeon who got his hands cut off.
Carol.	But his hands look like they were broken off.
Ivan.	Is it Chinese? Tibetan? Laos?

At first glance, this discussion may seem unfocused, even random. Students speak quickly, and they don't elaborate their assertions or sustain a particular topic for any length of time. Nonetheless, this discussion reflects strategies, ways of knowing that can be used in a variety of contexts. Perhaps because of the teacher's initial question, students begin by trying to identify the object as a member of a class of things. In some cases, the classes are large and relatively predictable: statues of Buddha, monks, Egyptian gods, Chinese gods. In other cases, the class is much more narrowly defined: "a girl who lost her hair," a "guy [who] struck his father," or "a surgeon who got his hands cut off." But in all these cases, students are *applying—sometimes seriously, sometimes whimsically—generic labels to a specific object*. And they are, simultaneously, *posing alternative interpretations* in the form of a wide and imaginative range of labels for the object. In a couple of instances they also support their claims by *focusing on specific features of the object*. When Ivan suggests that the statue represents a girl, Ken responds: "It's not a girl, but a man. Have a closer look." Carol rejects Paulette's suggestion that the statue represents "a surgeon who got his hands cut off" because "his hands look like they were broken off."

An excerpt from a subsequent day's discussion shows these tenth graders using additional strategies.

Ken.	It's an Egyptian priest.
Michael.	It's an Egyptian slave.
Bill.	It's an Egyptian king holding those two things—flags? emblems? and he has his hands crossed. . . .
Teacher.	Can you prove it?

Carol.	We can eliminate the Egyptian. Page 53 in our book gives a picture of an Egyptian. They wore head-pieces, and different clothing. The *World Book* has pictures of Aztecs. He doesn't look like them.
Michael.	Whoever made that must have been intelligent. You can't just sit down and make something like that.
Bill.	The Egyptians were intelligent.
Carol.	It doesn't have an Egyptian wardrobe on. It's not dressed for Egyptian weather. They wore head-pieces like scarves to protect themselves from the sun.
Bill.	Kings dressed like that, but did the peasants?
Michael.	I think he looks like a slave because he doesn't have a shirt on.
Mary Ann.	But that [outfit] took a lot of work to make.
Michael.	He has to be in the lower class.
Bill.	He's Babylonian, or maybe he's Assyrian.
Nell.	I think he's a Sumerian. Page 61 looks just like him.
Carol.	But there's a Sumerian woman on page 66 and the eyes and such are completely different.

In this session, discussion is less wide-ranging. The Rolling Stones and Chinese gods are no longer under consideration. Here students display a new strategy for testing claims. In addition to focusing on specific features, they eliminate alternative interpretations by *relating the specific features of the unknown object to objects that can be identified,* that is, statues depicted in their textbook. In a very few instances, they also appear to be *drawing on their own background knowledge.* Carol, for example, doesn't appear to be referring to the textbook when she rejects the "Egyptian" hypothesis because "It doesn't have an Egyptian wardrobe on. It's not dressed for Egyptian weather. They wore headpieces like scarves to protect themselves from the sun." And finally, these students don't simply ignore or dismiss each other's claims. Instead, *they challenge each other's assertions, testing some of the alternatives put forward by their classmates.* As noted earlier, Carol appears to draw on her background knowledge to question Ken's "Egyptian" hypothesis. When Michael asserts that the statue "looks like a slave," Mary Ann implicitly refutes his point by noting the amount of work the statue's "outfit" appeared to entail.

This analysis of students' language and thought is limited in at least two ways. First, one may argue, as John Mayher does, that our language expresses only "the tip of the iceberg of our thoughts" (142).

No written or spoken language can ever capture all the "psychological events" that occur while we are engaged in the meaning-making process. But this tip of the iceberg is our principal access to students' thinking. Granted, as Howard Gardner has pointed out, there are different types of intelligence that may be represented in different symbolic media. Further, as David Mallick has suggested, enacting a text may be a powerful way to understand it, as may be efforts to visualize a text (cf. Odell and Cohick). But for most of us, most of the time, the coin of the realm is written and spoken language. If we want to identify the meaning-making strategies students are using (or misusing or not using), we will have to look closely at their language, informing our analysis by an awareness of the interpersonal, cultural, or rhetorical contexts in which that language exists.

A second limitation of the preceding analysis is that it leaves unanswered any number of questions. Did these students consciously employ these strategies? Would they realize in retrospect that they were using them? If they needed to, would they be able to make deliberate use of these or other strategies? One may speculate about such questions, but given the evidence at hand, it simply is not possible to answer them with any confidence.

It is possible, however, to place some confidence in two conclusions. First, these students' language reflects patterns of inquiry, types of activities that can guide future efforts to reflect upon and make sense of unfamiliar information. Second, their strategies were effective. They were able to construct compelling arguments in support of the conclusions they reached.

Teaching for Meaning Making

The successful work of these tenth grade students leads to this question: If even relatively young students of "low average" ability have somehow developed sophisticated, effective meaning-making strategies, should we teachers try to intervene in a meaning-making process that seems to be working very nicely? If we do so, aren't we trying to fix something that isn't broken? The next several pages will develop a rationale for intervening, for encouraging students to try out new meaning-making strategies and to reflect on and, where necessary, modify the strategies they already are using. This rationale leads to still further questions. How do we choose from the enormous range of strategies suggested in current discussions of thinking and interpersonal interaction? And what does "teaching" these strategies entail? How do we conduct class in ways that help students engage in conscious, relatively systematic activity without overlooking the role of *surprise* in the meaning-making process?

Establishing a Rationale

Why should we try to influence students' meaning-making strategies? Well, sometimes we shouldn't. Any number of scholars (e.g., Barnes, Lindfors, Mayher, Shaughnessy, Tharp and Gallimore) have demonstrated a point that is exemplified in the preceding discussion of tenth grade social studies students: when students—of whatever age or ability—enter our classrooms, they bring with them information and meaning-making strategies that, potentially at least, are extremely valuable in the work we want them to do. Consequently, it would be foolish to assume that students can do only what we specifically teach them. There is much that they can (and must) do for themselves. Yet they still need substantial amounts of help from us.

We provide some of this help when we try to create a classroom environment in which students feel free to take risks, exercise independent judgment, and help determine the topics about which they will read and write. But we need to do more than this. In addition to creating conditions in which the meaning-making process can take place, we must also help students understand and use strategies they need in order to engage more effectively in that process. My rationale for this claim derives in part from Vygotsky's view of learning and in part from a further analysis of social studies students' efforts to identify a historical artifact.

According to Vygotsky, learning occurs when one is working in the "Zone of Proximal Development." This zone is the "distance" between what a student is able to do on his or her own and what the student can accomplish "under adult guidance or in collaboration with more capable peers" (*Mind* 86). In effect, Vygotsky is saying that an important element of our job as teachers is to see that students get help—either from us or from classmates—in doing something that they can't quite yet do on their own—at least not as well or effectively as they might.

As we look closely at students' work, we can begin to see what this help might entail. Specifically, we can identify strategies they should be encouraged to continue using as well as those they need to begin using or use differently. To illustrate this point, here is an excerpt from a discussion in which relatively able (class mean IQ, 125) eleventh grade students were trying to identify the same artifact as were the tenth grade students whose work was described earlier in this chapter (cited in Massialas and Zevin 87–95). As I'll suggest in a moment, the eleventh graders' work is, in some ways, quite different from that of the tenth graders. The differences suggest not that one group is superior to the other but that each group displays some valuable strategies that the other group could probably benefit from learning to use.

After the eleventh graders had spent a little more than a class period discussing the artifact, the following exchanges occur:

Ilyse.	Well, I think that if we agree that this is very old or the reproduction of something very old and that this man is from an advanced Caucasian culture, then it can only be from one place—the Middle East or ancient Greece.
Jim.	That's the "cradle of civilization" area. All of the earliest advanced groups . . . lived there as far as I know.
Dan.	That's what I remember, too. It's got to be from that area.
Lois.	Now all we have to do is figure out which one it is.
Mark.	Maybe it's of the Hebrew origin.
Roberta.	Maybe it's Babylonian or Persian.
Mike.	I still think it's Egyptian.
Jim.	It could be from the Mediterranean islands. Some advanced people lived there, but I don't remember their names.
John.	Wait a minute, it couldn't be Hebrew because they were forbidden to make idols or images of any kind by the Bible.

In this excerpt, the eleventh graders display a strategy that also appears in the tenth graders' discussion: they try to identify the object by relating it to their existing knowledge of history, geography, and religion. However, the eleventh graders used this strategy in a way that the tenth graders never did; they drew on their prior knowledge not simply to identify the object but also to maintain their personal relationships, providing support for others' comments and establishing a politely reasoned basis for their disagreements. For example, When Ilyse draws a conclusion based on what others have said ("if we agree . . . then . . ."), both Jim and Dan use their prior knowledge to support Ilyse's conclusion (e.g., "All of the earliest groups . . . lived there as far as I know"). And when John disagrees with Mark's suggestion that the statue might be Hebrew, he doesn't just dismiss that suggestion but, rather, draws on his own prior knowledge ("it couldn't be Hebrew because they were forbidden to make idols") to suggest a plausible reason for his disagreement. In other words, their use of prior knowledge represented an interpersonal as well as a conceptual strategy.

Furthermore, there was at least one fundamental difference in the ways these two groups approached their task. The eleventh graders showed that they had strategies for monitoring and directing their own work. Ilyse, for example, *summarizes their progress* ("we agree that this is very old") and *sets up a hypothetical relationship based on what they have done thus far* ("If we agree . . . then it can only be from one place"). This metacognitive work of monitoring and directing the meaning-making process also appears when Lois *rephrases their task* so as to help the group see what to do next ("Now all we have to do is . . .").

Although we may admire these eleventh graders' ability to guide their own efforts and to sustain their collaboration, their discussion is a bit troublesome. These eleventh graders seem more inhibited, less spontaneous than do the tenth graders. They do not begin their work by proposing a wide variety of possibilities. Further, they take a very circuitous, needlessly complex route to identifying the object. The student who first suggests that the artifact might be Sumerian is able to do so because she has made a special trip to a local museum, looking for artifacts that might correspond to the one she had seen in class. It's hard to fault this student's initiative. But sometimes problems have to be solved economically, using information that is immediately available.

As suggested earlier, there are limitations as to what one can conclude from looking at any one sample of talk or writing. To make confident generalizations about these students' habits of mind, we would have to work with them in a variety of situations over a period of time. But the excerpts do reflect somewhat different ways of thinking through a particular type of subject. Initially, the tenth graders were relatively uninhibited in brainstorming a wide variety of possible labels for the object. Once past this initial brainstorming session, the tenth graders tended to pay careful attention to specific features of the object and tried to relate those features to an immediately available, authoritative source of information, that is, their textbook. By contrast, the eleventh graders seemed relatively inhibited; certainly, they did not brainstorm as freely or imaginatively as did the tenth graders.

Further, they did not look very closely at the object, nor did they make use of readily available sources of information. They did, however, make much more use of their background knowledge of history, geography, and religion, and they were much more likely to monitor and direct their own inquiry. Insofar as these differences reflect these tenth and eleventh graders' patterns of meaning making, both groups may have a thing or two to learn.

Making Choices

But what are they to learn? How might their teacher decide which strategy(ies) might be useful to each group of students? Why these strategies rather than some others? And how do these strategies fit into a larger scheme of things, some comprehensive view of what people do when they try to construct meaning? There is no shortage of potential answers to these questions. We can draw on discussions of "thinking" strategies that range from the topics of classical rhetoric (comparison, consequence, etc.) to the categories of Bloom and colleagues' *Taxonomy* (e.g., analysis, synthesis, evaluation) to more recent formulations such as "critical" thinking (e.g., Sternberg), "creative" thinking, (e.g., Marzano et al.), "dialogical" thinking (Paul), "lateral" thinking (de Bono), reasoning (Toulmin, Rieke, and Janik), or "transactional" thinking (Marzano). Or we can draw on other approaches that emphasize the social aspects of that process (LeFevre) and, consequently, present ways to describe people's interpersonal strategies. These descriptions range from discussions of "conversational style" (Tannen) to explanations of "turn taking" (Heritage), Rogerian debate (Young, Becker, and Pike), interaction analysis (Bales), speakers' "purposes" (Roberts and Langer), and "dialogical collaboration" (Ede and Lunsford).

Any of these sources can be useful. But none, by itself, will give us and our students all the help we need. Consequently, we find ourselves having to do what we insist that our students must do— put things together for ourselves, testing, rejecting, combining, or modifying existing information until we can articulate something that makes sense for us and our students. Here, as with the rest of our lives, we must construct our own meanings. And it seems like we will probably have to *continue* to construct them. We may find an answer that seems to work well for a particular group of students at a particular time. But there's every reason to think that that answer will be challenged and modified as we encounter new students, new situations, new information about meaning making.

But still we have to start somewhere. If we are to change, it helps to have something in mind that we are changing from. In the next section of this chapter, I want to present a view of strategies for meaning making, a view that has evolved over several years of working with students in a variety of academic disciplines at educational levels ranging from second grade to graduate school. But before doing so, it seems only fair to acknowledge some biases—call them criteria— underlying my particular list of meaning-making strategies. All of these biases reflect one basic assumption: ultimately, any discussion of meaning-making strategies will have to be useful to teachers and to students of all ages and ability levels.

For one thing, it seems clear that any list of meaning-making strategies will have to be relatively brief and widely applicable.[9] We can't ask students to learn to use great long lists of strategies, as represented in the three-page outline of the activities of critical thinking cited by Marzano and his colleagues. Nor can we ask students to learn a completely different set of strategies for each task they undertake. If we did, they would spend all their time learning strategies and never get around to doing any substantive work. Consequently, any strategy or set of strategies will have to be relatively short and icsimple and yet adaptable enough to meet the various demands of different discourse communities or different academic subjects.[10] Further, the strategies will need to be as useful for interpersonal interaction as for reading and writing. They should be as useful for "critical" thinking as for "creative" thinking and as helpful in reflecting on one's emotions, values, memories, and personal experiences as in thinking through abstract, impersonal subjects. And finally, they should be as applicable to narration as to exposition or argumentation.[11]

In addition to being widely applicable and relatively simple, any list of strategies must have generative and descriptive power. These lists should help students understand specific actions they might take in order to begin, carry out, and assess the meaning-making process. Such strategies, of course, cannot pretend to be algorithms, recipes that if followed correctly will lead inevitably to a single, correct answer. But they can suggest actions readers and writers can take to get their minds going and provide the basis for imagination and insight. These strategies should also allow teachers and students to describe what students are currently doing as well as to determine what they might begin doing, stop doing, or do differently as they engage in the process of meaning making.

These criteria help explain not only what is included in my list of strategies (see below, "Identifying Strategies") but also what is excluded from that list. Conspicuously absent are some of the terms that often appear in discussions of thinking or meaning making. For example, the list does not contain familiar terms such as *analysis, evaluation, giving reasons, synthesis, making predictions, or metacognition.* Such terms are valuable in that they imply long-range goals. That is, we want students to learn to analyze more thoughtfully, to get better at the metacognitive work of monitoring and directing their own meaning-making processes. But such terms have relatively little descriptive or generative power.

Assume, for example, that we want students to give sound reasons for their claims or to synthesize material from several sources. Simply exhorting students to synthesize or give reasons may not be enough, especially if students lack an intuitive grasp of terms like *synthesize* or if students are dealing with particularly challenging topics. In such cases, we may need to suggest some of the things students might do in order to help themselves formulate reasons or arrive at a synthesis.

If we are to make appropriate suggestions about what students might begin doing (or stop doing or do differently), we must be able to describe what they are currently doing. Otherwise, our suggestions may be redundant or simply beside the point. In other words, we haven't given ourselves or our students much information if we can only say that a given student is doing a poor (or mediocre or excellent) job of synthesizing or giving reasons. Once we make such judgments, we need to be able to say what the student is doing that makes the work seem particularly strong or weak.

Identifying Strategies

The next several pages describe five basic meaning-making strategies: *selecting and encoding; creating/acknowledging dissonance; drawing on prior knowledge; seeing relationships; and varying one's perspective.* This list of strategies reflects theory and research in several areas: cognitive psychology, rhetoric, studies of interpersonal interaction, and discussions of "critical" and "creative" thinking. My understanding of these strategies has evolved over several years' experience in trying to describe the writing, talking, and thinking of my own students and those of other teachers, as well. That experience leads me to believe that some combination of these strategies is likely to come into play whenever students (or indeed, anyone) attempt to create meaning. These strategies appear not only when students examine and try to make sense of a particular subject but also when they do the metacognitive work of monitoring and directing their own meaning-making activities.

As Dan Kirby and Carol Kuykendall have pointed out, a list of meaning-making strategies may seem to imply that those strategies are discrete and unrelated. Further, a listing may imply that strategies are related in a linear sequence, that strategy X must always be carried out before strategy Y. However, any analysis of people's thinking (cf. the discussion of tenth and eleventh graders, above) makes it clear that these strategies are highly interrelated and occur in recursive rather than linear patterns.

Selecting and Encoding. The terms *selecting* and *encoding*, which I have adapted from the work of psychologist Robert Sternberg, can be defined separately, but for all practical purposes they are inextricably linked together. *Selecting* entails focusing our attention on some things and either reducing others to marginal awareness or ignoring them altogether. It also entails shifting the focus of our attention, moving back and forth between relatively small details and larger outlines.[12] *Encoding* entails representing our thoughts, feelings, observations, memories. Typically, we do this through written or spoken language. But we can also encode through numerical or scientific symbols, visual images, music, or any other communicative medium. Further, encoding can entail a process that Bloom and his colleagues label "translation," that is, putting "a communication into other language, into other terms, or into another form of communication" (89).

Because all language has the power to select, generalize, and evoke (see earlier discussion of Vygotsky), any use of language (i.e., any effort to select and encode) can function as an exploratory strategy. But in the field of composition studies, we have been especially aware of the exploratory value of informal, spontaneous language—journals, personal narratives, learning logs.[13] And specialists in interpersonal communication have been especially sensitive to the value of paraphrasing or summarizing as a way to clarify our own thoughts or to check for understanding of what someone else has said. If we want to understand other people's (or our own) meaning making, some of the most useful questions we can ask are: What are they focusing on? How are they representing what they focus on? What assumptions are implicit in those representations? How do those representations reflect speakers' or writers' membership in various discourse communities?

Creating/Acknowledging Dissonance. Dissonance entails a sense of uncertainty or an awareness of some sort of conflict. We feel dissonance in several different kinds of situations. There may be a conflict between us and our surroundings—a conflict, for example, between what we expect and what we encounter; between what we think (feel, perceive, remember, value) and what someone else thinks, feels, and so forth. Or the dissonance may arise within us—our thoughts about one subject may be inconsistent with our thoughts about another; we may realize that our values are inconsistent with our actions; or we may realize that there is some gap in our understanding of the world.

Most often, dissonance is expressed—in talk or in writing—as a question, a challenge, a disagreement, a criticism, a feeling of uncertainty. Sometimes we become aware of dissonance whether we mean to or not; as we read (or listen, observe) we find ourselves thinking, Wait a minute. That's not right. I don't get it. . . . In other cases, as I'll illustrate in the next section with references to Donald Murray's work, we deliberately set out to think of questions or play devil's advocate. In all cases, scholars such as Jean Piaget and Leon Festinger contend that an awareness of dissonance is the motivation for all human activity, whether cognitive, affective, or physical. The notion of dissonance is central to work in rhetoric (see Lloyd Bitzer's discussion of rhetorical "exigence"), problem solving (cf. Flower, *Problem-Solving Strategies*), Reading (cf. Langer 75–82), and interpersonal interaction (see, for example, Roberts and Langer's analysis of conversational turns in which participants in a discussion disagree, challenge, or "up the ante").

Drawing on Prior Knowledge. We don't approach any experience as a blank slate. In dealing with a routine event, we can draw upon what Roger C. Schank refers to as a "script," that is, "a set of expectations about what will happen next in a well-understood situation" (7). And even if subject matter is totally unfamiliar to us, we can compare it with our existing values, beliefs, and personal experiences as well as the information or theory we have gained from schooling, from reading, or from our general knowledge of our culture. If we are to understand—indeed, if we are even to remember—any experience, we must be able to relate it to and integrate it with what Kenneth Boulding has called our "image" of the world or what Reading theorists and researchers refer to as the mental *schema* we bring to bear upon any subject we read or write about. Summarizing a number of studies of reading, Janice Dole and her colleagues point out that prior knowledge may take several forms: knowledge about the specific topic at hand; more general knowledge about "social relationships and causal structures"; and understanding of ways texts are organized. It may also include knowledge of strategies—about their nature, about how they might be used, and about the circumstances under which they might be used (241).

Seeing Relationships. When we consider a body of information, we must not only relate it to what we already know, we must also consider ways in which some aspects of that information relate to others. Confronted with a lot of information, we may need to look for categories or subcategories within that information. Having focused on a fact, an action, a feeling, a concept, we may need to classify it, label it, or see how it's similar to some other fact.

This effort to find similarities is often closely linked to attempts to observe how something differs from other comparable things or how it conflicts with what one hopes, thinks, or expects. Or we may need to relate a given phenomenon to the setting in which it occurs or to sequences of events: What led up to or caused it? What are its consequences? What if the phenomenon were modified in some way?

The effort to see relationships is represented in familiar terminology: comparison, contrast, classification, analogy, cause-effect, and so forth. This terminology appears not only in rhetorical theory (cf. Corbett; Young, Becker, and Pike) but in discussions of *thinking* (see, for example, Sternberg 91–92, 112–14, 141–43, 191–92). For an explanation of ways to recognize these relationships in language, see my essay "Measuring Changes in Intellectual Processes as One Dimension of Growth in Writing."

Varying Perspective. Inevitably we approach any subject from our own perspective. But we can at least enlarge that perspective. In doing so, we might try to empathize with someone else (a literary character, an opponent in a debate), projecting ourselves into their role, trying to think and feel as they might feel or as we might think and feel if we were in their situation. Or we might deliberately seek out different interpretations of an issue or set of data.

We might begin, as philosopher Richard Paul suggests, by asking whether someone else might not have responses or interpretations that differ from our own. We can learn to engage in the "pro and con reasoning" that Thomas O. Sloan suggests is at the heart of rhetoric's tradition of challenging dogmatism. We can also alternate between playing what Peter Elbow has called the "doubting game"—in which we look for weaknesses in someone else's position—and the "believing game"—in which we try to look for information that tends to confirm someone else's assertion or try to think of circumstances in which that assertion might seem reasonable or at least plausible (*WWT*). As we vary our perspective, we may simply get a clearer notion of the ideas we want to refute through our own writing. But as Young, Becker, and Pike point out, there is an excellent chance that our own understanding of a subject will grow and that our own perspective will actually be changed.

Teaching Strategy, Encouraging Surprise

Having decided what sort of strategies we want to work with, how do we proceed? How do we conduct class in such a way that students learn to make the fullest, most effective possible use of strategy while remaining open to surprise, to the unexpected, unpredictable insights that are so crucial to the meaning-making process? How do we teach strategy while encouraging surprise? Obviously, these are the kinds of questions that don't lend themselves to neat, definitive answers. In my own experience at least, the answer seems to change somewhat with each class of students. Nonetheless, current work in the teaching of writing gives us a number of ideas as to how we might proceed. But these pedagogical ideas make sense only in light of some basic understandings.

For one thing, the strategies described above are not subject matter to be memorized and tested, nor are they skills to be "practiced" through exercises that are unrelated to the rest of what we are trying to teach. In other words, these strategies are not ends in themselves; they are, rather, means of helping students figure out something they see as worth figuring out. Moreover, these strategies are highly interrelated, and they work recursively rather than in a linear, rational manner. For example, the effort to draw on one's prior knowledge may lead to questions that lead to some unexpected insight into, say, cause-effect relationships. These insights may, in turn, lead back to further consideration of prior knowledge. Consequently, students need to work with strategies in contexts that allow exploration and speculation, contexts, in other words, that encourage surprise.

Introducing Strategies. In trying to think of ways to introduce strategies, we can draw on the work of some of our most respected teachers of writing. Consider the example Murray provides in *Write to Learn.* Murray does not use the term strategy, nor does he ever use a term like *cognitive dissonance.* But Murray does talk about "techniques" or "tricks of the trade" (88). And, as I'll explain in a moment, Murray repeatedly makes it clear that one of his favorite techniques is to acknowledge dissonance or deliberately set out to create dissonance.

In introducing his readers to various tricks of the trade, Murray demonstrates some of the things we might do in introducing students to any strategy. For one thing, when Murray recommends strategies, his recommendations are both specific and flexible. For instance, in explaining how students might sort through lots of potential material and focus their writing, Murray gives particular emphasis to dissonance, showing how students might focus on those aspects of their material that are most surprising (89–90). But he also suggests other focusing techniques, such as looking for a "revealing specific" (90) or calling up visual images that have personal meaning to the writer. (To relate Murray's suggestions to the list of strategies I described earlier: both of his suggestions entail allowing personal feelings or connotations to guide one's *selecting* [see earlier discussion of selecting and encoding].) In other words, Murray makes it clear that we need to have access to a variety of strategies. If one doesn't work—and no strategy works all the time in all circumstances—we need to be able to suggest alternatives.

Further, Murray is careful to provide a rationale for the strategies he discusses. Before recommending ways students might focus their writing, he carefully sets the context for his recommendations, talking about the "overwhelming problem" writers face when they have "too much to say, too many possibilities, no clear priority within the information [they have gathered]" (86). In this and other instances throughout the book, Murray dramatizes the importance of setting recommendations in a context that student writers can see as meaningful.

Finally, and probably most important, Murray reminds us of the need to provide models of the processes we want students to use. Without ever using the term *cognitive dissonance*, he repeatedly shows how he makes use of this strategy. He shows instances in which he uses questions to help himself find a subject (25), clarify rhetorical purpose (97), and to "check for meaning" of a draft (213–19). Further, he shows how his own composing is guided by an awareness of disparities—especially surprising disparities—between what he expected and what he finds, between what he had previously understood and what he is discovering, and between what he had hoped to do and what he is doing (25–26, 37, 89, 266–67).

As Murray's text demonstrates, providing examples of one's own composing processes can be extremely powerful. Such modeling both helps clarify the strategies we are encouraging students to use and also demonstrates that our recommendations have the authority of personal experience. But, of course, our own experience is not the only source of models. We can ask students to look at the work of their classmates, identifying the strategies that are reflected in a written text and listening to a classmate's account of strategies that helped produce that text. In addition, we can devise class activities that model the strategies we want students to use. (See, for example, George Hillocks's discussion [this volume] of ways to introduce students to inquiry processes.)

Encouraging Surprise. Obviously, it is not enough simply to introduce strategies and hope that students will somehow begin to use them. We also need to create classroom conditions that encourage surprise. In part, this means creating a climate of trust in our classrooms, a climate that encourages students to take risks and, thereby, increase the chances of surprise. No trust, no risk-taking. No risk-taking, no surprise.

Further, we need to combine work with strategy with occasions for exploratory language—freewheeling discussions, brainstorming, or freewriting/journal writing. Like Murray, I find it extremely important for students to ask questions throughout their writing process. But many of my students somehow have learned that it is the teacher's job to ask questions and the students' job to answer them. To help get them into a question-asking mode, I sometimes bring in a piece of writing that I suspect they will find problematic. Then I ask them to write for a few minutes, quickly listing every question they can think of concerning that piece of writing. "What sort of questions?" they invariably ask, apparently assuming that there are right questions just as there are right answers. My response is, any sort. Just ask questions and see where they lead. Then I ask students to talk with two or three classmates, trying to see where their questions were similar and where they were different, and noting additional questions that come up as they talk.

In the course of this talk, students may go beyond question-asking: Maybe their discussion leads them to some unexpected insight, which in turn leads them to reexamine the text at hand; maybe a question leads them to reflect on their prior knowledge. That's fine. The various strategies, after all, are interrelated. My goal is to show them that one way to approach a difficult topic is to begin by asking questions. If they'll do this in an exploratory, spontaneous way, they increase their chances of coming up with ideas they didn't have or couldn't have articulated when they started the question-asking process.

This same basic approach seems to apply to any of the other strategies described earlier in this chapter. Maybe students aren't making full use of knowledge they already possess; maybe they need to look at an issue from different perspectives; maybe they just need to quit editing every word before they put it on paper. In any of these cases, what seems to help is to ask students to use one of these strategies in informal, exploratory ways that encourage—*encourage*, not guarantee—surprise.

Practicing What We Preach

Ultimately, I suspect, if we want to help students with the mean-ing-making process, we ourselves will have to be continually engaged in that process—not just as writers who are trying to think through a particular topic, but as students of the meaning-making process itself. There are, after all, any number of questions that we have scarcely begun to consider. For example, from what I've seen, the meaning-making strategies described above appear to operate in a wide range of subject matters and grade levels. But David N. Perkins and Gavriel Salomon have argued that general cognitive strategies need to be supplemented by the "local knowledge" shared by insiders in a particular discourse community. In effect, they lead us to think about this sort of question: What does someone have to know in order to use a given strategy effectively in a given context? What kind of background knowledge does one have to have in order to ask a meaningful question in biology? And how is that knowledge different from or similar to the knowledge needed to ask a significant question in, say, history, or even in a different biology course?

So there are all sorts of new questions we need to consider. And, to complicate things, we can't even afford to become complacent about our current answers. The psychologist George Kelly begins one of his essays by asserting that the essay is, at best, filled with "half truths." His point is that all our knowledge is provisional, subject to ongoing scrutiny and revision. Consequently, it's likely that we will find ourselves continually rethinking the meaning-making strategies we hope to teach, redefining some, temporarily (or permanently) abandoning others, understanding new uses and new limitations of still others. If it's important for our students to engage in the meaning-making process, it's equally important for us to do so as well. After all, why should our students be the only ones to learn something from our courses? Why should they have all the fun?

Notes

1. For an earlier discussion of strategy and surprise, see Young, Becker, and Pike 71–77.

2. Richard Young ("Invention"; "Recent") has summarized the work of many who share this assumption. The assumption is also implicit in George Hillocks's discussion of "inquiry" (180–86) and in Judith A. Langer and Arthur N. Applebee's discussion of "reasoning operations." Further, the terms Doralyn Roberts and Judith Langer use to describe students' "intentions" in group discussions also imply strategies one might use in facilitating a group's efforts to construct meaning.

3. Over the years, a number of people in composition or English education have emphasized the importance of the unconscious in the composing process. See, for example, Emig, Kinney, Johnson, Mayher, Stafford.

4. See, for example, essays by Pat D'Arcy, Peter Stillman, Pat Belanoff, Mary Jane Dickerson, Nancie Atwell ("Building"), or Toby Fulwiler in Fulwiler's *Journal Book*.

5. Systematic approaches have been derived from a variety of sources including classical rhetoric (e.g., Corbett; Sloan), current work on problem solving (most notably, Flower *Problem*), philosophy (e.g., Paul), and linguistics (e.g., Young, Becker, and Pike).

6. Cognitve psychologist Robert Sternberg points out that we have to be able to "automatize" many of our cognitive processes; indeed, he suggests, the ability to do so may be one important aspect of intelligence (32).

7. See Hayakawa, *Language in Thought and Action* 154.

8. Hillocks, however, cites evidence that the use of freewriting does not necessarily enable students to produce more creative essays.

9. For a discussion of generic thinking strategies, see David Perkins's

Mind's Best Work. But see also Perkins and Gavirel Salomon's discussion of the importance of supplementing generic strategies with "local knowledge."

10. A number of people (e.g., Bazerman, Herrington, Odell ["Process"], Kinneavy) have argued that different discourse communities make different conceptual demands upon people in those communities. Thus, the questions asked by an anthropologist, for example, might differ significantly from the questions asked by a political scientist or a student of literature. However, in all of these communities, one fundamental intellectual act is asking questions.

11. Jerome Bruner and Roger C. Schank have discussed the unique features of narrative, and James Moffett has pointed out significant differences between "chronological" thinking (e.g., narration) and "analogical" thinking (as often represented in argumentation or exposition). However, as I have tried to illustrate in "Written Products and the Writing Process," some of the same conceptual processes are reflected in both exposition and narration.

12. For an explanation of one way this shifting of focus appears in written texts, see my essay "Written Products and the Writing Process."

13. In *Problem-Solving Strategies for Writing*, Linda Flower has argued that our efforts to compose formal discourse can be helped by what she refers to as the WIRMI strategy. Especially when writers are feeling stuck or uncertain, Flower recommends that they try to blurt out—in speech or writing—an ending to the sentence What I really mean is . . . (31).

Works Cited

Atwell, Nancie. "Building a Dining Room Table: Dialogue Journals about Reading." Fulwiler 157–70.

———. *In the Middle*. Portsmouth, NH: Boynton/Cook, 1987.

Bales, Robert F. *Interaction Process Analysis*. Chicago: U of Chicago P, 1950.

Barnes, Douglas. *From Communication to Curriculum*. London: Penguin, 1976.

Bazerman, Charles. *Shaping Written Knowledge*. Madison: U of Wisconsin P, 1988.

Belanoff, Pat. "The Role of Journals in the Interpretive Community." Fulwiler 101–10.

Bitzer, Lloyd. "The Rhetorical Situation." *Philosophy and Rhetoric* 1 (1968): 1–14.

Bloom, Benjamin S., M. D. Engelhart, E. J. Furst, and D. R. Krathwohl, eds. *Taxonomy of Educational Objectives: The Classification of Educational Goals. Handbook I: Cognitive Domain*. New York: McKay, 1956.

Boulding, Kenneth E. *The Image*. Ann Arbor: U of Michigan P, 1964.

Britton, James. "Shaping at the Point of Utterance." *Prospect and Retrospect*. Ed. Gordon Pradle. Portsmouth, NH: Boynton/Cook, 1982.

———. "Theories of the Disciplines and a Learning Theory." *Writing, Teaching, and Learning in the Disciplines.* Ed. Anne Herrington and Charles Moran. New York: MLA, 1992.

Britton, James, Tony Burgess, Nancy Martin, Alex McLeod, and Harold Rosen. *The Development of Writing Abilities.* London: Macmillan, 1975.

Bruner, Jerome. "Narrative and Paradigmatic Modes of Thought." *Learning, Teaching, and Ways of Knowing.* Ed. Elliot Eisner. Natl. Soc. for the Study of Educ., 1985. 97–115.

Burke, Kenneth. "Terministic Screens." *Language as Symbolic Action: Essays on Life, Literature, and Method.* Berkeley: U of California P, 1966. 44–62.

Corbett, Edward P. J. *Classical Rhetoric for the Modern Student.* New York: Oxford UP, 1965.

D'Arcy, Pat. "Writing to Learn." Fulwiler 41–46.

de Bono, Edward. *Lateral Thinking.* New York: Harper, 1970.

Dickerson, Mary Jane. "Exploring the Inner Landscape: The Journal in the Writing Class." Fulwiler 129–36.

Dole, Janice A., Gerald D. Duffy, Laura R. Roehler, and P. David Pearson. "Moving from the Old to the New: Research on Reading Comprehension Instructon." *Review of Educational Research* 61 (1991): 239–64.

Ede, Lisa, and Andrea Lunsford. *Singular Texts/Plural Authors: Perspectives on Collaborative Learning.* Carbondale: Southern Illinois UP, 1990.

Elbow, Peter. *Writing With Power.* New York: Oxford UP, 1981.

———. *Writing Without Teachers.* New York: Oxford UP, 1973.

Emig, Janet. "The Uses of the Unconscious in Composing." *College Composition and Communication* 21 (1964): 6–11.

Festinger, Leon. *Toward a Theory of Cognitive Dissonance.* Stanford: Stanford UP, 1957.

Flower, Linda. *Problem-Solving Strategies for Writing.* New York: Harcourt, 1981.

Flower, Linda, and Lorraine Higgins. *Collaboration and the Construction of Meaning.* Technical Report No. 56. Berkeley: Center for the Study of Writing, 1991.

Fulwiler, Toby. Introduction. *The Journal Book.* Ed. Toby Fulwiler. Portsmouth, NH: Boynton/Cook, 1987. 1–8.

Gardner, Howard. *Frames of Mind: The Theory of Multiple Intelligence.* New York: Bantam Books, 1983.

Ghiselin, Brewster, ed. *The Creative Process.* New York: NAL, 1952.

Hayakawa, S. I. *Language in Thought and Action.* New York: Harcourt, 1949.

———. *Symbol, Status, and Personality.* New York: Harcourt, 1963.

Heritage, John. *Garfinkel and Methodology.* Cambridge: Polity, 1984.

Herrington, Anne. "Writing in Academic Settings: A Study of the Context for Writing in Two College Chemical Engineering Courses." *Research in the Teaching of English* 19 (1985): 331–59.

Hillocks, George, Jr. *Research on Written Composition: New Directions for Teach-*

ing. ERIC Clearinghouse on Reading and Communication Skills, National Conference on Research in English, 1986.

Johnson, Sabina Thorne. "The Ant and the Grasshopper: Some Reflections on Prewriting." *College English* 43 (1981): 232–41.

Kelly, George. "The Autobiography of a Theory." *Clinical Psychology and Personality: The Selected Papers of George Kelly*. Ed. Brendan Maher. New York: Wiley, 1969.

Kinneavy, James. *A Theory of Discourse*. New York: Norton, 1970.

Kinney, James. "Tagmemic Rhetoric: A Reconsideration." *College Composition and Communication* 29 (1978): 141–45.

Kirby, Dan, and Carol Kuykendall. *Mind Matters: Teaching for Thinking*. Portsmouth, NH: Boynton/Cook, 1991.

Knoblauch, C. H., and Lil Brannon. *Rhetorical Traditions and the Teaching of Writing*. Portsmouth, NH: Boynton/Cook, 1984.

Koestler, Arthur. *The Act of Creation*. New York: Dell, 1964.

Langer, Judith A. *Children Reading and Writing: Structures and Strategies*. Norwood, NJ: Ablex, 1986.

Langer, Judith A., and Arthur N. Applebee. *How Writing Shapes Thinking: A Study of Teaching and Learning*. Urbana: NCTE, 1987.

LeFevre, Karen. *Invention as a Social Act*. Carbondale: Southern Illinois UP, 1987.

Lindfors, Judith Wells. "Speaking Creatures in the Classroom." *Perspectives on Talk and Learning*. Ed. Susan Hynds and Donald L. Rubin. Urbana: NCTE, 1990. 21–39.

Macrorie, Kenneth. *Telling Writing*. Rochelle Park, NJ: Hayden, 1970.

Mallick, David. *How Tall Is This Ghost, John?* Portsmouth, NH: Heinemann, 1984.

Marzano, Robert J. *Cultivating Thinking in English and the Language Arts*. Urbana: NCTE, 1991.

Marzano, Robert J., Ronald S. Brandt, Carolyn Sue Hodges, Beau Fly Jones, Barbara Z. Presseisen, Stuart C. Rankin, and Charles Suhor. *Dimensions of Thinking: A Framework for Curriculum and Instruction*. Alexandria, VA: Assoc. for Supervision and Curriculum Development, 1988.

Massialas, Byron G., and Jack Zevin. *Creative Encounters in the Classroom*. New York: Wiley, 1967.

Mayher, John. *Uncommon Sense: Theoretical Practice in Language Education*. Portsmouth, NH: Boynton/Cook, 1990.

Moffett, James. *Teaching the Universe of Discourse*. Boston: Houghton, 1968.

Murray, Donald M. *Write to Learn*. 2nd ed. New York: Holt, 1987.

———. "Writing and Teaching for Surprise." *College English* 46 (1984): 1–7.

Odell, Lee. "Measuring Changes in Intellectual Processes as One Dimension of Growth in Writing." *Evaluating Writing: Describing, Measuring, Judging*. Ed. Charles R. Cooper and Lee Odell. Urbana: NCTE, 1977. 107–32.

------. "The Process of Writing and the Process of Learning." *College Composition and Communication* 31 (1980): 42–50.

------. "Written Products and the Writing Process." *The Writer's Mind: Writing as a Mode of Thinking*. Ed. Janice N. Hays, Phyllis Roth, Jon R. Ramsey, and Robert D. Foulke. Urbana: NCTE, 1983. 53–65.

Odell, Lee, and Joanne Cohick. "Writing about Literature." *On Righting Writing*. Ed. Ouida H. Clapp. Urbana: NCTE, 1975. 42–47.

Paul, Richard W. "Dialogical Thinking: Critical Thought Essential to the Acquisition of Rational Knowledge and Passions." *Teaching Thinking Skills: Theory and Practice*. Ed. Joan Boykoff Baron and Robert J. Sternberg. New York: Freeman, 1987: 127–48.

Perkins, David N. *The Mind's Best Work*. Cambridge, MA: Harvard UP, 1981.

Perkins, David N., and Gavriel Salomon. "Are Cognitive Skills Context-Bound?" *Educational Researcher* Jan.–Feb. 1989: 16–25.

Piaget, Jean. *Six Psychological Studies*. New York: Vintage-Random, 1968.

Pike, Kenneth. "Beyond the Sentence." *College Composition and Communication* 40 (1964): 129–35.

Rapoport, Anatol. *Fights, Games, and Debates*. Ann Arbor: U of Michigan P, 1960.

Rico, Gabrielle Lusser. *Writing the Natural Way*. Los Angeles: Tarcher, 1983.

Roberts, Doralyn R., and Judith A. Langer. "Supporting the Process of Literary Understanding: An Analysis of a Classroom Discussion." Center for the Study of Literature, State U of New York at Albany.

Schank, Roger C. *Tell Me A Story: A New Look at Real and Artificial Memory*. New York: Scribner's, 1990.

Shaughnessy, Mina. *Errors and Expectations*. New York: Oxford UP, 1977.

Sloan, Thomas O. "Reinventing Inventio." *College English* 51 (1989): 461–73.

Stafford, William. "Writing the Australian Crawl." *College Composition and Communication* 15 (1964): 12–15.

Sternberg, Robert J. *Intelligence Applied: Understanding and Increasing Your Intellectual Skills*. San Diego: Harcourt, 1986.

Stillman, Peter. " 'Of Myself, for Myself.' " Fulwiler 77–86.

Tannen, Deborah. *Conversational Style*. Norwood, NJ: Ablex, 1984.

Tharp, Roland G., and Ronald Gallimore. *Rousing Minds to Life*. Cambridge: Cambridge UP, 1990.

Toulmin, Stephen, Richard Rieke, and Allan Janik. *An Introduction to Reasoning*. 2nd ed. New York: Macmillan, 1984.

Vygotsky, L. S. *Mind in Society: The Development of Higher Psychological Processes*. Ed. and trans. Michael Cole, V. John-Steiner, Sylvia Scribner, and E. Souberman. Cambridge, MA: Harvard UP, 1978.

------. *Thought and Language*. Cambridge, MA: MIT P, 1966.

Young, Richard. "Invention: A Topographical Survey." *Teaching Composition:*

10 *Bibliographical Essays*. Ed. Gary Tate. Fort Worth: Texas Christian UP, 1976. 1–43.

———. "Recent Developments in Rhetorical Invention." *Teaching Composition: 12 Bibliographical Essays*. Ed. Gary Tate. Fort Worth: Texas Christian UP, 1987. 1–83.

Young, Richard, Alton Becker, and Kenneth Pike. *Rhetoric: Discovery and Change*. New York: Harcourt, 1970.

8

Environments for Active Learning

George Hillocks, Jr.

During my first summer of graduate school, I took four semester-long courses, each condensed into five or six weeks.[1] Each was based on a set of pedagogical assumptions diametrically opposed to those I now accept. One, a course on Milton, met for two hours of lecture per day, five days a week, for five weeks. We "did," or perhaps more accurately, were scheduled to do all the English poetry, much of the English prose including the divorce tracts, midterm and final papers, four five-page reviews of four book-length studies of Milton, a midterm exam, and a final take-home exam. (During the same semester I took Shakespeare—fifteen plays, etc., etc.) From eight to ten each morning, we listened to the professor drone on and on about texts most of us had not finished trying to read. I remember dutifully forcing myself to eyeball and vocalize the words of *Paradise Lost*, struggling to wrest some kind of sense from what seemed to me to be labyrinthine syntax. By the time I finished a few lines, I realized, even when I understood them, that I had no idea of what that bramble had to do with what I had read earlier on the same page. I believed that death for me as a graduate student in English was imminent. I was terrified.

Then one day our prof did not appear in class; out of town hunting for a house to take a position in linguistics at a prestigious university, we learned. We had a sub for three days, a fairly well known Milton scholar, John S. Diekhoff. Instead of telling us what we *should* make of Milton's work, he asked what we *did* make of it. And he seemed to mean it. Why, he asked, did we think Adam had failed to obey the command of God. Why indeed, I wondered. If Adam were truly naive, as Milton claimed, why should he believe God's warning? If he were truly naive, how could he possibly understand what might await him outside the Garden? These, it turned out, were not the questions Diekhoff had in mind. But he allowed them, encouraged them.

We turned to some of the relevant passages concerning the warnings to Adam and Eve. I still remember how shocked I was that Milton's syntax had *cleared up*. I could read it with only minimal difficulty. It was as though scales had fallen from my eyes. Later I reread the poem with interest and understanding, or at least greater awareness of what was going on and of how the pieces fit together.

Even at the time, I recognized that this effect was more than serendipitous. In the more than thirty years since, I have had ample opportunity to think about it. The conceptual framework through which I examine it now allows me to see that in the first hour of class, Diekhoff had changed the learning environment radically. He refused the vacant despot's throne and took instead the role of learned and empathetic counselor. He allowed our ideas, no matter how poorly conceived, to become a legitimate part of the conversation about *Paradise Lost*. In doing that, he allowed us an important degree of control over classroom events as our ideas became the focus of discussion. As we revealed our knowledge or ignorance, he could respond to us as a friendly counselor might, helping his charges better understand what is for them new territory, but engaging them actively in the exploration. At the same time, this counselor retained control. We were still dealing with the themes and structures of Milton's work. Professor Diekhoff was our guide to the understanding we hoped to achieve.

What Diekhoff did is basic to what I have called elsewhere environmental teaching (Hillocks 1981, 1984, and 1986a), by which I mean teaching that creates environments to induce and support active learning. Such teaching stands in sharp contrast to at least two other instructional modes: the traditional mode that I have called "presentational" and what I have called the "natural process" mode. The first assumes that knowledge can be imparted from teacher or text directly to students prior to engagement in writing and that mastery can be achieved without the support of special teaching structures such as peer group collaboration, even when the knowledge imparted involves learning the use of complex strategies. Working in this mode, one professor (observed as part of a study of teaching writing in two-year colleges) divided his semester into eight two-week periods, one for each writing assignment. His procedure was to lecture on each "type" of writing (e.g., comparison/contrast), carefully explaining its uses, characteristics, and pitfalls before turning to several examples of the type, which students were to read and which the professor explained. To this point, the students did no writing other than to take notes on the lectures. After students had written the required composition, the professor evaluated their papers and requested revisions.

This professor assumed that teaching occurred when words of advice and analysis had been delivered to the students in the form of lectures, textbook readings, and comments on papers. Such teaching carries with it the assumption that students who have the talent and who put in the effort will succeed and, concomitantly, that many students will not put in the effort or do not have the talent. Those assumptions relieve whoever holds them of further responsibility for student failure. This appears to be the most common mode of teaching composition in high schools and colleges (Applebee 1981; Goodlad 1984; Hillocks 1981; Hillocks in progress b).

Those advocating the second mode, what I have called "natural process," reject the use of models, the assignment of topics for writing, and learning the "types" or structures of writing such as the "paragraph" or compare/contrast essay. Some supporters of this mode believe that students should find their own topics and structures, that they should engage in the process of writing, receiving comments from peers as they work through multiple drafts toward a final version that will have developed its own organic structure (Graves 1983). They believe that students learn best when left to their own devices. Most such theorists, however, are concerned with very young students in elementary and middle schools.

This natural process group has made three important breaks with the traditional "presentational" mode of instruction. First, it rejects the possibility of imparting knowledge about writing directly through lectures and textbooks without engaging the students in writing. Second, it focuses attention on the need for knowing and using general writing processes and provides some general procedures for prewriting, revising, giving and receiving feedback, and so forth. Third, and perhaps most important, the natural process mode insists on the need to develop positive dispositions toward writing.

The environmental mode shares certain features with the first two but stands in sharp contrast to both. As Applebee (1986) has pointed out, it shares process with "natural process." While it recognizes the importance of making general writing process an integral part of instruction, it moves well beyond general processes. Nor does it take a laissez-faire approach to process. On the contrary, it places great responsibility on the teacher to develop materials and activities that will engage students in specific processes requisite to particular writing tasks.

In this, it shares with "presentational" approaches the recognition that success in various writing tasks requires specific knowledge. However, it contrasts sharply with the "presentational" in both the kinds of knowledge presented and the way that knowledge is presented. Presentational approaches focus almost exclusively on what Berlin (1984) calls "arrangement" in current-traditional rhetoric (the arrangement of elements in forms of discourse and in the paragraph and through the principles of unity, coherence, and emphasis, p. 68). This knowledge is presented in lecture form, generally as a body of rules to be followed and examples to be emulated.

Environmental approaches, in contrast, provide environments that support students in learning strategies for developing both the content and form of discourse. Rather than lecture on the procedures to follow, this approach engages students in the necessary processes, for example, generating criteria for formal definitions, examining data to develop interpretive generalizations.

Further, proponents of the environmental mode assume with Vygotsky (1978) that students may operate well above their normal levels in tutorials, teacher-led discussions (provided they are true discussions), or in peer groups when provided with support appropriate to their current understanding. At the same time, the environmental mode shares with "natural process" the insistence on engagement, recognizing that without it no amount of support will enable reluctant students to work beyond their current independent levels.

Although the environmental mode shares certain features with the other modes, the differences among them appear to result in sharp differences in student writing. A synthesis of research on these three modes of teaching indicates that the presentational mode of instruction had the least impact on changing students' writing, with posttest scores only slightly better than pretest scores. The natural process groups made considerably more progress, but remained well below the average gain for all studies included in the analysis. The environmental treatment groups proved to have 2.3 times the effect of the natural process groups.[2]

When John Diekhoff entered our Milton class that hot August day many years ago, I believe he simply wished to engage us in conversation about *Paradise Lost*. Perhaps I romanticize that incident now. But as I recall, his questions energized us. Perhaps we were simply happy to be rid of our drone. Perhaps we had been suppressed for too long. While such factors undoubtedly played a part in the transformation of our class for those three days, I believe it would not have taken place without Diekhoff's ability to raise questions that we were able and willing to respond to, an ability based on knowledge born of experience. He knew that questions concerning Adam's motivation would be accessible to us, would engender some level of controversy, and would lead to more complex questions about Milton's theology and the structure of the poem.

At the same time, Diekhoff's seeds of transformation fell on fertile ground. We were, after all, an eager group of graduate students, hoping to become professionals in English, who would have responded to any semblance of interest in our opinions. We all had several years of English study behind us, including several graduate-level courses. We had selected the course on Milton, had already struggled with the text, and were committed to the project of interpreting it. A group of students with such a rich combination of positive dispositions toward the subject, knowledge, and experience is a luxury that most teachers of writing do not have. For most teachers of writing, at whatever level, creating environments for active learning is nowhere near the relatively easy task it was for John Diekhoff. Sometimes such environments seem to occur in classrooms serendipitously. However, my experience and that of my students indicates that maintaining them regularly requires careful, creative planning and reflective practice. Before moving to an examination of a classroom discussion, let us look at what such teaching entails.

Features of Environmental Teaching

In 1986, I described the environmental mode in operational terms as "characterized by (1) clear and specific objectives, e.g., to increase the use of specific detail and figurative language; (2) materials and problems selected to engage students with each other in specifiable processes important to some particular aspect of writing; and (3) activities, such as small-group problem-centered discussions, conducive to high levels of peer interaction concerning specific tasks" (1986a). These three dimensions or characteristics of instruction identified the studies included in the category of environmental teaching. Although this operational definition was useful to the small community of researchers who were familiar with the implications of the terms of the definition, it was not very useful to anyone who wished to put it into action.

Indeed, there are at least four dimensions of this mode of teaching that lie buried in my description, dimensions that are at least as important as those I made explicit. First, not only are the task objectives clear to teachers, but they are operationally clear to students. Second, the materials and problems engage students because they have been selected in view of (*a*) what students are able to do, (*b*) the likelihood of their interest to students, and (*c*) their power to engage students as real world problems. Third, students engage in complex tasks with support from materials, teachers, and/or peers before they proceed to independent work with such tasks. Fourth, students develop a stake or sense of ownership in the classroom proceedings because their ideas and opinions become the focus of classroom activity. Let me examine each of these in greater detail.

Goals and Objectives

The approaches to teaching that seemed to have the most powerful effects on student writing, as revealed in the synthesis mentioned earlier (Hillocks 1986a), always had clear objectives. Further, instructors appear to have made objectives operationally clear to the students by modeling the procedures, coaching students through them in the early stages, or using specially designed activities to facilitate learning the new procedures.

For example, in a series of studies (Hillocks, Kahn, and Johannessen 1983; Hillocks 1989; Hillocks in progress a) I have been focusing on a variety of approaches to teaching students to write extended, analytic definitions. The extended definitions involve comparing and contrasting cases to develop a series of criteria that delimit some particular, relatively abstract concept. Such definitions involve what is sometimes referred to as philosophical analysis. And they are found in the work of philosophers (e.g., Aristotle, *Nichomachean Ethics*), literary critics (e.g., Northrop Frye, *Anatomy of Criticism;* M. M. Bakhtin, *The Dialogic Imagination;* Robert Scholes, *Textual Power*); psychologists seeking to understand various cognitive phenomena (e.g., Stein and Trabasso, "What's in a Story: An Approach to Comprehension and Instruction"); composition researchers (e.g., Hayes and Flower, "Identifying the Organization of Writing Processes"); and so forth. In fact, such definitions are ubiquitous in research concerned with the systematic analysis of phenomena and in jurisprudence and legislation.

One activity intended to help students learn strategies necessary for defining (for the philosophical analysis of) complex concepts presented students with a series of scenarios involving courageous and seemingly courageous actions. The scenarios were developed on the basis of Aristotle's ideas of courage in the *Nichomachean Ethics.* In this activity groups of three or four students were to examine each scenario, make a decision about whether the actor was or was not courageous, and write a rule or criterion for guiding decisions in other cases. Although students are quite able to make decisions about whether or not the actors in the scenarios are courageous, they do not use explicit criteria in presenting definitions (McGhee-Bidlack 1991) and have considerable difficulty in devising them. The objective of this activity was to help students formulate specific criteria to use in deciding whether or not an action is courageous. (This goal is a step in learning the process of formulating such criteria whenever they may need to define abstract concepts.)

To make this objective operationally clear, teachers of each class led discussions of one scenario and helped students develop a criterion by which they might be guided in future decision making. The scenario for this teacher-led discussion puts Lois Lane dangling by her fingers from the edge of a thirty-story building while Superman flies to her rescue. He grabs her just in time and carries her safely to earth. The question for students is whether or not Superman might be considered courageous.

In the ensuing discussion, students usually recognize that some people may regard Superman as courageous because he rescues Lois Lane. Others recognize that although Superman rescues Lois Lane, his act involves no real risk or danger for him because of his supernatural powers. As the discussion develops, students usually reach the latter analysis. But that analysis, as it stands applies to only the particular incident. Additional discussion is usually necessary to reformulate student ideas as a rule. The question becomes whether or not the idea applies to everyone, or only to Superman. If it applies across the board, then how should the rule (criterion) be stated. Teachers lead the discussion until some rule emerges, perhaps one such as the following: "An action cannot be considered courageous unless it involves serious danger or risk to the person performing it." The purpose of such a discussion is to make the goal of the students' small-group discussions operationally clear, to give them a more precise idea of what their task is in small groups.

Once students begin working on additional problems in their small groups, the teachers circulate to various groups to determine from student talk whether they seem to understand the goal and, when necessary, to make suggestions and ask questions that will enhance understanding of the goal. At the same time, the group activity is, itself, an aid to understanding the goal of the larger sequence of instruction, in this case, the writing of an extended definition. Presumably this activity, along with several others in the unit, helps students learn strategies for developing clear criteria and examples for use in extended definitions.

Talk of clear objectives raises red flags. Many associate the term with behavioral psychology and the Tyler (1949) curriculum rationale, which they assume leads to mechanistic teaching. (See, for example, Cain 1989.) They appear to believe that working toward some goal in teaching and specifying or predicting what the outcomes ought to be leads to rigidity in teaching, a tendency to ignore the real needs of students, and a lack of insight into the teaching process (Cain 1989). In a certain sense, Cain and critics like her are right, especially if we restrict our thinking to what passes for clear objectives (what Cain refers to as behavioral objectives) in curriculum guides.

What constitutes a clear objective? What appear to be the clearest "behavioral" objectives are, in fact, often the most vague or the most trivial. Apparently simple statements (e.g., "to write better paragraphs"; "to write a short story") are not simply useless but harmful. They hide the complexity of the tasks they represent. When they stand alone, as they generally do, they provide no help in conceptualizing either the task or the instruction it requires. As a result, they suggest that some sort of simple-minded planning will suffice to help students reach the goals they represent.

On the other hand, statements of broad general purposes that may seem to pass as objectives are not very useful either. For example, the student teacher of whom Cain approves makes the following general statements of goals or objectives for teaching Shakespeare's *King Henry the Fourth, Part I*: "Through the study of literary works, we may increase our understanding of the commonality of human emotions as well as the range of differences in human experience. By reading and responding to a piece from a different time and culture, students move beyond their own experience to become aware of values, beliefs, and experiences different from their own as well as to recognize the universality of human emotions and reactions" (p. 15). This statement certainly represents a worthwhile goal.

As it stands, however, it is a goal difficult to translate into classroom activities likely to prompt meaningful discussions of the complex questions involved. In fact, Cain nowhere indicates that this goal is ever taken seriously. If it were taken seriously, one would expect the teacher to ruminate about it, at least considering how to raise such questions as (1) what we think the emotions are today and how they were viewed in Shakespeare's time; (2) what constitutes a universal "reaction"; (3) whether or not people from different cultures react in the same way to the same phenomena, or whether reactions are culturally dependent; and (4) how to involve students in thinking about the "universality of human emotions and reactions."

Cain's account of the teacher's thinking and planning indicates no such ruminations. Such global goals, though well intended, tend to serve as window dressing: they look good, they don't cost much, and they do not reveal what's really in the shop. Worse, they often seduce the planner into believing that something important is happening. The planner appears to believe that certain broad values are inherent in the literary work and readily transferable to readers upon the act of reading, viewed as a relatively passive process. Such belief ignores the idea that the reader constructs meaning from texts. Meanings do not transfer directly from the text to the student's head, especially not the meanings the teacher has constructed for herself.

If Cain's teacher expects students even to recognize the "universality of human emotions and reactions," the students must have an opportunity to construct the relevant ideas for themselves. That is, to be truly useful, the goal must be translated into specific activities and questions that can result in meaningful discussion and writing. For example, let us use as a test case act 5, scene 4 of *Henry IV, Part I*. As you will recall, in this scene Falstaff feigns dying at the hands of Douglas in order to escape death. He then rationalizes his deceit. Students might focus on Falstaff's speech in 5.5 after he has feigned death to escape Douglas's sword, interpret the scene to determine what emotions they think are involved, consider the extent to which Falstaff's reaction might be considered universal and why, and so forth.

In short, for Cain's teacher to attain the goal she sets, she will need to translate it into both specific activities that make concrete the global dimensions of the goal and also a narrative or analytical representation of it that will permit her to judge when students are engaged in increasing their "understanding of the commonality of human emotions as well as the range of differences in human experience." That is, a teacher needs some relatively specific image of student success in a unit of instruction. Such an image might take a variety of forms: memories of past student performance, sets of criteria of the sort that might be used in scoring writing or in identifying certain features of writing, examples illustrating the features of writing or discussion sought, and so forth. Clearly, it is not simply the objectives themselves that make for clarity. It is the context in which they appear.

Selection of Materials and Problems

To promote successful peer group and independent work, the problems and materials must be appropriate for the students, challenging yet within the realm of possibility when appropriate support is available, or to use Vygotsky's term, within the "zone of proximal development." If students can already do the tasks independently, ordinarily there is little pedagogical point in having them do the tasks in groups. On the other hand, the tasks should not be so difficult that students cannot handle them at all.

In a study by Carol Sager (1973), sixth grade students learned scales that they subsequently used to rate compositions. Working in groups, they then revised compositions that they had rated low. Sager believed that for this activity to be successful, the materials used had to be within the reach of sixth graders. For example, working with a scale for judging elaboration in writing, the students were asked to read a story entitled "The Green Martian Monster." The story was comparable to pieces that might have been written by one of the sixth graders in the class, although it was not written by any of them. They were told that it had received a zero on elaboration.

The Green Martian Monster

The Green Martian Monster descended on the USA. He didn't have a mouth. "Who goes?" they said. There was no answer. So they shot him and he died.

Clearly, this is a simple story. However, the task related to it is relatively challenging. Students were to list as many reasons as they could think of why a "mouthless, green Martian monster might land in the USA," list possible places the Martian might have landed, list possibilities for who "they" might have been, and list all the thoughts "they" might have had, and so on. This is a task that these inner-city sixth graders could do well and enthusiastically, with support coming in the form of earlier teacher modeling, the prompts listed above, peer group discussion, and teacher coaching.

There is no algorithm that I know of for arriving at the appropriate level of complexity in developing such tasks. Teachers who listen to their students and observe what they can and cannot do in classroom discussions, in dealing with texts, in writing, and so forth, will have innumerable clues as to what may or may not be appropriate. However, making the initial judgment about appropriateness remains an art, but an art the results of which are subject to careful scrutiny. Anyone who tries new materials, including new textbooks, must introduce that new material with a fair degree of trepidation, eagerness to see "how it works," and a willingness to scrap the new material and try something else.

In a sense, any trial of new materials is a pilot study. The courage scenarios alluded to above were piloted by a variety of teachers in a variety of settings over a period of years as well as in informal studies before they were ever incorporated in a formal research design.

It is important to judge new materials in terms not only of their level of challenge to students, but in terms of their interest for students. Sager reports that her students would discuss compositions at their recess breaks; continuing arguments about how a piece should have been rated or how it might have been improved. Students responding to the courage scenarios often engaged in heated debates about whether one character might be considered courageous or not. Groups would occasionally split on their decisions and write different criteria, with different factions supporting each.

Finally, the materials and activities are selected for their power to engage students in dealing with problems of the kind we encounter outside textbooks, problems that are fuzzy in definition, not so clear that only one solution is possible. Whenever a problem has a single solution, discussion, and probably learning, ends when someone finds the solution. When problems are real, they are amenable to a wide variety of solutions, for example, a definition of courage or a revision of "The Green Martian Monster." With such problems, discussion and learning can continue indefinitely. Undoubtedly, there is a place in education for algorithmic problem solving. But small-group discussion of the kind intended here is pretty clearly not the place.

Providing Support for Learning

A key element in the success of this mode of instruction appears to be that it helps students learn complex processes by engaging students in their use. The students' engagement in complex processes is made possible by providing them a variety of supports at the outset and gradually withdrawing the supports as students appear to become more fluent in their use. Traditionally, teachers and textbooks have recognized the connection between working on complex tasks and learning. However, they have simply asked students to undertake more and more complex assignments, with only verbal instruction from teachers and texts.

One important difference between traditional teaching and what I have called environmental teaching is the supported engagement in complex composing processes as preparation for independent writing. Because the tasks undertaken are more complex than students can be expected to manage on their own, this kind of instruction uses two important kinds of supports to secure student engagement: what I will call structural support and small peer group support.

Structural Support. By structural support I mean the provision of aid or the restructuring of the task so as to reduce its complexity while retaining its essential features. For example, writing an extended definition of an abstract concept entails finding or inventing examples, comparing and contrasting them, devising criteria, and so forth. One of the most difficult parts of that task is devising the criteria. One way of simplifying that task without changing its essential features is to provide examples from which the criteria are to be developed. Providing the examples allows students to concentrate on devising criteria and implies the kinds of criteria to develop.

Although some part of the task is taken over by the instructional environment, students must still use key strategies demanded by the task. As students become more adept at the task, the teacher withdraws part of the structure. That is, in later stages of teaching, students must undertake all phases of the task. In the case of definitions, for example, students must eventually invent their own examples as well as generate criteria and put all of that together into some sort of writing.

Another example is Lynn Troyka's work (1973 and Troyka and Nudelman 1975), which provides materials on argument designed for college freshmen in basic writing classes. Troyka's materials focus on a series of issues that can be seen from a variety of perspectives: pollution of waterways by a chemical plant in a community where employment is a problem, purchase of a fleet of taxicabs for service in a particular community, a prison uprising. Each set of material presents the situation. (For example, there is to be a meeting including officials from the chemical plant thought to pollute local waterways, officials of the tourist industry that has been harmed by the pollution, community members who need work, and so forth. The purpose of the meeting is to resolve the difficulty of pollution from the chemical plant.) Additional materials present sets of data relative to the issues involved and roles to be played by students in the proposed meeting (each role representing a different set of interests involved in the issue).

The structure of the learning environment established by the teacher and the materials simplifies the task of developing an appropriate argument by taking over some part of the task, while requiring students to deal with essential features of the task. The learning environment presents the situation, the points of view involved, and the data to be used. Students need not find and sift through data about some issue that they do not understand. Rather, they may devote their attention to the more limited task of developing a solid argument using appropriate grounds to support a claim that comes out of a particular point of view. As they present arguments to one another, students will see how those coming at the same issue from a different perspective will respond to their arguments. In the process, they learn more about developing a complete argument.

Eventually, students will have to move to finding their own problems, points of view, and evidence. Having done the simpler activities first appears to provide frameworks and schemata for developing new arguments. Troyka's research at the college level and Hamel's work at the high school level (Hamel 1990; Anderson and Hamel 1991) strongly suggest that this is the case for argument. The results of research related to a variety of other writing tasks strongly indicate the efficacy of this approach in structuring learning environments to make complex tasks more accessible to more students (Hillocks 1986a).

Small Peer-Group Support. Peer-group discussion or collaborative talk focused on specific kinds of problems, usually in small groups, is the second essential feature, perhaps the *sine qua non*, of what I have called environmental instruction. Results of the synthesis of research (Hillocks 1984, 1986a) strongly indicate that problem-centered peer-group interaction, the major feature differentiating these instructional groups from others in the study, is chiefly responsible for the gains made by the environmental groups.[3]

Any teacher who has ever used problem-centered small-group discussions as a standard part of classroom activity knows that the rate of active participation in small groups far exceeds that in teacher-led discussions. Students who never contribute at all in teacher-led discussions may become very active participants in small groups. The rate of response in some small groups has been as high as ten to fifteen responses per minute in some studies (e.g., Hillocks, Kahn, and Johannessen 1983). In small problem-centered group discussions, students feel free to argue actively with one another and to build upon each other's ideas. Further, their interaction appears to generate more response and the careful examination of ideas.

Teacher-led discussion in most classrooms, by way of contrast, tends to inhibit interaction. The desks are in rows so the students must speak to the backs of other students' heads. Nearly all student comments are funneled through the teacher and are seldom relayed back to other students. The number of turns available for individuals to respond is severely limited by the much larger size of the group in whole-class teacher-led discussions. The willingness of many students to venture an idea aloud in front of a group of between twenty and thirty peers and the teacher is often far less than it might be in a group of three to five peers. All of that, however, does not really tell us how small-group interaction is able to have such powerful effects. I shall return to that problem later.

Since I first used small-group discussion with ninth graders in 1960, small-group discussions have been an integral part of every class I have taught from seventh grade to graduate level. My own experience over those years and that of other teachers, many of them my own students, indicates that teachers must continue to support and coach if the small-group interaction is to have the kind of effect we hope it will. Certainly small-group discussions can flounder. The problem may be too difficult. Students may be distracted by an imminent holiday or school event. They may be frustrated by some relatively minor point in the problem. To insure that small-group discussions go smoothly, the teacher may circulate from group to group listening in for a moment or two, perhaps asking a question to redirect attention, perhaps suggesting an example, coaching students as their discussions are in progress but without taking over the central tasks of the discussions. This appears to be a very important part of maintaining group effort. When teachers do not monitor progress and make suggestions, students can get bogged down in relatively trivial problems or wander from the purpose of the small group.

Student Ownership

The activities that drive environmental teaching are ordinarily planned or invented by teachers. But not all activities invented by teachers result in what I have called environmental instruction. Only activities that result in high levels of interaction among students in regard to the materials and problems qualify. When the levels of interaction are high, and the interaction is *among* students rather than between the teacher and students in recitation fashion, student ideas and opinions become the focus of attention and substantially control the direction of classroom talk. This interaction gives students the necessary stake in what is happening. They become the authorities through their ideas.

The teacher's role is to coach and prompt, to ask questions that push at the edges of student ideas, and to sustain the interchange among students. If the teacher provides authoritative answers to the problems under discussion, the interaction among students ceases and learning is curtailed. For some teachers this appears to be a very difficult role. In one study, for example, observers noted one teacher who, when a disagreement arose among students in small-group discussions, would provide an authoritative answer. As the teacher moved from one group to another, he effectively ended real discussion. Students saw no point in pursuing the problem when they could see that the teacher would eventually provide "the right" answer. For one reason or another, this teacher could see no value in allowing students to work through the problem on their own (Hillocks 1989).

Students can develop a stake in what is happening in many other ways. They can make choices about topics they will study, texts they will read, data they will examine. For example, Deborah Stern, whose English program at Prologue Learning Center in Chicago was recognized by the National Council of Teachers of English as one of five outstanding programs for at-risk students in the United States and Canada, typically gives her students many different choices about what they will study. Her students are young adults who have dropped out of public schools. Nearly all the women in her classes are mothers. In one class, all had seen a friend or family member zipped by police into a body bag. Their young lives have encompassed drugs, prostitution, gangs, crime of various kinds, and poverty.

Not surprisingly, when given choices of what to study, they usually choose to study issues that concern them, "sex and violence," for example. With Deborah's guidance, they choose texts that they will read as a group and texts that they will read individually. They copy the lyrics of rap songs and bring them to class for study. When they write extended definitions of violence, they discuss examples from their own lives, from the rap songs they admire, and from the newspaper stories they have collected. The fact that students have choices does not mean that Deborah has relinquished control. On the contrary, students make choices within a carefully thought out rationale that begins with what she wants for her students: "to have some tools to think about the chaos of their lives. Sex and violence sometimes seem beyond their control. If we look at it here deeply, at least they may have something to help them understand what's going on and what choices they have."

Making choices of topics and texts, however, is not essential to students' having a stake in their own learning, as some theorists would have us believe. What is essential is structuring the learning environment so that students can and will want to gain entry to the ideas and materials and can contribute to the group's and their own understanding of whatever is at issue.

The Power of Environmental Teaching

The presence of all these supports, however, does not explain why problem-centered small-group discussion has such a powerful effect on learning and writing. Let me turn next to an excerpt from a transcript of a small-group discussion that involves four juniors in a small-town high school. Their teacher had volunteered to conduct a pilot study of the materials to be used later in a more formal study. What follows is the discussion of one of twelve scenarios, each describing an action that the students might or might not consider courageous.

The scenarios are based on the various distinctions Aristotle makes in defining courage in the *Nichomachean Ethics.* As indicated earlier, the instructional goal for students is to learn strategies for developing criteria, not to agree with Aristotle. (In fact, many of the students do not agree with Aristotle. Many, for example, take considerations of steadfastness in the face of great danger to be of greater importance than considerations of moral rectitude. For many, breaking into a bank to steal a fortune in the face of imminent danger is the epitome of courage.)

The class, of which the following discussion is a small part, begins with the teacher leading students in a discussion of one scenario about Superman. The teacher first asks students whether they think the character in the scenario is courageous or not. The reasons they give in response become the basis for developing a criterion. In this case, the students decide that a courageous act involves facing a real danger. In the scenario at hand Superman faces no real danger because his super powers make him immune to what would be real dangers to ordinary people. After this brief discussion, the teacher divides the class into their groups for discussion of the scenarios. In the following excerpt, four students are engaged in discussing scenario 6. From the beginning of their talk about scenario 6, they refer to the second scenario.

> Scenario 6: On Monday the fire had started on the oil derrick far out at sea. By Wednesday the men working on the derrick had been rescued, but the fire was out of control. "Red" Granger and his men were called in to fight the dangerous fire. "Red" and his men had fought many oil fires. They had the training and experience to put out the fire. Are "Red" and his men courageous when they fight the fire?

> Scenario 2: Out of the corner of his eye the Secret Service agent spotted a gun aimed at the President. Instantly, he threw himself in the line of fire, taking the bullet meant for the President. Was the agent's act of jumping in front of the bullet courageous?

Scenario 6 is based on the Aristotelian idea that the high levels of experience and the superior equipment of mercenary soldiers make their actions only seemingly courageous. Their experience and equipment provides them with such a high level of confidence that they need not overcome fear. In Aristotle's view, courage had to do with the balance between feelings of fear and confidence. If the mercenary has less to fear, there is less reason to consider him courageous. The students come close to a comparable analysis. Scenario 2 comes within the limits of the Aristotelian idea of courage, although it is possible that the agent's act is not deliberative, given the information available, and comes close to the foolhardy. Few high school students made this argument, however. Interestingly, however, even though the scenario generates little discussion of its own, it generates far more when it is considered in contrast to some other scenario, as it is below.

When I began my ongoing study of environmental teaching and small-group discussion, I believed that the changes in student writing came about because of the process of inquiry in which students engaged. They make comparisons and contrasts. They report what they see, make interpretations, ask questions, bring prior knowledge to bear, develop analogies, test their ideas, and all the while move in the direction of a solution to a fuzzy problem. One might argue that they use all the basic strategies of inquiry and that practice in using those strategies carries over into writing about other concepts.

As I began examining the transcripts from several pilot studies, I began to see that, at their best, the student discussions were extended arguments. Indeed, we can examine the entire discussion below in terms of Toulmin's analysis of argumentative structures (1958). Toulmin lays out the basic structure of argument as including claims, grounds, warrants, backing, and qualifications.[4] In the discussion below, the students are working toward a statement of backing for a warrant: "A person is not courageous when they're trained and familiar with a situation that is usual for them." The basic argument developed by this group, in abbreviated form, goes as follows:

CLAIM	"Red" and his men are not courageous.
GROUNDS	They "had fought many oil fires. They had the training and experience to put out the fire."
WARRANT	". . . because they're experienced . . . they're not actually putting themselves at risk."
BACKING	Courage requires steadfastness in the face of great personal risk (an idea developed earlier in the discussion). However, "a person is not courageous when they're trained and familiar with a situation that is usual for them." The idea that experience and training reduce risk in some instances (but not that of the Secret Service agent) remains implicit in the discussion.

The discussion moves in the direction of the criterion that serves as the backing in the argument that "Red" and his men are not courageous. In the course of its development, many other claims enter, each of which appears to clarify group ideas about the major argument. In the early part of the discussion, students engage in an argument that helps them consider a number of issues that, on their own, they would likely not consider. (A study of individual responses to the set of scenarios indicates that students consider a far narrower range of responses when working alone.) The argument they conduct is a constructive one as they continue to refine their ideas throughout.

The argument comes to a head when Amy restates Keith's ideas but she makes the point a bit more forcefully and in basic form: claim, grounds, warrant. "So this one is not courageous," she says. "They had the experience, so they're not doing anything out of the ordinary." In turn 16, Keith appears to build on the preceding turns in making the distinction between the two scenarios the clearest it has been. He points out the near certainty of harm in the Secret Service agent's action and the relative safety of the fire fighter's. Let us turn, then, to the portion of discussion itself. My commentary appears on the right. As the excerpt begins, the students have just completed their reading of the sixth scenario, the one about the fire fighters.

Discussion

Commentary

1. Scott: God, all these contradict the other ones.

2. Keith: Yeah.

3. Scott: Six contradicts the one with the agent, the security agent.

4. Keith: I don't think they're coura-geous/ because they're experi-enced,/ but they're not actually put-ting themselves at risk./ They're just doing another job./ It's not ac-tual. . . ./

Scott recognizes the connectedness of the scenario to preceding ones, making the continuity of context explicit, and sets up the pattern of contrast for the discussion. He makes the contrast specific in #3. Keith makes a claim about the ac-tion in #6, provides grounds for his claim, and provides a warrant explaining the connection between the claim and the grounds, the ma-jor parts of an argument in Toul-min's terms.

5. Scott: What did we have for num-ber 2?

Scott indicates that he will treat this analogically.

6. Keith: Yes.

7. Scott: Yes. Then this one has to be yes. It's a job.

He states the analogy briefly but fails to see that he has made doing a job the criterion.

8. Keith: No, not necessarily.

Keith indicates a reservation. He disagrees.

9. Amy: No, it's different./ You're not putting yourself in front of a bullet./

Amy also disagrees and presents grounds that pinpoint a major difference between the jobs. Uses contrast again.

10. Keith: Yeah./ Chances are that some people are going to die in car wrecks every day./ Just because you get in a car doesn't mean you're courageous./

Keith develops a different analogy based on Amy's point, taken to an extreme, to emphasize the difference in the likelihood of hazard. Uses prior knowledge as contrast.

11. Scott: But really, it's their job to do something like that./ And you have to be courageous to take a job like that in the first place.

Scott seems to maintain his original point but switches from the action in question to the action of taking the job with no experience.

12. Sue: He has fought many oil fires it says.

Sue refers to the printed text for grounds to reinforce the point about experience.

13. Amy: Yeah, that guy was going in front of many bullets.

Amy's sarcasm implies the impossibility of the agent's gaining experience.

14. Sue: This emphasizes their training and their fighting many of them. The other one was just like I saw them out of the corner of my eye.

Sue returns to the grounds given in the text and then implies that experience could not be useful to the agent. Attempts to analyze the difference.

15. Amy: So this one is not courageous. They had the experience, so they're not doing anything out of the ordinary.

Amy provides a claim based on the preceding discussion, indicates the grounds, and restates a warrant.

16. Keith: Yeah, even if the bullet doesn't kill him, he's pretty sure he's going to get hurt./

Keith makes explicit the point in Amy's and Sue's earlier comments (#13 and #14).

The students continue to disagree for a few more turns, testing each other's claims by relating them to other scenarios or to their prior knowledge.

17. Amy: Right. (agreeing with Keith)

18. Scott: Yeah, but in number five, when a person goes to Vietnam or something like that and after he stays there a course of time, he's well trained in that too. Does that make him not courageous any more?

Scott calls on prior knowledge for a contrasting example supporting his idea that at some point in their careers experienced people do not have experience. This point and the problems surrounding it eventually are lost.

19. Amy: No, he's not courageous to begin with because of the reason we gave.

Amy refers to an earlier scenario about a person who volunteered to fight because he thought it was expected of him.

20. Scott: No, I mean if a person was in Vietnam for a year . . ./

Scott begins to reiterate his idea.

21. Amy: No, we're still saying that he could still do something that would be courageous. We're talking about [unclear]

Amy appears to try to qualify how they are using the idea of experience.

22. Scott: I was getting into death. I don't want to get into death. When I get into death, I don't know what I'm talking about, man. I'll be rattling off stuff.

Scott backs off.

Eventually the students seem to have worked through their disagreements, and Sue begins to formulate a criterion, referring to a criterion the group had developed for a different scenario. They abandon their earlier argument mode and switch to a collaborative one.

23. Keith: I think anybody goes over there and they're well trained and stuff like that.

Keith indicates some level of agreement with Scott. (His tone of voice appears to be one of mollification.)

24. Scott: Yeah, like for a course of time.

25. Sue: OK, this one is . . ./

Sue brings the focus back to the task.

26. Scott: They've mostly seen everything that has to be seen.

27. Sue: A courageous person will . . . Same as number four?

Sue begins to formulate a criterion. She asks about repeating 4.

28. Amy: No.

Amy disagrees.

29. Scott: Let's read the book when it comes out.

Scott appears to give up.

30. Amy: He's not really in that much danger because of his training.

Amy nearly makes explicit the idea that training reduces risk.

31. Keith: I think they're a little bit courageous, but they're not. . . .

Keith seems to want to help Scott save face.

32. Amy: But it's their job and they're being trained for it, so they're being trained for it. And they put out similar fires too.

Amy objects and lists the relevant grounds.

33. Keith: They're not facing certain death or certain harm or whatever.

Keith makes clear the distinction the group has worked on in turns 8 to 16, 30, and 32.

34. Sue: Something they are trained and familiar with? [asking about criterion phrasing]

Sue asks about phrasing the criterion. From this point, the group collaborate on constructing the criterion that Sue records.

35. Keith: Yeah.

36. Sue: What would you say, "A person is not courageous when they are trained and familiar with . . ."?

They come very close to the way Aristotle expresses it.

37. Amy: A situation.

Students modify and build on each other's ideas in the following turns.

38. Sue: Usually a fatal situation?

39. Amy: No, they're trained.

40. Keith: So it's not going to be a fatal situation to them.

41. Amy: Yeah, they're going to know how to take steps to make it . . .

42. Sue: OK, what if you say, "A person is not courageous when they're trained and familiar with a situation"?

43. Keith: Well, it's usual for them. I think that's the big thing.

Keith's comment here appears to have been engendered by Scott's argument in turns 11, 18, and 20.

44. Amy: It's something they're used to.

45. Sue: So should I write that?

46. Keith: Yeah.

At first glance, the group seems to have lost sight of Scott's idea that undertaking a hazardous job "in the first place" is courageous. However, both Amy and Keith seem to recognize, as Scott did, that what may be commonplace and relatively danger-free for some persons in a particular set of circumstances depends upon their training for those circumstances and that the same persons acting in comparable circumstances without such training may be considered very courageous.

Scott's contributions, though they seem to go against the main-stream of the discussion, have made significant contributions to it. His initial comment, "all these contradict the other ones," sets in motion the strategy of contrasting and comparing, a strategy that is followed throughout, even in the final collaborative turns of the discussion. Second, his insistence on considering the courage of people undertaking something "in the first place," without the benefit of training, helps the group to make the important qualification that what is a "usual" situation for trained people may be quite dangerous for others.

Clearly, all students involved have made important contributions to the discussion. Working together the group have advanced their understanding of one dimension of courage from a rather general impression to a more complex and more explicitly defined concept. What makes small peer discussion groups such a powerful learning experience, one that enables them to deal with complex concepts in a far more sophisticated fashion than they can independently? I believe there are several important factors. First, students already have some ideas about the topic that they can bring to bear in discussion. Second, the problem is structured to provide support, in this case the scenarios, that make it unnecessary for students to think of their own examples. (Later, they move to an activity in which they develop both criteria and examples.) Third, the give-and-take of discussion in which students make use of various strategies of inquiry and develop several strands of argument, supported by the responses of their peers, enables them to internalize those processes such that they can use them again, independently, even as they take up new problems.

I believe that something else is involved as well. When John Diekhoff came into our Milton class that long ago August day, my guess is he had something in mind besides engaging us in discussion of concepts important to the study of Milton. I am sure he hoped we would enjoy the process of thinking about Milton, that we would develop not just the ability but the disposition to think about such issues. That is what environmental teaching is about, enabling students to enjoy thinking through complex problems with others and on their own.

Notes

1. Grants from the Benton Center for Curriculum and Instruction of The University of Chicago supported the preparation of this chapter.

2. The studies synthesized all tested two or more methods of teaching writing. By converting the pretest and posttest scores of all groups to standard scores, and aggregating the results for comparable methods, it is possible to compare and contrast the effects of different modes of teaching across studies.

For the environmental treatment groups the effect size was .44 standard deviations. That is, they gained .44 standard deviations more than did their control group counterparts. Another avenue for examining these results is the pre- to post-effect size. The environmental groups gained .75 standard deviations from pretest to posttest, three times the gain of the nearest competitor. A comparable gain on an IQ test would move the mean for the population from 100 to 107.5. Gains of this magnitude in educational research are quite unusual and cannot be ignored.

For a detailed explanation of the procedures used in this study, see Hillocks (1986a, pp. 93–112).

3. Note that small groups figure in "natural process" instruction as well, but there the process is not structured, not focused on a particular problem. In those studies, teachers simply asked students to respond to each other's writing, but without any specific teaching about what to look for in the writing or how to supply the feedback. The effect of the environmental treatments is more than twice that of the natural process treatments. For statisticians, the difference is significant at $p < .0001$. For a more complete explanation, see Hillocks (1986a).

4. In the following discussion, the term *warrant* refers to a statement that implies the abstract reason that Toulmin refers to as a warrant. The implied warrant, in the analysis of my current research (Hillocks in progress a), must be close to the surface of the text. For example, if a student says that an act is not courageous because the character is "just doing it for himself," our analysis takes that to imply the following warrant, that to be courageous, the act must be noble in nature and not done for some base reason. Since students do not ordinarily talk like that, we accept the implied warrant.

Works Cited

Anderson, Ellen M., and Fred L. Hamel. 1991. "Teaching Argument as a Criteria-Driven Process." *English Journal* 80.7: 43–49.

Applebee, Arthur N. 1981. *Writing in the Secondary School: English in the Content Areas.* NCTE Research Report No. 21. Urbana, IL: NCTE.

———. 1986. "Problems in Process Approaches: Toward a Reconceptualization of Process Instruction." *The Teaching of Writing.* 85th Yearbook of the National Society for the Study of Education: Part II. Ed. Anthony R. Petrosky and David Bartholomae, 95–113. Chicago: National Society for the Study of Education.

Aristotle. N.d. *Nichomachean Ethics*. Trans. W. D. Ross. *Introduction to Aristotle*. Ed. Richard McKeon, 308–543. New York: Random House.

Bakhtin, Mikhail M. 1981. *The Dialogic Imagination: Four Essays*. Ed. Michael Holquist. Trans. Caryl Emerson and Michael Holquist. Austin: U of Texas.

Berlin, James A. 1984. *Writing Instruction in Nineteenth-Century American Colleges*. Carbondale: Southern Illinois U P.

Cain, Beatrice N. 1989. "With Worldmaking, Planning Models Matter." *English Education* 21: 5–29.

Frye, Northrop. 1957. *Anatomy of Criticism*. Princeton, NJ: Princeton UP.

Goodlad, John I. 1984. *A Place Called School: Prospects for the Future*. New York: McGraw-Hill.

Graves, Donald H. 1983. *Writing: Teachers and Children at Work*. Portsmouth, NH: Heinemann.

Hamel, Fred L. 1990. "A Comparative Study of Two Teachers Teaching Exposition." Unpublished Master's paper. U of Chicago.

Hayes, J. Richard, and Linda S. Flower. 1980. "Identifying the Organization of Writing Processes." *Cognitive Processes in Writing*. Ed. L. W. Greg and E. R. Steinberg, 3–30. Hillsdale, NJ: Lawrence Erlbaum.

Hillocks, George, Jr. 1981. "The Responses of College Freshmen to Three Modes of Instruction." *American Journal of Education* 89: 373–95.

———. 1984. "What Works in Teaching Composition: A Meta-analysis of Experimental Treatment Studies." *American Journal of Education* 93.1: 133–70.

———. 1986a. *Research on Written Composition: New Directions for Teaching*. Urbana, IL: National Conference on Research in English/ERIC Clearinghouse on Reading and Communication Skills.

———. 1986b. "The Writer's Knowledge: Theory, Research, and Implications for Practice." 71–94. *The Teaching of Writing*. 85th Yearbook of the National Society for the Study of Education: Part II. Ed. Anthony R. Petrosky and David Bartholomae, 95–113. Chicago: National Society for the Study of Education.

———. 1989. "Two Modes and Two Foci of Instruction: Impact on Student Writing." Paper presented at the Annual Meeting of AERA.

———. In progress a. *Integrating Qualitative and Quantitative Data: Studies of Learning to Write under Three Foci of Instruction*.

———. In progress b. *Structures in the Teaching of Writing*.

Hillocks, George, Jr., Elizabeth A. Kahn, and Larry R. Johannessen. 1983. "Teaching Defining Strategies as a Mode of Inquiry: Some Effects on Student Writing." *Research in the Teaching of English* 17: 275–84.

McGhee-Bidlack, Betty. 1991. "The Development of Noun Definitions: A Meta-linguistic Analysis." *Journal of Child Language* 18: 417–434.

Sager, Carol. 1973. "Improving the Quality of Written Compositions Through Pupils' Use of Rating Scales." Unpublished doctoral dissertation, Boston U.

Scholes, Robert. 1985. *Textual Power: Literary Theory in the Teaching of English.* New Haven: Yale UP.

Stein, Nancy L., and Thomas Trabasso. 1982. "What's in a Story: An Approach to Comprehension and Instruction." *Advances in Instructional Psychology.* Ed. R. Glaser, 213–67. Hillsdale, NJ: Lawrence Erlbaum.

Toulmin, Stephen E. 1958. *The Uses of Argument.* New York: Cambridge UP.

Troyka, L. Q. 1973. "A Study of the Effect of Simulation-Gaming on Expository Prose Competence of College Remedial English Composition Students." Doctoral diss., New York U.

Troyka, L. Q., and J. Nudelman. 1975. *Taking Action: Writing, Reading, Speaking, and Listening Through Simulation-Games.* Englewood Cliffs, NJ: Prentice-Hall.

Tyler, Ralph W. 1949. *Basic Principles of Curriculum and Instruction.* Chicago: U of Chicago P.

Vygotsky, Lev S. 1978. *Mind in Society: The Development of Higher Psychological Processes.* Ed. Michael Cole, Vera John-Steiner, Sylvia Scribner, and Ellen Souberman. Cambridge, MA: Harvard UP.

9

Tribes and Displaced

Persons: Some Observations

on Collaboration

Jim W. Corder

I have come to notice, during the last three or four years, that I react, resisting almost instinctively, when I fall upon journal articles and books about collaboration. I don't actually growl or salivate, but I do twitch.

I need to know why.

Arguments and discussions that propose diverse kinds of collaboration in learning and writing are, I believe, generally wise and thoughtful, and they are characteristically marked by what are clearly the best intentions and hopes for students. If I resist them, then, is my resistance owed to failures of my own character and mind? I don't much like to think that, though I must say at the outset that I am not very good at handling participatory and collaborative enterprises, whether class discussions or otherwise. Still, I hold onto my self long enough to believe that there is more to account for my twitching than personal inadequacy, even if there's enough of that.

In the pages that follow, I hope to take three steps. First, I want to declare more specifically what I'm talking about and to situate myself, if I can, with regard to it. Second, I want to use a sporadic log I kept while preparing this paper to show what I believe I was thinking earlier. Finally, I want to try to isolate what seem to me to be, after all, some problematic features of collaboration.

1

In our field, the general term *collaboration* calls up almost immediately a range of specific interests, some of which I cannot consider or do not wish to consider.

I don't know how to deal with all that's entailed, for example, in *collaborative learning*, and that's probably not an enterprise for a solitary person. It's more likely to be, you might say, a collaborative project.

The *pedagogy of collaboration* doesn't at the moment interest me much, though I don't believe that I'm antagonistic, or deaf to its claims. I was the person responsible, some eighteen years ago, for changing the name of our first composition course from "Freshman Composition" to "Writing Workshop," and I believe I understood then, as I think I do now, the changes that required in goals and strategies. I'm only a little surprised that the word *workshop* has turned out to be not just a noun, but also a verb, and I'm a little startled that the participatory, experiential, collaborative class seems to have been accepted, with little controversy, as the model for all classes. I'm inclined to think that no method is splendid all of the time.

About the *writer-reader relationship*, I don't intend to say much except that of course it's collaborative, though we're not sure just how, despite the work of reading specialists and reader-response theorists. For example, is it a collaborative relationship, as I just said, or a competitive relationship, author and reader wanting to occupy the same place, each rhetoric seeking to displace the other? I steal *Gulliver's Travels* away from Jonathan Swift and make it mine, what was his as composition becoming mine as interpretation. Grandpa Durham existed as my version of him, not in his version of himself. His character as he lived and knew it was not identical to the character I came to attribute to him, though I wish I could have situated myself in his version, to see what he saw as he saw it. (One reason we grieve for ourselves upon the death of someone we love is that as we construct our version of the other, it becomes a complete version of ourselves, and in the death of the beloved we lose not just fragments of ourselves, but ourselves.) Still, the reader is not the sole author of *Gulliver's Travels*, and the grandson is not the sole author of the grandfather. Jonathan Swift and Grandpa Durham left the first tracks.

These things set aside, and other manifestations of collaboration being absent from my mind, I'm left with *collaborative writing*, which I do want to consider further. Before I go on, however, I think I should tell, not how students have succeeded or failed as collaborative writers in my classes, but how *I* have collaborated, if I have collaborated.

That is to say, since I have no elaborate or even clear research methodology, I ought at least to tell my experience of collaborative writing. By the phrase *collaborative writing*, I believe I intend to designate writing done jointly by two or more persons, where each person participates in the response to an occasion or need, the conception of the project, the discovery of its sources and possibilities, its design, style, and presentation to an audience. I have been on the campus where I now teach for thirty-three years, in all of them a member of the English faculty. During ten of those years, I was also chairman of the English Department. For five of those years, I was dean of the College of Arts and Sciences, and for two of those years, I was associate vice president for whatever came up. About seven years ago, I returned to the English Department hoping to find steady, honest, full-time work. During that same period of thirty-three years, I collaborated with *one colleague* in the composition of a textbook, and with *another* in writing three papers. The textbook was early, and I'd rather not ever see it again, and it was an instance of turn-taking, not collaboration. The three papers were late, and I believe each of them is a genuine conversation. I have collaborated many times with *editors*, a form of collaboration that, I think, has not been properly studied or appreciated. A good or a mean editor (and they may be the same person) is a powerful antagonist/friend/collaborator. I have collaborated with the *enemy*, that is, those who have assigned or expected me to participate in the composition of work that I could not regard as my own. If all the time and energy I have given to participating in the composition of committee reports, position papers, and "team" projects had been given to honest work, I would be among earth's most prolific authors. I have collaborated with the *world*, because that's not to be avoided, and with *myself*, pirating lines from earlier work, vandalizing passages I had intended to use elsewhere.

2

For various reasons, I kept an unsteady log from the beginning in the preparation of this paper. The log, I believe, turned out to have some uses. In the first place, keeping it afforded a reasonable way of keeping notes. Second, it helped me to see a little more clearly what I already thought about collaborative writing and what I came to think along the way. Third, it helped me to track where I went, if anywhere, between the beginning and the ending of the work, particularly as work in preparation for this paper first abutted, then mingled with work on intervening projects. Most important, keeping the log enabled me to see where I was already collaborating, even when I was feeling a little surly about the idea of collaboration. As I look back at the log, it seems pretty clear that I am believing in collaboration, relishing it, using it in a variety of ways to get on with my work. It's also clear that I am sometimes, perhaps more often, doubting and resisting the possibilities of collaboration.

In this section of the paper, I am going to depend on what the log may show, from time to time quoting from it. Sometimes I don't much like what I see when I look back at it. Sometimes, though, I'm okay. The beginning isn't very promising: it indicates no direction, and the self revealed badly needs at least a collaborative cosmetic touch-up.

> *Shortly before May 1, 1990*—Odell calls, invites me to do a paper sort of about collaboration. I tell him I'd like to work with him, but am doubtful: my habits of mind don't dispose me any more toward conventional scholarly writing.
>
> *Around May 10, 1990*—I do want to do the paper. I like the attention, the notice. I've begun to see some possibilities in combining scraps I've already written. I call Odell, tell that I can see what to do, though I can't, and still don't. . . .

Sometimes I look a little better; sometimes I am clearly uglier. At the start, I believe I was being a little belligerent, wanting to argue for the autonomy of the solitary writer—that is, myself. Early entries often show a churlish resistance to collaborative writing, which usually turns out to be a defense of my own identity; other entries plainly show both the inevitability and the desirability of collaboration.

Undated entries from about this same time show a conversation with my department chairman, who remarks that no one should ever *read* an academic paper to an audience. Within a couple of days, I have thought of a quick rebuttal. It takes the form of a drafted proposal for the 4Cs 1991 conference, titled "On Reading Academic Papers at Conferences Without, Perhaps, Even Looking Up." I'm thinking that he may want to pose a rebuttal, that we might make a session for the 4Cs program—in which, by the elegance of my prose and the righteousness of my argument, I would prevail. By the time I get my proposal drafted and show it to him, both of us have mostly lost interest.

But he has set me to thinking, reminding me of what I already know, that something is wrong when an academic reads a conference paper without noticing the audience. You might say we've collaborated. What I find my self thinking would not exist without his intervention. Our conversation and his presence effect a collaboration. I modify the draft and turn it into a single-paper proposal titled "Archival Essays, Conference Papers, and Writer-Reader Relationships," where, using certain personal essays and academic papers, I intend to speculate on the possibility that some writing has no audience, no other, but exists in solitude.

Among other failings, my log shows that I'm not especially well disciplined, at least not in the sense of pursuing one project at a time to conclusion. At the same time I am supposed to be thinking and writing about collaboration, I am at work on a personal book, tentatively called *Scrapbook*. The log remarks that

> it's a little about memory and nostalgia, about icons, about why some people and places and things register with us, even if erroneously, and some don't. My "research" sends me racing elsewhere, to others. I have been trying to understand my own impulses and thoughts about the use of images, about nostalgia, and so have been reading and talking back to Boorstin's *The Image* and Sontag's *On Photography*, on images, to Stewart's *On Longing*, Umphlett's *Mythmakers of the American Dream*, and Lukacher's *Primal Scenes*, on nostalgia.

Research and study are surely forms of collaboration, I think, and I have been collaborating gladly as I work on a particular section of *Scrapbook*.

The next dated entry in my spasmodic log is more than a little less than handsome:

Around May 20, 1990—I come across the brochure for the Lunsford and Ede book, *Singular Texts/Plural Authors*. It pisses me off:

> This study of collaborative writing, the most complete to date, chal-
> lenges the assumption that writing is a solitary act. Ede and Lunsford
> examine the theory and practice of collaborative writing, discuss
> their research on the collaborative efforts of writers outside the
> academy, and review both the history of the concept of the solitary
> author and contemporary challenges to it. . . .

I'm of course remembering the 1989 Penn State conference, where Lunsford was a principal speaker. I'm mad because I'm not a star, and she
is. I think she deconstructs herself in her speech: her *words* praise collaboration; her *performance* presents herself. She can't help it that she's striking. I grow quiet.

But not for long. I keep coming upon attacks against the "myth
of the great artist as solitary genius." I don't want to hold on to, can't
hold on to *great* or *artist* or *genius*, but I do want to hold on to *solitary*.
Perhaps the attacks are only enemies I have imagined to give me
nerve. I doubt that anyone would ignore altogether the role of the
individual.

Next the log shows this, as I return to work on a section of
Scrapbook:

> *Friday, June 8, 1990* - In a rush, I do the last five pages, and they're good.
> I don't know whether or not anyone else will ever know or think so. I
> don't care. I know. I am physically exhausted, completed enervated,
> almost unable to walk. Absolute exhilaration. Absolutely alone. Tentative
> conclusion: Why does it have to be one way or another? Either collabora-
> tion or solitude? If we paid attention, we'd know: You're always with
> other, but sometimes you're desperately alone.

Then another project intervenes. I had earlier promised to be
part of a four-person panel at a regional College English Association
meeting. The four of us are supposed to talk about classroom implications of contemporary literary theory. I don't know how to do what
I'm supposed to do. I scurry around, trying to read more. Some of
the theorists tell me again that the writer is not autonomous but is
only part of a social community that constructs and interprets discourse. The notion of the self as a source of meaning, they tell me,
is only a Romantic concept. I think this would surprise Alexander

Pope, who probably thought he was the author, though in company, of what he wrote, but I go on to hear the unavoidable lesson that the language by which we make and view the world comes from society, not from the individual. As I prepare for the panel discussion, I think about contradictions in our work. On Monday, we go to our literature classes and agree with Barthes that "the birth of the reader must be at the cost of the death of the author," but on Tuesday, we go to our composition classes and tell student writers to show themselves to us in their personal essays.

I read enough to begin to see that the literary theorists are collaborating with me, requiring me to think again and to revise, whether or not I wanted to participate, teaching me that rhetorical invention always already assumed social construction and intertextuality—none of us would have managed the vocabulary alone—while I answered back that it also always assumed that someone must choose the words. I began to be a little glad that these strange people—new literary theorists—came along. Where else to learn but from strangers? They've helped us to see our own field better. Perhaps they'll help us all to see, for example, that invention isn't a nice, simplified, little *step one* in a nice, simplified, little *writing process*, but an occasion to open our lives, whether as writers or as readers, to the geographies and archaeologies and sociologies of communities, tribes, texts, and selves, an invitation to create ourselves and to give ourselves away in the midst of plenty.

But the log shows an immediate lapse into more churlishness. We can seldom manage to enable two rhetorics to exist in the same space at the same time. How shall we ever collaborate in and serve community *and* free the self simultaneously? That is two rhetorics in competition, though neither exists entirely without the other. I read various papers that recommend collaborative writing, and I'm still angry, or perhaps I'm angry again, at what I read as recommendations that we submit to the group. Perhaps that isn't anyone's intention, but it is clearly a possible consequence of excessive devotion to collaboration: eventually the group is privileged, and then perhaps the corporation, and then perhaps the state.

Another project interrupts what I was thinking, or what I thought I was thinking, and I collaborate with anyone who will give me words to say.

The graduate students in our department have organized a symposium for area faculty and graduate students on rhetoric and composition pedagogy. It is scheduled for February 9, 1991. Much of the day is to be given over to discussion, but six of us are to make short presentations. I do what I can. I collaborate with myself. I go back to what I have already said about the possibility of two rhetorics occupying the same space at the same time. (I don't expect to have too many ideas; I hold on to those I have, and repeat them.) When divergent, non-isomorphic rhetorics come together—that is to say, when any two rhetorics come together—the consequence is sometimes happy. Insight and learning occur, and sometimes love and marriage. Sometimes, however, the consequence is not happy; our habits of competition are too strong. Sometimes one rhetoric expands to fill all available space, prevailing as the other is compressed into submission.

Over in the arena where we work, usually at least not a physically perilous place, in that arena where we read books, go to class, grade papers, write papers, devise pedagogies, and invent theories, it sometimes happens that one rhetoric catches or creates the fashion, and decides that the other is not only unworthy of courtship and matrimony, but is before that unworthy of notice.

In the 1940s and 1950s, when some of us were infected with the New Criticism, we decided that the old-fashioned biographical and historical studies of literature were no longer worthy of notice. In the 1960s and early 1970s, when some of us caught rhetoric, we decided that the New Critics were quaint and altogether errant for their failure to examine, among other things, the inventive contexts of writing. They were no longer worthy of notice. Lately, when some of us came down with deconstructive theory, we decided that the rhetoricians failed by not knowing that they were already inside a rhetoric. Along the way, collaborative writing replaces the work of the solitary writer, which is no longer worthy of notice, as once again we discard what was for what is new. The debate between those who see writing as invariably a collaborative act and those who have wanted to see writing as the work of a lone author is no longer much of a debate. For the moment, at least, those who propose that writing is collaborative and intertextual have prevailed, and they are supported by the practice of writing pedagogues. In my remarks to the symposium, I tried to advocate a fanatic eclecticism. Let's not decide one way or another, I recommended. Let's believe and enact this *and* that, *and* maybe also the other. Let's not foreclose possibilities.

But even if I'm charming, I don't do much good. Social constructionist and intertextual thought is engaging, sometimes exhilarating and provocative; it challenges the habits we call thought and recognizes that we are all rhetorical creations. It's late in the day to deny what social constructionism asserts, that, as Bruffee articulates it, in any discipline the entities "we normally call reality, knowledge, thought, facts, texts, selves, and so on are constructs generated by communities of like-minded peers" (774), that "the matrix of thought is not the individual self but some community of knowledgeable peers and the vernacular language of that community" (777). It's also late to deny the importance of the notion of intertextuality. The prevailing composition textbook pedagogies, James E. Porter says, "by and large cultivate the romantic image [Pope turns uneasily again] of the writer as free, uninhibited spirit, as independent, creative genius. By identifying and stressing the intertextual nature of discourse, however, we shift our attention away from the writer as individual and focus more on the sources and social contexts from which the writer's discourse arises" (34–35).

"The traditional notion of the text as the single work of a given author," Porter continues, "and even the very notions of author and reader, are regarded as simply convenient fictions for domesticating discourse" (35). The idea of Jefferson as author of the Declaration of Independence, for example, is "but convenient shorthand." In intertextual criticism, the idea of the "lone inspired writer" and the "sacred autonomous text" both "take a pretty hard knock" (40). In Porter's account, "Our immediate goal is to produce 'socialized writers,' who are full-fledged members of their discourse community, producing competent, useful discourse within that community" (42).

A considerable body of composition pedagogy appears to support this view of writing. A new law has been enacted for writing classes: You Have to Sit in Circles, Large or Small. We sit in circles. We brainstorm together. We edit ourselves and tutor ourselves. We write collaboratively.

Enough. At least I have sense enough left to declare that it's wrong to suppose any method will always be best. Still, it looks as if I'm working against collaboration (which is working against good sense) whenever I do anything. Worse: it looks as if I'm in danger of denying my own hopes for writing and talking, means, perhaps, that I don't know how to be myself and to be with others. Wasn't that a hope for writing and talking?

The log fizzles out here, in early spring 1991. I made no more

entries immediately pertinent to collaborative writing. I had gotten
busy trying to create out of nothing the paper I earlier proposed for
4Cs. I tried to use some personal essays and some academic papers
to speculate on the possibility that on some occasions authors may
be alone, with no audience or other near at hand. Both the scholar
and the essayist have a right, I think, to claim ownership of their
work. They were not alone when they began; each may have had an
audience at the end, even if unaware. Still, they have a right to claim
ownership, declaring themselves to be sole responsible authors. I may
wish that they would sharecrop their work with me, but it is not my
place to deny them their claims. And, besides, I'd rather know them,
not in here where I am, but over there, where they are, in their own
place, by their own testimony.

I am unconvincing, but at least I no longer have the log available
for self-reproach.

3

I have come, I think, to a peculiar place and have situated myself
there, ready to oppose arguments for collaborative writing. I call the
place where I am peculiar for at least two reasons. To oppose arguments for collaborative writing is odd, in the first place, because
collaboration is probably the prime hope citizens have for survival on
the planet, whether the immediate need is to raise a barn or to create
a new political reality. To set myself against collaborative writing is
strange, in the second instance, because my own log shows that I
was always collaborating in some way.

Then how am I to account for my resistance?

Part of it is owed to stubborn, selfish preoccupation with myself,
as I try to situate myself in a rhetoric and claim it, even when I can't
and know I can't. Some of what I hope is chiefly a latter-day selfishness
is owed to the nature of my working experience, which I sketched
earlier. I want to be displaced from the academic and administrative
groups I have previously lingered among, though I still long for their
notice and admiration. I no longer want to be identified by or with
these groups. Someone might remark that it's easy for me to say I
want to be displaced: I already have the power and the language of
males, of a discourse community, of tenure and rank.

Those, I think, are collectives of the past. In the new world, I am
already displaced. I look, and I'm not there. Displacement isn't simple,

and may not be possible. What I thought was myself is not, was constructed by others, and that is true. I am at best a member of my classes, not a teacher, and the classes ought to be participatory, experiential, and collaborative, for there is no one who knows, and that is true and always was. When I write, I do not write, for what I write is intertextual and collaborative as all past language writes me, and that is true. When I have written, I disappear as readers create the only self that they can find, and that is true. I am already displaced and have no place to get. Sometimes I'm pretty mad about the whole business.

But mostly I'm not. I want to be displaced. I haven't yet learned how to be myself. I don't want to be lost in a group. I don't want to learn how to be someone else. I can't be Maynard Mack, whose work I admired so much when I was in graduate school, and I probably won't turn out to be Jacques Derrida. I want to try to think my thoughts, which aren't altogether mine. I don't want to write in the languages of the academic communities I have almost belonged to for years. I hope this is the last piece that looks even a little like academic writing. That doesn't mean an end to study and research, quintessential forms of collaboration. It means that I want to do a scholarly sort of work but to write in a personal sort of way. What's "out there" is not just public; it's also immediate and personal. History and theory are present: they give joy, they change lives, they hurt. I want to write in my way, which isn't mine, and perhaps even help to stretch out the possibilities of prose. I want to be displaced.

But if selfishness, working experience, and ill-founded yearnings help to account for my resistance to collaborative writing, that is not all. Some of the arguments for collaborative writing exhibit problematic features and predict, I think, disastrous consequences. I'll commence with what seems to me the least consequential, but I come very quickly to significant problems.

Some arguments are predicated upon a peculiar sense of literary history. Lunsford and Ede remark that "our research, then, and that of others, such as Faigley and Miller, indicates that writing teachers err if, in envisioning students' professional lives upon graduation, they imagine them seated alone, writing in isolation, misplaced Romantic spirits still struggling in a professional garret to express themselves" (72).

And, in what becomes a familiar motif among arguments repudiating the notion of the autonomous individual as a source of meaning, Linda Brodkey writes:

The writer-writes-alone is a familiar icon of art and is perhaps most readily understood as a romantic representation of the production of canonical literature, music, painting, sculpture. And if the icon evokes in me and others an awe out of proportion to its content (it is after all also an image of economic, emotional, and social deprivation), that is probably because we have learned that we are to complete this scene not by projecting ourselves onto the image of the writer, but by assuming the role of reader. Even so, the scene of writing is a text many of us find ourselves reading when we think about writing or, worse, when we are in the very act of writing. (396)

Brodkey, I know, collaborates with me, whether or not either of us intends it so: I can't go on without her; she changes me. The influence of this scene of writing, Brodkey says, has been and is pervasive, for

all of us try to recreate a garret and all that it portends whether we are writing in a study, a library, a classroom, or at a kitchen table, simply because we have learned this lesson in writing first. Further, those of us who have since learned no other lessons, who can image no pictures of writing other than the writer-writes-alone, are the most likely to pass that lesson on to a new generation and are the least likely to reconceptualize writing in any of the ways it is being represented by research in composition. (397)

I find my self interested in *Romantic* with a capital and *romantic* with a lowercase initial letter, and I am full of questions. Both forms of the word are used by those who argue that the solitary author (presumably *Romantic* or *romantic*) is not a sole source of meaning. Was Milton Romantic or romantic? Was he sometimes alone? Was Pope Romantic or romantic? Was he sometimes isolated? Was writing his profession? Did Sigmund Freud and Charles Lyell sometimes write alone, sometimes in dreadful isolation against the world's expectations? Was Mozart Romantic or romantic? Was he sometimes alone in the middle of a crowd? Was music his profession? I'm led to a final question: Have advocates of collaborative writing sought to associate the concept of the "writer-writes-alone" with only a few moments in time (Romantic or romantic moments) so that they can more readily question its validity for other moments in time? I think so.

Some arguments seem uninformed about the nature of life in the garret. No writer was ever alone in a garret. It's always crowded there, noisy and raucous, filled with demanding voices, ugly voices, incriminating voices, enchanting voices. A solitary writer is always contending, conversing, collaborating—with crowds, with herself, with the voices in his head. If, for example, Pope was sometimes isolated, barred from the schooling of his time, he was always in company—with others, as the last third of *An Essay on Criticism* might attest, or with his own multivoiced self, as a reading of *The Rape of the Lock* against *Eloisa to Abelard* might attest.

Odd, isn't it, that in our rush to support collaborative writing we deny that the autonomous individual is a source of meaning, while over in another part of our lives we turn gladly enough to Foucault or to Derrida as sources.

Some arguments fail to distinguish among writers and among kinds of writing. Some arguments for collaborative writing appear to be concerned with all writing, though their intended aim may be job-related writing or the writing done within in specific academic discourse community. A model of distinction, I think, occurs in the Lunsford and Ede book: "Although some of our students will commit themselves to professions, such as creative writing, where solitary writing is the norm, most will work in situations where they are at least as likely to participate in a group brainstorming session for a proposal or edit a collaboratively written report on-line as they are to sit alone in their office, pen (or computer keyboard) in hand" (72).

But that distinction is not kept elsewhere. In "Writing as Collaboration," the examples that Reither and Vipond use indicate that they are chiefly interested in writing within academic discourse communities. But since they don't specifically say so, and since they have created and now recommend a curriculum for collaborative writing, one is left to suppose that they are talking about all writing, witness their claim for their course of study: "Perhaps most important of all, students learn that writing and knowing are collaborative acts—vital activities people do with other people to give their lives meaning" (866). Still, some people write when there is no one else in the room save the inescapable monologues and dialogues inside the head, the solo voices and choral ensembles that ring and echo around us.

I don't wish to argue with what is entirely appropriate, that advocates are concerned chiefly or solely with the kinds of writing entailed in social or political action, with job- or task-related writing, with team projects in professional settings, with writing that serves the corporation or state. It's past time to democratize and to demystify writing (it's only as hard as pulling your belly muscles out through your left nostril), to help composition students see diverse ways of proceeding in company or alone. But there is no particular need to attack one mode of writing in order to advance another, no particular need to attack the poet's way or the essayist's way or the dramatist's way or the novelist's way in order to support the group way, no particular need to resist the collaborative way in order to defend the author as sole source of meaning. The composing I is always plural, but the responsible I is typically singular.

And besides, we shouldn't make the prior decision for them that they won't write in the solitary way, whether to compose sermons or political protests, essays, poems, or songs, a letter to the editor, or some new barbaric yawp. If we make the decision for them, we are presumptuous, and we are, intentionally or unintentionally, serving an ideological program that they should have a part in deciding— you might say they ought to collaborate. I don't think we've paid enough attention to Donald Stewart's observations about the psychological differences among us at the end of "Collaborative Learning and Composition: Boon or Bane?"—some writers want and need collaboration, and that's no sin; some writers can't abide it, and that's no sin. They need to be alone so that they can hear the voices in their heads. Either decision—to go alone, or to collaborate—ought always to be possible for all writers. I thought that was one of the things we had learned from the concept of rhetorical invention, to look for the possibilities.

When the decision for collaboration is made beforehand, a program begins to take shape. Its end is not collaborative writing. Collaborative writing is a mode, not the end. The ultimate consequence, I believe, is the diminution or elimination of the individual as a source of meaning in order to serve whatever collective is at hand.

Some arguments for collaborative writing portend disaster. I think it's possible that one day I'll be shot for "selfish individualism" or "rampant individualism" or "self-serving anarchy" if I persist in smoking my pipe. The new tribal piety is powerful. Will I be shot if I don't engage actively in collaborative writing? Probably not. Or not soon. But maybe.

Probably I have already been shot and am not here, am only, as Bruffee says, "a construct largely community generated and community maintained" (777). Here or elsewhere, I could not speak better in praise of collaborative learning and writing than Stewart already has:

> I see several virtues in it and in the social constructionist theory which
> supports it: (1) its attempt to do away with the sterile and nonproductive
> authoritarianism of the traditional classroom; (2) its effort to involve
> students meaningfully and significantly in their learning; (3) its potential
> humaneness, especially when students are nourished both socially and
> intellectually by the groups in which they work; (4) its recognition of
> the role social forces play in the very nature of language and learning.
> These are powerful and commendable virtues. (63–64)

I'll add only that collaborative work may enfranchise some who might
otherwise be forever lost.

Still, merging the self with the group may mean the loss of the
self. I take it that this is what some want, an evolution of the self.
Attacks against what Brodkey calls a familiar icon, the "writer-writes-
alone," may have been necessary to free us from the requirement of
idolatry. Now, however, more is at stake, not just a dethronement
of the self, not just the decentering of the self, but the removal of the
self as a source of meaning. Lunsford and Ede explore the nature of
authorship, questioning "the concept of authorship as an inherently
individual activity": "By examining the history of this concept, we
hope both to demonstrate how 'constructed' our concept of authorship
is—not commonsensical or inevitable at all but a complex reflection
of our culture—and to explore the reasons why our culture has systematically (if unconsciously) emphasized those aspects of the writing
process that involve individual, rather than group, effort" (73). Their
study takes them to certain medieval discourses that do not evidence
our views of person, self, or authorship.

Exactly. We had not yet fallen into history, had not yet discovered
the perspectives of time and personality. When we did, what we
discovered was *not* that we are the autonomous, authoritative sources
of meaning but that we are what we've got, unattached from Heaven,
cut off from the past, which we at any rate misremember, lost among
jumbled rhetorics and making such noises as we can while we try to
do better the next time. I never was what Sampson calls the kind of
person "that one would expect to emerge from the very Western
metaphysics which Derrida deconstructs" (13). What Derrida decon-
structed was already in ruins.

But we did sometimes elevate solitary performers to magical,
mystical stardom. Now, I judge, we want to rid ourselves of them
and of ourselves altogether. But we don't have to give ourselves up
to be democratic.

When advocates of collaborative writing look to history, what they see is that the concept of individualism, with its corollary, individual authorship, was a Western invention, to them mistaken, and late besides. Some of us, Mara Holt remarks, still try "to exist in a world ignorant of social constructionist assumptions, a world that has privatized the individual" (103). LeFevre ties individual authorship to capitalism, with Foucault connecting the idea of private property and the idea of individual authorship. As I've already said, however, I think we became what we are not by virtue of capitalism or of Descartes, who was pretty tardy, but by falling into history. What those who turn to history do not do is acknowledge that the late Western invention of the concept of individualism was a great invention that may even yet enable us to cherish every solitary soul. "We are obliged to announce ourselves," Knoblauch says, "so that through the very process of self assertion, we grow more conscious of our axioms and submit that awareness to public debate" (139).

Absent the saved, cherished, announced self, what waits is a new collective as we disappear into the tribe, the group, the company, the corporation, the state. Perhaps we'll also fly yellow ribbons as we go. Holt remarks that privatized individualism is "powerless in the face of social and political reality" (108), but the privatized individual is the only hope for a continuing critique of the tribe. In their zeal to dethrone the precious canonical author—which needed to be done— and to desacralize the precious canonical text—which needed to be done—some have invariably privileged the interpretative community, the social construction, the intertextual matrix. They valorize the rhetoric of the tribe over the puny voice of the citizen. The new tribal piety is powerful. Will we then, after all, as Donald Stewart suggests, eliminate "non-social" types? Shoot solitary writers? Smokers? Jews?

Arguments for collaborative writing, like many academic arguments, evince the power of the tribal. Mostly, I'd rather wait, since the world is always unfixed, for what Robert Con Davis calls "the pedagogics for which there is no model, a pedagogy for teaching that which cannot be known in advance" (775).

I'm not much afraid (but a little) of being shot. I know that my colleagues (collaborators, you might say) mean nothing but good, and I know that none of them was behind the door when the brains were passed out.

But academics will do tribal dances.

The power and appeal of arguments for collaborative writing

illustrate the peril they hold. Almost every good academic idea that comes along tends, for a while at least, to generate pedagogical monism. Though the university ought to be the last home for such thinking, we're all too often likely to say that it's either this idea or obsolescence and maybe damnation, not that both your vision and another's should be enacted. We will do tribal dances. Tribal magic is powerful and wrong. When you join the tribe and accept the tribal rhetoric, thereby the tribal magic, then any outsider who does not immediately accede is already a fool and may be a villain. Participatory, experiential, collaborative classroom experience is already the best, noncontroversially accepted as part of the tribal magic. So is collaborative writing. Yet we are many, and our students are more, and we're not all alike. Perhaps we should at least remember what John Trimbur suggests, to think of collaboration not merely as a process of creating a tribal rhetoric but "more important as a process of identifying differences and locating these differences in relation to each other" (610).

Can we keep on becoming for a while yet, learning, accepting, sorting, rejecting, hunting for that blessed day when we can fully belong and give way to community *and* fully emerge, ourselves, each a blessed self, freely, lovingly becoming a self in the presence of others? Won't that be a time? Some of us take our pleasure, our strength, and our energy from others, learning with them and through them, seeing with them and through them. Some of us take our pleasure, our strength, and our energy from what we catch inside our private headbones, turning our experience, looking at it this way and that, trying to see what sense we can make of it. Why should we ever imagine that any one conceptualization of writing would serve us all? We are too various, too lovely, for any single vision to hold us.

I know only to back off and to hope. I cannot deny that writing entwines us all, cannot deny that writing is community intertextualized in collaboration. If I denied that, I would be denying my own hopes. I can't claim ownership for the author; neither can I deny the author's ownership. If I did either, I would be denying my own hopes, that we can come together, reading and hearing each other. Won't that be a time?

As I don't have to make a case for collaboration—rhetorical invention has already told us that it is so—so I don't have to make a case for private ownership. It already exists. No matter the inevitability of collaboration and intertextuality, some writer found the words that make any piece of writing. The spells we live by were handed to us by someone who found the words—"Tranquility Base here, the Eagle has landed," "Kilroy was here," "Up yours," "All right, then, I'll go to hell," "I tremble for my country when I remember that God is just"—but you'd do better to say your own. We're nothing much, and we're our best hope. We need to have things both ways—centered and de-centered, private and collaborative—plus a third and fourth and fifth way that we haven't yet imagined. To be displaced is to be lonesome, but to be tribalized is to be lost.

Works Cited

Brodkey, Linda. "Modernism and the Scene(s) of Writing." *College English* 49 (1987): 396–418.

Bruffee, Kenneth A. "Social Construction, Language, and the Authority of Knowledge: A Bibliographic Essay." *College English* 48 (1986): 773–90.

Davis, Robert Con. "Pedagogy, Lacan, and the Freudian Subject." *College English* 49 (1987): 749–55.

Holt, Mara. "Towards a Democratic Rhetoric: Self and Society in Collaborative Theory and Practice." *Journal of Teaching Writing* 8 (1989): 99–112.

Knoblauch, C. H. "Rhetorical Constructions: Dialogue and Commitment." *College English* 50 (1988): 125–40.

LeFevre, Karen Burke. *Invention as a Social Act.* Carbondale: Southern Illinois UP, 1986.

Lunsford, Andrea, and Lisa Ede. *Singular Texts/Plural Authors: Perspectives on Collaborative Writing.* Carbondale: Southern Illinois UP, 1990.

Porter, James E. "Intertextuality and the Discourse Community." *Rhetoric Review* 5 (1986): 34–47.

Reither, James A., and Douglas Vipond. "Writing as Collaboration." *College English* 51 (1989): 855–67.

Sampson, Edward E. "The Deconstruction of the Self." *Texts of Identity.* Ed. John Shotter and Kenneth J. Gergen. Newbury Park, CA: Sage Publications, 1989.

Stewart, Donald C. "Collaborative Learning and Composition: Boon or Bane?" *Rhetoric Review* 7 (1988): 58–83.

Trimbur, John. "Consensus and Difference in Collaborative Learning." *College English* 51 (1989): 602–16.

10

Writing Assessment and

Learning to Write:

A Classroom Perspective

Lee Odell

In a recent essay, Dennie Wolf has argued that we need to find ways to make assessment "an episode of learning." Specifically, Wolf contends that assessment of writing should allow students to reflect upon their current work and determine ways in which they need to refine or improve on that work. Implicit in Wolf's argument is the assumption that assessment should provide formative information as well as summative.[1] That is, evaluation should do more than simply determine how well students are performing at a given point in their schooling. It should help us and our students see what they need to do if they are to improve in their subsequent work. Beyond providing grades or rankings, evaluation should contribute to students' development as writers.

The prospects for such a contribution may seem none too good. Typically, evaluation means only summative evaluation. Too often, the only thing students learn from an evaluation of their work is what sort of grade they got, how their writing compares to that of other students, or whether their work meets the standards established by a school, state, or national assessment program. Further, these summative judgments often reflect a limited, highly questionable perspective. A number of scholars such as C. H. Knoblauch and Lil Brannon have pointed out that when many teachers evaluate students' writing, they adopt what James Britton and his colleagues call the "teacher-as-examiner" role (122–28). That is, these teachers tend to become preoccupied with matters of grammatical correctness, and, ignoring the purposes students are trying to accomplish, they judge students' writing by the extent to which students' style, organizational strategies, and ideas conform to the teacher's preferences.

Unfortunately, our own experiences suggest that this teacher-as-examiner role may be more widespread than we would like to think. Why else would so many of our students focus strictly on matters of form and grammatical correctness when we first ask them to work in peer response groups? Why else would they persist in coming to us—even when their expertise on a given topic far exceeds our own—and asking, Am I on the right track? Is this what you want?

In spite of all these problems, Wolf's basic premise seems right. We can make evaluation play an important role in the development of students' writing abilities. But in order to do this, we cannot begin our thinking about evaluation by focusing narrowly on specific evaluation procedures—on ways to train readers to make reliable judgments, for example, or ways to set up an assessment program. We have to begin by thinking more generally about the evaluation process itself. What do students need from this process? What must it do for them in order to contribute to their growth as writers? As we answer these questions, we can determine the extent to which existing assessment procedures meet students' needs. And we can better understand the challenges we still must meet if evaluation is to help students develop as writers.

Rethinking Students' Needs

Part of what students need from an evaluation process is opportunity—the opportunity to write about meaningful subjects for real audiences and purposes, the opportunity to explore their topics over a reasonable length of time, the opportunity to discuss their ongoing work with others. But they need more than this. If evaluation is to contribute to students' development as writers, they need an evaluation process that does two things for them: (1) provides them with information they can use in revising a particular text or in creating subsequent texts and (2) allows them to play an active rather than a passive role in assessing their own work.

Obtaining Information

As do all writers, our students need to know how readers react to their writing, whether readers felt inspired, entertained, confused, informed, bored, persuaded, moved. And ultimately, they need to know whether their writing does what they hoped it would do for the reader(s) they were trying to address. But most of the writers we work with are likely to need more than this. They will probably need information about the discourse community(ies) in and for which they are writing and about the strategies that will help them communicate effectively in a particular community. Of course, writers may not always have to be consciously aware of this information. When the writing is coming smoothly and easily, a writer may be able to rely on a tacit understanding of community and on habitual strategies that don't even require conscious effort.[2] But occasionally writers have to be able to step back and reflect on what they have done and what they still need to do. In such moments, writers often need to become aware of both community and strategy. A good evaluation process has to help writers develop this awareness.

Discourse Community. When we write and when we evaluate writing, we do so as members of one or more discourse communities— groups of people with their own particular values, knowledge, and ways of doing things. These communities may comprise an academic discipline (cf. Bazerman) or a business or government organization (see, for example, Paradis et al. or Winsor]. Or they may comprise a particular office (cf. Odell, "Beyond"), a single course within a discipline (cf. Herrington), a single classroom (cf. Fish), or even a particular family or social group (cf. Heath).

Whatever their size, these communities confront writers with a variety of expectations—about ways to present ideas, for example, or even about which ideas are worth presenting. These expectations imply values by which writing is to be judged, and these values may vary widely from one community to another. Consequently, neither evaluators nor writers can function very intelligently until they have some sense of the ground rules of a particular discourse community.

Strategies. Elsewhere in this volume (*"Strategy* and *Surprise"*) I have argued that the meaning-making process entails strategies, mental activities that can guide our efforts to formulate our ideas, feelings, reactions. Other writers have suggested that there are still other kinds of strategies—strategies, for example, that help writers make beginning paragraphs more appealing,[3] sentences more cohesive and emphatic,[4] writing more organized,[5] or voices more engaging.[6]

Not all of these strategies will appear in a written text. Some strategies for exploring a topic may serve only to start writers thinking about their subject matter. For example, Gabrielle Rico recommends that writers begin the composing process by "clustering," brainstorming freely and widely about one's associations to a given phrase (28–44). These associations may or may not appear in the text; sometimes they have served their purpose if they stimulate the creative process and lead to new insights. Other strategies may not appear because a writer tried them and then abandoned them—maybe they didn't seem consistent with the direction the rest of the text was taking; maybe they didn't seem appropriate given the writer's evolving sense of audience and purpose.

Nonetheless, we routinely talk about a text as reflecting a writer's actions. If we say, for example, that a text is "organized," we imply that the writer has *done* something—grouped facts into categories, set up a plausible time or cause-effect sequence, used terms that give us a clear sense of what to expect in subsequent sentences. Similarly, terms such as *well-thought out* or *perceptive* imply a writer who is thinking or perceiving—anticipating and refuting counterarguments, selecting details that create a unified effect, looking closely at the objects or persons being described. If students are to continue to grow as writers, an evaluation of their writing should help them see what they are currently doing and what they might continue doing or do differently as they try to communicate in a particular discourse community.

Active Participation

Conventionally, students have been assigned a rather passive role in the evaluation process. On occasion, they may have felt they could argue about the fairness of a grade or the appropriateness of a comment at the end of an essay. But that's been about the extent of their involvement in the evaluation process. And that's too bad. Whatever their age or ability level, students don't come to us as blank slates, empty vessels that we must fill with our knowledge before they can contribute to the evaluation of their writing (or to their education in general). They have information and abilities that can let them play a very active role in the evaluation process. For one thing, they can help construct the assignments on which they will be evaluated. That is, they can help determine the audience, purpose, and subject matter for their writing. They can also help establish the criteria that are specifically appropriate for the assignment they have helped construct. And they can take responsibility for monitoring and assessing their ongoing efforts to do that assignment. What's more, students *need* to do these things if they are to develop the independence and self-direction that will let them continue to grow as writers long after they leave our classrooms.

Constructing Assignments. For many years, the evaluation of writing was done with no explicit reference to audience and purpose. Students were simply assigned topics, and their work was judged by criteria that were presumed to apply to all writing done for any audience or purpose. Thanks to the work of people such as Wayne Booth and Richard Lloyd-Jones, we have come to realize that writers must work within a rhetorical context, that they must have an awareness of their audience(s), their purpose(s), and the voice that seems appropriate given their sense of audience and purpose. Consequently, writing assignments are now very likely to make some reference to audience and purpose. For example, students may be asked to try to persuade members of the school board or to tell a story that will entertain their classmates. Such assignments are an improvement over earlier practice if only because they acknowledge the importance of rhetorical context. But such assignments are still problematic, for they relieve students of the obligation of constructing their own rhetorical contexts.

The term *construct* may raise questions here. After all, writers usually have to work within some constraints. They have to be guided by factual information about what the audience knows or believes or cares about. And especially in the enormous amount of writing they have to do at work,[7] writers are likely to have a specific purpose they must accomplish—to make a recommendation, to explain a procedure, to sell a product. So how much latitude do writers actually have in defining their audiences and purposes? And are we doing students a service if we give them a latitude that does not exist outside our classrooms?

With regard to *voice* and *purpose*, these questions seem to arouse little controversy. No one seems to doubt that writers have at least a degree of latitude in deciding upon the voice they will create, or upon the purpose(s) they will attempt to accomplish, or the role(s) they will adopt in relation to their readers.[8] There are, of course, occasions on which a writer's basic purpose may seem to be well-defined in advance. Typically, for example, academic discourse seeks to inform and/or persuade. But even if academic writers accept one or another of these purposes as a given, the writers must still make their own decisions as to a variety of related purposes: Will they seek to allay readers' misgivings? To overwhelm the opposition? To raise an issue and encourage debate? To provide a definitive answer?

With respect to *audience*, however, there is a good bit of controversy. Is the audience, in Lisa Ede and Andrea Lunsford's words, an entity that must be "addressed," a person or group of people who have verifiable characteristics writers must analyze and then accommodate in their writing? Or is the audience something that is "invoked," a composite of writers' conjecture and of their vision of the sort of person they would like to have read their work? After surveying opposing viewpoints on this matter, Ede and Lunsford argue that these viewpoints are not mutually exclusive. Sometimes writers address actual people with distinctive, analyzable characteristics; sometimes writers invoke audiences that differ from the audience(s) addressed. And sometimes a writer's conception of a particular audience may represent both analysis and invocation ("Audience" 181).

Ede and Lunsford's argument should help us avoid doctrinaire oversimplifications of a complex process. But it must not blind us to this fact: whether the audience is invoked or addressed, it is always *constructed*. Even when writers have access to an abundance of verifiable information about their audience, even when they are addressing classmates or friends, their sense of audience is not simply the sum total of all the factual information they have access to. It is, rather, a mental construct, a product not merely of "facts" but also of the writer's processes of selection, synthesis, and inference. Inevitably these processes are guided not only by the information at hand but also by the values, hopes, expectations, and purposes with which writers approach that information. Thus writers' understanding of their audience, and, indeed, of the entire rhetorical context, can never be a passive reflection of "reality"; rather, it is an effort to construct that reality in a way that will be as personally meaningful and useful as possible. The context writers construct will influence not only what they do as writers but how their efforts are evaluated.

Establishing Criteria. If students are to get better at writing, the evaluation process will need to help them understand what "getting better" means. And understanding—rather than passively accepting what someone else tells them—means that students will have to take an active role in establishing the criteria by which their writing is to be judged. In part, this means that students will have to help define the terms used in evaluation. For instance, both teacher and students might examine examples of a particular type of writing, talking about ways in which the text does or does not seem "organized" ("sensitive," "logical," "perceptive") and in the process coming to a consensus as to what *organized* may mean in a particular context. This is particularly important, since, as I'll argue later in this essay, many familiar evaluative terms—*organized, perceptive, logical*—are not nearly so clear as we might like to think.

Taking an active role also means helping decide which criteria are specifically appropriate for a given rhetorical context. As Lloyd-Jones has pointed out, the qualities that are important in one context—for example, in a letter to a close friend—may be less important in another—in a statement to a school board, for example. Sometimes writers need to give extensive background to orient and engage readers. At other times, readers can supply this information for themselves. Sometimes it makes good sense to include personal reactions, observations, feelings; sometimes this sort of information is inappropriate or irrelevant. Sometimes writers need to anticipate and refute counterarguments, and sometimes they don't.

As is the case with defining criteria, students need to be involved in determining the criteria by which a given piece of writing is to be judged. This may mean that we work with the entire class, speculating about what a given assignment appears to require and then later testing and revising those speculations by looking at sample texts. Or it may mean that we invite individuals to reflect on their ongoing efforts, helping articulate the qualities that seem most important for the kind of work they are trying to do. In all cases, the evaluation process must continually engage both teachers and students in trying to figure out what criteria are specifically appropriate for the task at hand.

Monitoring. Dennie Wolf points out that all writers need to be able to step back from their work, reflecting on it not as a writer but as a disinterested third party, an "onlooker" to the process in which they have been profoundly engaged. As Wolf argues, these reflections can become part of the ongoing process of rethinking the goals they are trying to accomplish and assessing their efforts to accomplish those goals.

We have reason to believe that writers of all ages and ability levels can learn to do this sort of work (e.g., Dyson 104–6). But to understand the complexity of this process, it may help to see it in the work of a sophisticated writer such as Donald Murray. As part of showing students how the process of writing relates to the process of learning, Murray includes information about his own effort to plan and write an essay in which he tries to understand the significance of his grandmother's death. Among other things, this information includes a series of drafts of the essay and marginal notes intended to capture his reflection on those drafts.

These notes show Murray monitoring his own efforts in various ways. At several points he reflects on matters that affect the entire essay. In one note, for example, he tries to reassure himself about the genre he has chosen ("The genre seems right. It is a familiar essay—not an argument, a short story, a poem. It really isn't a profile or character sketch."). And he continually questions himself about the main point he is trying to make ("What do I think I am saying in this piece? That you can never run away from home?"). He also focuses on specific passages, wondering whether the voice in a particular paragraph seems "too personal," or worrying that a transition is "clumsy," or that the information in a particular paragraph is "all jumbled up." In all this, he is continually giving himself instructions about how he should proceed. For example, after asking himself if he's trying to say "that you can never run away from home," he goes on to note, "If that's true I've got to tie this—and other experiences— to now. Do I do that?"

What am I trying to do? Am I succeeding? As one might expect from a writer of his ability, Murray considers these and related questions with exceptional sensitivity and sophistication. But, in some form, these questions are within the grasp of all writers. If our students are to improve as writers, we need to give them the opportunity to do this sort of work, and we need to help them do it better.

Reevaluating Evaluation Procedures

Devising evaluation procedures that will meet students' needs as writers will require a good bit of work. Fortunately, we do not have to start completely from scratch. We can draw on procedures that are currently used in certain large-scale assessments. There are, of course, a number of such procedures.[9] But for classroom purposes, there are two that seem especially important—Primary Trait scoring, which was developed during the 1970s, and Portfolio Assessment, which has received widespread attention in our profession only during the past few years. Each can help us meet some of our students' needs as developing writers. Yet each has some significant limitations. Neither procedure, by itself, will let us give our students all the help they need.

Primary Trait Scoring

This approach to assessment begins with a couple of assumptions that are well documented in rhetorical theory and in composition research. The first is that all meaningful writing works to accomplish some significant goal. These goals may vary widely, ranging from attempts to get something off one's chest to clarifying the meaning of some personal experience to changing someone's opinion or enabling someone to carry out an unfamiliar task. But in all cases there is a goal, a purpose. (See, for example, Booth; Kinneavy; Broadhead and Freed.)

Primary Trait scoring further assumes that different rhetorical purposes (e.g., explaining, persuading, expressing) engage writers in very different types of rhetorical tasks. Consequently, Primary Trait scoring also assumes that the features (i.e., the "traits") that are especially important (i.e., "primary") for a particular task or type of task might not be equally important for other tasks.

One of the strengths of Primary Trait evaluation is that it can provide students not only with judgments about the success of their writing but also with information about some of the strategies they are using in trying to do a particular type of writing. For example, Claudia A. Gentile cites a Primary Trait scoring guide for persuasive writing that describes some of the strategies that distinguish a "partially developed argument," which would receive a 3 on a 6-point scale, from a "developed refutation," which would receive a 6 on that scale (22).

The partially developed argument "states [an] opinion and gives reasons to support the opinion," and in addition "attempts to develop the opinion with further explanation" (22). The paper does not, however, develop or elaborate on that explanation. By contrast, the developed refutation not only states an opinion and gives reasons but elaborates on those reasons by using "rhetorical devices" such as "sequence of events, cause and effect, comparison/contrast," and so forth. Further, this paper contains a "discussion and/or refutation of [an] opposing point of view," a discussion that "summarizes [the] opposite point of view and discusses why it is limited or incorrect" (22).

As I'll point out in a moment, there are reasons for feeling some reservations about Primary Trait scoring. Nonetheless, Primary Trait scoring can help us give our students a certain amount of useful information. If a student asks us why a particular piece seemed only "pretty good" rather than "excellent" (or why it received a 3 rather than a 6; a C rather than an A), we can mention some of the good things the student has done (e.g., stated an opinion, given some reasons) and also some of the things the student needs to do the next time he or she does this type of writing (e.g., elaborate reasons by using certain rhetorical devices; summarize and note limitations of an opposing point of view).

One further and largely unmentioned benefit of Primary Trait scoring is that it provides a strong rationale for asking students to help establish the criteria by which a given piece of writing will be evaluated. In an early discussion of Primary Trait scoring, Lloyd-Jones makes it clear that criteria or traits are not chiseled in tablets of stone. Although Lloyd-Jones does not use the term *transaction*, his discussion (45) suggests that these traits are arrived at through a transactional process that is essentially the same as the process that goes on when we read any text, for any purpose. This notion of *transaction*, of course, comes from the work of Louise Rosenblatt and other scholars who see all reading processes as interactions between what we already know and the new material we encounter in texts. In these interactions we try to fit new material into our existing views of the world and we also revise those views as they are challenged by new material.

When we and our students set out to articulate the criteria by which we intend to judge a set of papers, we bring with us some assumptions about the world, about the structure of written texts, and about the demands of a particular type of writing (cf. Dole et al. 241). If, for example, we are reading material intended to explain a set of procedures to a novice in a field, the work of Linda Flower, John R. Hayes, and Heidi Swartz leads us to expect that explanation to contain "scenarios," passages that elaborate on a general instruction by mentioning typical sequences of actions that the reader might be expected to carry out (52–53). If we are reading persuasive discourse, we might anticipate that there will be some place where the writer tries to anticipate and refute counterarguments.

Although we have these expectations, we cannot assume they constitute absolute rules to which a given set of papers must conform. Good writers have a way of surprising us, showing us that a given rhetorical task may be approached in more than one way, that our initial expectations may be too limited or just plain wrong. Further, as Lloyd-Jones suggests, we may have to revise our sense of what is desirable in light of what it is reasonable to expect in a given group of papers. Thus criteria are—or should be—the result of a very complex transaction, one that involves the expectations of teachers and students and also the characteristics of a particular paper or set of papers.

Despite these strengths, there are several reasons for approaching Primary Trait scoring with some caution. One is that the term *Primary Trait* has recently been applied to scoring guides that appear uninformed by current theory and research and that have little value in helping students improve their writing. In its *Writing Framework*, The National Assessment of Educational Progress (NAEP) characterizes very different types of writing—persuasive, informative, and expressive narrative—with some of the same undefined evaluative terms— *well-written, organized, clear*. The scoring guides give no indication that, for example, the features that make a persuasive text seem well-written may be quite different from those that make an expressive narrative text seem well-written. Consequently, these scoring guides provide us almost no help in working with students. Although NAEP has used Primary Trait scoring effectively in other contexts (see Gentile and Lloyd-Jones), this misuse of the label *Primary Trait* makes it difficult to develop consensus about the actual strengths and weakness of this approach to evaluation.

Another cause for concern is that Primary Trait scoring is often associated with large-scale writing assessments such as those conducted by NAEP. As is usually the practice in such assessments, the writing tasks and the criteria for those tasks have been determined by the organization that conducts the assessment. Consequently, students have not had a chance to determine for themselves the goals they might be best able to accomplish or the audiences they might be most interested in addressing. Moreover, students and their teachers have been left out of the process of negotiating criteria, and students have not had access to these criteria at the time they would be most useful—while they are planning and revising their work.

These problems can easily be offset in an individual classroom, where students can be more actively involved in the entire assessment process. Other problems, however, seem inherent in Primary Trait scoring. Although this approach to scoring has made us much more aware of rhetorical purposes for writing, it has not been concerned with the larger social or institutional contexts in which a text exists. It has not invited us to think about the ways the values and practices of a discourse community might influence the writing process or the evaluation of a particular text.

Moreover, even the most useful Primary Trait evaluation guides · (e. g., those cited by Gentile and Lloyd-Jones) focus our attention on only certain types of strategies, ignoring others altogether. For example, even those guides that identify specific persuasive strategies fail to help us understand the strategies students have used (or might have used) in, say, creating an introduction that engages the intended reader or in creating a voice that is suited for a particular audience and purpose.

Portfolio Assessment

As Wolf has made clear, this approach to assessment rests upon several beliefs, but one of the most compelling may be the belief that, in the words of Robert Tierney, Mark Carter, and Laura Desai, "traditional assessment [is] both limited and subversive" (4). In the scholarly community, if not in the popular culture, there is a long tradition of criticizing the profound limitations of standardized tests that purport to assess writing (cf. Della-Piana et al.). But even when a writing assessment requires students to produce a piece of writing, that assessment limits the conclusions we can draw about a student's writing ability. If a student does well on an individual writing assessment, there is still the problem that Lloyd-Jones has noted: the ability to write, say, an effective formal report does not necessarily imply the ability to do well on some other type of writing, such as a narrative of personal experiences designed to convey one's feelings and reactions.

These and other limitations of traditional assessment can subvert the goals of a good writing program. If the test measures students' ability to do only one type of writing, there will be a strong temptation to focus instruction on that one type, rather than giving students opportunity to work in a variety of modes and write for a variety of audiences and purposes. Further, as a number of scholars have pointed out (see especially Elbow and Belanoff 4–6), most testing situations allow students no opportunity to do most of the things that we spend our time trying to teach students to do—identify a meaningful topic, define a rhetorical context, seek feedback, revise, and so on. Traditional assessments, then, can belie the values on which good writing programs are based. (For a discussion of ways to overcome some of these limitations, see Odell and Hampton forthcoming.)

A powerful alternative to such assessments is to evaluate students not on their work on a single, teacher-/evaluator-assigned writing task, but rather on their portfolios, collections of several types of writing that they have done over the course of a semester or year. (For suggestions as to how to help students develop portfolios, see essays in *Portfolios: Process and Product* by Pat Belanoff and Marcia Dickson.) These portfolios provide a way of meeting many of the needs students share with all other writers. Because the writings in the portfolios are done over a period of time, rather than in a one- or two-hour assessment session, students have the opportunity to discuss their emerging drafts with peers and teacher. These discussions can help students get a better sense of what counts as a good argument (or description, story, etc.) in a given discourse community; these discussions can also figure into students' efforts to monitor and assess their ongoing efforts. Moreover, the use of portfolios allows students to take a very active role in the evaluation process, since they have opportunity to negotiate criteria by which their work will be judged and have some choice as to which pieces of writing will be evaluated.

The principal weakness of Portfolio Assessment is that, at least in published discussions of this assessment procedure, it doesn't provide students with much information about the strategies that appear (or that might appear) in their work. For example, only four of the twenty-three essays in *Portfolios: Process and Product* talk in any detail about ways to describe students' texts. (See essays by Holt and Baker; Smit, Kolonosky, and Seltzer; Rosenberg; and Larson.)

And even when discussions of portfolios do suggest ways to describe students' texts, they often run into substantial problems. For instance, in *Portfolio Assessment in the Reading-Writing Classroom*, Tierney, Carter, and Desai present a list of "features to notice" in examining student portfolios. Since these authors are concerned with portfolios that reflect both reading and writing, these features are grouped under a variety of headings, some of which clearly pertain mainly to reading, some to writing. Those features that pertain to reading or "response" to literature seem quite helpful. They imply strategies (e.g., relating texts to personal experiences; writing about different story elements [98]) that might enhance a student's response to a text.

But when it comes to matters that are clearly pertinent to writing, this list of features is much less helpful. For assessing matters of "style" and "development," Tierney, Carter, and Desai's text suggests one pay attention to such matters as "strong voice," "attention to audience," or "depth of thought." All of these imply global reactions a reader might have to a piece of writing, and any of them might constitute a summative evaluation, such as, This paper is excellent because it creates a strong voice and reflects careful attention to the audience. But, as presented, none of these provides much information about the text under discussion. For example, what is there in a text that makes it seem attentive to audience? Does it focus on questions the reader is likely to need answered? Does it elaborate instructions through the use of scenarios? Does it allude to knowledge/values the reader is likely to bring to the text? Does it avoid rehashing material the reader already knows? Does it create a narrative that has no inappropriate jumps in time or causal sequence? Does it use language that a particular reader is likely to find especially evocative?

The same kinds of questions occur with regard to topics like "depth of thought." What is there in the text that gives the reader this impression? Does the text show that the writer has anticipated consequences of a recommendation? Is it that the writer's claims are consistent with some other set of values? Has the writer avoided logical contradictions? Has the writer included details that imply why characters felt or acted as they do? Is the text answering questions that are specifically appropriate for readers in a given discourse community?

Obviously, no general list of "features to notice" can include all of this. And maybe the effort to present such a general list is part of the problem. The things that are worth noticing in, say, an account of a personally moving experience may not necessarily be the same things that are important in a summary of data or an explanation of how to carry out a complex process. In any case, the preceding list of features to notice is not a list of features of texts but rather a list of impressions a reader might come away with after reading a text. They are a good beginning point for further description and analysis. But they leave undone the difficult task of deciding what a writer is doing effectively and what he or she needs to begin doing or do differently.

Meeting Challenges

Clearly, one challenge that lies ahead of us is to find some way to combine Primary Trait and Portfolio Assessment. Specifically, we need to work out evaluation procedures that will help us and our students describe the work that appears in portfolios and that will make our descriptions more sensitive to the rhetorical context for a given piece of writing. But important as it is to develop new evaluation procedures, it seems to me that our greatest challenge is to become more reflective about our current practices and more willing to examine and rethink the basic values that underlie our efforts.

Part of becoming more reflective about current practice is making sure that the language of evaluation is clear enough to be informative to student writers. Unfortunately, this is not always the case. For example, in a workshop on writing assessment, one participant remarked that a particular essay did not seem very organized. But another participant disagreed rather heatedly. After a series of marginally polite exchanges, it became apparent that the two participants were, implicitly, operating on two different definitions of the same term. For one reader, the essay seemed organized because the writer had grouped facts into general categories. For the other, the essay seemed to lack organization because the writer did not indicate at the outset just which categories he was going to discuss.

Each of these definitions made perfect sense for the type of writing the student was doing (an evaluative essay comparing two different restaurants). But for a time these two workshop participants, both of them experienced teachers of writing, had difficulty not only in articulating the specific definition they were using but even in acknowledging that the term *organized* might have more meanings than the one they were, implicitly, operating with. Each assumed that the term *organized* was unambiguous. Consequently, both teachers overlooked an important feature of the essay and thus unnecessarily limited the kind of information they could provide to the writer.

In addition to becoming more careful about the language we use, we need to make sure that we are not, inadvertently, taking the teacher-as-examiner role and thereby preventing students from taking an active role in establishing criteria and monitoring their own efforts. I assume that readers of this volume want to avoid the stance of teacher-as-examiner. But this may be harder to do than we think. For one thing, that's the role that many of our students expect us to play. As William Perry has shown, students often assume that we have definitive answers, although we may not reveal them immediately because we want to make our students think for themselves. When we deny having these kinds of answers, students can become, to put it mildly, skeptical. For example, early in the term, a student in a colleague's writing class asked exactly what he had to do to receive an A in the course. When my colleague suggested that there was no simple answer to such a question, the student was not at all happy. According to my colleague, the student "looked at me as though I was either a fool or a knave. A fool because I did not have an answer to a fundamental question about my subject. Or a knave because I had that answer and wouldn't tell him."

Further, this skepticism may be more justified than we would like to think. In the course of our own education, we have spent a lot of time in classrooms where the teacher expected to be treated as the unquestioned authority. Consequently, there is always the chance that we will, wittingly or not, do unto others as we have been done unto. We may not be so blatant as a teacher who wrote this comment on a student paper: "I can almost hear myself talking here. It's nice to know someone was listening. A+." But sometimes we convey much the same sentiment. Intending, for example, to invite students' opinions, we may ask questions ("Yes, but don't you think the author really meant . . . ?") that are not questions at all, but rather clear assertions of the opinion we want students to give us.[10] Or hoping to get students to see the need to substantiate their more debatable assertions, we may become especially critical of statements with which we happen to disagree, passing by other statements that are no less debatable but that we find more compatible with our own views.

One way to keep ourselves from slipping into the teacher-as-examiner role is to accept yet another challenge: that of continually questioning and rethinking the criteria underlying our judgments about writing. Specifically, we need to test those criteria by seeing if they actually account for the effectiveness of writing we intuitively admire. As we do this, we engage students in the process of articulating criteria, we give them practice in identifying strategies that help make a particular piece of writing effective, and we help our classrooms become the kind of discourse communities in which people are free to venture their own opinions and take responsibility for their own learning.

Consider, for example, the criterion that says writing should "show, not tell." The assumption here is that writers should give us the information we can use to come to our own conclusions as to whether something is wonderful or logical or inspiring or boring. This is especially the case in personal experience expressive writing, where we want students to cut back on the generalizing and editorializing and, instead, give us very concrete images that let us see or hear exactly what is going on in a given scene.

By and large, this is probably a very useful criterion. But last semester a student, assigned to find a piece of writing that seemed especially effective and then analyze the qualities that contributed to the essay's effectiveness, came up with the following brief essay from the collection *On the Road with Charles Kuralt*.

The Christmas Tree

Trees just do not grow up here on the high plateaus of the Rockies— everybody knows that. Trees need good soil and good weather and up here there's no soil and terrible weather. People do not live here. Nothing can live up here and certainly not trees. That's why this tree is a kind of miracle.

The tree is a juniper, and it grows beside US 50 utterly alone, not another tree for miles. Nobody remembers who put the first Christmas ornament on it—some whimsical motorist of years ago. From that day to this, the tree has been redecorated each year. Nobody knows who does it. But each year, by Christmas day, the tree has become a Christmas tree.

The tree, which has no business growing here at all, has survived against all the odds. The summer droughts somehow haven't killed it or the winter storms. When the highway builders came out to widen the road they could have taken the tree with one pass of their bulldozer. But some impulse led them to start widening the road just a few feet past the tree. The trucks pass so close they rattle the tree's branches. The tree has also survived the trucks.

The tree violates the laws of man and nature. It is too close to the highway for man, and not far enough away for nature. The tree pays no attention. It is where it is. It survives.

People who live in Grand Junction, thirty miles one way, and in

Delta, Colorado, fifteen miles the other way, all know about and love the tree. They have Christmas trees of their own, of course, the kind of trees that are brought to town in trucks and sold in vacant lots and put up in living rooms. This one tree belongs to nobody and to everybody.

Just looking at it makes you think about how unexpected life on earth can be. The tree is so lonely and so brave that it seems to offer courage to those who pass it—and a message. It is the Christmas message: that there is life and hope even in a rough world.

As far as anyone in the class could see, there is a lot more telling than showing in this essay. Kuralt tells us that the tree is a "miracle," a "message"; that it is "lonely," "brave"; that it "offers hope." He generalizes about the harsh winters and summers, about what trees "need" if they are to survive, and about the attitudes of people in two Colorado towns, "all [of whom] know about and love the tree." He gives us a little bit of concrete information—that the tree is solitary, that trucks sometimes "rattle its branches," and that it is a juniper. But how big is the tree? What is its shape? What sort of ornaments do people put on it? If we saw it for ourselves, would it give us the same assurance it provides for Kuralt? How do we know that the tree isn't wizened, scrawny, more pathetic than inspiring? How do we know that all those decorations don't just make the tree gaudy, trashy? Kuralt's implicit answer is "Trust me on this."

And indeed my students and I were willing to do just that. The kinds of questions I've just mentioned struck us as inappropriate. We liked the voice in this piece—the knowledgeable traveler who picks up some detail of life in an out-of-the-way place and helps us understand its significance. We liked the rhythms of the sentences and the evocative power of some of his observations (for example, his comparison of this tree with other, domesticated trees that are "brought to town in trucks and sold in vacant los and put up in living rooms"). We were willing to forgo being "shown"; we were quite happy to let Kuralt tell us.

This one essay, of course, doesn't prove that telling is better than showing or that we should never look for specificity of detail. But it does suggest that none of us, teachers or students, have the final answer as to what constitutes "good writing." Like our students, we teachers have to be continually engaged in articulating the criteria by which writing is to be judged, rethinking those criteria depending on the particular rhetorical context or discourse community in which writing is done.

In addition to reflecting on our terminology, evaluation practices, and criteria, we also need to meet one further challenge: we need to find some way to reconcile the divergent roles we must play in the evaluation process. In recent years, scholars such as Robert Probst have begun to argue that we need to abandon the role of teacher as examiner and, instead, adopt the role of reader or, more specifically, the role of one reader in a community of readers that also includes students' peers. Yet Cheryl Geisler argues that we also need to function as a "coach," someone who is not the intended audience for a piece of writing but who has some expertise that can help the writer address a particular reader. And finally, we have to function as evaluators, people who make judgments about the quality of a completed text. Each of these roles makes different demands, each entails different relationships to student writers.

In the reader role, both we and student peer reviewers act as though we are members of the primary audience for a text, and we try to help the writer understand how well the text works for members of that audience. As readers, we essentially follow Elbow's advice in *Writing Without Teachers*: we point out words or phrases to which we had a strong reaction; we summarize what seemed to us the key ideas; we talk about the places where we felt confused, engaged, annoyed, inspired. In doing this, we accept no obligation to make suggestions, we claim no special expertise, and we make no pretense of being dispassionate. We are just one reader in a community of readers, all of whom are trying to come to their own understanding of the writing and to give the writer the fullest possible account of what went on in their minds as they read the writing.

By taking the role of reader—especially as just one among a group of readers—we oblige students to take a more active role in the process of monitoring and assessing their own work. They can no longer count on someone else—that is, us—to do the hard work for them. They have to come to their own decisions as to what is and is not working in their writing; they have to figure out for themselves what they need to do next.[11] So the role of reader is extraordinarily valuable. But it may not be adequate.

As we encourage students to identify the audiences they wish to address, it becomes increasingly likely that those audiences will not include us. If we allow students to write to, say, the manager of the school food services, and if we mean it when we say that the writing must actually be sent to that manager, our obligations change somewhat. It is no longer enough simply to give our own personal responses; indeed, those responses are now valuable principally insofar as they help the writer anticipate how the intended reader might react. We have to do more than respond; we have to help. Our role is no longer simply that of reader; it is also that of advisor, mentor, coach.

In this role, we are obliged to have certain kinds of expertise. For example, we should have some skill in constructing a rhetorical context. We should be able to help students articulate the assumptions they are making about their audience, perhaps testing those assumptions against what we know about comparable audiences, perhaps showing students ways to gain additional information about their intended reader. We also should be able to describe the student's work: What kinds of arguments is he or she making? What features of the text make it seem cohesive (or not cohesive)? What is there in the text that creates expectations as to what the writer will say next? What are the features of diction, syntax, or content that are contributing to the "voice" of the text?

We should also be able to identify places where there may be a mismatch between the text and what the student wants the text to do: Are there places where arguments seem irrelevant to the audience's values or concerns? Are there places where, given the student's audience and purpose, the voice seems too harsh (too sarcastic, too timid, too exuberant)? And finally, we should be able to make suggestions that are based not simply on some generalized notions about "good writing" but on our understanding of strategies employed by other writers who are successfully doing something comparable to what the student is doing. For example, we should be able to show students how other successful writers make their writing seem more cohesive, how they develop a certain kind of argument, how their choice of words creates a particular voice.

In functioning as readers and coaches, our obligation is simply to help students get better at what they are trying to do. But eventually we have to tell them whether or how well they have actually succeeded in their efforts. We have to adopt the role of evaluator.

There are a number of things we can do to keep this role from becoming simply that of teacher-as-examiner. We may couch our judgments not in terms of abstract criteria but rather in terms of personal responses: This is much better, or This is really well thought out (or persuasive, informative, funny, moving). We may involve students not only in articulating criteria but also in applying these criteria. We may legitimately postpone making a final judgment, giving students an entire semester to revise the pieces that go into a portfolio. But sooner or later we must look at completed texts and make a decision about how well those texts do the job the writer has set out to do. In this role, we are no longer the collaborators in making meaning or even the helpful mentors. Instead, we are the persons who must make a fair, informed judgment that will stand up under careful scrutiny.

Reader, coach, evaluator—how are we supposed to reconcile these different roles? My own strategy is to acknowledge forthrightly that at different times I do different things and then to plan class activities that show students how to perform the various roles— reader, coach, evaluator—for themselves. Is that the best way to do it? Is there a strong reason for proceeding differently? And how do my students interpret all this? They know that both their classmates and I will make judgments about their work. So how does that knowledge affect their perceptions of our efforts to function as readers or coaches?

I don't have definitive answers to these questions any more than I know for sure exactly how we can manage to play all three roles. But I do know this: If we don't play—and show students how to play—those roles, someone else will. For instance, they may turn to a friend, who may be a very sensitive reader, or who may be what Karen Spear calls a "teacher surrogate," simply passing on the *ex cathedra* judgments he or she has heard over the years (*never* use the pronoun I; *always* have three paragraphs in the "body" of the essay; *always* begin each paragraph with a topic sentence). And if we don't make reliable evaluations of our students' work, there will ultimately be plenty of legislators, administrators, and publishers of standardized tests who will see that those evaluations get made for us.

Such challenges as these give an unexpected twist to Wolf's view of the connection between evaluation and learning. By drawing on the best aspects of different evaluation procedures, we can devise procedures that help students improve their writing. But students aren't the only ones who have a thing or two to learn here. Even as we devise useful evaluation procedures, we cannot assume that the procedures themselves will accomplish everything we want done. Instead, we will need to be continually engaged in examining our practices, rethinking our values, and trying to answer questions (e.g.,

How can we reconcile our diverse roles in the evaluation process?) for which we currently have no adequate answers. In other words, if assessment is to be an episode of learning, a good bit of that learning will have to be ours.

Notes

1. For a further discussion of summative and formative evaluation, see Odell, "Defining."

2. For further discussion of tacit information processing strategies, see Robert Sternberg's discussion of "automatization," 248–54.

3. See, for example, Donald Murray's discussions of writing "lead" paragraphs.

4. See Joseph Williams's text *Style, 10 Lessons in Clarity and Grace.*

5. See, for example, the discussion of "accessibility" by Janice Redish et al.

6. See, for example, Ken Macrorie's discussions of "honest voice" or Walker Gibson's book *Tough, Sweet, and Stuffy.*

7. See Paul Anderson's survey of the amount of job-related writing associated with various occupations and professions.

8. See, for example, Peter Elbow's discussion of "voice and writing" (*Power* 281–303), Linda Driskill's discussion of writer/audience relationships, 51–80, or Walker Gibson's *Persona.*

9. For a survey and critique of several of these, see Odell and Cooper, "Procedures."

10. See Douglas Barnes's discussion of ways teachers cue students as to what is an acceptable comment.

11. As Richard Beach notes, however, not all students may be able to make effective use of all the information they receive from a group of readers.

Works Cited

Anderson, Paul V. "What Survey Research Tells Us about Writing at Work." Odell and Goswami 3–83.

Anson, Chris M. *Writing and Response: Theory, Practice, and Research.* Urbana, IL: NCTE, 1991.

Barnes, Douglas. *From Communication to Curriculum.* London: Penguin, 1976.

Bazerman, Charles. *Shaping Written Knowledge.* Madison: U of Wisconsin P, 1988.

Beach, Richard. "Showing Students How to Assess." Anson 127–48.

Belanoff, Pat, and Marcia Dickson, eds. *Portfolios: Process and Product.* Portsmouth, NH: Boynton/Cook, 1991.

Booth, Wayne. "The Rhetorical Stance." *College Composition and Communication* 14 (1963): 139–45.

Britton, James, Tony Burgess, Nancy Martin, Alex McLeod, and Harold Rosen. *The Development of Writing Abilities (11–18)*. London: Macmillan, 1975.

Broadhead, G. J., and R. C. Freed. *The Variables of Written Composition: Process and Product in a Business Setting*. Carbondale: Southern Illinois UP, 1986.

Della-Piana, Gabriel, Lee Odell, Charles R. Cooper, and George Endo. "The Test Scores Decline: So What?" *Educational Technology* 16 (1976): 30–39.

Dole, Janice A., Gerald G. Duffy, Laura R. Roehler, and P. David Pearson. "Moving from the Old to the New: Research on Reading Comprehension Instruction." *Review of Educational Research* 61 (1991): 239–64.

Driskill, Linda P. *Business and Managerial Communication: New Perspectives*. Fort Worth: Dryden-Harcourt, 1992.

Dyson, Anne Haas. "Talking Up a Writing Community: The Role of Talk in Learning to Write." *Perspectives on Talk and Writing*. Ed. Susan Hynds and Donald L. Rubin. Urbana, IL: NCTE, 1990. 99–114.

Ede, Lisa, and Andrea Lunsford. "Audience Addressed/Audience Evoked: The Role of Audience in Composition Theory and Pedagogy." *College Composition and Communication* 35 (1984): 155–71.

———. *Singular Texts/Plural Authors*. Carbondale: Southern Illinois UP, 1990.

Elbow, Peter. *Writing with Power*. New York: Oxford UP, 1981.

———. *Writing Without Teachers*. New York: Oxford UP, 1973.

Elbow, Peter, and Pat Belanoff. "State University of New York at Stony Brook Portfolio-based Evaluation Program." Belanoff and Dickson 17–29.

Fish, Stanley. *Is There a Text in This Class?* Cambridge, MA: Harvard UP, 1980.

Flower, Linda, John R. Hayes, and Heidi Swartz. "Revising Functional Documents." *New Essays in Technical and Scientific Communication: Research, Theory, Practice*. Ed. Paul V. Anderson, R. John Brockman, and Carolyn Miller. Farmingdale, NY: Baywood, 1983. 41–58.

Geisler, Cheryl. "Reader, Parent, Coach: Defining the Profession by Our Practice of Response." Forthcoming in *Reader*.

Gentile, Claudia A. *Exploring New Methods for Collecting Students' School-Based Writing*. Princeton: National Assessment of Educational Progress, 1992.

Gibson, Walker. *Persona*. New York: Random, 1969.

———. *Tough, Sweet, and Stuffy: An Essay on Modern American Style*. Bloomington: Indiana UP, 1966.

Heath, Shirley. *Ways with Words*. Cambridge: Cambridge UP, 1983.

Herrington, Anne. "Writing in Academic Settings: A Study of the Context for Writing in Two College Chemical Engineering Courses." *Research in the Teaching of English* 19 (1985): 331–59.

Holt, Dennis, and Nancy Westrich Baker. "Portfolios as a Follow-up Option in a Proficiency-Testing Program." Belanoff and Dickson 37–45.

Kinneavy, James. *A Theory of Discourse*. New York: Norton, 1970.

Knoblauch, C. H., and Lil Brannon. *Rhetorical Traditions and the Teaching of Writing*. Portsmouth, NH: Boynton/Cook, 1984.

Kuralt, Charles. *On the Road with Charles Kuralt*. New York: Ballantine, 1985.

Larson, Richard L. "Using Portfolios in the Assessment of Writing in the Academic Disciplines." Belanoff and Dickson 137–49.

Lloyd-Jones, Richard. "Primary Trait Scoring of Writing." *Evaluating Writing: Describing, Measuring, Judging*. Ed. Charles R. Cooper and Lee Odell. Urbana, IL: NCTE, 1977. 33–66.

Macrorie, Ken. *Writing to Be Read*. Rev. 2nd ed. Rochelle Park, NJ: Hayden, 1976.

Murray, Donald M. *Write to Learn*. 2nd ed. New York: Holt, 1987.

National Assessment Governing Board. Writing Framework for the 1992 National Assessment of Educational Progress. Prepublication Draft. Princeton: National Assessment of Educational Progress, 1992.

Odell, Lee. "Beyond the Text." Odell and Goswami 249–80.

———. "Defining and Assessing Competence in Writing." *The Nature and Measurement of Competency in English*. Ed. Charles R. Cooper. Urbana, IL: NCTE, 1981. 95–136.

Odell, Lee, and Charles R. Cooper. "Procedures for Evaluating Writing: Assumptions and Needed Research." *College English* 42 (1980): 35–43.

Odell, Lee, and Dixie Goswami, eds. *Writing in Non-Academic Settings*. New York: Guilford, 1985.

Odell, Lee, and Sally Hampton. "Writing Assessment, Teacher Professionalism, and Improvement of Instruction." *A Rhetoric of Doing*. Ed. Stephen Witte, Roger Cherry, and Neil Nakadate. Carbondale: Southern Illinois UP, forthcoming.

Paradis, James, David Dobrin, and Richard Miller. "Writing at Exxon ITD: Notes on the Writing Environment of an R&D Organization." Odell and Goswami 281–307.

Perry, William. *Forms of Intellectual and Ethical Development in the College Years*. New York: Holt, 1970.

Probst, Robert E. "Transactional Theory and Response to Student Writing." Anson 68–79.

Redish, Janice C., Robbin M. Battison, and Edward S. Gold. "Making Information Accessible to the Reader." Odell and Goswami 129–53.

Rico, Gabrielle Lusser. *Writing the Natural Way*. Los Angeles: Tarcher, 1983.

Rosenberg, Roberta. "Using the Portfolio to Meet State-Mandated Assessment." Belanoff and Dickson 69–79.

Rosenblatt, Louise. *The Reader, The Text, The Poem: The Transactional Theory of the Literary Work*. Carbondale: Southern Illinois UP, 1978.

Smit, David, Patricia Kolonosky, and Kathryn Seltzer. "Implementing a Portfolio System." Belanoff and Dickson 46–56.

Spear, Karen. *Sharing Writing: Peer-Response Groups in English Classes*. Portsmouth, NH: Boynton/Cook, 1987.

Sternberg, Robert J. *Intelligence Applied: Understanding and Increasing Your Intellectual Skills*. San Diego: Harcourt, 1986.

Tierney, Robert J., Mark A. Carter, and Laura E. Desai. *Portfolio Assessment in the Reading-Writing Classroom*. Norwood, MA: Christopher-Gordon, 1991.

Williams, Joseph. *Style: 10 Lessons in Clarity and Grace*. 3rd ed. New York: Harper, 1989.

Winsor, Dorothy A. "An Engineer's Knowledge and the Corporate Construction of Knowledge." *Written Communication* 6 (1989): 270–85.

Wolf, Dennie Palmer. "Assessment as an Episode of Learning." Ms. Harvard Graduate School of Education, Cambridge, MA, n.d.

Contributors

Index

Contributors

Jim W. Corder is professor of English at Texas Christian University. He is the author of various textbooks, of articles on rhetoric appearing in *Rhetoric Review, College English, College Composition and Communication, Rhetoric Society Quarterly, Pre/Text,* and elsewhere, and of the books *Lost in West Texas, Chronicle of a Small Town, Yonder: Life on the Far Side of Change,* and *Hunting Lieutenant Chadbourne* (forthcoming).

Sally Hampton works in the Fort Worth, Texas, school system where she is responsible for that district's writing and reasoning skills program. She directs a National Writing Project site and serves on the New Standards Project Language Arts Advisory Board and the Texas Committee on Student Learning. She is currently working on an assessment project focusing on differences between work-world writing and writing taught in schools.

Shirley Brice Heath is a professor of English and Linguistics at Stanford University. An anthropological linguist whose primary interests are in language socialization and the sociocultural contexts of language use by young people of diverse cultures, she is the author of *Ways with Words: Language, Life, and Work in Communities and Classrooms* (1983) and coauthor (with Shelby Anne Wolf) of *The Braid of Literature: Children's Worlds of Reading* (1992).

Anne J. Herrington is an associate professor of English and director of the writing program at the University of Massachusetts at Amherst. She is coeditor (with Charles Moran) of *Writing, Teaching, and Learning in the Disciplines.* Her research on writing in the disciplines has appeared in *College Composition and Communication, Research in the Teaching of English, College English,* and a number of collections. Her current research project, conducted with Marcia Curtis and a group of first-year college students—primarily students first placed into basic writing classes—examines those students' perceptions of their development as writers and their experiences with writing in their composition and other college courses.

George Hillocks, Jr., received his B.A. in English from the College of Wooster, a diploma in English studies from The University of Edinburgh (Scotland), and his M.A. and Ph.D. in English from Case Western Reserve University. He taught secondary school English in Euclid, Ohio, where he was director of the United States Office of Education funded Project English Demonstration Center from 1963 to 1965. He taught English at Bowling Green State University where he served as director of Freshman English programs. Since 1971 he has been at the University of Chicago where he is currently professor in the departments of Education and English Language and Literature. He has contributed articles to *College English, Research in the Teaching of English, American Educational Research Journal, American Journal of Education, English Journal, English Education,* and other journals as well as chapters to various books. He is coauthor of *The Dynamics of English Instruction* and author of *Alternatives in English, Observing and Writing,* and *Research on Written Composition: New Directions for Teaching.* He is currently working on a book that attempts to integrate the various theories implicated in the teaching of writing.

David Kaufer is associate head of the English Department at Carnegie Mellon and coordinator of the undergraduate and graduate writing programs. His research interests are cognitive, social, and historical theories of writing, computer systems to support academic and industrial writing, and theories of logic and rhetoric. With Cheryl Geisler and Christine Neuwirth, he has published a textbook on academic wriring: *Arguing from Sources: Exploring Issues Through Reading and Writing.* He is (with Kathleen Carley) publishing a forthcoming book on the impact of print on sociocultural organization and change in the nineteenth century. For the past few years, he has (with Chris Neuwirth) been supported by the National Science Foundation to develop new technologies for collaborative writing.

Beverly J. Moss is an assistant professor of English at the Ohio State University and specializes in rhetoric and composition. She conducts research on literacy in African-American churches and on the teaching of composition. She is currently editing a book, *Literacy Across Communities.*

Lee Odell is a professor of composition theory and research at Rensselaer Polytechnic Institute. He has served as chair of the Conference on College Composition and Communication and is currently chair of the NCTE Assembly for Research. He has edited several books: *Evaluating Writing* and *Research on Composing,* both with Charles

Cooper, and *Writing in Non-Academic Settings,* with Dixie Goswami. Currently, he is working on ways to incorporate work-related writing tasks into the academic curriculum.

Jane Peterson is assistant chair of the Communications Division of Richland College, where she teaches English and developmental writing and coordinates the supervision of part-time faculty. A past chair of the Conference on College Composition and Communication and one of five community college participants in the 1987 English Coalition Conference, she now serves on the editorial boards of the *Journal of Basic Writing, Teaching English in the Two-Year College,* and *College Composition and Communication.* She has published articles on teaching and technical writing and coauthored (with Judy Lambert) a basic writing text, *From Course to Course.*

Keith Walters is currently an assistant professor in the Linguistics Department at the University of Texas at Austin. His research interests include sociolinguistic approaches to literacy, African-American English, and Arabic/French code-switching, as well as linguistic variation and change in developing countries.

Richard Young is a professor of rhetoric and English literature at Carnegie Mellon University. His continuing research interests are rhetorical invention, research methodologies, and the pedagogy of writing. At present he is working on problems of language learning in undergraduate education. From 1978 to 1983 he was head of the Department of English at Carnegie Mellon, during which time he oversaw the development of its graduate programs in rhetoric.

Index